AMERICAN CLIPPER SHIPS
1833-1858

"MANDARIN," 776 TONS, BUILT AT NEW YORK, IN 1850
From a painting by Charles R. Patterson, reproduced by courtesy of
Arthur H. Harlow & Co., New York City

AMERICAN CLIPPER SHIPS

1833-1858

By

OCTAVIUS T. HOWE
and
FREDERICK C. MATTHEWS

VOLUME II

MALAY—YOUNG MECHANIC

DOVER PUBLICATIONS, INC.
NEW YORK

Published in Canada by General Publishing Company, Ltd., 30 Lesmill Road, Don Mills, Toronto, Ontario.

Published in the United Kingdom by Constable and Company, Ltd., 10 Orange Street, London WC2H 7EG.

This Dover edition, first published in 1986, is an unabridged republication of the work originally published as Publication Number Thirteen of the Marine Research Society, Salem, Massachusetts, in 1926–27. A few obvious typographical errors have been tacitly corrected. In the original edition the frontispiece of each volume appeared in color.

Manufactured in the United States of America
Dover Publications, Inc., 31 East 2nd Street, Mineola, N.Y. 11501

Library of Congress Cataloging-in-Publication Data

Howe, Octavius T. (Octavius Thorndike). b. 1851.
American clipper ships, 1833–1858.

"Originally published as Publication Number Thirteen of the Marine Research Society, Salem, Massachussetts, in 1926–27"—T.p. verso.
Includes index.
Contents: v. 1. Adelaide—Lotus—v. 2. Malay—[etc.]
1. Clipper-ships—United States.   I. Matthews, Frederick C.   II. Title.
III. Series: Publication no. 13 of the Marine Research Society.
VM23.H62   1986   623.8'224'0973   86–1986
ISBN 0-486-25115-2 (v. 1)
ISBN 0-486-25116-0 (v. 2)

ILLUSTRATIONS

AMERICAN CLIPPER SHIPS
1833-1858

AMERICAN CLIPPER SHIPS

MALAY

CLIPPER ship, built by John Taylor, at Chelsea, Mass.; launched Aug. 26, 1852. Keel, 164; over all, 178 x 33: 2 x 19: 1; 868 tons, old measurement; 821 tons, new measurement. She had fine lines and her sharp, wedge-shaped bow, with but slight flare, was ornamented with the bust of a Malay chief. She was rakish in rig, crossed three skysail yards and had studding-sail booms on the royals. Her original owners were Silsbee, Stone & Pickman of Salem, which was her hailing port.

During her first twenty years, the *Malay* was engaged in trade between New York or Boston and the Far East, Australia or California. She made five Cape Horn runs to San Francisco, as follows: arrived out Jan. 9, 1853, in 116 days from Boston; Jan. 31, 1860, in 149 days from New York; Feb. 2, 1861, in 126 days from Boston; July 16, 1863, in 148 days from New York and Dec. 29, 1872, in 150 days from New York. On all of these passages she sailed during the season unfavorable for making fast runs, and her average from port of departure to the line is 34 days, with 44 days, in 1872, as the longest. Her experience in the North Pacific was nearly as unsatisfactory. On her run out in 1863, there were only 12 days on which she made 200 miles or upwards, while on 97 days she logged under 100 each. Off the Horn she lost foretopmast, had boats stove, the cabin filled and the false stem and head washed off. The ship had to be put before the wind on several occasions to canvas and batten the bows. On arrival at San Francisco, it was found that damage to ship and cargo amounted to $6300. Of her passages over the course in question, the only instance where she had an opportunity to show what she could do was on her maiden voyage in 1852-1853, when she made the run from off Cape St. Roque to 50° South, Atlantic, in 17 days, and from 50° South, Pacific, to the equator, in 20 days.

In 1859, when near Cape Virgin, 74 days out from New York, she met the *Panther*, 61 days from Boston for San Francisco. Captain Gannet of the *Panther* noted in his log: "Came up with and quickly passed the clipper ship *Malay*, bound in the same direction." As a sequel, however, the *Malay* reached San Francisco, three days in the lead.

On the first of her four voyages to the Antipodes, the *Malay* left New York, Oct. 14, 1853, and was 90 days to Hobart Town. Had the average seasonable run of 35 days to the line and 65 days to the meridian of the Cape. On running her easting down she had no one day of steady winds throughout and her log is replete with entries of gales and hard squalls, single, double and close reefs and heavy seas. On the following passage she left New York, Dec. 2, 1854; was 32 days to the line and 49 days thence to Sydney. She encountered much ice, both bergs and float, and for several days Captain Hutchinson had a most anxious time. On her third run over the course she sailed from Boston, Nov. 28, 1855; was 32 days to the line and 57 days thence to Melbourne. On her fourth run she left Boston, Nov. 30, 1856; was 23 days to the line; passed Rio, 32 days out; was on the meridian of the Cape on the 48th day and 21 days thereafter was 950 miles from Melbourne; here, however, she struck a belt of calms and took 11 days to make port, her passage totaling 80 days. These four runs show an excellent average of 85 days.

On all the occasions of her visits to San Francisco, referred to, the *Malay* crossed the Pacific in continuation of her voyages and her performances here are, again, much better than average. On two occasions she went to Manila in 44 and 43 days respectively and two of her runs were to Hong Kong in 48 and 60 days. In continuation of her voyages to Australia she proceeded to Calcutta or China. Of her homeward passages from the Far East, records are available of the following and in no instance was her departure taken during the season of favorable monsoons. Manila to New York; 127 days, in 1853; 117 days, in 1862 and 124 days, in 1865. On this last passage she had a heavy gale, lasting two days, off the Cape, during which the head was knocked off and the stem started, causing a bad leak which was finally gotten under by driving wedges and continually pumping. In 1854, she was 107 days from Calcutta to New York and in 1855, 115 days from the same port to Boston. In 1859, she went from Shanghai to New York, in 106 days.

Following the arrival at San Francisco, in December 1872, after her last Cape Horn passage, the *Malay* became a regular packet between the Californian port and Hong Kong and was a popular ship in the trade. Her last run over this course was in 1875, she reaching San Francisco, Mar. 30th, 84 days out, nearly a complete wreck. It was considered nothing short of a miracle that she had survived the terrific weather encountered. Everything forward was started, rails and stanchions carried away, as also the booby hatch, allowing a large quantity of water to get below; in addition a bad leak developed. A considerable proportion of the cargo was jettisoned and later, that in the lower hold became so hot as to threaten the destruction of the ship by fire. After arrival and survey at San Francisco, the ship was sold to Nicholas Bichard of that port and was repaired and rerigged as a barkentine. She was operated in the Pacific, doing some coasting, but her principal work was off shore, with lumber, she frequently returning with coal from Newcastle, N. S. W. She often received rough treatment by the elements, but on being overhauled in June 1885, she was found to be still staunch and sound, in some ways being as strong as when new.

The last arrival of the *Malay* at San Francisco, was on July 9, 1891, in 67 days from Newcastle. After loading a cargo of railroad ties for Mollendo, she sailed Aug. 22nd. In the South Pacific very heavy weather was encountered; the deck load was lost, the deck badly damaged and a severe leak started. She put into Tahiti, in distress, where, in October, she was condemned.

Capt. Nat. Brown, Jr., was the first master of the *Malay*. After him came Capt. S. Hutchinson, who was followed by Captains Willcomb, Dudley and Clough, the latter being in command for several years prior to her sale in 1875. Thereafter she had a number of different masters, all well known in the Pacific, including Captains Love, Peterson, Hunt, Morehouse, Panno and Callicott.

MAMELUKE

MEDIUM clipper ship, built in 1855, by E. & H. O. Briggs, at South Boston, for Curtis & Peabody of Boston; 195 x 38: 10 x 24; 1303 tons. She is said to have been a sister ship of the *Fair Wind* and both had two complete decks and beams for a third. With her three skysail yards and all other spars and rigging taut and trim, she made a handsome appearance. She was a large carrier for her type; her freight list on her second passage from New York to San Francisco being $22,600, which was only some $700 less than that of the clipper ship *David Crockett,* 400 tons larger in register, both carrying the same class of freight and loading at the same time.

The *Mameluke* sailed from Boston, Oct. 3, 1855, under command of Capt. Elisha Whitney; was 39 days to the line; 73 days to 50° South; 15 days thence to 50° in the Pacific, passing Cape Horn under skysails; crossed the equator, 114 days out and was ten days within 600 miles of San Francisco, arriving Feb. 19, 1856, in 139 days from Boston. At San Francisco, she delivered her cargo of 2400 tons in perfect condition; took on 76 passengers, among them Mr. W. W. Cleaveland, a member of the firm of Flint, Peabody & Co., agents for the ship, and was 49 days to Hong Kong. From Hong Kong she went to Manila where she loaded for New York; was 34 days to Java Head; off the Cape, 69 days out; crossed the line on the 96th day and arrived at New York, Oct. 28, 1856, in 126 days from Manila. On her second voyage she arrived at San Francisco, July 5, 1857, in 179 days from New York. Captain Whitney reported having had strong head winds after leaving port and did not cross the line until 60 days out, probably a record slow run for a first-class ship. She was 104 days to the Horn, off which she was 27 days, in strong gales; crossed the equator, 149 days out. From San Francisco she went to Singapore and Calcutta. In 1859, while bound to Calcutta from Singapore, she ran on a sand bar and sustained considerable damage. On arrival at Boston, permanent repairs were made and she loaded for San Francisco. Capt. Samuel W. Pike, formerly of the clipper ship *Meteor*, succeeded to the command and arrived at San Francisco, Aug. 12, 1860, in 143 days from Boston. Sailed, again, Sept. 3rd; reached Baker's Island the 25th, loaded 1700 tons of guano and sailed Oct. 18th; passed Cape Horn, Nov. 21st and arrived at New York, Jan. 26, 1861, in a leaky condition. On Mar. 12th, Captain Pike, who had left the *Mameluke* to take the clipper *Sea Serpent*, was presented with a beautiful chronometer, by the insurance companies of New York and Boston, "in appreciation of his skill, perseverance and energy in bringing the *Mameluke* into port, in a leaky condition, from Baker's Island."

Captain Porter now took the *Mameluke* and sailed from New York, Mar. 4, 1861, for Liverpool making the fast run out of 16 days; thence went out to Calcutta, in 100 days; loaded there for London and sailed Jan. 2, 1862; left Sand Heads, the 5th, and arrived at London, May 16th, in 121 days' passage. Arrived at New York, July 26th, in 37 days from London, in ballast. Again loaded for San Francisco, on what was to be her last voyage as an American ship, and arrived out Feb. 18, 1863, in 137 days from New York. Captain Porter reported being 44 days to the line; 88 days to the Horn; 15 days from 50° to 50°; crossed the equator, Jan. 29th; off the Platte, in a heavy gale, had mainmast sprung and bulwarks and water casks stove in. Sailed from San Francisco, Mar. 21, 1863, and was 58 days to Callao.

After this voyage, the *Mameluke* was sold to J. Edminster Naylor of London, and became the British ship *Milton*. While under the British flag she was commanded by Captain Smith, as late as 1869, having been repaired in 1868. In 1874, her owner was given as W. S. Lishman and hailing port, Newcastle, England; tonnage, 1287, British measurement.

MANDARIN

EXTREME clipper ship, the second clipper to be built for the California trade; launched in June 1850, shortly after the *Celestial* had left the ways in the yard of William H. Webb, New York. The *Mandarin* was built at New York, by Smith & Dimon, who had previously built the famous tea packets *Rainbow* and *Sea Witch*, the latter, known in her early career as the fastest sailing ship afloat, but the new comer was designed to be even faster. She was one of the smallest of the clipper fleet, was called a perfect little gem and during her career of 14 years she fully sustained the high character of New York-built ships, both in general appearance and speed. Of but 776 tons, old measurement, she measured 151: 6 x 33: 6 x 19: 3. She was owned by the prominent New York firm of Goodhue & Co., and after Jan. 1, 1862, by Weston & Gray, the junior partners who succeeded to the business on the principals retiring. Her first commander was Captain Stoddard, who, after three years service, was succeeded by Captain Parritt who remained in the ship until her loss.

The *Mandarin* made ten round voyages and was lost while homeward bound on the eleventh. Of her outward passages, three were from New York to San Francisco, as follows: in 1850, 128 days; in 1852, 115 days, on which occasion she arrived off the entrance to the Golden Gate, 110 days out, but was driven off shore in a hard gale; in 1853, 123 days. On neither of these passages did she have any opportunity to show what she could do in the way of speed. On the third, which was her last westward run around Cape Horn, she was one of six first-class clippers which entered the Golden Gate within a few hours of each other, Dec. 10-11, 1853. Her time was beaten six days by the *Witch of the Wave*, four days by the *Raven;* was equaled by that of the *Hurricane*, while she beat the celebrated large flyers, *Trade Wind* and *Comet*, two and five days, respectively. On account of light and adverse winds, no remarkable work was done by any of the six, the *Raven's* best day being 310 miles; *Witch of the*

Wave's, 289; *Trade Wind's*, 270 miles. The *Mandarin's* best day, 249 miles, was 14 miles under that of the *Comet* and *Hurricane*.

The second, seventh and all subsequent outward passages from New York, made by the *Mandarin*, were to China. Present available data gives her fastest passage as 95 days, although she is said to have made several runs in very close to 100 days, all, however, performed in the unfavorable season. All of her ten homeward passages were made from China and of these, only in one instance did she leave the China coast during the season of the northeast monsoon. In that case she sailed in January 1858 and reached New York, Apr. 14th, in 100 days from Shanghai, 85 from Anjer and 47 days from the Cape. Captain Parritt reported having much light and squally weather, the steady trades expected at that season being conspicuous by their absence. Her fastest homeward passage was in 1853, leaving Woosung Feb. 19th, when the season was getting poor; passed Anjer in 16 days and was at New York in 89 days from Woosung, 73 days from Anjer and 30 from St. Helena. Capt. Robert Bennett Forbes, one of the best authorities on the China trade and the work of the clippers engaged therein, regards this run of the *Mandarin* as fully equal to the best ever made over that route, considering the season in which it was performed. Her other eight homeward runs were made during the unfavorable season, on one of which, 1856, she had the long run of 41 days from Foo Chow to Anjer; yet her whole average is under 118 days, which is considered very good sailing.

The fifth voyage of the *Mandarin* was from Norfolk, Va., to Melbourne, sailing Sept. 13, 1854, and arriving out in 106 days. In the North Atlantic her mainmast was so badly crippled that she could not carry a press of sail and she was not up with the line until 40 days out. The following year, however, she eclipsed all records and her time of 70 days from New York to Melbourne has never been equaled by sailing vessel from any eastern American port to Australia, to the present day. Leaving New York, Dec. 21, 1855, she was 21 days to the line and two days later passed Cape St. Roque;

on the 39th day out she crossed the meridian of Greenwich. From off St. Roque to Melbourne her time was 47 days, quite fast but some ten days longer than record. She was fortunate in having the rare experience of meeting with favorable winds in each section of the 13,000-mile voyage, a combination requisite in making fast or record passages. From Melbourne she went to Hong Kong, in what was stated to have been a record run, but dates of departure and arrival are not now obtainable and the correctness of the "record" report is not confirmed.

On what was to be her last voyage, the *Mandarin* sailed from New York on Dec. 9, 1862, and arrived at Shanghai, Apr. 14, 1863. She remained trading on the coast until the summer of 1864 when she loaded at Hong Kong and Whampoa for home. On Sept. 26th, Captain Parritt wrote from Batavia, to his owners, as follows; "The *Mandarin*, while under my command, in the China Sea, to the northward of the Thousand Islands, on August 9th, at 7 P.M., struck an unknown reef in 12 feet of water." The passengers, crew and a portion of the cargo were saved by the steamer *Ambon* which had been sent from Batavia to assist.

MANITOU

BUILT at Petty's Island, N. J., in 1855; 1401 tons; Stilwell S. Bishop, Philadelphia, owner. Reported missing in 1859, while on a voyage from New York to San Francisco.

MARY

MEDIUM clipper ship, built in 1854, by Benjamin Dutton, at Marblehead, Mass., for Edward Kimball of Salem; 179 x 37 x 21; 1148 tons, old measurement. She was launched Dec. 6th, coming off the ways fully rigged, ballasted and ready for sea. Sailed from Boston, Jan. 8, 1855, under command of Capt. William Churchill, and went to Havre via New Orleans. On returning to New York, she loaded for San Francisco and sailed Oct. 9th, arriving out Mar. 9, 1856, in 152 days' passage. As Captain Howes reported having put into Rio and being 95 days thence, it would appear that she was detained there about ten days. She had had a long run from New York to St. Roque, 39 days; was 24 days off the Horn and over two weeks within four days' sail of the Golden Gate. From San Francisco she made the run to Calcutta in 100 days, and sailed from Sand Heads, Oct. 19th, making the passage to Boston in 107 days.

Capt. John Bridgeo now assumed command and the *Mary* left Boston, May 22, 1857, and arrived at San Francisco on Sept. 11th. These dates give her run as 112 days although her captain gave details showing 109 days, as follows;—29 days to Cape St. Roque; thence 25 days to 50° South; 14 days rounding the Horn; 18 days from 50° South, Pacific, to the line, and from there, 23 days to port. Her time of 59 days between the two equator crossings, as also her 41 days running up the Pacific, is particularly good. From San Francisco she was 83 days to Calcutta; sailed thence Feb. 2, 1858, and made the run of 114 days to London.

In 1858, the *Mary* struck on a coral reef in the Bahama Islands and the inhabitants of the Keys came off to wreck the ship, as was their custom, but Captain Bridgeo and his crew succeeded in getting her off, much against their opposition and attempts at bribery. At his arrival at New Orleans, the captain received a handsome reward for himself and crew. She was then, for a time, engaged in trans-Atlantic trade and on July 22; 1860, arrived at New York with 206 passengers from Havre. In 1862 she was registered as owned by J. P. Turner of Marblehead.

The *Mary* sailed from Boston in March 1862 and made a voyage around the world, going to San Francisco and thence to Calcutta and London. She was 165 days, 79 days and 118 days respectively on the different legs of this round, arriving at London in May 1863. In January 1864, she was reported to have put into St. Thomas with seven feet of water in her hold, being bound to Boston from Cadiz. Captain Bridgeo subsequently gave up his command to take the new

Marblehead bark *Hellespont*, to engage in the African trade, Captain Hall succeeding him in the *Mary*. On June 23, 1865, she arrived at San Francisco after a passage of 157 days from Boston. Had light winds in the South Atlantic and off the Horn had the foremast sprung. Was 36 days from the Pacific equator crossing to port, in light winds and calms, and was unable to enter the harbor for six days after sighting the Heads, due to strong northerly winds, accompanied by a dense fog. Completing this voyage she returned East via Callao. On Jan. 6, 1867, she sailed from New York for San Francisco, Captain Hall still in command. Off Cape Horn she sprang a bad leak and was forced to put into Callao in May. Her cargo was discharged and forwarded to destination by two other vessels. The *Mary* was condemned and sold for $15,000, Peruvian money, the insurance companies taking a loss of $73,000. The ship was repaired and went under the British flag, retaining her old name.

In 1869 the *Mary* loaded 1187 tons of guano at the Chincha Islands and sailed from Callao, Nov. 30th, for Cork. On Dec. 11th, during a severe storm she sprang a bad leak, became unmanageable and two days later was abandoned with 14 feet of water in the hold. The captain took one boat and the mate another but they soon became separated. After intense suffering from thirst and exposure, the captain's boat was picked up by the ship *Iona* and her occupants landed at Payta, Peru. Somewhat later those in the other boat were also rescued.

MARY BANGS

BUILT by Paul Curtis, at East Boston, Mass., in 1856; 177 x 36 x 23; 958 tons; W. H. Bangs & Co., of Boston, owners. Wrecked near Altata, Mexico, in November 1874.

MARY L. SUTTON

MEDIUM clipper ship, built in 1856, at Mystic, Conn., by Charles H. Mallory, who was her owner during her whole sea life. Length over all, 216 feet x 40: 8 x 23; 1448 tons, old measurement. While a good carrier, she had fine lines and was a beautiful ship in all respects. Her bow was very graceful, her round stern particularly neat and she had ample sheer. She had Howes' double topsails and crossed three skysail yards. A finely carved image of the lady after whom she was named was the figurehead. She became one of the most popular of the high-class ships engaged in the California trade and her sailing record compares very favorably with celebrated flyers designed primarily for speed. In the North Atlantic and also in the South Pacific she made runs equal to the fastest. Her average of five passages from San Francisco to New York, direct, is 95 days; that of her eight runs from New York to San Francisco, is 118½ days, while the mean of six of these is 110 5/6 days.

On her maiden voyage, the *Sutton* sailed from New York, Apr. 6, 1856, under command of Captain Rowland and crossed the line in 24 days and 15 hours, having skysails set in light winds all the way except for 50 hours; logged 3893 miles; was up with Cape Horn, 60 days out; made the run from 50° to 50°, in nine days, in light winds and calms. From latitude 57° South, Pacific, to the equator, she was 17 days, a run which has never been beaten. Crossed the line, 82 days out, and reached San Francisco, July 26th, 111 days from New York. Sailed from San Francisco, Sept. 29th, and arrived at New York, Jan. 2, 1857, in 95 days. Had made her landfall Dec. 23rd, 85 days out. Sailed from New York, Apr. 1, 1857, Captain Sisson in command; was 35 days to the line, and 71 days to 50° South; made the Cape Horn passage in eight days, in light easterly winds and fine weather, the first fair winds she had experienced for 65 days. Crossed the equator in the Pacific, 100 days out, and was 40 days thence to San Francisco, having had one spell of 12 continuous days of calms during which she made a distance of only eight miles. Completing this voyage she was 118 days from the Sandwich Islands to New Bedford, with whale oil.

On her third voyage the *Sutton* arrived at San Francisco, Sept. 24, 1858, in 116 days from New York, Captain Spicer in command. She then made a round voyage to Hong Kong. On the outward run was 49 days, being dismasted in a typhoon in the Bashee Straits. On the return to San Francisco she lost her foretopmast and had the foremast sprung, but was only 41 days on the run. Sailed from San Francisco, July 16, 1859, and was 110 days to New York, via Rio. From New York she returned to San Francisco, arriving May 12, 1860, in 103 days; was 18 days from the Pacific equator crossing to destination. Left San Francisco, June 13th, and was 100 days to New York. Went back to San Francisco in 106 days, arriving Mar. 11, 1861. Sailed May 9th and was 95 days to New York. Reached port in company with the clipper ship *Golden Eagle* which had left the Pacific port eight days before her and whom she had met near the line in the Atlantic.

The *Sutton* then made a rapid round voyage between New York and Havre, the return run being 24 days. She then loaded for San Francisco and reached destination June 15, 1862, in 115 days' passage. Off the Horn lost foretopmast and had bulwarks stove; was 100 miles from the Golden Gate when 112 days out. Sailed from San Francisco, Aug. 19th, and went back to New York in 98 days. Light and baffling winds prolonged her run from port to the Atlantic equator crossing to 82 days but she covered the distance thence to New York in the very fast time of 16 days. She returned to San Francisco in 114 days, arriving June 15, 1863; was 17 days from 50° South, Pacific, to the equator, crossing on the 87th day out. At San Francisco, Captain McKnight assumed command and, leaving port Aug. 26th, made the run to New York in 94 days.

The last arrival of the *Sutton* at San Francisco was on Aug. 5, 1864, in 144 days from New York, Captain Rowland in command. On Oct. 9th, she arrived at Baker's Island to load guano. Sudden and severe squalls from the westward were prevalent that fall, with an unusual rainfall, and the phosphatic guano became of the consistency of pea soup. A number of ships were wrecked on the different Line Islands through their tailing on the reef from the mooring buoys. On Nov. 20th, during one of these squalls, the *Sutton* struck and soon became a total loss. Captain Rowland and his crew got ashore safely and were several months on the island. The ship was insured for $40,000, being at the time classed A 1.

MARY OGDEN

BUILT by Chase & Davis, at Warren, R. I., in 1854; 169 x 32 x 22; 969 tons; G. Buckley of New York, owner.

MARY ROBINSON

MEDIUM clipper ship, built by Trufant & Drummond, at Bath, Me., in 1854; 215 x 38: 6 x 22: 6; 1371 tons, old measurement. Owned by E. M. Robinson of New Bedford. She was of beautiful model and well sparred; her fore and main yards were each 76 feet long and 20 inches diameter and the topsail yards were 60 feet by 16 inches. Her outward voyages from eastern ports were mainly to San Francisco and her cargoes were always delivered in first class condition. Her first master was Captain Crocker who was succeeded by Captain Harding. Captain McCleave was in command during the last five years of her career.

From New York or Boston, the *Robinson* made six passages to San Francisco, averaging 127 days, the fastest being 115 days, in 1864, her last run. Off Cape Horn she was in company with the *Carrier Dove* whom she led into San Francisco by 18 days. On this run she was 23 days from New York to the line and was in 50° South, Atlantic, 49 days out, but was 17 days rounding the Horn and thence had light winds clear to port. Her maiden run, in 1854, was 139 days from Boston, via Valparaiso, 46 days. She was 30 days off the Horn in heavy gales and continual snow storms. Captain Crocker reported her best day's run as 300 miles; best speed, 15 knots; made 12½ knots within seven points of the wind. Three of her homeward passages were from Callao to Hampton Roads, with guano in 83, 81 and 86 days respectively. In 1858 she was 58 days from San Francisco to Melbourne and thence 40 days to Honolulu,—a very fast passage. From Honolulu she went to Jarvis Island to load guano for New York.

During the summer of 1864 the *Robinson* went from San Francisco to Howland's Island to load guano. There had been that season a most unusual period of very bad weather with numerous and heavy squalls from the westward and during one of these she was driven on the reef, but came off not materially damaged. On the night of June 27th, however, a particularly heavy squall came up suddenly and she again went on the reef. The rudder was knocked off and she began leaking, having some 1300 tons of guano aboard. The following night she slid off the reef at 8 P.M. and went down in deep water, taking the moorings with her. All hands were saved and arrived at San Francisco, Sept. 1st, in the bark *Harrison,* which had also been ashore at the Island but got off. The insurance on the *Robinson,* ship and cargo, was $75,000.

MARY WHITRIDGE

MEDIUM clipper ship, built in 1855, by Hunt & Wagner, at Baltimore, Md., for Thomas Whitridge & Co., of that city; 168 x 34 x 21; 978 tons, old; 862 tons, new measurement. She was a fine sailer and a successful ship and with the clipper *Golden State,* shares the honor of having an active career of some 30 years, principally in the China trade. She was singularly fortunate as to mishaps.

The first voyage of the *Whitridge* was from Baltimore (June 24, 1855), to Liverpool. From Cape Charles to Rock Light she was but 13 days and 7 hours,—a remarkable passage. On the return she was 30 days from Rotterdam to New York. She then went out to San

Francisco in 114 days and this, with a similar run of 138 days made in 1859, were her only Cape Horn voyages. For a number of years, on different occasions, she operated between San Francisco and Hong Kong, becoming a prime favorite on the route. She has to her credit three westward passages of 44 days each and one eastward run in the fast time of 39½ days. In 1858 she took a cargo of Chinese coolies from Swatow to Havana in 89 days. During the two years prior to December 1864, she was trading on the coast of Asia. On Mar. 27, 1865, she left Akyab for Falmouth and on subsequent arrival at New York, via Bermuda, where she put in on account of a leak, she was thoroughly overhauled and repaired. She then became a regular packet between New York and China and so continued with minor interruptions for over 15 years. She was one of the best known American ships in North China ports, particularly in Shanghai and Foo Chow. In 1876 she made a call at San Francisco from Hong Kong and, after making a round voyage to Peru, returned to China.

Sometime prior to 1886 she was unrigged and converted into a barge for operation on the Atlantic coast. While coal laden and in tow, she was lost off the coast of New Jersey on Feb. 22, 1902. Her captains were, consecutively, Robert B. Chesebrough; William Andrew Cressy, brother of Josiah P. Cressy; Benjamin F. Cutler and George Freeman.

MASTIFF

BUILT by Donald McKay, at East Boston, Mass., in 1856; 1034 tons. Owned in Boston and afterward by Warren Delano of New York. Burned at sea, Sept. 10, 1859, when five days out from San Francisco, bound for Hong Kong.

MATCHLESS

CLIPPER ship, built in 1853, by Isaac Taylor, at Chelsea, Mass., 1053 tons; Capt. Symes Potter; owned by Nathaniel and Benjamin Goddard of Boston.

She was launched June 30, 1853, and sailed from Boston, Sept. 6th and when two days out experienced a severe hurricane which carried away her three topmasts and the head of her foremast. The decks were swept and the vessel leaked so badly that Captain Potter bore up for Boston. Repairs took more time than was expected and it was not until Oct. 20th that she resumed her voyage. She arrived at San Francisco, Feb. 8, 1854, Captain Potter reporting his run as 109 days; 58 days to the Horn and off it ten days; crossing the equator in the Pacific, Jan. 19, 1854, and was off San Francisco Heads 18 days later but was detained in the fog for two days. The real time seems to have been 110 or 111 days and the *Ringleader*, which left Boston the same day and arrived a few hours after the *Matchless*, reported her run as 110 days. The *Matchless* sailed from San Francisco, Feb. 23, 1854, and arrived at Singapore, Apr. 23rd in 58 days, and at Calcutta, May 28th, in 93 days from San Francisco; thence 99 days to Boston.

From Boston she went to Calcutta and sailed from there Apr. 18, 1855, arriving at Boston, July 6, 1855, in 89 days. Sailed from Boston, Aug. 9, 1855, and arrived at San Francisco, Dec. 19th, in 131 days. She reported 37 days to the line; was becalmed 14 days in the Atlantic; off the Horn 18 days, in heavy gales; crossed the equator, Nov. 25th; thence light winds to port. She sailed from San Francisco, Jan. 6, 1856; was 62 days to Hong Kong, loaded at Shanghai and thence 124 days to New York.

The *Matchless* sailed from New York for Manila, July 13, 1857, still under Captain Potter and was reported lost after having passed Anjer on Oct. 3rd. No particulars.

"MALAY," 868 TONS, BUILT AT CHELSEA, MASS., IN 1852

From a Chinese painting showing the ship off Hong Kong

"MARY," 1148 TONS, BUILT AT MARBLEHEAD, MASS., IN 1854

"MIDNIGHT," 962 TONS, BUILT AT PORTSMOUTH, N. H., IN 1854
From a painting made in China from lines drawn in London

"N. B. PALMER," 1399 TONS, BUILT AT NEW YORK, IN 1851

From a painting made at Hong Kong, in 1858, owned by the Vose Galleries

MESSENGER

EXTREME clipper ship, built by Jacob Bell in New York; launched Apr. 22, 1852; 201: 3 x 36: 6 x 21: 8; draft 20 feet; old register, 1351 tons; new measurement, 1026 tons. The heaviest dead weight cargo she ever loaded was 1302 short tons; wheat cargo, 1224 short tons, showing her to be so sharp as not able to carry her register in dead weight. Her original owners were Slade & Co., of New York, for whom she made one round voyage, when she was sold to William Platt & Co., of Philadelphia, who had been greatly pleased with the performances of their clippers, *White Squall* and *Trade Wind*, predecessors of the *Messenger* from the Bell yards. In 1863 she was reported sold at New York and in 1869 her hailing port was Boston, the managing owner being R. F. C. Hartley of New York. In 1875 she had the same register and probably continued the same ownership and hailing port until her sale in 1879, when, under command of Captain Gilkey, on a voyage from New York with a cargo of petroleum, she put into Mauritius, leaky, and was condemned and sold for £1010 sterling. She had jettisoned 300 cases of petroleum and the balance of her cargo was forwarded by the German bark *Norma*.

The original cost of the *Messenger* was reported as $105,000, and she was in every way a beautiful ship, of fine model, trim in spars and rigging and a credit to her builder. She was one of the most successful vessels engaged in the California, East India and China trade. Her captains were many: Frank Smith, for the first two voyages; Samuel Kennedy for two; Captains Corning, Manton, Woodside, Small, Bailey and Hooper, each had a try at her; Capt. Waldo Hill was in command the longest, some six years or so, being succeeded by Captain Gilkey. Captain Sturges had her when she was sold in 1879.

To San Francisco the *Messenger* made seven trips from New York and two from Philadelphia; fastest, 109 days in 1866; slowest, 138 days in 1867; average of the nine, 127 days. On all of these passages except that made in 1866, when fairly favorable weather throughout was encountered, she was handicapped in one way or another. On the first voyage, at noon on the 76th day from New York, she was 20 miles north of the latitude of Valparaiso and this in the face of the fact that for the prior 70 days the winds had been such that she had been unable to lay her course for any consecutive 24 hours. Thirteen days thereafter she crossed the equator and then had calms and light winds for practically all of the remaining 35 days into port. Her best day's run on the passage was 300 miles, under skysails and royal stunsails. On another day she logged 285 miles on the wind. Captain Smith was well pleased with the performances of his ship and predicted that with a fair chance, she could hold her own with the fastest clippers, a prophecy which was later fulfilled. On her second passage out, a continuance of light winds and calms prevailed. For 40 days the average was under 50 miles. She was within 600 miles of the Golden Gate for 17 days and close to the California coast for 12 days with the sea as smooth as glass. Practically the same experience was had on the third run, the time from the Horn to the line being 37 days; thence into port, 32 days, the final 11 days being passed within a distance of 800 miles from the Golden Gate.

On the next trip she had bad weather off the Horn, losing jibboom, etc. The usual run of light winds accompanied her on her fifth outward passage (1862), this time, however, occurring in the Atlantic, for she was 40 days to the line and 80 days to the Cape. However, she ran from the Pacific equator crossing into San Francisco Bay in 20 days; whole time from New York, 137 days. The commencement of the following voyage was very good with 20 days to the line and 49 to the Horn, but there good fortune stopped. Twenty days were spent in strong westerly gales and light winds were experienced in the Pacific; for seven days the ship was within 150 miles of destination; total passage, 127 days. On the longest westward passage, 138 days (1857), she took 25 days to the line; 61 to 50° South; 17 days rounding the Horn, during which lost nearly an entire suit of sails in very heavy weather; and was 33 days from the equator into port. Her last westward Cape Horn passage was in 1873, in 136 days, being 87 days between the two equator crossings, with 23 days of very heavy westerly gales off the Cape, during which shifted cargo. Under these stated conditions, her average of 127 days would appear to be very good and on one of the later runs she is said to have made 1032 nautical miles in three successive days, an average of 344 daily.

Of the return voyages from San Francisco, two were by way of China; one via Calcutta; one each, direct to New York, Philadelphia and Queenstown and on three occasions she took guano cargoes from Peru or the Pacific Islands. Completing her first voyage, she left Whampoa, Jan. 11, 1852, the favorable season, and reached New York in 94 days, being 73 days from Anjer; but the remarkable portion of the trip was her 17 days from the Atlantic equator crossing to Sandy Hook. The other passage from China was from Shanghai, whence she took her departure Oct. 24, 1854, the northeast monsoons not yet having set in; was 22 days to Anjer, crossed the equator 67 days out, and reached New York, Jan. 22, 1855, in 90 days from Shanghai and 68 from Anjer, an excellent passage for the season. Her passage from San Francisco to Philadelphia, in 85 days, in 1853-1854, when she was off the Capes of the Delaware, Jan. 3rd, 82 days out, is the sixth shortest passage recorded from the Pacific Coast to any Eastern port. She was up with Cape Horn when 38 days out (the record being the *Flying Dutchman's* 35 days), but after getting well clear of the Cape she did some wonderful work which is believed to have never been surpassed. She averaged 200 miles for 35 days, running up the Atlantic, and after passing the Abrohlos banks, off Brazil, in 18° South, she made by log, 3016 miles in 12 days. She had no cargo except a few specimens of California products among which was a ten foot long section from a giant redwood tree, 92 feet in circumference at the ground and 66 feet at ten feet above. It had required 150 days labor to cut out the section, which was then bored through and burned out, leaving a shell two feet thick.

Her run from Calcutta to Philadelphia, in 1856, was made in 95 days. In 1863 she was 100 days from San Francisco to New York and made the distance from latitude 17° South in the Atlantic to Sandy Hook, in 26 days. In 1873 she took a cargo of wheat from San Francisco to Queenstown in 122 days, her freight list being $26,000.

In 1856, Captain Corning took the *Messenger* from New York to Bombay in 90 days, excellent time considering the fact that she faced the adverse monsoon in the Indian Ocean. On the 44th day out from New York, she was some 400 miles south of the Cape of Good Hope and 20 days from the equator crossing. From Bombay she was 104 days to Liverpool, where Capt. Benjamin D. Manton took command and had a good passage of 80 days out to Melbourne. Thence went to India and China. In August 1859, Captain Manton was convicted at Hong Kong of cruelty to sailors and sentenced to three month's imprisonment and a fine of $250. The affair caused much indignation as it was proven that his crew had been insolent and mutinous. All of the American and most of the British merchants joined in a petition to the acting governor which resulted in the fine being remitted and the imprisonment order revoked. The ship had been on the China coast for some time "kidnapping coolies," as it was called, and in the spring of 1860 got away from Macao with her freight of Chinese laborers who were landed at Havana after a passage of 105 days. Going out to China, direct from New York, the *Messenger* then took a second living cargo to Havana, of 544 coolies, making the run in 102 days. Captain Bailey, whose ship *Golden Rocket* had just been captured and burned by the Confederate privateer *Sumter*, took the *Messenger* from Havana to New York, arriving July 27, 1861, and reporting a hard time off Hatteras; lost and split sails; had New York pilot on board for four days.

At San Francisco, in 1854, the *Messenger* had a record dispatch. She arrived off the Heads on Monday, July 17th; entered at the Custom House at 10 A.M. the next day; discharged her full cargo of assorted merchandise in 26 working hours, from three hatches, using double teams of horses for hoisting, and the work was done so carefully that the bill for damages was under $10. She cleared on

Wednesday afternoon; finished taking in 450 tons of ballast, swept decks and was ready for sea on Thursday at 1: 30 P.M. The time occupied from crossing the bar inward until the ship was on the Pacific, under full sail bound for China, was only 97 hours, during 35 of which she was idle; first, on account of arriving too late on Monday to enter at the Custom House and second, on account of the tow boat not being able to take her to sea Thursday afternoon.

While in the harbor of San Francisco, early in 1873, it was noted that the clipper ships *Young America, David Crockett, Fleetwing* and *Lookout* were also in port. All five ships had met at the same place in August 1855 and it was a matter of comment that after 18 years of service in all oceans and all parts of the world, the brave old ships once more found refuge within the friendly portals of the Golden Gate.

In September 1875, the *Messenger,* Captain Gilkey, crossed from Hong Kong to San Francisco in 47 days and went up to Puget Sound and took a cargo of lumber to Iquique, Peru. Captain Gilkey continued in the ship for some three years in trade between New York, China and Japan. In May 1879 she was reported about ready to sail from Port Louis, Mauritius, for San Francisco, but she was condemned there and sold to C. W. Turner of Lyttleton, N. Z., who had her rig changed to that of a bark. She proceeded to Newcastle, N. S. W., in ballast; was off the southwest coast of Tasmania when 23 days out, best day 330 miles. Arrived at Lyttleton, Aug. 21, 1879, from Newcastle and sailed again on Sept. 10th, in ballast. Two days later she went ashore on Farewell Spit, coast of New Zealand, and became a total wreck. In San Francisco, where she was always held in great favor by importers, the news of her loss was received with much regret.

METEOR

MEDIUM clipper ship, built in 1852, by E. & H. O. Briggs, at South Boston; 195 x 36 x 24; 1067 59/95 tons. She was built to the order of James Huckins of Boston, but during construction was sold by him to Curtis & Peabody of the same city. She was launched Oct. 27, 1852, and is described as a splendid ship, with a sharp bow ornamented with the representation of Atalanta picking up the golden apples. She is said to have been modeled after the *Northern Light* but was more nearly the tonnage of the *Boston Light,* an after production of the same builders.

Capt. Samuel W. Pike of Newburyport, later master of the *Sea Serpent,* was appointed commander of the *Meteor* and she sailed from Boston, Nov. 17, 1852, and arrived at San Francisco, Mar. 10, 1853. Her captain reported a passage of 110 days but the dates give 113 days. She was ten days off the Horn in severe gales and for eight days was within 400 miles of port. Continuing her voyage she left San Francisco, Mar. 30th, and arrived at Calcutta, June 21st; sailing thence Oct. 13, 1853, she had a 95 days' passage to Boston. On her second voyage she arrived at San Francisco, June 25, 1854, in 124 days from Boston. Was 19 days to the line; 60 days to the Horn and seven days off it; 40 days from the Horn to the equator and thence had light winds to port. Left San Francisco July 12th and was 55 days to Hong Kong, thence to Calcutta; sailed from Calcutta, Dec. 28, 1855, and was off Cape Cod on Mar. 31st, 93 days out, but had to haul off and arrived at Boston, Apr. 5, 1855, in 98 days from port of departure.

On her third voyage she left Boston, May 12, 1855, and arrived at San Francisco, Aug. 30th, in a passage of 110 days. Was 20 days to the line; passed through the Straits of LeMaire on July 4th; was becalmed off the Horn for two days; crossed the equator, Aug. 4th; was north of latitude 31° 11', on Aug. 20th, an excellent run from the line, but light winds kept her ten days from there to destination. Left San Francisco, Sept. 21st and was 13 days to Honolulu and 40 days, sailing time, to Hong Kong. Left Hong Kong for Melbourne,

Jan. 20, 1856, arriving at port of destination, Mar. 22nd, sailing thence Apr. 7th for Hong Kong. Arrived at San Francisco, Nov. 14, 1856, in 62 days from Hong Kong. Sailed from San Francisco, Dec. 12th and made the fast run of 38 days to Hong Kong. From Hong Kong she went to Rangoon, sailing thence in August, and was 110 days to Falmouth, Eng. She arrived at San Francisco, July 23, 1859, Captain Melville in command, who had replaced Captain Pike, reporting her passage as 114 days from New York. Was 29 days to the line; 63 days to the Horn and off it 15 days in heavy weather. Was 15½ days from 50° South, Pacific, to the equator and then had light winds to port. The above run of 15½ days is the record or near it. She left San Francisco, Aug. 9, 1859, for Calcutta, via Manila, and sailed from Calcutta, Jan. 23, 1860, arriving at Boston, Apr. 28th, in a passage of 96 days.

On her next voyage she left Boston, May 30, 1860, and arrived at San Francisco, Oct. 12th, a passage reported as 133 days though the dates give 135 days. Was 30 days to the line; passed through the Straits of LeMaire, Aug. 7th, in company with the *Black Prince* which arrived at San Francisco seven days after the *Meteor*, was 15 days from 50° to 50°; crossed the equator, Sept. 13th, and had light winds and calms to port. Left San Francisco, Nov. 18, 1860, and arrived at Falmouth, Eng., Feb. 24, 1861, in a passage of 98 days; thence to Calcutta in 94 days. From there she went to Hong Kong and during 1862 was engaged in trade between that port and Singapore and Bangkok, under command of Captain Woodward. About this time she was sold to go under the British flag.

MIDNIGHT

THE clipper ship *Midnight* was launched Apr. 17, 1854, from the yard of Fernald & Pettigrew, at Portsmouth, N. H. She was a handsome vessel with sharp ends and was coppered and masted while on the stocks. Captain Pierson of Boston superintended her construction; 175 x 36 x 20: 10; 962 tons, old measurement; 838 tons, new. She was owned by Henry Hastings of Boston.

She sailed from Boston, June 30, 1854, under command of Capt. James B. Hatch, and arrived at San Francisco, Oct. 25th, in a passage of 117 days. She reported 66 days to the Horn; crossed the equator in 115° West, 93 days out, after which she had light winds to port; was off the Horn eight days in strong gales. Sailed from San Francisco, Nov. 6th; arrived at Singapore, Jan. 2, 1855, and at Calcutta, Feb. 2nd; thence in 101 days to Boston, arriving June 20, 1855; making the round in ten days less than a year. On her second voyage she arrived at San Francisco, Dec. 29, 1855, in 144 days from New York. She reported 31 days to the line; 54 days to Cape Horn, off which she was 22 days in heavy weather; crossed the equator, Dec. 6th, after which had light winds and calms to port. Sailed from San Francisco, Mar. 1, 1856, and arrived at New York, June 9th, reporting 99 days' passage. Her next voyage to San Francisco was 143 days from New York, arriving out Jan. 2, 1857. Reported being 24 days off the Horn in heavy weather and had 27 days from 50° South in the Pacific to picking up the southeast trades; crossed the equator Dec. 12th. All ships arriving about this time reported similar experiences off the Horn and in the South Pacific. Sailed from San Francisco, Jan. 21st, for Aracan, Bay of Bengal; arrived at Hong Kong, Mar. 6th; at Singapore, Mar. 14th, and proceeded to Aracan.

The *Midnight* left Boston, Dec. 2, 1858, Captain Brock in command, and arrived at San Francisco, Apr. 5, 1859, in a passage of 124 days. Sailed from San Francisco, Apr. 27th, and arrived at Valparaiso, June 8th, in 48 days; thence to Boston. Arrived at San Francisco, May 17, 1860, in 120 days from Boston. Reported 62 days to the Horn, off which she was 15 days in severe weather; crossed the equator, Apr. 29th, in 112 days; carried the trades to 28° North, thence had moderate weather. Sailed from San Francisco, June 24, 1860, and arrived at Melbourne, Aug. 18th; passage, 54 days. From Melbourne she went to Calcutta and is said to have sailed from Colombo for London prior to June 6, 1861. From London she crossed to New York, arriving Nov. 11, 1861. Arrived at San Francisco, July

8, 1862, in 142 days from New York. Reported 23 days to the line; 60 days to the Horn and off it 24 days in strong westerly gales, during which she lost an entire suit of sails and sprung her bowsprit. Sailed from San Francisco, Aug. 10th, and arrived at Boston, Nov. 29, 1862, in 111 days.

Her next arrival at San Francisco was on June 12, 1863, in 132 days from Boston. Captain Brock reported that in a hurricane, Feb. 3rd, in 38° 50′ North, 58° West, he had every sail blown away; lost booby hatch, binnacle boats, water and coal casks and one man overboard; was hove to over 12 hours with the dead eyes under water. Sailed from San Francisco, July 10th; was off Honolulu 12½ days out and arrived at Hong Kong, Aug. 31st. From China she went to New York and here Captain Crosby took her for one voyage and arrived at San Francisco, June 10, 1865, in a passage of 142 days. Sailed from San Francisco, July 29th; was off Honolulu, Aug. 12th, and proceeded to Hong Kong. Sailed from Whampoa on Nov. 30th; passed Anjer, Dec. 10th; Cape of Good Hope, Jan. 12th; the equator, Feb. 5th, and arrived at New York, Feb. 26, 1866, in 87 days from Whampoa. Shortly after clearing the Straits of Sunda, on Dec. 15th, the *Midnight* spoke the clipper bark, *Benefactress,* which arrived at New York four days before the *Midnight,* in 87 days from Amoy.

The *Midnight* arrived at San Francisco, Aug. 31, 1866, Captain Brock reporting 119 days from New York, which port he left May 3rd. Crossed the line, June 3rd; was 60 days to 50° South, Atlantic, and then had the phenomenally short run of seven days to 50°, Pacific; crossed the equator, Aug. 10th, and was on the coast ten days in fog, near the Roads three days, and came to anchor off the Heads, Aug. 30th; actual sailing time 117 days. Returned to New York in 112 days.

In the summer of 1870 the *Midnight* was at Singapore and the United States consul there sent to Boston on her, some of the crew of the clipper ship *Fearless,* who had been treated cruelly by the captain and mate on their outward voyage from Boston. During

1871-1872 the *Midnight* continued in trade between China and Boston or New York and sometime in 1872 Captain Kendrick succeeded Captain Brock. She arrived at New York in March 1873, having left Hong Kong, Dec. 13, 1872, passing Anjer, Dec. 24th. In 1874 she loaded at Hong Kong and arrived at San Francisco, June 4, 1874, after a passage of 59 days. Sailed from San Francisco, July 15, 1874, for Honolulu, Baker's Island and Liverpool; charter, £4.5.0 per ton; arrived at Liverpool, Jan. 1, 1875.

While on a voyage from New York for Yokohama, under command of Captain Tucker, the *Midnight* put into Amboyna, leaky, some time in January 1878 and discharged cargo. She was condemned, given up to the underwriters and sold for £540. Her valuable cargo of petroleum, coal and hardware was forwarded by another vessel. She was said to have been well insured.

MINNEHAHA

MEDIUM clipper ship, launched from the yard of Donald McKay, at East Boston, Mass., Mar. 22, 1857. She was a handsome ship in every way, with good lines and while generally spoken of as a fast sailer, yet such records of her passages as are available do not include any noteworthy run. Her capacity for dead weight cargo was 2300 tons, against her register of 1698 tons, old measurement. In May 1862 she was sold at New York for $62,500, to Samuel G. Reed & Co., of Boston, who continued as owners until her loss.

The maiden voyage of the *Minnehaha* was to Australia and for some years she is said to have been operated in trade with the Far East, with Captain Beauchamp in command. In January 1862, when homeward bound, she rescued the crew of the bark *Waverley*, Moulmain for Queenstown, and landed them at Table Bay, Feb. 4th. Under command of Captain Hopkins she sailed from New York, July 21, 1862, with a cargo of coal for the Pacific Mail Steamship Company at San Francisco. In the South Atlantic, very heavy gales caused such a leak to develop that she put back to Rio, arriving on her 70th day out from New York. A portion of her cargo had to be discharged and after a stay in port of 35 days, making repairs, she resumed her voyage on Nov. 6th; was 31 days from Rio to 50° South; 38 days thence to the Pacific equator crossing and 34 days thence to San Francisco, arriving Feb. 17, 1863, in 103 days from Rio. On crossing the bar, inward bound, she shipped a sea which carried away the stern rail and filled the cabin. From San Francisco she went to Callao in 48 days; thence to England with guano.

On her only other visit to San Francisco, she reached that port, Nov. 20, 1864, in 189 days from London, with coal, Capt. David Bursley in command. Off the Platte, in a pampero of 16 hours duration, she was hove on beam ends; the head was carried away, the bulwarks, galley and round house stove, and the cargo shifted. She was 32 days rounding the Horn in strong westerly gales and 37 days from the equator to destination in light head winds and calms; was 12 days making the last 200 miles. Completing this voyage she again returned east via Callao.

On Oct. 20, 1867, the *Minnehaha* arrived at Honolulu, in 29 days from Yokohama, Captain Bursley being still in command. On Nov. 20th she arrived at Baker's Island, 16 days from Honolulu, and was brought to her moorings. For ten days the weather was calm but then heavy squalls came up; all shipping escaped however by putting out anchors, running extra lines, etc. A calm of three days then ensued, followed by heavy squalls with rain, the wind blowing stronger than had ever before been experienced at the Island. On Dec. 3rd the head moorings of the *Minnehaha* carried away and her bow swung on the reef. The stern moorings then gradually hauled in and she soon lay broadside on the reef. Twenty-four hours later not a stick forty feet long was to be seen. No lives were lost, the crew having got ashore in time but without being able to save much of their belongings. The storm lasted 60 hours and also caused the loss of the ship *Washington*, of Boston, on McKean's Island.

The Minnehaha was insured for $56,000.

MISCHIEF

EXTREME clipper ship, launched by James M. Hood, at Somerset, Mass., Mar. 26, 1853; 146 x 29 x 16: 6; 548 tons. She was described as a particularly handsome little clipper, having the sharpest ends ever put on a ship and her initial passage from New York to San Francisco was expected to be under 90 days. Her dead rise was 26 inches. Her original owners were W. H. Merrill and Capt. Martin Townsend, her hailing port being New York. After arrival at San Francisco in November 1853, she was reported as being sold for $22,000 and Captain Logan assumed command.

On her maiden voyage she left New York, May 19, 1852, and put into Valparaiso leaky, Aug. 15th, 88 days out. Arrived at San Francisco, Nov. 9th, in 133 sailing days from New York and 45 days from Valparaiso. From San Francisco she was 15 days to Honolulu and 30 days thence to Hong Kong. Returned to San Francisco, her passage being reported as 43 days. Went back to Hong Kong, being 11 days to Honolulu and 38 days thence to destination. On her run from Hong Kong to San Francisco it was stated that she was detained near the Loo Choo Islands for five days, making the run thence to destination in the very fast time of 29 days, the whole passage from Hong Kong to the Golden Gate being equivalent to 38 days.

She left Foo Chow, under Captain Lawrence, on Sept. 14, 1854, and went down the China Sea in very heavy weather; entered the north end of Gaspar Straits, Oct. 18th; was detained in the Straits of Sunda, Oct. 20th, for five hours on account of a revolt in the crew; arrived off Sandy Hook, Jan. 5, 1855, 76 days from Java Head and reached New York, two days later, in 116 days from Foo Chow. She then crossed to Bremen where she was sold to Meyer & Stucher. Subsequently she was sold to parties in Denmark and in the late 60's and early 70's appears as the bark *Sleipner*, of Copenhagen, owned by A. W. Hansen & Co.

MONARCH OF THE SEAS

BUILT by Roosevelt & Joyce, at New York, in 1854; 223 x 43 x 29; 1971 tons; Lawrence Giles & Co., of New York, owners. Sold at New York in 1863. Resold at Liverpool in 1865. Left Liverpool, Mar. 19, 1866, and was never heard from.

MONSOON

CLIPPER ship, built in 1851 by Trufant & Drummond, at Bath, Me., for George Hussey of New Bedford, which was her port of registry; 158 x 32: 7 x 21; 773 tons, old measurement. She was of sharp model and gained the name of being a fast sailer. In August 1852, after returning to Boston from her first voyage, it was advertised that for eight consecutive days she had averaged 293 miles and on one day had logged 346 miles.

On her first passage to San Francisco, the *Monsoon* reached port Jan. 6, 1853, in 130 days from Boston. Captain Winsor reported having had a succession of light winds throughout and being four days off the Heads in thick fog. She went to Singapore in 50 days from the Golden Gate; thence 35 days to Calcutta and 102 days from there to New Bedford. Captain Baker assumed command and leaving Boston, Jan. 4, 1854, was 19 days to the line; 60 days to Cape Horn, crossing the equator on the 97th day; then had the very fast run of 16 days to sighting land but was blown off and did not pass through the Golden Gate until May 4th, seven days later, in 120 days from Boston. Went to Callao in 48 days; thence 85 days to Baltimore. On her last Cape Horn passage to San Francisco she left New York, Feb. 27, 1855; was 30 days to the line; thence all light winds to destination except for the 30 days rounding Cape Horn; reached destination Aug. 2nd, 154 days out. Completing the voyage she crossed to China and reached New York, Apr. 7, 1856, in 109 days from Foo Chow and 94 days from Anjer. Sailed from New York, July 26, 1856, and arrived in Hobson's Bay, Nov. 11th. It was reported that she hove to off Sydney and was driven into a cove where she lost her anchors and was obliged to substitute a cannon. From Melbourne she went to Singapore, Calcutta, China and home.

Under Captain Loring she left New York, Aug. 1, 1861; passed Anjer, Nov. 19th, and arrived at Hong Kong, Dec. 31st. Went to Bangkok and Singapore, sailing from the latter port, Mar. 21, 1862; passed Anjer, Mar. 30th; the Cape, May 11th; had light winds to the line, June 9th, and arrived at New York, July 6th.

Loaded for Australia, arriving at Newcastle, Jan. 19, 1863; thence to Shanghai and Manila. On Dec. 30, 1864, she arrived at San Francisco with 1000 tons of sugar from Manila, Captain Loring reporting very severe weather throughout the run of 73 days. Sailed from San Francisco, Feb. 9, 1865; was 19 days to the line; 40 days thence to Cape Horn; crossed the equator May 17th and was thence 21 days to New York, arriving June 7th, in a passage of 117 days.

In 1865 the *Monsoon*, which up to that time had been owned by George Hussey, was reported sold for $23,000 and the register of 1866 gives her owners as Ruger Bros., and Captain Closson as her commander. From 1870 to 1875 she appears in the registers as the Norwegian ship *Monsoon*, hailing port, Krageroe, J. Duces, owner.

MORNING GLORY

BUILT at Portsmouth, N. H., in 1854; 1114 tons; J. Goodwin of Portsmouth, owner. Sold to go under the British flag, in 1864, and renamed the *British Crown*.

MORNING LIGHT (1)

THE extreme clipper ship *Morning Light* was built at Portsmouth, N. H., by Tobey & Littlefield and was their first production. Launched Aug. 25, 1853, for account of Glidden & Williams of Boston. Tonnage 1713, old measurement; 1589 tons, British measurement; length of keel, 205 feet; deck, 220 feet; over all,

235 feet; extreme breadth of beam, 43 feet; depth of hold, 27 feet. She had three decks, the 'tween decks being seven feet four inches each. As the stern post was at right angles with the keel, the stem had 30 feet forerake; the dead rise at the half floor was 20 inches, swell of sides, six inches, and sheer, three feet and six inches. She had sharp ends and the bow was carried up in its angular form, to the rail, which was above the bowsprit. The figurehead was an archer with bended bow and quiver; the graceful oval stern was ornamented with a carved, gilded chariot in which an Aurora was seated. She was in hull, spars and rigging an exceedingly beautiful ship, her lofty masts and immense yards making her a conspicuous member of the clipper fleet and at sea she was said to loom up like a line-of-battle ship. Her cost was $117,000 and for solidity of construction she could not have been excelled. Capt. E. D. Knight left the *Queen of the Seas* to take command of the *Morning Light*.

Prophecies made for an exceedingly short run on the maiden voyage of the new clipper were not realized, due to unfavorable conditions of winds and weather. She had the long time of 37 and 42 days to the line and St. Roque, respectively, and was not in the Pacific, northbound, until the 82nd day out; thence to the equator crossing, her 24 days time was fair, while her excellent run of 15 days from the line, to within 500 miles of the Golden Gate, was offset by the ten days thereafter into port. She had left Boston, Oct. 3, 1853, and reached San Francisco, Feb. 11, 1854,—a passage of 131 days. From San Francisco she went to Callao, in 51 days, with light winds throughout. From Callao to New York, with guano, she had a continuation of light and adverse winds and was 84 days making the run. Was 33 days to the Horn; 58 days to the line and was within 500 miles of New York for seven days. Arrived out, Oct. 16, 1854.

On her second voyage she arrived at San Francisco, Apr. 12, 1855, Captain Knight reporting her passage as 112 days, her log beginning Dec. 21, 1854. With fair winds in the North Atlantic it would have been close to 100 days, but as it was she did not pass St.

Roque until 35 days out; was 60 days to the Horn, off which she had six days of heavy weather; crossed the equator, Mar. 23rd, in 111° West, 92 days out, and for four days was within 200 miles of her destination. As before, she went to Callao and loaded guano, this time for Spain, and arrived at Valencia, Jan. 11, 1856; thence crossed from Cadiz to Boston in 26 days.

The *Morning Light* made three more passages from New York or Boston to San Francisco but in none of them did she equal the time made on her second voyage and in all she seemed to encounter the same unfavorable weather conditions. Her third passage, from Boston, was made in 124 days; her fourth, from the same port, this time under Captain Thomas, was made in 141 days and on this trip, with her usual luck, she was 32 days off the Horn. Her fifth voyage was 128 days from New York, during which she lost her figure-head in a heavy gale which lasted 48 hours; but she ended up in good style by making the run from the equator to San Francisco in 18 days.

The *Morning Light* commenced her last voyage under the American flag by taking her departure from Cardiff, Aug. 21, 1861. She had her usual hard luck as to weather conditions and her run to Valparaiso was a long one of 88 days, but her passage from Valparaiso to San Francisco, 37 days, is within one day of the record and taking into consideration the fact that she was becalmed three days off the port of departure, her 34 days actual sailing time is the fastest, by two days, ever made. From San Francisco she went to Callao and then to Queenstown and in April 1863 was sold at London for £9000 sterling to sail under the British flag. Her new owners, James Baines & Co., renamed her *Queen of the South* and employed her in Colonial trade.

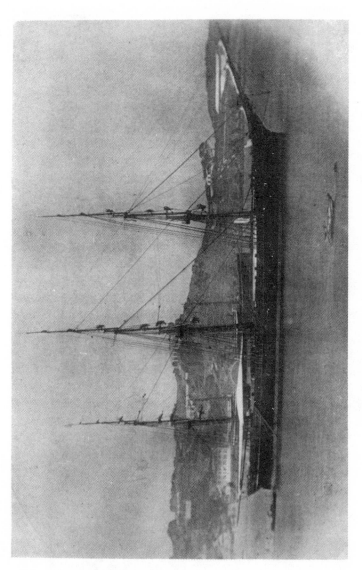

"N. B. PALMER," 1399 TONS, BUILT AT NEW YORK, IN 1851
From a photograph made in Amoy, in 1867

"NIGHTINGALE," 1060 TONS, BUILT AT PORTSMOUTH, N. H., IN 1851

From a lithograph by N. Currier, after the drawing by C. Parsons made in 1854

"Northern Light," 1021 tons, built at South Boston, Mass., in 1851

"Northern Light," 1021 tons, built at South Boston, Mass., in 1851

MORNING LIGHT (2)

EXTREME clipper ship, built in 1853, by William Cramp, at Kensington, near Philadelphia; 162 keel; 172 deck x 34 x 19; 938 tons. Capt. Benjamin Johnson was her first commander and she was owned by Bucknor & McGammon of Philadelphia.

The *Morning Light* was very sharp with a wedge-shaped bow and little sheer and lines so fine that her capacity for such a cargo as bulk guano was but 1017 tons. She carried three royals instead of the three skysails then in vogue; had single topsails and looked every inch a clipper. She was launched Aug. 15, 1853, and sailing from Philadelphia, Sept. 25, 1853, arrived at San Francisco, Feb. 9, 1854, in a passage of 136 days. She reported being off the Horn for 25 days and within eight miles of the Cape, twice, each time being driven back by furious westerly gales. Was five days on the California coast before being able to get into port. Maury divides her run as follows: 38 days to the line and 41 days to St. Roque, then 21 days to 50° South and 24 days thence to 50° in the Pacific; 25 days later crossed the equator in 113° West and had a good run to the coast of 18 days, off which she was detained five days by adverse winds. She sailed from San Francisco, Feb. 24, 1854, and was 46 days to Iquique, this being the fastest passage to the West Coast from San Francisco made about that time. It was particularly remarkable in that the *Morning Light* was but 12 days from the Golden Gate to the equator in 109° West and only 18 days thence to her highest southern latitude, 34°, both splendid runs. She sailed from Arica, May 18th and arrived at Philadelphia in 89 days.

On her second passage she arrived at San Francisco, Mar. 14, 1855, in 121 days from Philadelphia, went on to Calcutta in 92 days and was 104 days from Sand Heads to the Delaware Capes. On her third voyage she had the long passage of 144 days; from Philadelphia to San Francisco; thence to Callao in 49 days and arrived at Baltimore, via Hampton Roads, in 89 days. She again sailed from Philadelphia, Aug. 28, 1857, with a cargo of coal for Panama, on Government account and was damaged by a pampero off the

Platte and obliged to put into Rio for repairs. In 1860 she was 140 days from home port to San Francisco, thence to Baker's Island where she took on a load of guano; was obliged to put into Sydney, leaky, and arrived at New York, June 28, 1861, Captain Johnson still in command.

In 1859 the *Morning Light* was sold at auction for $26,000.

In the fall of 1861 she was purchased for the United States Government from J. B. Sarby, agent, for $37,500 and was equipped with eight cannon and used as a cruiser. On Feb. 28, 1862, she arrived at New York from a cruise in the Gulf under command of Commander H. T. Moore. In 1863 she was attached to the West Gulf Squadron and her officers were Acting Masters, John Dillingham, H. W. Washburn, W. W. Fowler and L. H. Partridge; Masters' Mates, George H. Rice and J. L. Chambers; Acting Assistant Surgeon, John W. Shrify; Paymaster, W. S. Blunt.

Early in 1863, off the coast of Texas, she was surprised and captured by the Confederates, set on fire and totally destroyed.

MORNING STAR

CLIPPER ship, launched Oct. 4, 1853, from the yard of Tobey & Littlefield, at Portsmouth, N. H.; 187 x 36: 2 x 23: 8; 1105 tons. She was of fine model and heavily sparred. Her owners were T. B. Waters & Co., of Boston and Captains William L. and Nathan F. Foster were successively in command until she was sold foreign, in 1863.

On her first voyage she left Boston, Nov. 15, 1853, and was 15 days to New Orleans; thence 31 days to Liverpool; thence to Boston in 24 days. Loaded for San Francisco, sailing July 2, 1854, and arriving out Nov. 27th in 148 days. She thereafter made five similar runs as follows:—138 days; 102 days; 125 days; 105 days and 115 days. Average for the six runs, 120 5/6 days, a good showing when account is taken of the particularly unfavorable conditions prevailing on the first two runs. On the 102 day passage, which was in 1857, she crossed the line in under 20 days; was up with the Horn on the 50th day; was on the equator in the Pacific, 78 days out; was 13 days between 5° South and 5° North, and off the California coast several days in light winds and calms. In 1860 she was only 60 days from the equator crossing in the Atlantic to the Pacific crossing and had it not been for light winds and calms for the final ten days of the run it would have been made in two figures.

Of her homeward trips, two were from Calcutta, in 101 days and 105 days, to Boston and London respectively. In 1857 she was 92 days from Callao to Havre. In 1860 she was 122 days from San Francisco to New York. She went from San Francisco to Calcutta in 73 days and from Hong Kong to Singapore in ten days. While at Callao, in the summer of 1857, ready to sail for Havre, the ship being gotten under way, the mate was stabbed by one of the crew, the remainder of them drawing knives and pistols. The mutiny was finally quelled by an armed force from H. B. M. ship *Monarch*.

On Mar. 23, 1863, when 74 days out from Calcutta for London and near the equator in the Atlantic, the *Morning Star* was fallen in with by the Confederate privateer *Alabama*, but the cargo being owned by neutrals, the ship was released under a bond of $60,000 and allowed to proceed. Shortly after her arrival at London she was sold for £6500 sterling and became the British ship *Landsborough*, owned by Smith, Bilbrough and Co., of that port. From 1865 to 1871, inclusive, she is listed as owned by Mackey and Co., of Liverpool and commanded by Captain Maxwell. She made some passages on the "Black Ball Line" of Australian packets and according to one report was lost in the late seventies. Mitchell's Register reports her loss as in 1890.

MOUNTAIN WAVE

MEDIUM clipper ship, built by Joshua Magoun, at Charlestown, Mass.; launched Dec. 13, 1852. Owned by Alpheus Hardy & Co., of Boston, while under the American flag. A small ship of but 708 tons, foreign measurement, and 17 feet draft, she had fine lines and was called a superior ship. Her first master was Capt. John Paine who was succeeded by Captain Humphrey. Later she was commanded by Captains Isaac Fessenden, Charles Hopkins, George Hardy and Captain Sears.

The first voyage of the *Mountain Wave* was from Boston to San Francisco, arriving out May 28, 1853, in 130 days, with light winds throughout. From San Francisco she went to Callao in 57 days and from that port was 90 days to Hampton Roads. On her second voyage she sailed from Boston, Nov. 24, 1854; was 43 days to the line; put into Rio when 56 days out and was 98 days thence to San Francisco, arriving May 13, 1855; was 25 days off the Horn in heavy gales, having head rails stove; from 50° South, Pacific, to San Francisco, was 56 days in light breezes, the topsails not being reefed once.

These two passages were all that the *Mountain Wave* made to California. In 1858 she was 140 days from Boston to Honolulu, returning thence to New Bedford in 128 days. She then went out to China and for a time operated on that coast. On Dec. 30, 1860, while bound from Iloilo to Melbourne, she encountered a heavy gale off the coast of Mindanao, losing sails and having bowsprit and foretopgallant mast sprung; put back to Iloilo, arriving Jan. 4, 1861. From then until February 1863, she was engaged in trade between China and the Philippines and Melbourne and Otago. On Mar. 9, 1863, she left Manila for New York, in company with the ship *Danube*, of and for Boston. The two ships were together on the run down the China Sea and through the Straits of Sunda; were in sight of each other daily in the Indian Ocean until up with the south end of Madagascar, when, the wind coming out ahead, they went off on separate tacks and did not again see each other. Captain

Whidden of the *Danube* considered it the most even sailing ever reported, considering the length of time and great distance covered. The *Mountain Wave* arrived at New York, July 4th, 117 days from Manila, 100 from Java Head and 70 days from the Cape. The *Danube* arrived at Boston, July 11th.

On June 21, 1864, the *Mountain Wave* arrived at New York, 18 days from New Orleans, with a cargo of iron. Her captain, Charles Hopkins, had formerly commanded the *Santa Claus* which foundered in August 1863. Captain Hopkins later took the brig *Lorana* and died aboard her at Havana, in 1866.

The *Mountain Wave* sailed from Boston, Jan. 12, 1865, for Calcutta, Captain Sears in command. On Feb. 21st she put into Rio with loss of sails and spars. Later she was sold to parties who renamed her *Maria del Gloria* and altered her rig to that of a bark. Registers then gave her hailing port as Fayal.

MYSTERY

CLIPPER ship, launched from the yard of Samuel Hall, at East Boston, Mass., Jan. 11, 1853; deck, 185; over all, 196 x 37 x 23; 1155 tons, old measurement; 1074 tons, new measurement. Dead rise, 19 inches; swell of sides, six inches; sheer, three feet. She had long, sharp ends and a handsome semi-elliptical stern. A mermaid rising from the sea was the figurehead. She was owned by Crocker & Sturgis and D. G. & W. B. Bacon of Boston.

The *Mystery* made but one complete voyage under the American flag, being sold after arrival at London, in March 1854, for £17,000, to go under the British flag without change of name. She had sailed from Boston, Feb. 6, 1853, under command of Capt. Peter Peterson; was 18 days off the Horn in heavy westerly gales, during which carried away the head and was damaged on deck; put into Valparaiso, Apr. 30th, 83 days out, short of water; sailed May 4th; was 20 days to the equator and 32 days thence to the Golden Gate, having had no trades and being off the California coast 14 days in calms and fogs. Arrived at San Francisco, June 25th, in 135 sailing days from Boston and 52 from Valparaiso. Then crossed to Shanghai, in 44 days, and loaded for London; left Woosung, Nov. 18th and arrived at Deal, Mar. 14, 1854, in 116 days' passage; 98 from Anjer.

After being sold she was engaged in trade, principally between London and India. Left Deal, June 28, 1854, and was 101 days to Bombay; returned to London in 98 days. Left Deal, July 12, 1855, and went out to Sydney in 92 days; thence to Calcutta and from there had the long passage of 147 days to Deal. Sailed from London, Nov. 5, 1856, and was 102 days to Bombay, arriving back at London, Aug. 8, 1857, in 112 days from Bombay.

In 1861, the *Mystery* is listed as owned in Liverpool by W. Coltart and from 1863 to 1871 as owned in London by J. M. Walsh. From 1861 to 1863 she was commanded by Captain Matthews.

N. B. PALMER

EXTREME clipper ship, launched Feb. 5, 1851, by Westervelt & Mackay, at New York, for account of A. A. Low & Brother, of that city, who remained owners until 1873. She was one of the most famous of the American clipper fleet and for years was certainly the most popular vessel entering the harbors of either Hong Kong or Shanghai, where her captain, Charles Porter Low, had the reputation of being a most lavish entertainer as well as a navigator of signal ability. Captain Low took great pride in his handsome ship, the model of which attracted much attention when exhibited at the Crystal Palace Exposition, in London, in 1851. On the occasion of the celebration of the Queen's birthday at Hong Kong, in 1863, the *Palmer* was acknowledged to be the "gem of the harbor," as she was literally covered with flags and in the evening illuminated with lanterns.

The *Palmer* was 202:6 x 38:6 x 21:9; 1399 tons, old measurement; 1124 tons, new measurement. She proved to be one of the fastest sailing ships ever built and was an excellent sea boat, especially in heavy weather. Of her outward passages from New York, the first three were made to San Francisco; thereafter, while she was American owned, all were to Hong Kong with the exception of two to Shanghai, there being 17 all told. On her first run out to the Golden Gate she was 23 days to the line; 48 days to 50° South; 66 days to the same latitude in the Pacific; 88 days to the equator and 19 days thence to port, a total of 107 days, arrival date being Aug. 21, 1851. On her second passage she was 24 days to the line from Sandy Hook and passed Cape Horn 57 days out; had heavy gales with much rain, hail and snow and very high seas, storm after storm succeeding each other for 35 days or until the ship was well into the Pacific; put into Valparaiso, Aug. 16th, 85 days out, to land two seamen who had attempted to murder the first and second officers. For 18 days near the Horn, Captain Low was without any assistance from his officers and on account of his turbulent crew and the continual storm, was obliged to keep the deck continually, not getting any chance to sleep below. At Valparaiso most of his sailors deserted but he was able to secure a new and efficient crew and made the run from the Chilean port to San Francisco in 41 days; total time from New York, 130 days or 126 actual sailing days. The third and last passage of the ship from New York to San Francisco was in 121 days; arrival out, Jan. 26, 1854. Light and variable winds in the North Atlantic prolonged the run to the line to 32 days; 18 days were spent off the Horn in storms, with much hail, snow and cold weather; crossed the equator in the Pacific, 96 days out.

Of the 15 passages made from New York to Hong Kong, six were made in 100 days or less, as follows:—in 1858, 88 days, her fastest outward run to China, Captain Higham, formerly her chief officer, in command; in 1859, Captain Frisbie had 100 days; the other four were under Captain Low,—100 days in 1860, 97 days in 1861, 90 days in 1868 and 93 days in 1870. In 1869, Captain Low had 93 days to Shanghai pilot. Of her homeward runs from China, Captain Higham had also the honor of making the fastest, Shanghai to New York (1858-1859) in 82 days, 64 from Anjer, and 35 from the Cape. In 1859-1860, the *Swordfish* was also 82 days over this course; these runs have never been beaten. The *Palmer's* run from Anjer is within two days of record. In 1852, Captain Low had 84 days from passing Macao to anchorage in New York harbor; in 1857-1858, 100 days from Hong Kong. In 1865, Captain Steele, also a former chief officer in the ship, had 92 days from Hong Kong. In 1855, Captain Frisbie was 99 days from Manila, home. On arrival of the ship at New York, Jan. 15, 1861, in 108 days from Amoy, it was noted as a remarkable coincidence that it was the fourth successive year in which she had reached that port from China between noon of the 15th and noon of the 16th of January.

In 1861, the *Palmer* was 45 days from Hong Kong to San Francisco and in 1863 was 44 days over the same course. In 1854 she went from San Francisco to Honolulu in ten days, averaging over 200 miles daily. Sailed from Honolulu, Apr. 23rd, with a cargo of whale oil; crossed the equator, six days out; passed the Horn, 38 days out, and was on the equator in the Atlantic on the 57th day, but light winds and calms delayed her arrival at New York until July 14th, or 82 days from Honolulu, a passage that has been equalled but never beaten.

Outside of fast complete passages, the *Palmer* is credited with the following performances:—in 1868 and again in 1872, she was 72 hours from Woosung to off Pedro Blanco, where she hove to and sent letters into Hong Kong by pilot. In 1851 she was 75 hours from Shanghai to anchorage in Hong Kong, having logged 846 miles. In 1856, on a passage from New York to Hong Kong, she averaged 335 miles for four days and 288 miles daily for 12 days. On May 26, 1852, when three days out from New York for San Francisco, she made 396 nautical miles, from noon to noon, which, with her, was less than 24 hours. In all of the instances quoted Captain Low was in command for although on three different occasions he had remained ashore for a voyage or more he had always later on resumed command and was in charge on her arrival at New York from China, in February 1873, when Messrs. Low decided to sell the ship. The mate, Mr. Nairn, was then temporarily put in charge and Captain Low retired from the sea. He had made his first voyage in 1842, as boy on the *Horatio,* a well-known China merchantman, and five years later was master of the *Houqua,* which he left to take the *Samuel Russell* and later, the new *N. B. Palmer.* Captain Low died at Santa Barbara, Cal., Feb. 22, 1913, a few days after having been stricken with paralysis. He was 89 years of age.

Captain Low's very interesting "Reminiscences" include several accounts of the *Palmer* when she met and incidentally raced different famous clipper ships. In 1852, when 15 days out from New York, bound for San Francisco, he came up with the *Gazelle,* which had taken her departure six days before him. Being in the doldrums, the two ships were in company for several days, alternately one getting a breeze and forging ahead and then the other. On reaching the southeast trades, however, the *Gazelle* was soon left "a long way astern." In the North Pacific, 95 days later, the two ships again met, the *Palmer* having put into Valparaiso while the *Gazelle* had been badly damaged by collision off Cape Horn. In May 1868, when 14 days out from New York bound for Hong Kong, the *Palmer* came up with the clipper ship *Game Cock,* which had left five days before her, and, as Captain Low puts it, "we were in company five days when we left her out of sight astern." A particularly interesting reminiscence, however, is the account of the meeting of the *Palmer* and *Flying Cloud* in the South Atlantic, July 1, 1852, both ships being bound from New York to San Francisco. The *Cloud* had passed Sandy Hook on May 14th, the *Palmer* getting away the 22nd. In the North Atlantic, Captain Low had more favorable winds and weather than were experienced by Captain Cressy, so that on crossing the line, the *Cloud* was only three days ahead. South of the line the *Cloud* had two heavy gales, losing some sails and having the head of the foremast sprung, while her rival with good weather was steadily overhauling her. At noon on July 1st, in about 32° South, Captain Low, when taking his observations, made out a ship dead to windward, which he thought might be the *Cloud*, then out from port 49 days against his 41 days. Here would be an excellent opportunity for a trial of speed between rivals which were believed by competent judges to be of equal capability; on the occasion of their maiden passages the prophecy had been made that each would reach San Francisco in not over 95 days after leaving New York. The *Cloud* had eclipsed this by five days while the *Palmer* was 107 days, the difference being practically all due to the extra detention of the latter in rounding Cape Horn. From San Francisco to China and from there home, however, she had turned the tables on the *Cloud*. Captain Low had always been confident that his ship could outsail his rival going before the wind, but conceded that on a wind he would be beaten by at least a mile an hour. When he sighted the *Cloud* both ships were running before the wind under all sail and Low hauled up close to the wind with studding sails shaking, until the *Cloud* was alongside. Captain Cressy appeared much chagrined on learning the length of the *Palmer's* time from New York and continued going ahead at full speed while Low's ship was at a standstill. Shortly after the *Palmer* had filled away, the wind hauled ahead and the studding sails had to be taken in and the ship braced sharp on a wind, the *Cloud* in the meantime getting quite a start. The next day, 24 hours after the meeting, the *Palmer* was only 12 miles astern, much to the satisfaction of her captain, who had not anticipated being able to so nearly hold his own.

An incident unparalleled in the maritime annals of the port of San Francisco was the mooring at her specified berth and wharf, of a large fully laden ship without the assistance of towboats or others. According to Captain Low's account, the pilot had anchored the *Palmer* in the stream and refused to obey the orders of the agents to bring her up to the wharf. Low, however assuming all responsibility, hove up the anchor, set all sails including skysails and on the ebb tide, with a light beam wind, went along nicely until close enough to the wharf, when the main yard was backed and the ship was brought alongside with scarcely a jar. The assembled crowd cheered most heartily and the feat was long remembered as being the prettiest piece of seaman-ship ever done in San Francisco. This was on Aug. 21, 1851.

While under American registry, the *Palmer* was singularly fortu-nate as to mishaps. On Feb. 28, 1853, when homeward bound from Whampoa, she struck on the reef known as Broussa Shoal, near the North Watcher Island, Java Sea, while going eight knots, but got off by kedging, the ship leaking seven inches an hour. The captain put into Batavia, discharged cargo and had to go to the Onrust Navy Yard for repairs. On examination, a piece of coral nearly two feet in diameter fell out of the beam ends, which, had it come out at sea, would have caused the ship to founder in less than an hour. Al-though repairs went on under great disadvantage, only four Euro-peans, ten Chinese and six Manila-men being available for work, yet, by Mar. 28, 1853, the repairs were nearly completed and the vessel ready to reship her cargo. Nearly all of the *Palmer's* crew were then taken sick with Java fever and Captain Low shipped the crew of the condemned ship *Sumatra* in their place. In December 1864, shortly after leaving Hong Kong for New York, she was found to be leaking and put back. On arrival at New York she was thoroughly overhauled and practically rebuilt.

After her sale in the spring of 1873, she was engaged in trade from New York to Antwerp or Hamburg, mostly carrying oil out-ward and empty barrels on return. Records show various returns to port on account of having been on beam ends and cargo jettisoned. On Jan. 10, 1892, she was abandoned in latitude 45° North, longi-tude 43° West. She had been under the Norwegian flag, hailing from Arendel and operating under original name.

NABOB

MEDIUM clipper ship, built by John Taylor, at Chelsea, Mass.; launched Jan. 21, 1854; 193 deck x 38 x 24; 1246 tons. During her life she was owned by William Appleton & Co., and by their successors Hooper & Co., on the retirement of Mr. Appleton from the firm. She was a handsome ship of fine model with convex lines. An eagle was her figurehead. Although not an extreme clipper she was reasonably sharp and yet a good carrier having, in 1861, on a voyage from California to England, loaded 1566 short tons of wheat, a cargo 25 per cent greater than her register, old measurement. She established an excellent record for speed, the following instances being very close to record:—Lizard to Boston, 18 days, 6 hours, in 1855;—Boston to the equator, 17 days, 21 hours, in 1856;—New York to Hong Kong, in 1857, in 85 days, being only 52 days from St. Roque to destination, against the 54 days of the *Oriental* on the record run of 81 days in 1850;—Foo Chow to Bermudas, 82 days—to Sandy Hook 89 days and into New York harbor 91 days, in 1860. In 1869, when homeward bound, she was dismasted when about 600 miles from Mauritius and is said to have covered the remaining 10,000 to New York, under jury masts, in 76 days. Running her easting down on one voyage, an authority quotes her as averaging 246 miles a day for nearly a month.

Although designed for the East India trade, the demand for tonnage in trans-Atlantic business was so great when she came out, that her initial voyage was to Liverpool via New Orleans. She made two westward Cape Horn passages, both to San Francisco, in 1855 and 1861 respectively. A complete list of her voyages follows.

She left Boston, Mar. 1, 1854; was 26 days to New Orleans; thence 38 days to Liverpool; thence 97 days to Melbourne; went on to Shanghai and was about 114 days from there to London. She then crossed to Boston and her time of 18 days, 6 hours, was equalled by only one other vessel, according to Lieut. Maury's tables of 1859. Arrived at San Francisco, May 21, 1856, in 113 days from Boston, having crossed the equator 17 days and 21 hours from port. Went to Callao and was 104 days thence to New York; then had 85 days out to Hong Kong and it was on this voyage that she was but 52 days from St. Roque, which is said to be the record. She then went up the coast to Shanghai and was 120 days from there to New York; returned to Shanghai in 105 days; loaded at Manila and was 102 days to New York, the final 76 being, as stated, under jury masts. Went again to Shanghai; passage 102 days; loaded at Foo Chow; passed the Bermudas, 82 days out, and then had a succession of gales and was under double- or close-reefed topsails for six days, with a very heavy sea, taking her pilot 89 days out and reaching New York, Mar. 23, 1861, in 91 days from Foo Chow. She then went out to San Francisco in 142 days, having light winds and poor trades throughout, excepting off the Horn where she had very heavy gales. She then took a cargo of wheat to Queenstown and on coming to anchor there, Mar. 7, 1862, after a passage of 120 days, grounded on the Camden Bank but was assisted off and towed into dock, leaking badly. This mishap cost $5000.

From Queenstown she went to Liverpool and loaded coal for Shanghai, sailing June 25, 1862. On Nov. 6th, when 134 days out, off the north coast of Luzon, she encountered a typhoon and was thrown on her beam ends, necessitating the cutting away of her masts. The vessel partly righted but the hold was nearly full of water and the *Nabob*, with her crew lashed to the rigging, drifted on the rocks. Luckily she went on at high tide and as the water ebbed, though the ship broke in two, they were able to launch the long boat and Captain Baxter and part of the crew attempted to make a landing. A tremendous sea was breaking along the shore and for ten miles they skirted the coast, seeking a safe landing place. No such place was found but as a choice of evils they finally turned the boat's bow to the beach and were soon among the breakers; before they had gone 100 yards the boat capsized and of the 18 in the boat, 12 were drowned, one swam ashore and Captain Baxter and four others, clinging to the boat, were swept out to sea. By great exertion they were able to right the boat, bail her out and paddle almost to the wreck, but here the tide took them and finding they could not reach her they made signs to those on board to throw them a keg of water which they finally secured. The next day those in the boat and those on the vessel were rescued from the shore. The survivors were well treated by the authorities, the port being Aparri, and were sent on to Manila. According to one report 17 men and the steward's wife were lost in the wreck.

The first commander of the *Nabob* was Captain Dewhurst, who was succeeded by W. H. Bartlett, the succession then passing to William Cole who was referred to as "Commodore" of William Appleton's ships and one of the firm's most successful masters. In 1857, Capt. John Baxter assumed command and continued in charge until the ship was lost.

NAPIER

MEDIUM clipper ship, launched Aug. 23, 1854, from the yard of William & George Gardner, at Fell's Point, Baltimore, for Dawson & Hancock of Philadelphia; 225 x 42: 6 x 28; 1811 tons, old measurement; 1424 tons, British measurement. She had three complete decks and drew, loaded, 23 feet. With short but fairly sharp ends she had a long, flat floor and was a large carrier. Her spars were but a trifle shorter than those of the *Great Republic*. She carried 40 foremast hands. With a lively sheer, she was in every way a handsome ship and very strongly built. Reported cost, $140,000. As to sailing ability, it is stated that on her run to San Francisco in 1860, her log showed a speed of 16 knots at times, while on a prior occasion she had made 316 miles in 24 hours.

The *Napier* made three passages to San Francisco, arriving out on her first, Sept. 23, 1856, under Captain Stafford, in 140 days. On the second, she reached destination, Feb. 19, 1860, 119 days out, Captain Keith in command. Captain Logan had her on her third, reaching San Francisco, May 13, 1863, in 131 days from New York. Her runs from New York to the line are 29, 27½ and 31 days respectively and to passing Cape Horn, 65, 59 and 68 days. In 1856 she was 45 days from the Cape to the equator crossing, thence 30 days to the Golden Gate. In 1863 she was 650 miles from San Francisco, when 119 days out.

In 1856 she was 57 days from San Francisco to Callao, thereafter taking guano from the Chincha Islands to Hampton Roads. In 1860 she went over the same course, reaching Hampton Roads in a very leaky condition on Dec. 28th, in 88 days from Callao. In 1863 she was 122 days from San Francisco to Liverpool. In 1859, under Captain Kennedy, she left Singapore in ballast for New York and reached destination Aug. 11th, in 82 days. In 1861-1862 she was employed between New York and Liverpool, Captain Marshall in charge. In August 1862 she was reported sold at New York for $55,000.

After arrival at Liverpool, in November 1863, from San Francisco, the *Napier* was sold to J. R. Graves of the former port and Captain White assumed command. As a British ship, under her original name, she was running until Apr. 1, 1871, when she arrived at Baker's Island from Melbourne. She had loaded 1380 tons of guano when, during a gale, the bridle chain parted and she stood out to sea. Two days later, Apr. 24th, she returned and attempted to make fast but struck the reef and remained. A portion of the keel floated up; she soon had 11½ feet of water in the hold and was abandoned. Three days later she slid off the reef and sank. Captain Williams was in command at the time of her loss.

NATIONAL EAGLE

MEDIUM clipper ship, built by Joshua T. Foster, at Medford, Mass., in 1852; 179 x 36 x 24; 1095 tons, new measurement. She was designed for both carrying and sailing ability and was a successful ship. The *West Wind*, built in the same yard in 1853, was a sister ship but had no figurehead, while the *National Eagle* was ornamented with a large gilded eagle having outspread wings. Her original owners were Fisher & Co., of Boston. In 1865 she was purchased by John Bates and others, of Cohasset, for $41,-000 and in 1870 her owners were given as Hinckley Brothers & Co., of Boston. Later, she was owned by Capt. S. C. Jordan who commanded her until he bought into the new ship *Joseph S. Spinney*, in 1874. When lost in 1874 she was rigged as a bark and owned in New York.

The *National Eagle* was first engaged in the triangle run between Boston, New Orleans and Liverpool. On July 29, 1853, while bound to Liverpool with cotton, she put into Boston with yellow fever on board. Capt. Knott Pedrick was down and his wife, the mate and several of the crew had succumbed to the disease. Following her return to Boston after the completion of this voyage, she loaded for San Francisco; sailed Jan. 6, 1854, and made the passage out in 134 days, with Capt. George Matthews in command. Returned to Boston via Calcutta and for some years thereafter, with a few intermissions, she continued trading between Boston and India, her outward cargoes generally being ice. She became one of the best known American ships arriving at Calcutta.

In 1863 she went to San Francisco from Philadelphia in 126 days, Captain Matthews being still in command, and returned to Boston direct in 112 days. In 1867, under command of Captain Christopher Crowell, she was 139 days from Boston to San Francisco and thence to New York in 116 days. The following year she returned to the Pacific Coast port, under Captain Nickerson, in 121 days from New York; then went to Hong Kong in 41 days; returned to San Francisco in 44 days and thence to Liverpool in 116 days.

On Dec. 15, 1857, the *National Eagle*, Captain Matthews, left Boston for New Orleans and received her pilot off the mouth of the Mississippi, Jan. 5, 1858; thence went to Liverpool in 28 days and from there was 103 days to Calcutta and thence 100 days to Boston. On Dec. 15, 1858, the captain's daughter, who was accompanying her father, noted in her diary:—"About noon today we saw a ship astern; she had a great spread of canvas and seemed to be rushing over the waves. She gained on us very fast and about 5 o'clock was abreast and passed within gunshot, going, our captain says, about 13 knots, while we were making 10. It was the clipper ship *Phantom*, of Boston, like us, homeward bound and she glided away from us like a phantom indeed." This incident occurred near the Cape of Good Hope and as a sequel it is noted that the *Phantom* led the *Eagle* about two weeks into their common destination. The best day's work recorded on this round voyage of the *National Eagle* was 230 miles.

During some of her later years Captains George Bray and John Freeman, Jr., had command of the *National Eagle* and for a while she was engaged in trade with ports on the East coast of Central America, taking home hardwood timber. She met her fate in 1884 when bound to Trieste, being driven ashore in a gale near the town of Pola on the Adriatic Sea and becoming a total loss.

NEPTUNE'S CAR

CLIPPER ship, launched Apr. 16, 1853, from the yard of Page & Allen, at Portsmouth, Va., for Foster & Nickerson of New York; 216 x 40 x 23:6; 1616 tons, old measurement. She was a sharp ship, built after a New York model and was in every way a splendid clipper. She remained under the American flag until February 1863, when she was sold at auction at Liverpool for £8000 sterling, to Barclay & Co., and in Lloyds of 1870 she is still so listed under her original name.

On account of dullness in the California and China trade when she came out, her first voyage was a round to England. On Feb. 9, 1854, she arrived at San Francisco, 115 days from New York, Captain Forbes in command. Had heavy gales off the Horn for ten days; crossed the equator in the Pacific, 91 days out, and was 12 days within 800 miles of the Golden Gate. From San Francisco went to Singapore in 56 days; thence to Calcutta and from there was 109 days to New York, arriving Oct. 29, 1854.

Captain Patten replaced Captain Forbes and the *Car* arrived at San Francisco, Apr. 25, 1855, in 101 days from New York. Crossed the line on the 24th day out, 294 miles west of the *Westward Ho* which had passed *Boston Light* the day before she had left Sandy

Hook, also bound for San Francisco. The *Car* was 54 days to Cape Horn and crossed the equator on the 79th day; then, however, she was practically becalmed for eight days which effectually spoiled a very fast passage. In the southeast trades in the Pacific she ran 310, 310 and 313 miles on three consecutive days, often logging 16 knots. The *Westward Ho*, previously referred to, arrived at San Francisco the day before the *Car* and there was much discussion in the newspapers as to which ship made the fastest passage. The actual time was found to be:—*Neptune's Car*, 100 days and 23½ hours from New York and the *Westward Ho*, 100 days and 18 hours from Boston. Both vessels proceeded from San Francisco to Hong Kong, sailing the same day, and although Captain Hussey of the Boston clipper offered to back his ship for a large amount and the *Car* had no backers, yet the latter made the run in 50 days against her competitor's 61 days. The time made, however, indicates more of a drifting match than a trial of speed. The *Car* loaded at Foo Chow for London and made the run from Anjer in 81 days. From London she crossed to New York and on the passage was struck by lightning, slightly damaging her foremast and injuring several of the crew.

She next arrived at San Francisco, Nov. 15, 1856, in 136 days from New York. Was 80 days to the Horn, off which she was 18 days in heavy gales; crossed the equator 107 days out and was close to the San Francisco Heads for ten days. The passage had been a sad one; Captain Patten was sick with brain fever and became deaf and blind; the first officer was under arrest for insubordination and Mrs. Patten, then only 19 years of age, in addition to caring for her helpless husband, navigated the vessel and took her safely into port. As a recognition of her services the sum of $1399 was raised and paid to Mrs. Patten a year later and she was called the "Florence Nightingale of the Ocean." At San Francisco, Captain Bearse took command of the *Car* and sailing on Mar. 12, 1857, made the passage to New York in 99 days. It was stated that she had logged 385 miles in one day on this run. Captain Patten died at Boston in July 1857, aged 30 years.

The *Neptune's Car* was again at San Francisco, Mar. 4, 1858, in 125 sailing days from New York, via Rio, 82 days. Captain Bearse reported being obliged to put into Rio, Nov. 8, 1857, on account of the foremast being badly sprung; was in port 34 days; off the Horn 25 days and 24 days from the equator to port. Sailed from San Francisco, July 3rd, for Hong Kong and was idle there for several months, thence going to Singapore where she loaded part cargo and sailed May 5, 1859, for Penang. Left Penang, May 24th, and arrived at New York, Aug. 24th, in 92 days' passage, 37 days from the line. Capt. Caleb Sprague, formerly in the clipper ship *Gravina*, then took command and arrived at San Francisco, Apr. 23, 1860, in 114 days from New York. Was 24 days to the line; 60 days to the Horn and 91 days to the equator; light winds predominated most of the passage. From San Francisco she went to Callao; thence in 73 days to Hampton Roads and three days from there to New York, arriving Dec. 27, 1860. About this time J. D. Fish of New York, was reported to have become the managing owner.

The last arrival of the *Neptune's Car* at San Francisco was Oct. 28, 1861, in 186 days from New York, via Callao. Off the Horn she had three days of very heavy weather, the last two of which were a perfect hurricane. Her decks were swept, bowsprit sprung, jibboom snapped off like a pipe stem, foretopgallant and main-royal masts carried away and other damage received. The ship became leaky in her topsides and the crew mutinied, refusing to pump. Captain Sprague had the ringleaders put in irons and steered for Callao for necessary repairs. Shortly after arrival at San Francisco the ship was seized by the United States authorities on the ground that partial ownership was held by Southerners. After some delay, she sailed from San Francisco, Jan. 31, 1862, and crossed the equator 13 days out, exceptionally fast time; on the 41st day was up with Cape Horn; then had easterly winds to Trinidad and then light winds and calms to the line, which was crossed on the 78th day out; then had 20 days to New York, arriving May 9th, in a passage of 98 days.

The *Neptune's Car* left New York, July 24, 1862, under command of Captain Reed, for London, and on her return, reached New York, Oct. 19th, in 28 days from the Downs, in ballast. She then recrossed to Liverpool and was sold as heretofore stated.

NEPTUNE'S FAVORITE

MEDIUM clipper ship, built by Jotham Stetson, at Chelsea, Mass., in 1854; 194: 4 x 39: 8 x 23: 8; 1347 tons, old measurement; 1194 tons, British measurement. Owned by H. A. Kelly & Co., of Boston. She was finely modeled and established the reputation of being a fast ship. From her start she was a popular vessel, particularly in England, with which country many of her voyages were made.

On her maiden voyage she sailed from Boston, June 24, 1854, Capt. Oliver G. Lane in command, for St. George, N. B., where she loaded for Liverpool and was 16 days crossing the Atlantic. Recrossed to Philadelphia and on her second voyage left that port, Dec. 8, 1854, for San Francisco. Arrived out after a passage of 115 days of which 20 days were spent off the Horn in strong gales; had sails split and bulwarks stove; crossed the equator 94 days out. From San Francisco went to Shanghai in 42 days and was thence 112 days to London. Beat the *Sovereign of the Seas*, *Sweepstakes* and *Chrysolite*, the latter by over two weeks. She then crossed to Boston and went out to San Francisco in 113 days, arriving Apr. 8, 1856. Captain Lane reported 22 days to the line; 46 days to 50° South; 15 days rounding the Horn; and 85 days to the equator. When 102 days out was 200 miles from the Golden Gate. Then went to Shanghai in 45 days and left that port, Feb. 13, 1857, for London. From London she went to Melbourne in 90 days; thence 48 days to Callao; sailed thence, Apr. 20, 1858, for England. On her fifth voyage she reached San Francisco, Mar. 23, 1859, in 117 days from New York, under command of Captain Emmerton who had succeeded Captain Lane. Went to Callao in 54 days and loaded guano at the Chincha Islands for England. Sailed from Callao, Sept.

9th and on Oct. 31st, when 52 days out, put into St. Thomas, leaking badly. Her cargo was discharged and forwarded by another vessel. Under date of Dec. 15th she was reported to be still in port but would soon proceed to the United States for repairs.

On her sixth voyage, the *Neptune's Favorite* left New York, May 27, 1860, and arrived at San Francisco, Oct. 12th, in 137 days' passage. Captain Emmerton reported 33 days to the line; was ten days from 50° to 50°; made Cape Horn, 66 days out; had very light winds in the South Pacific and was not up with the equator until 101 days from New York; had light, baffling winds and calms for 36 days to port. In the North Atlantic was in company with the *Black Prince* and also saw her near the Straits of Le Maire; led her into San Francisco seven days. The *Favorite* herself, however, was beaten eight days by the *Challenger*, whom she had met two days after leaving New York. Completing this voyage the *Favorite* was 50 days from San Francisco to Callao; sailed thence Feb. 6, 1861; anchored in Lynnhaven Roads, near Cape Henry, Apr. 27th, 81 days out. No pilot responding to signals, she proceeded to New York the following day.

The seventh voyage was the last made by the *Neptune's Favorite* under the American flag. She arrived at San Francisco, Feb. 2, 1862, in 146 days from New York; had 15 days of calms in latitude 30° North, Atlantic, and did not cross the line until 41 days out; passed through the Straits of Le Maire on the 70th day; was 19 days rounding the Horn; had very light winds in the South Pacific, being 33 days from 50° South, to the equator; thence 26 days to destination, being off the Heads for four days. In the North Atlantic she was in company with the *Prima Donna* which had left New York three days before her. Both ships had identical experiences until reaching 50° South, Pacific, where the *Favorite* was two days in the lead. The *Prima Donna* then found good winds and trades, catching up with her opponent and passing her, being seven days in the lead on crossing the equator, and maintaining this until arrival at San Francisco, Jan. 23rd, in 139 days from New York.

From San Francisco the *Favorite* was 48 days to Callao and left there, guano laden, Aug. 5, 1862, for Queenstown. After arrival and on proceeding to London she was offered for sale and early in 1863 was sold for £8000, a sum higher than that realized for any other vessel of her size and age sold about that time. She was renamed *Mataura;* hailing port Glasgow; owner D. Swan. In November 1865 she was at San Francisco, Captain Stewart, in 67 days from Sydney. In October 1868 she was again at the same port from Hong Kong, 112 days, damaged in very heavy weather. Was surveyed and classed A 1½. In November 1869 she reached San Francisco in 162 days from Ardrossan, under Captain Watts. Completed this voyage by going to Liverpool in 116 days. In Lloyds, 1874, she is listed as owned by L. T. Merrow; hailing port Glasgow; not classed. There was also an iron ship named *Mataura* hailing from Glasgow at the same time.

NIGHTINGALE

THE extreme clipper ship *Nightingale* was one of the most beautiful, as she was certainly the most interesting, of any of the ships built during the clipper era. Her story, were all the facts known, would be as romantic and exciting as anything in marine fiction. Constructed with all the finish and luxury of a yacht; launched under a load of debt which necessitated an early sale at auction; a pioneer to the gold fields of Australia; a winner in the English tea races; a slave ship, war vessel and California clipper, the *Nightingale,* wherever she went, excited admiration and interest. During her 42 years of strenuous service she sailed on every ocean; the Pacific (or Behring) sea knew her as far north as 65°; the Indian Ocean had her keel cleaving its waters in the high latitudes of 54° and up to nearly 56° South; in the Atlantic she had been to 58°, off the Horn, while her last hailing port, Krageroe, is about the same latitude North. The elements were not always kind to her and underwriters had to pay many heavy claims. She had more than her share of mutinies and for a time the "taint of a musky ship" stigmatized her;

but up to the last of her long sea life she is said to have retained much of the beauty and speed that characterized her as a clipper of the fifties.

She was designed and built by Samuel Hanscomb, Jr., at Portsmouth, N. H., who planned to make her surpass in model, speed and beauty any thing afloat and Captain Miller, her reputed original owner, took personal charge of her lavish interior decoration. She measured 185 feet on deck; was 36 feet beam and had 19 feet depth of hold. The original figure of tonnage was 1060, which was subsequently reduced by new measurement rules to 722 tons, and again, later, to 657 tons. Her draft was 19 feet. Her ends were sharp as was also her bottom and her 36-inch dead rise, at half floor, was equalled by but few of the clippers. Her spars were beautifully proportioned and her masts raked, counting from the fore-mast, $1\frac{1}{4}$, $1\frac{1}{2}$ and $1\frac{3}{4}$ inches to the foot. The height of her masts and spread of her yards, in feet, were as follows:

MASTS

	Foremast	Mainmast	Mizzen
	72	77	63
Topmast	42	45	35
Topgallant	22	24	19
Royal	14	15	10
Skysail pole	10	11	9

YARDS

	Foremast	Mainmast	Mizzen
	68	71	54
Topmast	53	57	42
Topgallant	30	42	$31\frac{3}{4}$
Royal	$24\frac{1}{2}$	32	25
Skysail	$21\frac{3}{4}$	25	21

The bow of the *Nightingale* was ornamented by a bust figurehead of the famous singer Jenny Lind, and the stern with a representation of the same lady in a reclining posture with a nightingale perched on her finger. The name *Nightingale*, appeared in letters of blue and gold on the stern and was repeated on bow and quarter.

The keel of the *Nightingale* was laid in the early part of February 1851, and on the 17th of this month the following advertisement appeared in the "Boston Journal":

TRANS-ATLANTIC EXCURSION TO LONDON

The elegant new clipper ship, Sarah Cowles, 1100 tons burthen, commanded by Captain F. A. Miller, now building expressly for conveyance of passengers on the GRAND TRANS-ATLANTIC EXCURSION to the WORLD'S FAIR, landing the same at the port of Southampton, England, will be despatched from this port about May 20th. In the designing and construction of this splendid specimen of naval architecture, intended for this great mission, nothing will be overlooked. Parties, families and all who contemplate joining the excursion, are informed that the model and drawings of the ship with plan of cabin, staterooms and berths may be seen and rates of passage made known at the office of DAVIS & COMPANY, 76 STATE STREET.

This advertisement appeared as above until Apr. 18th, when the name *Nightingale* was substituted for *Sarah Cowles*. May 7th, the following advertisement was inserted in the "New York Commercial Advertiser":

TRANS-ATLANTIC EXCURSION TO THE WORLD'S FAIR

Rare opportunity for a cheap and delightful trip to London. Captain Miller, so favorably known to the public on both sides the Atlantic as a noble navigator and gentleman, goes out in command of the *Nightingale*. To sail from Boston on or about June 10th. Rate of passage to London and back: first cabin staterooms, $125. Ladies' cabin, berths, $125. Saloon staterooms, $110. Saloon berths, $100.

For tickets apply to Adams & Company, 16 Wall Street.

The *Nightingale* was launched June 16, 1851, but by this time her builder was in financial difficulties, caused—the "Boston Journal" says—by Captain Miller's refusal to accept her because she did not come up to specifications. Money was due the mechanics who worked on her and the vessel was mortgaged to parties in Boston. All the creditors agreed, however, that the vessel must be finished and Governor Goodwin and Captain Yates were appointed agents until her financial troubles were settled. The *Nightingale* was towed to Boston, July 19, 1851, by the tug *R. B. Forbes* and for nearly six weeks she lay at her wharf while her agents attempted to unravel her financial tangle. It was found impossible to do this without a public sale and the beautiful clipper ship, thoroughly bolted and coppered; well-found in boats and tackle; cabin containing ten staterooms with bedsteads in place of berths; ladies' cabin with eight staterooms; water tank holding 4500 gallons; accommodation for 250 passengers, was offered at public sale to satisfy the mortgage held on the vessel. The auction was held at Number 22, Long Wharf, on Sept. 6, 1851, in the presence of a large number of shipowners and merchants and after a few moments of listless bidding the *Nightingale* was knocked down to Davis & Co., for $43,500. Davis & Co. were ship brokers who had advanced money on the vessel and it is probable that the auction was merely to enable the owners to give a clear title to the ship, since it is hardly possible that, at a time when clippers were in great demand, a vessel like the *Nightingale* should have brought only the sum stated. Soon after, she was sold to Sampson & Tappan and for many years remained registered in their name.

Her new owners put her on the berth for Sydney, thus becoming pioneers in the trade between United States Atlantic ports and Australia. Clearing on Oct. 17, 1851, for "Oceania and China," and sailing the following day, the *Nightingale* went out under command of the veteran navigator John H. Fiske. In common with others sailing about the same time she encountered adverse winds and unfavorable weather in the North Atlantic and it was not until the 39th

day that she was up with Cape St. Roque. She crossed the meridian
of Greenwich in 39° 50′ South, 17 days from St. Roque, having
experienced very variable weather; best day's run, 263 miles. It is
noted, however, from Lieut. Maury's list of 268 voyages over this
particular route, made during a period of over ten years, that the
Nightingale's 17-day run was beaten only four times and equalled
but twice and of these six runs, one only was made during a corresponding season of the year. The whole passage from Boston to
Sydney was 90 days and was disappointing to all concerned, but that
portion of the run from St. Roque to port, 51 days, was very fair,
although in a subsequent trip the *Nightingale* made it in 44 days.

From Australia the *Nightingale* proceeded to Canton and thence
to Shanghai to load tea for London. She found on the coast as com-
petitors the British clippers *Stornoway*, *Chrysolite* and *Challenger*
and the American clippers, *Challenge* and *Surprise*. The *Nightingale* and *Challenger* were at Shanghai and the others at Whampoa.
The season was getting to be the worst for a voyage down the China
Sea and although the *Nightingale* left only a few days later than
the others it took her an excessively long time—61 days from Shanghai—to getting clear of Sunda Straits. Thence to London, however,
she was but 72 days, on this portion of the voyage beating all but the
Challenge, though on the whole voyage she was ten days slower than
her tardiest competitor, the *Challenger.* Her run from the Cape of
Good Hope to Deal was only 39 days. Captain Fiske was so chagrined over the result of his first round voyage that he left the *Nightingale* on arrival at London and the owners sent out Capt. Samuel W.
Mather to take command. Sampson & Tappan, however, had not lost
faith in the sailing qualities of their ship and offered to match her
for £10,000 sterling, on a voyage to China and return, but there
was no response.

The second voyage of the *Nightingale* was a round from London
to Shanghai and return. On the outward run Captain Mather was
80 days to Anjer and 112 days to Shanghai, beating everything but
the American *Challenge* which had 78 days to Anjer. On this pas-

sage the *Nightingale* encountered some very heavy weather in the South Atlantic, losing sails and having her bowsprit sprung. From Shanghai to London she had her revenge on the British *Challenger,* beating her two days. From London she crossed over to Boston and had a rough passage, anchoring off Boston Light in a snow storm with only four men fit for duty; the tug *R. B. Forbes* had to go down to assist in raising her anchor. She was towed to the wharf, arriving Feb. 24, 1854.

From Boston she went to New York and loaded for Melbourne in R. W. Cameron & Co.'s Australian "Pioneer Line." With some 125 passengers the *Nightingale* left New York, May 20, 1854, and anchored in Hobson's Bay, Aug. 2nd, 75 days out. She had had a tedious run of 29 days to the line, but her time of 46 days thence to Melbourne was excellent. Her best day's run was 365 nautical miles, an average of 15.55 knots, the log frequently showing better than 16, with strong, steady breezes. As an instance of how sail was carried, the following is taken from the account of a passenger:—In the dog-watch, 4 to 6 P.M. when the chief officer came on deck to relieve the second officer, he swiftly cast his eye towards the horizon in the direction of the wind, then at the struggling canvas and particularly at the maintopgallant sail which threatened to blow away. As nautical etiquette forbids the officer in charge to alter canvas when the captain is on deck, without his command or consent, the chief officer, after his hurried survey, said: "Captain Mather, that maintopgallant sail is laboring very hard." "It is drawing well, let it stand, Mr. Bartlett," was the reply. At 6 o'clock, when the second officer in turn relieved the first, he, also, gave a rapid glance around and said: "Captain Mather, that maintopgallant sail is struggling hard." "It holds a good full, let it stand, Mr. Macfarland," was the answer.

From Melbourne, the *Nightingale* proceeded in ballast to Whampoa, there loading merchandise, mostly raw sugar, and with a number of Chinese as passengers went up the coast to Shanghai, whence she took a cargo of tea to London. The passage occupied 91 days with but 70 days from Batavia Roads. Continuing in this triangular run for several years she averaged very good passages and one of 88 days from Shanghai to New York, in 1856, was excellent. In 1859 she made her first visit to San Francisco, Captain Peterson in command, having had the long passage of 148 days from Boston, with unfavorable weather conditions throughout. She then crossed to China and loaded at Foo Chow for New York. She left Foo Chow, Oct. 9, 1859, passed Anjer, Nov. 10th, signaled the *Argonaut*, Dec. 14th, and arrived at New York, Jan. 30, 1860, beating the *Argonaut* eight days. Time of passage, 113 days and 81 days from Anjer.

At New York, the *Nightingale* was sold to unknown parties and for the next eight months her history is involved in mystery. It has been stated that she went from New York to Rio and was there sold to a Brazilian merchant who employed her in the slave trade under the flag of his country, but there seems a reasonable doubt whether such was the case. In the life of Commodore George Hamilton Perkins, U. S. N., by Carroll Storrs Alden, is a letter written home by the Commodore, then Acting Master of U. S. steamer *Sumter*, from which we quote an extract:—"Apr. 15, 1860; The clipper ship *Nightingale* of Salem, shipped a cargo of 2000 negroes and has gone clear with them. * * * The *Nightingale* is a powerful clipper and is the property of her captain, Bowen, who is called 'Prince of Slavers.' " As the *Nightingale* arrived at New York Jan. 30, 1860, and is said to have shipped a cargo of slaves prior to Apr. 15, 1860, there is a maximum of 73 days during which she must have discharged her cargo and completed her sale and other business at New York, made her passage to Rio, been sold there and fitted out as a slave ship, sailed to the west coast of Africa, collected and received aboard her slaves and then sailed from her port of departure. It is fair to say that it would take at least 50 days, actual sailing time, to go from New York, via Rio, to Kabenda or any point on the African coast in that vicinity and that would leave only 23 days to complete all we have indicated above. This seems extremely improbable and if we accept the date of Commodore Perkins' letter as correct, and there seems no reason to doubt it, we are driven to the conclusion that the *Nightingale* fitted out as a slave ship at New York and sailed from that or some other Eastern port direct to the west coast of Africa. The passage from New York to Kabenda would take some 40 to 45 days and even sailing direct, the time allowance seems short; but Captain Bowen had been on the African coast before in command of the slave ship *Sultana* and probably everything was arranged before the arrival of the *Nightingale* at New York. The fact that the *Nightingale,* in 1860, was listed as owned and commanded by Captain Bowen, with New York as a hailing port, and that in 1861 she was certainly sailing under the American flag, tends to confirm this view. So much for mystery and surmise.

It is known that the *Nightingale* returned to New York in the late summer of 1860 and there loaded a cargo of grain and sailed, Sept. 18th, for London, where, on arrival, she was fitted out as a slave ship. The "London Times" of July 13, 1861, has the following item:—"Ship *Nightingale* of Boston, 810 tons, owned and commanded by Frederick Bowers (Francis Bowen) arrived in Liverpool from New York, November 1860. November 24, 1860, she sailed for St. Thomas with a cargo valued at $21,000, consisting of guns, powder and cotton cloth. It was well known in certain circles before she sailed that she was a slaver." The *Nightingale* was reported at St. Thomas, W. C. A., Jan. 14, 1861, and while there was boarded by H. B. M. *Archer* and U. S. S. *Mystic* and her papers found in order. She continued to dodge about the African coast until Apr. 20-21st, when she was seized by the U. S. sloop of war, *Saratoga.* A letter from Commodore Taylor of the *Saratoga,* to the Judge of the District Court at New York, tells how the capture was made.

"U. S. S. *Saratoga,* Kabenda, April 21, 1861.

"To the Judge of the U. S. District Court at New York City:

"For some time the American ship *Nightingale* of Boston, Francis Bowen, Master, has been watched on this coast under the suspicion of being engaged in the slave trade. Several times we have fallen in with her and although fully assured that she was about to engage in this illicit trade she has had the benefit of the doubt. A few days ago observing her at anchor at this port, I came in and boarded her and was induced to believe she was then preparing to receive slaves aboard. Under this impression the ship was got under way and went some distance off but with the intention of returning under cover of the night; which was done and at 10 P. M. we anchored and sent two boats under Lieutenant Guthrie to surprise her and it was found that she had 961 slaves aboard and was expecting more. Lieut. Guthrie took possession of her as a prize and I have directed him to take her to New York. She is a clipper of 1000 tons and has *Nightingale* of Boston on her stern and flies American colors.

"Alfred Taylor, Commander U. S. Navy."

The day of the capture Lieutenant Guthrie was put in command of the prize and ordered to proceed to Monrovia, Liberia, and there deliver the African captives to the Rev. John Seyes or his successor, the agent appointed to receive and provide for slaves recaptured by United States cruisers. Lieutenant Hayes of the Navy and Lieutenant Tyler of the Marines were ordered to report to Lieutenant Guthrie for duty and the latter was given as a prize crew, six petty officers, six ordinary seamen, six landsmen, two boys, one corporal of marines and five privates of marines. The *Nightingale* sailed from Kabenda, Apr. 23, 1861, and soon after her departure African fever broke out and of the 961 African captives only 801 were landed at Monrovia; nor did the prize crew escape the infection for Lieutenant Guthrie, Lieutenant Tyler and several of the crew were attacked and one of the landsmen died of the fever.

The *Nightingale* anchored off Monrovia, May 7, 1861, and landed the recaptured Africans. No provision had been made for these half-starved negroes among whom African fever was raging. There was little surplus food in Monrovia and the mortality among them, after landing, must have been appalling. The *Nightingale* sailed from Monrovia, May 13th, and arrived at New York, June

13, 1861. The day of his arrival Lieutenant Guthrie made his report to the Secretary of the Navy, from which the following are extracts.

"I have the honor to report my arrival here today in command of the American ship *Nightingale*, 32 days from Monrovia. * * * The *Nightingale* was seized in the act of receiving their negroes aboard on the night of the 20th of April, about midnight, and I regret to say that an American named Francis Bowen and a Spaniard named Valentino Cortina affected their escape during my watch on deck on the night of the 22nd of April. * * * The first person named was known to be the commander of the *Nightingale* prior to her capture, and the latter was represented as such at the time. * * * After filling up with water and purifying the ship we sailed from Monrovia for New York, Monday, May 13th. Our crew had become so debilitated and sickly from the effects of the climate and from continual labors and exposures that it became very difficult to carry sail and manage a ship of this size. At one time there were only 7 men on duty, 3 in one watch and 4 in the other."

The *Nightingale* lost two of the crew from ship fever on the passage from Monrovia and brought back as prisoners the three mates of the slaver, named, Hind, Winslow and Westervelt. It will be noticed from the report of Lieutenant Guthrie that Francis Bowen, the real, and Valentino Cortina the pretended commander of the *Nightingale* made their escape from the vessel soon after her capture. As Bowen told the story he was allowed to escape by Guthrie who was, himself, a slave holder. In fact all the officers of the prize *Nightingale* were Southerners. John J. Guthrie was a citizen of North Carolina, Charles W. Hayes of Alabama and H. B. Tyler of Virginia. Francis Bowen is said to have returned to the United States but was never recaptured; later, in 1872, turning up as commander of the steamer *Virginius*, a supposed Cuban filibuster.

The case of the *Nightingale* came before the district court June 26, 1861, and no defence being offered she was promptly condemned and July 6th, at Marshal's sale, was purchased by N. L. McCreedy, acting for the United States Government. The purchase price was $13,000. She was equipped with four 32-pound guns and Aug. 21, 1861, arrived at Hampton Roads under command of Acting-Master D. B. Horne, with orders to proceed to Key West and report to Flag Officer Marvin, commander of the Gulf Blockading Squadron. She arrived off Fort Pickens, prior to Sept. 19, 1861, with a cargo of coal from New York. Was aground northward of the bar at the Southwest Pass of the Mississippi River in the early part of October 1861 and coal and pig iron were thrown overboard in an effort to lighten her, so that the *G. B. McClellan* might extricate her from her muddy berth; but it was found impossible to move her and Oct. 12th, under orders from Lieutenant Belden, Acting-Master Horne prepared to abandon and fire the *Nightingale*, if necessary, on the near approach of any rebel flotilla coming down the river. The Confederate steamer *Ivy* came down the river but when within ten miles of the *Nightingale* turned back and at a later period the latter vessel was pulled off the bank.

Nov. 19, 1861, the *Nightingale* arrived at New York, ten days from the Southwest Pass. Dec. 26, 1861, she was at Key West, under command of Lieutenant Delano, with a cargo of naval stores. Feb. 25, 1862, she was at Ship Island, with coal. During most of the year 1862 she was a supply and store ship to the Eastern Gulf Blockading Squadron. In 1863 she was an ordnance vessel at Pensacola under command of E. D. Brunner. In the early months of 1864 she was reported at Key West with Brigadier-General Newton and Staff aboard; at this time she was armed with four 8-inch guns. May 17, 1864, Acting-Lieutenant E. D. Brunner was ordered to proceed, when ready for sea, to Boston and report to the Commander of the Navy Yard:—"Your crew will be composed of men whose time will have expired and who are sent north to be discharged. The *Nightingale* is sent north because she is supposed to be infected with yellow fever, which for the safety of the squadron requires her to be withdrawn from this neighborhood." She arrived off Boston, June 9, 1864, and Feb. 11, 1865, was sold at auction in Boston, to D. E.

Mayo, for $11,000. During her ownership by the Government, $11,-000 had been spent on her in repairs.

The *Nightingale* was now once more a merchant trader and in October 1865 was advertised to sail from Boston for San Francisco under command of Capt. D. E. Mayo. She arrived at San Francisco, Mar. 9, 1865, in 119 days from Boston, with a freight list amounting to $21,107. Soon after her arrival she was purchased for the price of $23,381 by the Western Union Telegraph Company which at that time had commenced the exploration of a proposed telegraph line, which, by means of a cable via Behring Straits, was to unite the New and Old World. Under Captain Scammon, the company's chief of marines, the *Nightingale* made several passages between San Francisco and Petropaulovsky and Plover Bay, all being quite fast runs; the final trip from Plover Bay being made in the fast time of 22 days. In January 1868, the *Nightingale* went from San Francisco to Victoria and sailed thence for New York but was obliged to put into Valparaiso, leaky; was repaired there at the cost of $6000 and sailed again, July 6, 1868, arriving at New York, Sept. 7, 1868. About this time she was sold to Samuel G. Reed & Co., of Boston.

The *Nightingale* continued in trade between New York, San Francisco and China, until late in 1876 when she was sold and went under Norwegian colors, retaining her old name but later was rerigged as a bark. In 1868, on a passage from Hong Kong for San Francisco, she lost her foretopmast and several yards, sprung her mainmast and was obliged to put into Yokohama for repairs. She had strong gales coming out of Yokohama and for several days before reaching San Francisco was under bare poles in a hurricane; the damage on the voyage amounted to $22,000. In 1871, from New York for San Francisco, she put into the Falkland Islands, leaky, with her crew mutinous and the mate, Edward B. Hunt, dead from a knife wound. She returned to Rio and two weeks later sailed for port of destination. In 1876 she was sold at auction at the Merchants Exchange, San Francisco, for $11,500, and her purchaser, George Howes, loaded her with oil and sent her to New York where she was sold for

$15,000 to sail under Norwegian colors. The next year she arrived at Philadelphia, June 12th, and on the night of the 27th, while lying in the stream, dragged her anchor and went ashore on the bar, but was got off without much injury.

Up to 1860, the *Nightingale* was commanded in turn by Captains Fiske, Mather and Peterson. After her sale by the United States Government, Captain Mayo took her out to San Francisco and was succeeded by Captain Scammon. Capt. H. F. Sparrow and Captain Cutter then had her for a couple of years each. In 1876, Captain Palmer was in command, giving place to Captain Norris. During the last years of her life the *Nightingale* was engaged in the lumber trade in the North Atlantic, hailing port, Krageroe, Norway. Apr. 17, 1893, the Norwegian bark, *Nightingale*, Captain Engebrilsen, on a voyage from Liverpool for Halifax, was abandoned at sea. The officers and crew were taken off by a passing vessel.

NONPAREIL

MEDIUM clipper ship, launched from the yard of Dunham & Co., at Frankfort, Me., in November 1853; 220 x 41: 6 x 22: 5; 1431 tons, old measurement; 1097 tons, British measurement. Capacity for such cargo as wheat in bags, 1540 short tons. Her original owners were her builders and their friends in Frankfort and early in January 1854, she was sent to Boston to be sold by Summers & Swift. They advertised that she was built of the best materials; was well sparred and furnished; designed and fitted out as a first-class packet and a REAL clipper: statements that were substantiated in her after career. The market for clipper ships was not as good in 1854 as it had been, and for weeks the *Nonpareil* lay at Grand Junction wharf, East Boston, awaiting a purchaser. She was finally put on the berth for New Orleans and six days before sailing was sold to Thomas Richardson & Co., of New York and Philadelphia, for $76,000.

Under command of Capt. Edward Dunn, the *Nonpareil* sailed

from Boston, Mar. 6, 1854, and arrived at New Orleans, Apr. 6th. The new clipper *Panther*, which had left Boston two days ahead, reached port the same day. From New Orleans, the *Nonpareil* went to Liverpool and for a time was operated between that port and Philadelphia. Leaving Philadelphia, Mar. 27, 1855, she arrived at Liverpool, Apr. 12th, in 16 days,—a very fast passage. According to newspaper accounts she made the run from the Delaware Capes in 13 days, a run claimed to be equivalent to 12 days from New York. Shortly after her arrival at Liverpool she was chartered to carry troops and stores from Marseilles to the Crimea, for account of the French Government. While at anchor off Seraglio Point, Constantinople, soon after her first arrival out, she was run into by a French steamer, losing bowsprit, cut-water, figurehead and being otherwise damaged. She was then taken to Toulon, in tow of a French steam frigate, arriving in September 1855, and thence sailed for Liverpool. Left Liverpool, Dec. 10, 1855, and arrived at Philadelphia, Feb. 9, 1856, in 61 days' passage. She had favorable winds for the first 12 days, with every prospect for completing a fast passage, but thereafter experienced a succession of westerly gales during which she lost two suits of sails and was finally reduced to one topsail, which was close-reefed; had to run south to latitude 24° for warmer weather and then had westerly winds. For three weeks she was within 250 miles of the Delaware Capes.

Captain Dunn, who had been sick during the whole of this passage and unable to come on deck, was succeeded by Captain Foulke, formerly in the *Philadelphia* (originally the *Fanny McHenry* and in later years the *Sanspareil*) also belonging to Richardson & Co., and the *Nonpareil* sailed from Philadelphia, Apr. 17, 1856, for Liverpool, arriving May 14th, in 27 days' passage. She continued as a packet between Philadelphia and Liverpool until the fall of 1858, one of her outward passages being via Savannah. Her best outward runs were made in 20 and 22 days respectively; the best homeward was 32 days.

Under command of Capt. B. G. Green, she sailed from New York,

Dec. 12, 1858, and arrived at San Francisco, Apr. 7, 1859, in 115 days' passage. Was 23 days to the line; 56 days to the pitch of the Cape; 96 days to the equator crossing, and 19 days thence to port. Crossed from San Francisco to Shanghai and sailed thence Oct. 2, 1859; passed Anjer, Nov. 12th, and arrived at New York, Feb. 7, 1860, in 128 days' passage. Other arrivals at New York about the same time were; *Nightingale*, 113 days; *Argonaut*, 116; *Witchcraft*, 117; these from Foo Chow: the *Pampero*, 101 days from Shanghai. The *Pampero* had also the shortest run from Anjer, 79 days; *Nightingale* was 81 days; *Nonpareil*, 87 and *Argonaut*, 89 days.

The *Nonpareil* arrived at San Francisco, Aug. 24, 1860, in 129 days from New York. Was 29 days to the line; passed Cape Horn 63 days out, and crossed the equator on the 97th day. Sailed from San Francisco, Oct. 7th, and arrived at Falmouth, England, in 106 days. Then crossed to New York, in ballast, in 40 days. Arrived at San Francisco, Oct. 22, 1861, in 124 days from New York. Was 31 days to the line and passed Cape Horn on the 59th day out; was 15 days between the 50's; crossed the equator 97 days out, and made the South Farallon, Oct. 20th. Off Cape Horn was in company with the clipper ship *Euterpe*, from New York for San Francisco, and led her into port 11 days. The *Nonpareil* sailed from San Francisco, Dec. 29, 1861, and was 138 days to Falmouth; discharged at Liverpool and was 32 days thence to New York, arriving July 17, 1862.

In May 1863, the *Nonpareil*, after having completed a round voyage to New Orleans as an army transport, was reported sold at New York to go under the British flag without change of name; her actual ownership, however, was said to still remain with Richardson & Co. On May 11, 1863, she left New York for Shanghai; thence went to Liverpool and the statement has been published that she made a very fast return passage of 84 days, but confirmation of this is lacking. She then had a long passage from Birkenhead to Shanghai, taking the Eastern passage through the Straits of Gilolo. On July 17, 1865, she arrived at San Francisco in 52 days from Hong Kong, having had light winds throughout. Sailed from San Francisco, Nov. 8, 1865, and arrived at Falmouth, Eng., Feb. 16, 1866, in a passage of 100 days. For the following five years she was engaged in general trade, chiefly between England and the Orient, and on June 30, 1871, was reported at Bombay from Newcastle, leaky, but chartered for New York. Sailed from Bombay, June 27, 1871, and on Oct. 11th, she foundered at sea. Three lives only were saved out of her crew of 22 and three passengers. The survivors had supported themselves for five days on the deck house, without food or water, when they were picked up by the schooner *Delmont* and landed at Martinique.

About 1865, Mr. Richardson died and his ships *Nonpareil* and *Sanspareil*, became the property of the Globe Navigation Company of Liverpool. In 1869 the *Nonpareil* was sold to W. S. Lishman of Newcastle, Eng. Capt. Edward Worrall Smith, an American, later prominent as a commander of Pacific Mail steamers plying between China and San Francisco, was master of the *Nonpareil* after she went under the British flag. He is said to have been succeeded by Capt. C. P. Low, and he, by Captain Evans. Captain Johnson was in command at the time of her loss.

NOONDAY

MEDIUM clipper ship, built in 1855, by Fernald & Pettigrew, at Portsmouth, N. H., for Henry Hastings of Boston. She had fuller lines and was somewhat larger than the *Midnight*, a product of the same builders in 1854, for the same owner. The *Noonday* was 200 feet, over all, x 38: 6 x 23: 6; 1189 tons, old measurement; dead weight carrying capacity, 1500 short tons; capacity for weight and measurement general cargo for California, about 2100 tons. She was a fine looking ship and carried only one skysail, the main.

On her maiden voyage, under command of Capt. William Blackler Gerry, whose last ship, the *Cahota*, had been sold at Calcutta in 1854, the *Noonday* sailed from Boston, Oct. 17, 1855, and arrived at San Francisco, Mar. 4, 1856, in a passage of 139 days. She was forced by southerly winds from the start to within 90 miles of the Azores and was not up to the line until 32 days out. Was then close hauled to off Rio and had no chance to set studding sails. Thereafter encountered light winds and calms to the Horn, which was made on the 66th day. From Staten Island had strong westerly gales for two weeks, during which the mainyard was sprung and some head gear carried away. In latitude 32° South, Pacific, she met with good trades and covered the distance thence to the equator in the good time of 14 days, averaging 190 miles daily. From the equator to destination was 35 days, in light and head winds.

The *Noonday* completed three other passages from eastern ports to San Francisco, being lost on the fourth when about to take her pilot near the Farallon Islands. Captain Brock, who had her on her second passage, reported on arrival out, May 13, 1857, that this run was 117 days from Boston. Her next arrival out was on Feb. 10, 1860, Captain Henry, formerly in the *Romance of the Seas*, in command; passage, 126 days from Boston. In 1861, reaching San Francisco, Aug. 26th, Captain Henry reported being 146 days from New York. On these several passages, her time from port of departure to the line in the Atlantic was 26, 27 and 24 days respectively; to 50° South, Atlantic, 52, 61 and 73 days; rounding the Cape, 20, 21 and 12 days; from 50° South, Pacific, to the equator, 21, 21 and 29 days; from equator to destination, 24, 23 and 32 days.

Her first two voyages were completed by her return east from San Francisco, via Calcutta. On the second, she was forced to put into Batavia, August 1857, for repairs, having struck a rock near the Banda Islands. It was found that 50 feet of her keel had been knocked off and a hole stove in her bottom. In 1860 she took guano from Callao to Hampton Roads, in 85 days. On this passage, while in the South Pacific, she met the *Flying Mist*, and Captains Henry and Linnell had quite a "gam." The ships were very near each other, now one and again the other being slightly ahead. Captain Henry, a great man to "carry on," had his foretopmast studding-sail slyly set, and the *Noonday* then forged ahead rapidly. In 1861, the *Noonday* loaded wheat and other California products for London and made the passage from San Francisco in 117 days.

On Jan. 1, 1863, the *Noonday* was approaching the entrance to San Francisco harbor, 139 days out from Boston, weather clear, sea smooth but with a long swell on, the ship under all sail to mainsky-sail and topgallant studding sails and making nine to ten knots. When about eight miles west of the north Farallon, she struck a rock but glided clear. The shock was not sufficient to carry away any of the spars or rigging. However, her bottom had been stove and she immediately started to fill. Captain Henry and his crew had only time to save a portion of their effects and take to the boats before the ship sunk in 40 fathoms. The pilot boat *Relief*, some two miles distant, picked up all hands. It appears that the rock which caused the disaster was covered by 18 feet of water; its existence was known to pilots but it had not been charted; it subsequently received the name of Noonday Rock.

The *Noonday* had 2012 weight and measurement tons of general cargo, which with the vessel, was estimated worth about $450,000.

It is noted that the *Midnight* met her fate in the Banda Sea, not far from where the *Noonday* narrowly escaped being wrecked in 1857, some 20 years later.

NORSEMAN

BUILT by Robert E. Jackson, at East Boston, in 1856; 812 tons; Cunningham Bros. & Co., of Boston, owners. Sold in Siam in 1863.

NOR'WESTER

CLIPPER ship, launched in April 1854, from the yard of S. Lapham, at Medford, Mass.; 185:6 x 38:6 x 23; 1267 tons, old measurement; 1133.63 tons, new measurement. Her original owners were J. T. Coolidge & Co., of Boston. From 1864 she appears to have belonged to R. F. C. Hartley and others, also of Boston.

She left New York on her first voyage, June 14, 1854, and was 122 days to San Francisco; thence to Honolulu and from there to Boston in 93 days, according to published statements. Voyage number two was from Boston to Calcutta in 91 days, returning to Boston in 95 sailing days. Number three was from Boston to San Francisco in 132 days and Calcutta to Falmouth in 135 days. Number four, Cardiff to Singapore in 126 days and Calcutta to Boston in 106 days. Five was, Boston to San Francisco in 131 days and Calcutta to Boston in 113 days. Number six was, Boston to San Francisco in 139 days; thence to Hong Kong in 37 sailing days; return to San Francisco in 55 days; thence to Melbourne, from which port she was engaged in trade with Otago, N. Z., for something over a year. Then went to Singapore in 48 days and finally returned to New York. She then loaded for San Francisco, arriving out Jan. 17, 1865, in 195 days and being 164 days from Portland, Me., where she had put in leaking badly, from a hole knocked in her bottom by the anchor. Completing this voyage she was 125 days from Callao to Hamburg and arrived at New York in January 1867. She then went out to Port Stanley, Falkland Islands, and loaded 1463 tons of coal for San Francisco, the cargo of the condemned ship *Charles Cooper* from New York. This passage occupied 72 days, practically all light winds and calms, with royals continually set for the final 57 days. At San Francisco she was chartered to load guano at McKean's Island, for Hamburg, but was compelled to leave the Island through having parted moorings in a heavy westerly swell; arrived at San Francisco, Sept. 1, 1868, in 66 days from McKean's, with 200 tons of guano on board. Went to Puget Sound, loaded a cargo of lumber for Callao and put into San Francisco, Jan. 21, 1869, for a crew. Sailed Feb. 1st and was reported at Callao, Apr. 9th. She was subsequently engaged in general trading but did not again pass through the Golden Gate.

Her passage from Boston to Calcutta in 1855, is claimed to be the second best on record. Taking her departure June 22nd, she was 31 days to the line; her run of 36½ days from the meridian of

Greenwich in about 38° South latitude to the Hoogly pilot grounds was particularly fast; total time from port to port, 91 days; from port to pilot, 89 days. Sailed from Calcutta, Dec. 11, 1855, and Sand Heads the 15th. On Jan. 24, 1856, off Algoa Bay, lost foretopmast, main topgallant mast and jibboom in a gale. Passed the Cape of Good Hope, 51 days out, put into St. Helena on account of cholera having broken out among the crew and arrived at Boston, Mar. 22, 1856, actual sailing time being given as 95 days.

On her passage to Hong Kong from San Francisco, in 1861, she took her departure on Jan. 12th, with 500 Chinese passengers and arrived at Honolulu in 9 days and 14 hours. Sailed the 28th and arrived at Hong Kong, Feb. 25th, in 37 sailing days from San Francisco. In 1869 the *Nor'Wester* sailed from Callao with guano for Hamburg and on Mar. 8, 1870, put into St. Barts in a sinking condition. Her cargo was landed and the ship repaired, her cargo being forwarded by the *Messenger* which was sent from Boston for that purpose.

On May 10, 1871, the *Nor'Wester*, Captain Small, on a voyage from Liverpool for Philadelphia, put into Fayal, leaky. She discharged cargo and it was thought the leak was stopped but after reloading she was found to be still leaking and Captain Small, after discharging 300 tons of his cargo and hiring seven extra men to pump, sailed again June 10th and reached his port of destination. On Feb. 23, 1873, while on a voyage from New Orleans for Liverpool, she put into Key West, having been on fire for several days, with the flames coming through the main deck. She was run ashore and with men from naval vessels, an attempt was made to check the fire but pumping proved ineffectual and the ship became a total loss. About half of her cargo of 2934 bales of cotton was saved of which some 500 bales were damaged by water only.

The first captain of the *Nor'Wester* was Frank C. Eldridge who later was to take command of the steamer *Voyageur de la Mer* for the Pasha of Egypt. In 1856, Capt. Michael Gregory, formerly of the clippers *Sunny South* and *West Wind*, and in 1859, Capt.

William T. Savory, were in command. Capt. Robert B. Almy then had her several years and was succeeded by Capt. M. V. B. Mosher. In 1871, Captain Small had her in charge. Captain Sedgeley was master at the time she was burned.

NORTH WIND

EXTREME clipper ship, launched Apr. 30, 1853, and was the first production of Abraham C. Bell, the son of Jacob Bell, although he had completed the clipper ship *Jacob Bell*, which was in frame when his father died. The dimensions of the *North Wind* were: length of keel, 176 feet; of deck, 186 feet x 35: 8 x 21; 1041 tons, old measurement. She was very sharp and could carry only slightly more than her register. Grinnell, Minturn & Co., of New York were her owners.

She sailed from New York, July 27, 1853, for San Francisco, under command of Captain Hildreth. Anticipations of a short passage were soon dispelled for she had the long run of 38 days to Cape St. Roque and was not up with the parallel of 50° South until the 59th day; 29 days were spent battling heavy gales off Cape Horn, during which her figurehead was carried away, boats stove and other damage received. Had calms and light winds in the Pacific, being 51 days from 50° South to San Francisco, making her total on the passage, 138 days. From San Francisco she went to Callao in 48 days; left there, guano laden, Apr. 29, 1854, and was 77 days to Hampton Roads. She then made a round voyage between New York and Havre, going over in 23 days and returning with 317 passengers in 29 days. Her next voyage was from New York to Calcutta in 99 days, returning to New York in 98 days. Then loaded for San Francisco, arriving out, July 30, 1856, in 110 days' passage. Captain Gore, then in command, reported having fine weather off the Horn; crossing the line in the Pacific, 85 days out, being becalmed off the California coast for three days. She then crossed to Hong Kong in 48 days, going thence to Shanghai with rice and loaded finally at Foo Chow for London. Sailed Aug. 17, 1857, and put into Hong Kong, Aug. 31st, considerably damaged and partly dismasted. Repaired and sailed Dec. 19th and was 96 days to London.

In April 1860, the *North Wind* arrived at Port Philip Heads, Melbourne, from London, being only 67 days from the Downs, which was called at the time a record passage. Later, she went on to China and loaded at Amoy for New York, sailing Sept. 18, 1860; was 43 days to Anjer and then four days getting clear of Java Head. Arrived at New York, Jan. 26, 1861, in 130 days from Amoy and 55 days from the Cape. Captain Norton, then in command, reported unfavorable weather conditions throughout the whole voyage. Captain Jewett then took the ship; sailed from New York, Mar. 1, 1861, for London and was back at her home port, May 12th, the return run being 24 days. On May 24th she left New York for Havana, thence to Matanzas and left that port, July 15th, for Cronstadt. On Mar. 13, 1862, she reached Cardiff from London and loaded coal for Galle, Ceylon; sailed Mar. 27th and arrived out June 26th. Later proceeded to Singapore and from that port to London. Left port, Jan. 17, 1863, for Cardiff, to load coal for Singapore and put into Deal, two days later, damaged by collision with the British ship *Golden Fleece*, outward bound for Shanghai. Sailed from Cardiff, Feb. 23rd, and arrived at Singapore, May 27, 1863. Left Singapore in September but got ashore on a reef off Bintang Island; was towed into Singapore, Oct. 2nd, and found to be but slightly damaged.

While at Cuba, in July 1861, the *North Wind* was referred to as a British ship although her American captain, Jewett, was in command. A different account was that she was sold at Singapore, in June 1863, to go under British colors. However, her subsequent career seems to have been short and one report is that she was wrecked in 1871, yet her name does not appear in the registers of 1868.

NORTHERN LIGHT

MEDIUM clipper ship, launched Sept. 25, 1851, by E. & H. O. Briggs, at South Boston, Mass.; 171: 4 x 36 x 21: 9; 1021 tons. She was designed by Samuel H. Pook and was quite sharp below the water-line, with 40 inches dead rise. The figure-head was a full-length angel, in flowing drapery, with one arm extended overhead, the hand bearing a torch with a golden flame.

She sailed from Boston, Nov. 20, 1851, and arrived at San Francisco, Mar. 8, 1852, in 109 days' passage, Capt. Bailey Loring in command. Had lost jibboom and topgallant mast in the South Atlantic. From San Francisco she went to Acapulco and returned, being 15 days going down and 25 days returning. Then went back to Boston in 100 days from San Francisco. Capt. Freeman Hatch assumed command and took his ship out to San Francisco in 117 days, returning direct to Boston in 76 days and 8 hours, which is the record for this run to this date. There is carved on his grave-stone in the cemetery at Eastham, Mass., the following;—"Free-man Hatch, 1820-1889. He became famous making the astonishing passage in clipper ship *Northern Light*, from San Francisco to Boston in 76 days, 6 hours—an achievement won by no mortal before or since."

The third passage of the *Northern Light* was from Boston to San Francisco and return (1853-1854); 122 days out and 91 days return. The fourth voyage was 123 days outward; thence to Calcutta and 91 days from that port to Boston. She had been reported as sold at auction in April 1854, by her original owner, James Huckins, to Captain Doane, for $60,000. Her fifth voyage was from Boston to Calcutta and return (May 1855-February 1856); Capt. Seth Doane in command. On the homeward run she left in company with the clipper ship *North Wind*, for New York and both had practically the same passage,—about 102 days. The following voyage was 89 days from Boston to Manila and return to home port in 107 days; 78 days from Anjer. Her outward voyage is believed to be the record to the present time. On the seventh voyage, left Boston Dec. 11, 1856, and on Mar. 23, 1857, 102 days out, made Angaur Island, the southernmost of the Pelew group. There-after, for seven days, had a hurricane, which became a perfect ty-phoon; part of the time with tarpaulin in mizzen rigging or under bare poles the ship rolling almost yard arms in the water, with decks filled and the vessel straining badly; blew the maintopgallant mast over the side although the sails were all snugly furled and the yards pointed to the wind. Captain Doane had been in a number of typhoons in the China Seas and off the Bashee Islands but had never seen anything comparable to the present instance. Completing this voyage the ship loaded at Manila and was 115 days to Boston; 78 days from Anjer. During 1857-1858 she made another round be-tween Boston and the East Indies, after which she returned to the California trade and arrived at San Francisco, Sept. 13, 1859, in 116 days from Boston. Crossed to Shanghai in 45 days; went to Manila and from there was 53 days to San Francisco, with very heavy gales throughout, during which lost jibboom, sprung bow-sprit and stove bulwarks. From San Francisco went to Acapulco; thence to Boston, arriving there Sept. 20, 1860. Again went out to San Francisco in 134 days' passage and returned to New York in 106 days. Here Captain Lovell assumed command and crossed to Havre. Left that port, Dec. 25, 1861, in ballast for New York. On the night of Jan. 2, 1862, was in collision with the French brig *Nouveau St. Jacques,* which soon foundered, her crew getting aboard the ship. The latter, however, was so badly damaged that she was abandoned a few hours later, all hands being picked up some by the *Norma* and landed at Falmouth and the remainder by the *Bremer-haven* and landed at Cowes.

On Feb. 24, 1853, the day after the arrival of the *Northern Light* in 117 days from Boston, there reached San Francisco, the New York-built clippers *Contest* and *Trade Wind,* in 100 and 102 days respectively from that port. At the time there was much dis-cussion as to the merits of the clippers modeled and built in New York and in Boston and the appearance together at the Pacific Coast port of three first-class vessels, with the fact that they were to sail for home nearly in company, was a matter of much interest in maritime circles. Each ship had its admirers and a number of wagers were placed. The principal of a Boston house, who was in San Francisco at the time, offered Captain Hatch of the *Northern Light,* a suit of clothes if he should arrive at Boston before the *Trade Wind* reached New York. The *Contest* was not thought of in the offer as she was supposed to be the fastest of the three, in ballast trim. The *Trade Wind* got away Mar. 10th, the *Contest* left the San Francisco Heads, Mar. 12th, at 3 P. M., and the *Northern Light* sailed the 13th and arrived at Boston, May 29th, in a 76 days' and 8 hours' passage. The *Contest* arrived at New York, May 31st, in 79 days and odd hours; and the *Trade Wind* was 84 days on the way. The *Northern Light* reported 38 days from the Golden Gate to Cape Horn, against the *Contest's* 39 days. The *Light* was off Rio, 52 days out, and crossed the line on the 60th day, against the *Contest's* 61 days. The Boston ship was then favored with fine winds and strong trades from the line clear to Boston Light, making the distance in 16 days, whereas the *Contest* ran into a calm belt in 37° 30' North, and for three days made 71, 33 and 102 miles respectively; at noon, May 30th, she was 80 miles from Sandy Hook. The *Trade Wind* was off Cape Hatteras when 78 days out, thereafter encountering calms, light winds and fogs. There was much rejoicing in Boston over the result of the impromptu "race." Newspaper reports were that the *Northern Light* had spoken the *Contest* and "passed her with ease." One account was that Captain Hatch, on catching the *Contest* near the Horn, signaled that he couldn't sail in company for he "couldn't hold his horse." It is only fair, however, to quote the *Contest's* log, which is full and complete:—"April 20, daylight, discovered a ship off the lee bow; at noon, ship abeam; made her out *Northern Light;* distance made, 196 miles. April 21, *Northern Light,* 4 points abaft the beam; made 240 miles. April 22, *Light* 4 miles astern; 298 miles; April 23, *Light* 15 miles astern and out of sight in course of day; 240 miles." Best day's run of *Northern*

Light on passage, 355 miles; of *Contest*, 320 miles. Round voyage of *Northern Light*, Boston to San Francisco and return, seven months and one day; of *Contest*, between New York and San Francisco, 6 months and 15 days.

The time made by the *Northern Light* from latitude of Rio to Boston Light, 24 days, is believed to be the fastest on record to this date.

OCEAN CHIEF

CLIPPER ship, built by J. and C. Morton, at Thomaston, Me., in 1854, for their own account and sold for $85,000, soon after being launched, to James Baines & Co., of Liverpool, to be operated in their "Black Ball Line" of Australian passenger packets. She was 190 x 39 x 23 feet; 1228 tons, old measurement. She was designed by Samuel H. Pook who had drawn the plans of the *Red Jacket* and many other very fast clippers with which the *Ocean Chief* fully ranked. She was in every way a beautiful ship.

The first passage of the *Chief* was from Liverpool to Hobart Town in 72 days, the fastest on record to that time. On the return she was 84 days from Sydney to Liverpool. The two following outward passages were from Liverpool to Melbourne and were made in 80 and 75 days respectively. Thereafter she maintained a consistently good record but her career was comparatively short. She met her fate while in port at Bluff Harbor, New Zealand, being totally destroyed by fire, which was supposed to have been set by some of the crew.

OCEAN EXPRESS

MEDIUM clipper ship, built in 1854, by J. O. Curtis at Medford, Mass.; launched July 10th. Length between perpendiculars, 215: 2; over all, 240 x 41 x 24: 5; 1697 tons, old measurement; 1483 tons, new measurement. She had two decks and beams for a third,—a lower 'tween deck. Dead rise, 14 inches; swell of sides, 18 inches; sheer, 42 inches. A gilded eagle was her figurehead. Her original rig of single topsails was altered to Howes' double topsails after her first voyage. She was well sparred and a handsome ship, with easy, graceful lines and for over 20 years was one of the prominent and most popular ships trading to and in the Pacific. She proved satisfactory as to carrying capacity and sailing ability and the prophecy of her builder that she would be "First in speed, first in beauty and first in the world of waters," although exaggerated, was not an entirely idle boast. While under the American flag she was owned by Reed, Wade & Co., and their successors, Samuel G. Reed & Co., of Boston.

On her maiden voyage she sailed from Boston, Aug. 22, 1854, and was 99 days to Callao. Her fine time of 18 days from Cape St. Roque to 50° South, Atlantic, and 15 days from a similar latitude in the Pacific to destination, were offset by her 35 days from Boston to the line and the 29 days taken in rounding the Horn. From Callao she went to Liverpool in 87 days; thence in 36 days to New York. Sailed from New York, Nov. 11, 1855, for San Francisco, with a freight list of $60,441 and made the passage in 135 days, with light or head winds throughout. For 63 days her daily average was only 66 miles and she had only 22 days of 200 miles or over, the average of these being 224; the S. E. trades in the Pacific were so light that during 11 days she covered only 560 miles. Her log showed 15,858 miles made during the passage, the daily average being only 117. From San Francisco she went to Callao in 45 days; thence in 92 days to Philadelphia.

Subsequent passages made by the *Ocean Express* to San Francisco, from Atlantic ports, were as follows. From New York: 125 days (122 days and 21 hours, land to land) in 1858; 136 days in 1859; 139 days in 1860; 148 days in 1867 and 133 days in 1869. From Boston: 137 days in 1871. From London: 129 days in 1864. From Liverpool: 129 days in 1868. A further passage from New York was in 1862, when she sprung aleak off Cape Horn and put back to Rio for repairs; reached San Francisco, Jan. 2, 1863, 75 days from Rio and 208 days after leaving New York. In none of

"OCEAN EXPRESS," 1697 TONS, BUILT AT MEDFORD, MASS, IN 1854

"OCEAN HERALD," 1658 TONS, BUILT AT DAMARISCOTTA, MAINE, IN 1853

From the painting by François Roux, in the Musée de Marine du Louvre

"OCEAN ROVER," 777 TONS, BUILT AT PORTSMOUTH, N. H., IN 1854
From a painting showing the ship entering Hong Kong, Feb. 20, 1865

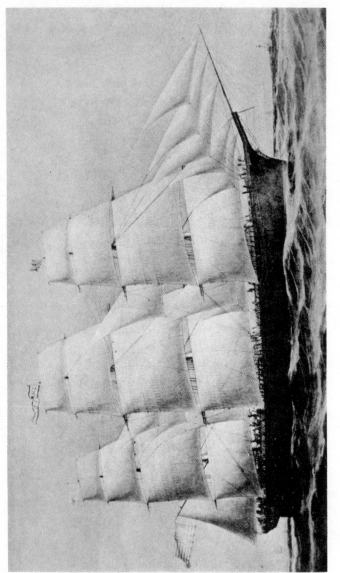

"Oracle," 1196 tons, built at Thomaston, Maine, in 1853

these passages did she have any chance to make fast time in whole or in part except in two instances when she made the run from the Pacific equator crossing to San Francisco in 16 and 17 days respectively. On her passage in 1858, her fastest, her two best days were only 252 and 258 miles. From ports of departure to the line, her shortest run was 23 days; longest, 44 days; average, 31 days. From port to 50° South, Atlantic, the figures are 55, 84 and 66 days. From port to the Pacific equator, 89, 126 and 108 days. From the equator to San Francisco, her longest run was 36 days and the average is 26 days. On one occasion she was within 600 miles of the Golden Gate for 12 days and in another instance within 700 miles for 18 days.

Of return voyages, eight were to Atlantic ports from Peru or the Pacific guano islands, the fastest being those of her first two,— 88 and 92 days to Liverpool and Philadelphia, as heretofore referred to. The others averaged something over 100 days. Three returns were from San Francisco to Great Britain with grain, the fastest being in 1867; 106 days to Liverpool with 2000 long tons of wheat which had been laden by hand, bag by bag, in 44 working hours. Her best time from San Francisco to Callao was 45 days. In 1857 she made a round voyage between New York and Liverpool when it was claimed that on the outward run she sailed by observation, 364 miles in 24 hours. During the winter of 1861-1862 she was engaged as a United States Army transport and reached New York, Jan. 30, 1862, from Port Royal.

During her career as an American ship, the *Ocean Express* had many mishaps and insurance companies suffered severely. In June 1861, bound to New York from Baker's Island, she put into Rio leaky and was in port one month repairing. Her mishap in 1862, previously referred to, was very costly. In 1868 she arrived at Callao from San Francisco, in a leaky condition. In July 1870 she left Bahia, in ballast, for San Francisco; put into Montevideo, Sept. 9th, in distress, leaking; temporary repairs were made and she went home to be rebuilt; insurance loss, $60,000. In September 1859, while proceeding to sea from San Francisco, beating out through the Golden Gate in a fog, she stranded but received only slight damage. In December 1861 she was ashore on a shoal near New York and for a time it was feared that she would become a wreck, but fortunately she was floated not materially damaged. An incident in her career occurred in August 1855. While lying off the Rock Light, Liverpool, with the pilot in charge, ready to sail for New York, the crew mutinied and refused duty, claiming that the mate overworked them. They had no fault to find with the captain or the ship. Two of the ringleaders were arrested and taken before the American Consul who advised the captain to return on board and again to ask the other men to work, which he did, but they refused and the whole of them, 30 in number, were landed and turned adrift, forfeiting their clothes and outfits, the English authorities not being at liberty to deal with the case. Another incident was in 1867, when, the ship being two weeks out from New York, bound for San Francisco, it was discovered that nearly all the water supply had been lost. For the remaining four months of the passage water was procured by condensing.

Following her arrival at San Francisco, in December 1871, the *Ocean Express* went to Peru where she was sold for 75,000 soles. On returning to San Francisco, in December 1872, she was under the flag of San Salvador and her master, Captain Bollo, reported having made the run from Callao to the coast of California in 31 days, which is very close to record time. For several years she was operated in the lumber trade between Puget Sound and Peru or Australia, part of the time being under Costa Rican colors and again under Peruvian. In 1875-1876 she went to New York where she was sold for $30,000 and went under the German flag, being renamed *Friedrich*; hailing port Bremerhaven. Subsequently she was sold to Norwegians and in registers of 1890 her home port is given as Porsgrund. In that year she was reported as having been abandoned in the North Atlantic ocean.

The first master of the *Ocean Express* was Captain Cunningham who was succeeded by Capt. Levi J. Hutchinson who was followed by Captains Hotchkiss, Willis, Hale, Horace H. Watson, Cushing, Warsaw and Horton.

OCEAN HERALD

BUILT at Damariscotta, Me., in 1853; 1658 tons; Everett & Brown of New York, owners. Sold to go under the French flag in 1856. Renamed *Malabar*.

OCEAN PEARL

MEDIUM clipper ship, built at Charlestown, Mass., in 1853, by J. Magoun; launched Aug. 15th. She was 847 tons, old measurement; had but 13 inches dead rise, but is said to have been sharper than many of the medium clippers. She is described as a beautiful vessel in every way, alow and aloft. A billet served for a figurehead. She was owned by Alpheus Hardy and Joshua Sears of Boston, whose fleet also included the *Conquest, Mountain Wave* and *Wild Rover*. Mr. Hardy was listed as the managing owner of the *Pearl* at the time of her loss.

Under command of Capt. Winthrop Sears of Yarmouth, Mass., the *Ocean Pearl* sailed from Boston, Sept. 12, 1853, and arrived at San Francisco, Jan. 25, 1854, in a passage of 135 days. The *Winged Arrow*, which had left Boston in company, reached San Francisco ten days ahead, but the *Pearl* had 20 days of very heavy weather off Cape Horn and was detained four days outside the Heads at the Golden Gate, in a dense fog. From San Francisco she had the good run of 44 days to Singapore, thence proceeding to Calcutta. From there she went to Boston in 101 days, arriving Sept. 24, 1854. Sailed from Boston, Dec. 1st and was 80 days to Valparaiso, thence going to Honolulu and being 33 days from that port to Hong Kong. Arrived at Boston, Nov. 16, 1855, in 121 days from Manila.

On Jan. 13, 1857, she arrived at San Francisco from New York, in a passage of 158 days, Captain Crowell in command. Was off the

Horn 30 days in heavy gales and had very light winds in the North Pacific; was close in to the Golden Gate for five days, her pilot being on board for three days. Completing this voyage she returned East via Callao. She then went out to San Francisco in 137 days from Baltimore, returning East via Manila. On June 29, 1860, she was again at San Francisco in 132 days from New York and after making a round voyage to Hong Kong, returned East. In July 1862, after having completed a voyage to New Orleans, with troops and stores for General Butler's Expedition, she loaded at Baltimore for San Francisco and arrived out Feb. 5, 1863, after a passage of 155 days from Cape Henry. Was 86 days to the Horn and then had 20 days of strong westerly gales; was within 700 miles of the Golden Gate for 14 days in strong gales from northward. Then made another round voyage between San Francisco and Hong Kong and finally returned East via the West Coast of Mexico.

On Oct. 27, 1864, the *Ocean Pearl*, Captain Hardy, on a voyage from New York to Lisbon, put into Tarragona. She had received her pilot and anchored but before she could get "pratique," a southwest gale sprang up and she went ashore and became a total wreck. The crew were saved by boats from the British ship *Calypso*.

OCEAN ROVER

BUILT by Tobey & Littlefield, at Portsmouth, N. H., in 1854; 162 x 43 x 23; 777 tons; R. H. Tucker and others, of Boston, owners. In March 1867 she was purchased from Salem parties by Captain Carleton and others. Wrecked on a reef in the Guigana River, north of Pernambuco, Brazil, July 18, 1870, while bound for Baker's Island from Hamburg.

OCEAN SPRAY

B UILT by George Dunham and others at Frankfort, Me., in
1852; 174 x 37 x 23; 1089 tons; Veasie & Co., of Bangor, Me.,
owners. Abandoned in 1857 during a voyage from London to Madras.

OCEAN TELEGRAPH

E XTREME clipper ship, launched from the yard of J. O. Curtis, at Medford, Mass., Mar. 29, 1854, for Reed, Wade &
Co., of Boston. Length between perpendiculars, 212 feet; over all,
227 x 40 x 23; 1495 tons, American, old measurement; 1244 tons,
British measurement; actual capacity for weight and measurement
goods from Eastern ports to California, 2260 tons. Her 'tween
decks were nine feet high and she had beams for a lower 'tween
deck. The bow raked boldly forward, flaring gracefully and was
ornamented with a beautiful carved female figure with forks of
lightning playing around. She was very sharp, with a long, clean
run tapering like that of a pilot boat. Her light and graceful stern
was ornamented with carved work surrounding a figure of Neptune.
She had a fine sheer and every line and moulding harmonized her
whole length. No expense was spared to make her one of the most
perfect ships ever built. She spread 11,000 yards of canvas in a
single suit of sails, although she had no studding sails on the mainmast. Capt. George H. Willis, formerly master of the clipper ship
Star of the Union, was placed in command.

The *Ocean Telegraph* was never operated in trade with China
or the East Indies and all of her outward passages, eight in number,
were from New York to San Francisco. The average of seven of
these is under 117 days and that of the whole eight, which included one exceptionally long run, is only 121 days. She made five
passages from San Francisco direct to New York, of which four
were under 100 days each. The average of the five is 96 4/5 days.
As will appear, portions of a number of these different runs were
very close to record.

On her maiden voyage she reached San Francisco, Nov. 24, 1854, Captain Willis reporting 65 days to the Horn, off which had bulwarks stove and lost part of deck load. Crossed the equator 101 days out and made the California coast 100 miles south of the Golden Gate, 16 days thereafter; was then seven days to port, due to a dense fog. From San Francisco went to Callao in 50 days; loaded guano at the Chincha Islands for New York. When eight days out from Callao was found to be leaking ten inches per hour. Returned and discharged a portion of her cargo which was forwarded per ship *Arcole*. Resumed the voyage and made the run to New York in 58 days, the fastest passage over that route for many years if, indeed, it does not stand to this date. Her next outward passage to San Francisco was made in 118 days. Was within 100 miles of destination when 110 days out. Went to Honolulu and took a cargo of whale oil thence to New York in 92 days. Her third outward voyage was very long,—150 days, she being 46 days to the line, with adverse winds, and 40 days off the Horn, during 12 days of which she did not make one mile. Completing this voyage she returned direct to New York in a 98 days' run. The following passage out was 105 days and 20 hours; was off Rio, 35 days out, although she had fallen to leeward of St. Roque and had to tack to north and east. Her time of 50 days to the Horn was the fastest during that season. From the equator crossing to San Francisco she was only 19 days and on the whole passage had but one good day's run,—300 miles. At San Francisco she was put on the berth to carry passengers to New York in "Moore and Folger's Line," the cabin rate being $100 as against the exorbitant steamer rate of $135 for steerage. She went home this time, also, in 98 days. The fifth voyage was under Captain Potter, 125 days outward and 106 days return. Captain Little was in command on voyage six performed in 109 days. Was up with the Horn, 55 days out, but had no trades in the South Pacific; made the run from the line to destination in 18 days. Returned home arriving at New York, Aug. 9, 1860, 70 days from Callao in ballast. The next voyage was 125 days outward and

90 days return direct to New York. Had passed the Horn 42 days out and crossed the Atlantic equator when only 63 days out,—remarkably fast time. From the line to Sandy Hook had nothing but light winds and calms and arrived July 5, 1861. Soon after her arrival she went into the dry-dock to be stripped, caulked and repaired. Her eighth and last voyage as an American ship was 112 days outward, arriving at San Francisco, Feb. 15, 1862, Captain Little still in command. The return was to Queenstown, for orders, with guano from the Peruvian deposits.

In 1863 she was sold at London to James Baines & Co., for £7060 and for a time was operated in their "Black Ball Line" of Liverpool-Australian packets under her new name, *Light Brigade*. She continued registered as the ship *Light Brigade*, with the same ownership, as late as 1870, but in 1875 she appears as the bark *Light Brigade*, owned by Williams & Co.; hailing port London. In 1878, under Captain Peabody, she made a short run across from Baltimore, being only 15 days from Cape Henry to Cork. Her last days as a sailing vessel were spent in the Quebec deal and lumber trade and in February 1883 she was reported as arriving at Queenstown, 19 days from New York, leaking badly. Some time thereafter she was unrigged and converted into a coal hulk for use at Gibraltar, where she served many years.

ONWARD

MEDIUM clipper ship, built by J. O. Curtis at Medford, Mass., for Reed, Wade & Co., of Boston; launched July 3, 1852. Length between perpendiculars, 167 feet; over all, 175 x 34: 6 x 20: 6; 874 tons, old measurement. Dead rise, 20 inches; sheer, 27 inches; swell of sides, six inches. Her lines were convex; for a figurehead she had the Goddess of Liberty robed in the American ensign, the right hand pointing forward, the left, grasping the emblems of harvest; one foot rested on a carved representation of the globe. The stern was curvilinear, ornamented with an American

Indian, surrounded with gilt work. Under the name and hailing port, the words "According to Law" appeared in carved, white letters. The fore and main lower masts were "made" spars, 26 and 27 inches in diameter; the mizzen was a single stick, 23 inches in diameter; in length, the lower masts were 70, 75 and 69 feet, and their yards, 66, 70 and 50 feet; the topmasts were 41, 43 and 32 feet long and their yards, 50, 54 and 44 feet. She was well built, her construction being superintended by Capt. Jesse G. Cotting who became her first commander.

The *Onward* made three passages from Boston or New York to San Francisco, arriving at destination on her maiden trip, Dec. 1, 1852, in 125 days from Boston and was only 19 days from the equator crossing to port. On Jan. 25, 1854, she passed through the Golden Gate, 150 days out from New York. Capt. Thomas F. Wade, who was in command, reported being 45 days to the line, 74 days to 50° South, in light winds, and 28 days rounding the Cape in heavy gales. On her third outward passage she reached San Francisco, Oct. 15, 1856, 158 days from New York, Captain Luce in command. Was 71 days to 50° South, and 26 days rounding the Horn, encountering heavy gales and a great quantity of ice; had a hurricane of 18 hours' duration during which her deck houses and rigging were considerably damaged. Of the 40 days between the Pacific equator crossing and destination, 20 were spent in practically a dead calm. Of her homeward passages, the first was from Honolulu to New York in 113 days. Her second was from Shanghai to London, she being 89 days from Anjer. She then went out to Melbourne and back to London in 114 days from Calcutta. Completing her last voyage as a merchant ship, she arrived at New York, June 21, 1861, in 115 days from Shanghai, 101 days from Anjer and 45 from the Cape.

On Sept. 9, 1861, John Ogden, who had purchased her in 1857, for $32,000, sold her for $27,000, to George D. Morgan, United States Government Agent, and she became a sailing cruiser of the fourth class. Her equipment was one 30-pounder Parrott rifle and eight 32-pounders. Her crew numbered 103 men. She remained in commission until June 20, 1865, and at first was under command of Acting Volunteer-Lieutenant J. F. Nickels. Later her Acting-Master was William H. Clark. Official naval records show that she was well thought of and her commanders were zealous in duty. In January 1863 she captured the British brig *Magicienne*, which Lieutenant Nickels believed intended to run the blockade. The justification of this action was not upheld, however, and the brig was later restored to her owners. On different occasions the *Onward* was sent on cruises in search of the Confederate privateers *Florida*, *Alabama* and *Shenandoah*, besides which she operated off the coast of Brazil as a protection to unarmed homeward bound merchantmen.

After the close of the Civil War, the *Onward* was used as a store-ship by the Navy, being stationed at Callao for a number of years. Finally, her days of usefulness being over, she was sold at that port, Nov. 1, 1884, for the small sum of $1850.

ORACLE

BUILT by Chapman & Flint, at Thomaston, Me., in 1853; 1196 tons. Owned in New York. Sold to go under the British flag, November 1862. Reported renamed *Young England*.

ORIENTAL

CLIPPER ship, built by Jacob Bell, at New York, in 1849, for A. A. Low & Brother of that port, for the China trade; 185 x 36 x 21; 1003 tons, old measurement. She was somewhat larger, though quite similar in model, to the *Samuel Russell*, built by Brown & Bell for the Messrs. Low in 1847, but neither ship had the extreme lines of the clippers brought out a few years later for the California trade. The *Oriental* cost, ready for sea, $70,000.

On her maiden passage she sailed from New York, Sept. 14, 1849, under command of Capt. Nathaniel B. Palmer and arrived at

Hong Kong, by the Eastern passage, on Jan. 1, 1850, in a run of
109 days. Sailed from Whampoa, Jan. 20th, and passed Anjer 11
days later; arrived at New York, Apr. 21st, in 81 days from Whampoa, 70 from Anjer and 42 days after passing the Cape. Sailed from
New York, May 18, 1850, under command of Capt. Theodore D.
Palmer, a younger brother of her former master, and crossed the
line in 25 days, logging 3904 miles with 264 as the best day. On
her 45th day out she was on the meridian of the Cape with the
best day 300 miles on which occasion she was under double reefs
a portion of the time. From June 19th to July 21st, 33 days, her
daily average was 239 miles and for the 11 days between July
10th and 21st, she averaged 264; best, 302 and poorest, 228. Passed
St. Paul's, 58 days out, and entered Prince's Straits, July 29th, 71
days out; had sailed by log, 14,160 miles and by observation, 14,-
521 miles, an average of 204¼ miles per day. Arrived at Hong
Kong, Aug. 8, 1850, 81 days from New York, the fastest on record
to the present time.

At Hong Kong, the agents of the *Oriental*, Messrs. Russell &
Co., of which firm A. A. Low had at one time been a member,
where offered by British merchants the unprecedented rate of £6
sterling, per ton of 40 cubic feet, to take a cargo of tea to London. Other ships had been getting £3.10 per ton of 50 feet. This
highly remunerative freight, amounting to about $48,000 for the
1618 tons she loaded, was ample inducement for the *Oriental* to be
diverted from her projected return to New York. She sailed Aug.
28th and was 21 days to Anjer, against the monsoon; passed the
Lizard, 91 days out, and entered the West India dock at London,
Dec. 3rd, in 97 days from Hong Kong, the fastest passage from
China to England up to that time. She was also the first American
ship to load in China for London direct, under the new regulations
of trade, and her arrival caused much comment, the English press
being replete with articles about her fast passage, her model and the
probable effect her advent would have on British ships engaged in
the trade. Shipbuilders, particularly those of Aberdeen, were ap-

pealed to, to bring out models which could successfully compete with their new rivals, the American clippers. Admiralty surveyors took off her lines while she was in dock.

The *Oriental* immediately obtained a charter for a round voyage between London and China and sailed Jan. 14, 1851; passed Anjer, 89 days out, and arrived at Hong Kong, May 11th, in 116 days' passage. Returning, she reached London, Nov. 20th. She again went out to Hong Kong, arriving May 5, 1852, in 116 days from London. Loaded at Shanghai for New York; sailed Sept. 1st; passed Anjer the 29th; was ten days off the Cape in light winds and arrived at New York, Dec. 16th, in 106 days' passage. It was two years and seven months since she had taken her last departure from New York, during which time she had sailed 95,000 miles.

Captain Fletcher now assumed command and sailed from New York, Jan. 27, 1853, for San Francisco. When 42 days out and nearly up with the Horn, she had the head of the foremast badly sprung and for three days was forced to make her course north by east, the wind being southwest. From the Falkland Islands to 50° South, 78° West, had very heavy weather. When 98 days out was only 50 miles from the Golden Gate but ran into a calm and did not enter port until two days later, May 7th, in 100 days from New York. Thence crossed to Shanghai in 41 days, and later went to Foo Chow to load for New York. Is said to have been the first ship to enter the river Min after the port of Foo Chow was opened to trade. On Feb. 25, 1854, while proceeding down the river to sea with a cargo valued at $175,000, and assisted by a number of native boats, she struck on a point of rocks and soon sunk in deep water. A good breeze was blowing but the tide was strong and it was stated that the boats did not obey the directions of the pilot. The crew and passengers were saved but the ship and cargo were total losses. The valuation of the ship was given as $50,000.

ORPHEUS

MEDIUM clipper ship, built by Rice & Mitchell, at Chelsea, Mass.; launched Mar. 1, 1856. Length over all, 200 feet x 42 x 23; 1272 tons, old measurement; 1067 tons, new measurement; dead weight capacity, 1500 short tons. Her original owners were W. F. Weld & Co., of Boston, who, when they commenced disposing of their large fleet of sailing vessels in the early '70's, sold the *Orpheus* to C. L. Taylor & Co., of San Francisco. During her career she had many different masters, all for short terms except Capt. Sturgis Crowell of Hyannis, who was in command some six years. Among her other captains were, Richard Mitchell, Sr.; Isaiah Chase; Levi Howes; Wilson; Smith; Sawyer.

The *Orpheus* was of fine model and established a good record for sailing ability. On her run of 112 days from New York to San Francisco in 1868, she made the very fast time of 19 days from 50° South, Pacific, to the equator, and 16 days thence to destination, which total of 35 days is equal to that made by the *Flying Cloud*. In 1859, her passage from New York to San Francisco being 114 days, she was in company with the famous clipper ship *Young America*, in latitude 45° South, Atlantic; 43 days thereafter both ships crossed the parallel of 30° North, in the Pacific,—very fast and even sailing. The *Orpheus* was several degrees to westward of her larger rival and then ran into a calm belt, covering but 44 miles in six days. The *Young America* found good winds and passed through the Golden Gate seven days in the lead.

Contrasting with these two passages is the *Orpheus'* maiden run of 180 days from Boston to San Francisco, in 1856. On this passage she fell to leeward of Cape St. Roque and in beating around she was 40 days on soundings. She was not up with Cape Horn until 98 days out and after getting into the Pacific found head winds instead of the expected trades. Was 41 days from the Cape to the equator and 41 days thence to destination. She had two other long passages to San Francisco, that in 1860 being 144 days and in 1865, 146 days from New York. On the first of these she was 40 days to the line and 26 days rounding the Horn in very heavy weather. On the 1865 passage, a good run of 26 days to the line was offset by a long spell of bad weather off the Cape, which continued to latitude 40°, Pacific. She was not up to the equator until 115 days out.

In 1862, the *Orpheus* was 135 days from New York to San Francisco and the following year her time was 126 days. On both occasions light or head winds and calms generally prevailed. In 1867 she was 500 miles from the Golden Gate when 111 days out from New York, but to cover that short distance took 15 days. In 1869 she had moderate or light weather excepting 20 days off Cape Horn, where, in addition to very heavy gales, she encountered a large quantity of ice; time on this passage, 132 days. In 1873 she was 127 days from Boston; was 700 miles from the Golden Gate on the 113th day out. Her last deep-water voyage was a light-weather run from Ardrossan to San Francisco in 1875, in 139 days.

The foregoing eleven passages to San Francisco are all the westward Cape Horn runs made by the *Orpheus*. In 1857-1858 she was 138 days from Philadelphia to Hong Kong. In 1861 and in 1863 she was 125 and 111 days respectively from San Francisco to Liverpool. In 1867 she took wheat from San Francisco to New York, via Hampton Roads, in 119 days, gross. Four of her passages from Manila to New York were made during the unfavorable season. In 1862 she was 59 days working down the China Sea to Anjer and was two weeks off the Cape in very stormy weather, all conditions being particularly bad that season.

During the fall of 1875, the *Orpheus* made a voyage to Puget Sound from San Francisco, returning with a cargo of coal. She was proceeding north on her second trip when, during the night of Nov. 4th, she was run down by the steamship *Pacific* which had left Victoria, B. C., some hours before, for San Francisco, full of freight, overloaded with passengers and in a very tender condition. The steamer sunk with 273 out of the 275 souls aboard. The *Orpheus* lost foretopmast and maintopgallant mast, with all her starboard rigging. After making such repairs as were possible, Captain Sawyer

stood in for the land and at 5 A. M. of the 6th, the light on Cape
Beale was mistaken for that of Tatoosh and the ship went ashore
and became a total wreck. The crew were landed safely. The vessel
was valued at about $30,000 and was insured for $20,000. The wreck
was sold for $380.

OSBORNE HOWES

MEDIUM clipper ship, launched from the yard of Hayden
& Cudworth, at Medford, Mass., July 27, 1854; 186 x
35:9 x 23:9; 1100 tons, old measurement. She was named after
the senior member of the Boston firm of Howes & Crowell, who
were her owners. Capt. Nehemiah D. Kelley of Brewster, who was
in command for the first four years, called her a good sailer, she
having made on one occasion, 325 miles under all sail, including
skysails and topgallant studdingsails. She has not, however, any
complete fast voyage to her credit.

She first left Boston, Aug. 23, 1854, and was 151 days to San
Francisco. Except for 25 days of heavy gales off Cape Horn, nothing but light winds were experienced and her royals were set con-
tinuously from the latitude of Valparaiso to destination. On her
second voyage she reached San Francisco, Apr. 30, 1856, in 124
days from New York, with light weather throughout except for 21
days while rounding the Horn. On July 30, 1857, she was again
at San Francisco, in 147 days from New York. Had the good run of
22 days to the line but thereafter experienced unfavorable weather
and lost an entire suit of sails battling gales for 25 days while rounding the Cape. She then made a round voyage between San Francisco and Hong Kong being 47 days on the outward and 60 days on
the return passage. Arrived at San Francisco, Feb. 8, 1859, in 136
days from Boston, Captain Crowell in command. Was 41 days to
the line, 80 days to 50° South; near Cape Horn, was in company
with the clipper ship *Fleetwing* for four days, the latter having had
identically the same weather and length of passage from New York

as had the *Howes* from Boston. Both ships were over three weeks
rounding the Cape and both had excellent runs up the Pacific, under
40 days, but the *Howes* reached destination three days in advance
of the *Fleetwing,* having been only 16 days from the equator crossing. Her last westward Cape Horn run was in 1860, she reaching
San Francisco, Nov. 30th, in 177 days from Liverpool. Captain
Baxter, who was in command, reported being 42 days to the line;
90 days to 50° South; 142 days to the Pacific equator crossing; off
the Horn had the main and foretopsail yards and jibboom sprung,
the tiller broken off, the figurehead started and a number of sails
split and saw many huge icebergs. After crossing 50° South, Pacific, had 12 days of hard gales and could scarcely show a close
reefed foretopsail. It is noted in the log on Aug. 31st, in 58° South,
63° West, that she saw a ship and a bark six miles astern steering
directly for a solid block of field ice, the weather being somewhat
thick with night coming on.

Homeward bound on her first voyage the *Howes* arrived at Baltimore, Sept. 12, 1856, in 105 days from Callao, via Hampton Roads.
Her second return was 71 days from Callao to Hampton Roads.
Her third, Callao to Boston, in ballast, was in 86 days. On her
fourth, she went from San Francisco to Calcutta and thence to
Liverpool. On her fifth, she left McKean's Island, guano laden,
Mar. 30, 1861, for New London. Off the Horn she sprung a leak
and on June 12th, put into Rio; had jettisoned 125 tons. Discharged 150 tons, caulked from the copper up, and took out and repaired the foremast. After completing the voyage she made a round
voyage between New York and Havre. Sailed from New York,
Mar. 6, 1862, and had the long passage of 142 days to Shanghai.
Arrived at San Francisco, Mar. 9, 1863, in 55 days from Manila,
with very heavy weather after passing the coast of Japan. Captain
Cottrell was in command and his ship loaded grain at San Francisco for Liverpool.

In June 1864 the *Osborne Howes* was at Calcutta, from New
York, and was sold to go under the British flag without change of

name; purchase price reported as 84,000 rupees. Her name appears in registers of 1870 but not thereafter.

PAMPERO

EXTREME clipper ship, built by Charles Mallory, at Mystic, Conn.; launched Aug. 18, 1853; 202: 3 x 38: 2 x 21; 1375 tons, old measurement. She was the largest vessel that had been built at Mystic, up to that time, and was in every way a superior ship and proved to be a fast sailer. J. Bishop & Co., of New York, were her principal owners. Capt. Calvin Coggin was in command until 1859, when William Lester, who had been an officer aboard from her first voyage, succeeded. After the sale of the *Pampero* to the Government, in July 1861, Captain Lester took the *Flying Childers*, and then in turn, the *Invincible* and *Swallow*.

On her maiden voyage the *Pampero* left New York, Oct. 8, 1853, and when 30 days out lost fore and main topgallant masts and had mizzen mast sprung. Was up with the Horn, 56 days out; crossed the equator on the 88th day; 17 days thereafter, then being 105 days out, she was close to the California coast enveloped in a dense fog which prolonged the passage to 109 days, although Captain Coggin reported only 105. Passing through the Golden Gate, Jan. 25, 1854, she was in company with the *Onward*, 143 days, and the *Bald Eagle*, 115 days from New York, and the *Ocean Pearl*, 135 days and the *Kingfisher*, 115 days from Boston. The *Kingfisher* had crossed the equator, Jan. 5th, the other four the day previous and all had practically the same run up to the coast and were then held up by fog. The *Pampero* sailed from San Francisco, Feb. 15th, and arrived at Hong Kong, Mar. 24th, a remarkably fast run of 36 days. She left Whampoa, Apr. 18th; passed Anjer, May 20th, and arrived at New York, July 31st, in 104 days' passage, 72 days from Anjer. Time of the round voyage, 9 months and 23 days.

The *Pampero's* second voyage was in 125 days from New York to San Francisco, being 60 days to the Horn and 94 days to the

"Phantom," 1174 tons, built at Medford, Mass., in 1852

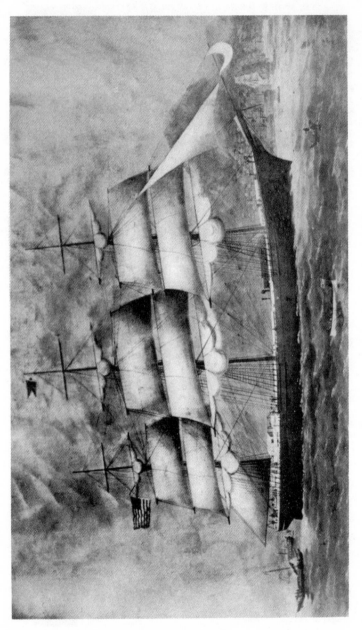

"Prima Donna," 1529 tons, built at Mystic, Conn., in 1858

SHIPPING CARD ADVERTISING THE "PRIMA DONNA"
From the Peabody Museum, Salem, Collection

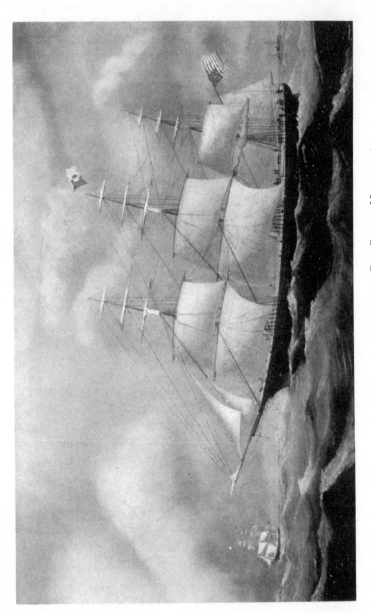

"Queen of Clippers," 2361 tons, built at East Boston, Mass., in 1853

equator crossing. When five days from destination had a heavy gale which stove bulwarks and hatch and damaged some 'tween-deck cargo. From San Francisco she returned to New York via Shanghai and London. Again went out to San Francisco, passage 123 days, with light winds prevailing throughout. Proceeded to Honolulu in a 15 days' run and was thence 91 days to New York, arriving Mar. 6, 1857. She then went out to Shanghai, direct, and operated on the China coast for some time. Finally left Shanghai, Oct. 20, 1859, and Woosung the 22nd; passed Anjer, Nov. 11th and while in the Straits of Gasper, signalized the *Nonpareil*, Captain Green, from Shanghai, Oct. 2nd, for New York. Dec. 11th she signalized the *Argonaut*, Captain Norton, from Foo Chow for New York, and arrived at New York, Jan. 29, 1860, in 99 days from Woosung and 70 days from Anjer. Reached port nine days ahead of the *Nonpareil*. Loaded for San Francisco and arrived out, July 31, 1860,—a passage of 119 days. Had 23 days to the line; 51 days to 50° South; rounded the Horn 55 days out; crossed 50° South, in the Pacific, 71 days out and the equator 21 days later. Off the Horn lost figurehead, bulwarks and mainrail and also had some severe weather in the North Pacific. From San Francisco she arrived at New York, Jan. 8, 1861, in 102 days. Then crossed to Havre in 34 days and reached New York in return, June 10, 1861, losing several men overboard on the passage which occupied 30 days.

In February 1860, after her return from China, a twenty-one forty-eighth interest was sold at auction, bringing the small sum of $11,200. On July 7, 1861, she was purchased from J. Bishop & Co., by George D. Morgan, acting for the U. S. Government, for $29,-000 and being rated as a fourth-class vessel of war, she was assigned to the West Gulf Blockading Squadron as a store and guard ship. In August 1861 she was loaded with coal at New York and proceeded to Key West, but most of her four years' naval service was spent at the passes of the Mississippi. At first she had a crew of 50 men and an armament of four 32-pounder cannon, but one 20-pound Parrott rifle and one 12-pound brass rifle were later added. Among her commanders were: Acting-Masters C. W. Lamson, Charles Huggins, Oliver Colburn and Lt.-Commander H. Wilson. Her last employment was transporting army stores from New Orleans to Pensacola, after which she proceeded to New York and went out of service. On Oct. 1, 1867, she was sold at New York, at auction, for $6000. The cost of repairs while in the Government service totalled $12,931.

PANAMA

EXTREME clipper ship, launched from the yard of Thomas Collyer, at New York, Oct. 11, 1853, to the order of N. L. & G. Griswold of that city, and was the third ship belonging to that firm so named. All of these had been so successful that after number three was condemned and sold in 1867, the Messrs. Griswold had a fourth *Panama* built. The subject of our sketch was 192: 4 over all x 35: 7 x 19: 4; 1139 tons, old measurement; 867 tons, new measurement. She was very sharp below the water-line, with convex lines above and rather flaring bows. Her actual capacity for measurement freight was about 1450 tons, while for dead weight it was slightly under her original register.

The *Panama* proved to be a very fast sailer and when on the loading berth at San Francisco was advertised as "The fastest ship afloat." This encomium was agreed with by officers who had made a number of trips in her, who stated that she had never met her match at sea. She holds the record from San Francisco to Liverpool, 86 17/24 days, and from Tome, Chile, to Liverpool, 56 days. She also has to her credit a run of 101 days from New York to San Francisco; one of 85½ days from Shanghai, 67 days from Anjer, to New York; 74 1/3 days, Sandy Hook to Melbourne; 87 days, Foo Chow to New York; 37 days, San Francisco to Shanghai. The total number of days occupied on her six passages from New York to San Francisco is 670, an average of 111 2/3; slowest, 120 days. She made one run from Liverpool to San Francisco in 116 days, being 19 days from off St. Agnes, Scilly Islands, to the line and 93 days thence to destination. In 1864, on her passage of 101 days from New York, she was 20 miles southeast of Cape Horn when 47 days out and crossed the Pacific equator on the 81st day. In 1866, her run out being 108 days, she was again on the equator, 81 days out. Her other Pacific equatorial crossings were, in order, 87, 94, 94, 91 and 86 days. From New York to the line she was 22, 31½, 31, 21, 19 and 22 days, respectively. In 1860 she was eight days from 50° South, Atlantic, to the same latitude in Pacific.

She was built for the California and China trades but on account of low freight rates prevailing when she was first ready, she was diverted to the European run and made the trip from New York to Liverpool in 30 days, returning home in 22 days having sprung her bowsprit in a heavy gale. Went back to Liverpool where she loaded for Shanghai and sailed May 27, 1854, arriving out in 107 days. Sailed from Shanghai, Oct. 27th, and arrived at New York, Jan. 21, 1855, in a passage of 85½ days; 67 from Anjer and 41 days from the Cape. Loaded for San Francisco and took her departure from New York, Mar. 8th. Her captain, W. P. Cave, who had been in command from her maiden voyage, reported experiencing an extraordinary amount of head winds and calms during his passage of 112 days; had no southeast trades in the Atlantic where they were expected to blow heaviest. Her best work was running down the northeast trades in the North Atlantic where for several days she averaged 260 miles. Off the Horn she sprung the foremast. Completing this voyage she was 51 days from San Francisco to Hong Kong. Loaded for home at Foo Chow, sailing Oct. 25, 1855, and reached New York in 113 days; 81 days from Anjer.

The following voyage was 74 days and 8 hours from Sandy Hook to Melbourne; thence to China. Sailed from Shanghai, Dec. 12, 1856, and arrived at New York, Mar. 19, 1857, 97 days out and 77 from Anjer. Left New York, again, May 6th, and was 117 days to San Francisco in a succession of light winds and calms the whole passage. Was becalmed three days while in sight of Cape Horn; had but one gale, in 42° South, Pacific, which lasted 30 hours, it being a perfect hurricane for 16 hours. From San Francisco she went to Shanghai in 37 days and thence to Hong Kong, from which port she sailed, Feb. 18, 1858, and was 52 days to Melbourne. Reached Hong Kong on the return, June 22nd, being four months and four days on the round. From then until the autumn of 1859 she continued in trade between those two ports. Finally loaded at Foo Chow for New York and sailed Dec. 6, 1859; passed Anjer, the 15th, nine days out; the Cape of Good Hope, Jan. 17th, 42 days out, and arrived at New York, Mar. 2, 1860, in 87 days from Foo Chow; 78 from Anjer.

Captain Soule now took command and took the *Panama* to San Francisco in 120 days from New York, reaching destination Oct. 1, 1860. Was 31 days to the line, 57 days to 50° South, eight days thence to 50°, Pacific, and crossed the equator 94 days out. Had heavy weather off the Falkland Islands but was three days off the pitch of the Cape in light, baffling winds; had strong head winds and light trades in the South Pacific and was 29 days from 50° to the equator. Aug. 5th, off the Horn, saw the clipper ship *Challenger* and saw her again a week later. The latter reached San Francisco three days after the *Panama*, in 128 days from New York, but reported having even more adverse weather conditions on the run than her rival. The *Panama* sailed from San Francisco, Oct. 27th, and arrived at Liverpool, Jan. 21, 1861, in 86 days and 17 hours' passage, which was just 7 months and 19 days after the date she had left New York. This is a record over that course. The following voyage was 116 days from Liverpool (112 days from off the Scilly Islands) to San Francisco; thence 54 days to Coquimbo. Left Tome, Chile, on Feb. 20, 1862, and anchored in the Mersey, Apr. 17th, in 56 days' passage. From Liverpool she went out to Shanghai and for nearly a year was on the China coast, between the ports of Hong Kong, Foo Chow and Shanghai. Left Hong Kong, Aug. 1, 1863, the poorest season and was 44 days to Anjer. Arrived at New York, Nov. 30th, in 121 days from Hong Kong, 77 from Anjer and 50 from the Cape. Had very light winds from St. Helena. Sailed from

New York, Feb. 2, 1864, and made the Farallon Islands at 10 A. M. May 13th, in 20 days from the line and 101 days out. Completed this voyage by going back to New York in 107 days' passage with very heavy weather most of the run, the ship receiving some damage and losing a number of sails. Went back to San Francisco in 111 days; thence to Hong Kong and arrived at New York, Jan. 21, 1866, from Whampoa, Sept. 20, 1865, in 123 days and 58 days from the Cape.

On her last passage to San Francisco she left New York, Apr. 10, 1866; was 22 days to the line; thence 59 days to the Pacific equator crossing and then 27 days to port; total 108 days. Loaded wheat for Sydney and arrived out Oct. 17th, in a 49 days' run. From Australia she went to China and thence to Bangkok, where she loaded rice for Pernambuco for orders. Put into Bahia, Aug. 4, 1867, in distress and leaking badly and with seven feet of water in the hold. Discharged and was surveyed, condemned and sold, the reported consideration being $2000, and her purchasers residents of Buenos Ayres, who had her repaired for trade between that port and New York.

An incident in her history is related that while in Hong Kong harbor, early in 1867, Chinese thieves one night stripped a large amount of her copper from one side.

PANTHER

MEDIUM clipper ship, launched early in 1854, from the yard of Paul Curtis, at Medford, Mass.; 193: 7 x 37: 5 x 24; 1278 tons, old measurement; 1185 tons, new measurement; capacity for dead weight cargo, 1700 short tons. She was of fine model and very strongly built, being diagonally braced with iron straps. Her original owners, R. C. Mackay & Sons of Boston, were prominent in trade with India and the first three voyages of the *Panther* were to Calcutta, with railroad iron from England.

She left Boston, Mar. 4, 1854, and soon encountered a very heavy storm and was 32 days on the run to New Orleans; thence 37 days to Liverpool and from there, 99 days to Calcutta. On this latter passage she is said to have made 3000 miles the first 17 days. From Calcutta she was 100 days to London and then went back to Calcutta in 93 days. On the return she had very severe weather in the Bay of Bengal and in the Indian Ocean and did not clear the Cape until 70 days out. Left London on her third voyage, May 21, 1856, and Deal, seven days later; 92 days thereafter she was off the Sand Heads. On leaving Calcutta she encountered bad weather and sprung a leak and was forced to return to port. She finally left the Sand Heads, Jan. 16, 1857, and arrived at Boston, Apr. 17th, in a fine run of 91 days. She was off the Cape, 44 days out.

The *Panther* left Boston, July 9, 1857, and was 143 days to San Francisco. Thereafter she made five other passages from American-Atlantic ports to San Francisco, arriving out as follows: Feb. 3, 1860, 139 days from Boston; May 10, 1863, 140 days from New York; May 1, 1865, 170 days from New York; Nov. 19, 1867, 165 days from New York; Dec. 23, 1868, 142 days from New York. For a ship recognized as a fast sailer and having a good record in her other work, these Cape Horn passages seem to be anomalous but the race is not always to the swift and an inspection of the memoranda from her logs, explains the situation. On all of the passages in question, particularly unfavorable weather was encountered and in not a single instance did she have an opportunity to make a showing. From her port of departure to the line in the Atlantic, light or head winds caused her average time over that section to be 35 days, 30 days being her shortest run, while on two occasions she was 40 days. Her average time in rounding the Horn was 33 days, the shortest being 20 days. In two instances she was driven back from the Cape, once being forced to the eastward of the Falkland Islands and another time, back and around Cape St. John. In November 1859, while near the eastern entrance to the Straits of Magellan, 61 days out from Boston, she met the clipper ship *Malay*, 74 days out from New York, and Captain Gannett noted in the log of the *Panther*, "Came up with and quickly passed her." Luck, however, then deserted the

Panther and her rival passed through the Golden Gate three days in the lead. On July 9, 1857, she left Boston a few hours after the *Goddess* and led her two days to the line and four days to the Platte. Here, however, she encountered a pampero followed by continuous heavy gales which forced her to go to eastward of the Falkland Islands. The *Goddess* escaped these storms, had a fine run through the Straits of Le Maire and led her much faster rival 13 days to San Francisco. In 1863 the *Grace Darling* and the *Panther* were in company in latitude 38° South, Pacific, and the former, taking a more westerly course, reached San Francisco one day before her competitor, a faster ship.

In 1858, the *Panther* made the fine run of 38 days from San Francisco to Valparaiso, returning over the same course in 50 days. She then went to Calcutta; left the Sand Heads, Mar. 28, 1859, and was 99 days to New York; being 12 days north of Bermuda. In 1860 she went from San Francisco to Callao and was 92 days thence to New York, via Hampton Roads. She then crossed to Liverpool and went out to Calcutta and Bombay. Arrived at Boston, Aug. 31, 1862, from Calcutta. Had light head winds and calms in the Bay of Bengal with no trades in the Indian Ocean and a long succession of westerly gales from Madagascar until west of the Cape. In 1862 she went to Liverpool from Callao. In 1865, to Liverpool from Baker's Island, and in 1866-1867 made a round voyage between New York and the East Indies. In 1867 she was 116 days from San Francisco to New York.

Soon after arriving at San Francisco, in December 1868, from New York, on which passage Captain Johnson had a most anxious week off the Horn while surrounded by huge icebergs, the *Panther* was sold to Pope & Talbot of San Francisco and made some passages with lumber from her owners' Puget Sound mills to ports in the Pacific. On her return to San Francisco from the first of these, she being 62 days from Newcastle, N. S. W., Captain Kilton reported having made the run to within 800 miles of the Golden Gate in 48 days, which is very fast time. In 1870 she made a round voyage between San Francisco and Hong Kong, being 44 days going over and the same length of time on the return; both good runs. She then went to Liverpool in 117 days from San Francisco, returning to the Golden Gate in 139 days, arriving Aug. 31, 1871. Thereafter she was operated in the Pacific Ocean in the off-shore lumber trade or coastwise.

The *Panther* left Nanaimo, B. C., Jan. 17, 1874, with a cargo of coal for San Francisco. In a strong head wind and blinding snow storm, while in tow of the tug *Goliah,* she stranded off Vancouver Island but came off with eight feet of water in the hold. Her tug was then forced to cast her off and she again went ashore on a reef. After 30 days of fruitless efforts to get her off, she was abandoned, her sails and rigging being all that was saved. She was valued at $40,000 and was insured. There was no loss of life.

In 1854, the captain of the *Panther* was Nat. G. Weeks. From 1857 until 1862, Capt. John P. Gannett was master. Captain Lathrop succeeded, he being followed by Captain Johnson in 1866. Captain Kilton took her after her sale at San Francisco and was succeeded by Capt. John W. Balch who was in her when she was lost.

PHANTOM

MEDIUM clipper ship, although of quite sharp model, with lines concave below and convex above the water. Built by Samuel Lapham, at Medford, Mass., and launched Dec. 8, 1852. Shortly before launching she was purchased by Crocker & Warren of New York, and Crocker & Sturgis of Boston and later she was owned by D. G. & W. B. Bacon of Boston. She was very strongly built and diagonally braced. Keel, 179; deck, 195; over all, 200; beam, 37: 11; depth of hold, 21: 6; 1174 tons, old measurement. Dead rise, 20 inches; sheer, two feet; rounding of sides, six inches. The stem ended in a billet about which twined a gilded vine. Her mainmast was 86 feet long; maintopmast, 48; topgallantmast, 26; royal, 18 and skysailmast, 13 feet. Mainyard, 80 feet; topsail yard,

61½; topgallant, 45; royal, 36 and main skysail yard, 29 feet long. In comparison with the *Flying Cloud*, which was longer by some 30 feet with two feet greater beam, the *Phantom* was nearly as lofty, with yards but slightly shorter, so that the sail area differed but little. She could stand hard driving and has a fine record for speed.

On her first voyage the *Phantom* left Boston, Jan. 6, 1853, under command of Capt. Alvin H. Hallett, and arrived at San Francisco, Apr. 21st, in a passage of 105 days. Passed Rio, 33 days out, and Cape Horn on the 55th day. During the 15 days from 50° to 50°, she had a continuation of very heavy gales, during which part of the stem was washed away, cabin filled with water and the patent steering apparatus broken. The rudder head and jury tiller were later carried away and on several occasions the sea made a clean breach over her; the ship laboring hard and the crew much used up with exposure. Captain Hallet rigged up a tackle by which she was steered into port. She crossed the equator 90 days out and thence had the excellent run of 15 days to the Golden Gate. Homeward bound she had another serious mishap and was obliged to put into Rio on account of a bad leak. Had loaded guano at the Chincha Islands and the published account of her run from Callao to Rio was 32 days. She arrived at New York, Feb. 16, 1854, in 65 sailing days from Callao. On Feb. 14th, during a fog she grounded on Flynn's Knoll, off Sandy Hook, but was got off without injury.

She sailed from New York, Aug. 13, 1854, for London, passed the Lizard in 20 days, and returned from London to New York in 30 days. On her third voyage, the *Phantom*, under command of Captain Peterson, sailed from New York, Oct. 25, 1854, and arrived at San Francisco, Feb. 23, 1855, in 121 days' passage. Was 35 days to the line and 69 to Cape Horn, off which had the mainmast sprung in two places; crossed the equator in Pacific, 96 days out. From San Francisco went to Hong Kong in 46 days; sailed from Foo Chow, July 26th, and arrived at New York, Nov. 27th, in 124 days. Sailed from New York, Jan. 18, 1856, and arrived at San Francisco, Apr. 29th, in a passage of 102 days and 9 hours. Was 20 days and 9 hours from Sandy Hook to the line; 49 days to Staten Island, where she was becalmed three days and was off the Cape ten days; crossed the equator, Apr. 8th, 81 days out, and was within 800 miles of destination for eight days in light winds. Then went to Hong Kong in 42 days; thence to Manila and back. Sailed from Whampoa, Oct. 17th, and arrived at New York, Feb. 1, 1857, in 106 days.

The fifth voyage was from New York, sailing Mar. 17, 1857, to Hong Kong in 97 days; left Shanghai, Sept. 10th, and was thence 114 days to New York. Sailed from New York, Feb. 15, 1858, and arrived at San Francisco, June 21st, in 125 days. Went to Manila in 54 days; sailed from there Oct. 5th and arrived at Boston, Jan. 20, 1859, in 103 days' passage. On her outward run on this voyage she passed in sight of Cape Horn, 58 days out, but had adverse winds nearly all the way thence. The seventh voyage was from Boston, Mar. 13, 1859, to Honolulu, July 12th, in 120 days; thence to Foo Chow in 27 days; sailed from there Nov. 8th and arrived at New York, Feb. 26, 1860, in a passage of 110 days.

Capt. Henry Sargent now took command of the *Phantom* and leaving New York, Apr. 26, 1860, was 99 days to Shanghai; sailed from there Oct. 17th, and arrived at New York, Jan. 29, 1861, in 104 days. On her ninth and last departure from New York, she left Apr. 11, 1861; was 84 days to the Horn, off which had 18 days of strong gales; thence had light winds to San Francisco, arriving Aug. 26th, in a 137 days' passage. Went to Shanghai in 56 days and thence to Hong Kong. Sailed from there Apr. 1, 1862; discharged her pilot the 3rd; passed the Japanese coast the 14th; received the San Francisco pilot off the bar, 6: 30 P. M., May 6th; anchored in San Francisco Bay the next morning, 36 days and 18 hours out, anchor to anchor; 33 days and 22 hours, pilot to pilot, and 24 days from the coast of Japan. This latter portion of the run is not exceptionally fast but her time from pilot to pilot is within two days of the record.

The *Phantom* sailed from San Francisco, May 30, 1862, for Hong Kong. On July 13th, at 4: 15 A. M., having had thick, rainy weather for ten days previous, she ran on the Pilot Reef, off Pratas Shoal, while going eight knots. She began immediately to make water and after remaining by the wreck for some hours and cutting away the masts, the captain decided to abandon her and the same day, at 5 P. M., all hands, 26 in crew and officers and 12 Chinese passengers, left in five boats. A portion of the crew arrived at Hong Kong on July 19th. Captain Sargent with those in his boat and the treasure, $50,576, which the *Phantom* had had aboard, were picked up by a bark and landed at Shanghai on July 22nd. Two boats were captured by pirates near Swatow and their occupants were detained until ransomed by Chinese merchants at the rate of $25 each. They finally reached Hong Kong on Aug. 27th. The *Phantom* was insured for $66,000 and had but little cargo aboard, a portion of which was saved.

Captain Peterson, who was in command of the *Phantom* for five voyages, claimed that she never had been beaten on a wind, by any vessel, and that only when going free had she been outsailed, even by the extreme clippers. At times she averaged 14 knots for 20 hours and once made 336 miles and on another occasion 345 miles in a day. Her log of Mar. 14, 1853, New York to San Francisco, shows "47° S.—83° W., 67 days out, spoke and passed the clipper ship *Tornado*, 69 days out from New York; from 1 A. M. to noon, making 15 knots."

PHOENIX

CLIPPER ship, built at Cape Elizabeth, Me., and launched in February 1854; 217 over all x 41: 6 x 24 feet; 1458 tons, old measurement. She was of beautiful model, with elegantly fitted cabins and was sold shortly after arrival at New York, Feb. 28, 1854, for $90,000, to Charles Carow, to be operated in trade between New York and Liverpool. She was heavily sparred and very lofty, crossing besides her three skysail yards, moon-sail yards on the fore and main masts.

Soon after her launch she sailed from Portland, Me., Captain

Crabtree in command, and arrived at New York, Feb. 25, 1854. On the night of the 23rd, during a blinding snow storm, she came in contact with the schooner *William E. Baird*, Captain Crowell, of and from Boston, cutting her almost in two. The *Baird* floated only a few moments, but all her crew were saved with one exception. The *Phoenix* sailed on her maiden voyage for Liverpool, Mar. 22, 1854, and after two round voyages across the Atlantic, the last westward run being made in 18 days and on which she had often logged 16 knots, she loaded at New York for San Francisco. Sailed Feb. 1, 1855; had very heavy weather in the Gulf Stream and was 24 days to the line; was 18 days rounding the Horn in furious gales and 30 days from 50° South, Pacific, to the line; thence had 31 days of light winds and for the final 15 days was within two days' sail of the Golden Gate. She had left New York drawing 22 feet yet had frequently logged 15½ knots and had made in one day 334 miles. She arrived at San Francisco, June 5, 1855, in 124 days from New York, Captain Hoxie in command. Sailed from San Francisco, June 28th, for Hong Kong and passed Honolulu, July 7th, in 8 days and 17 hours, land to land. Loaded at Manila for New York and arrived home Feb. 29, 1856. During 1857-1858 she was regularly employed between New York and Liverpool.

POLYNESIA

MEDIUM clipper ship, launched July 2, 1852, from the yard of Samuel Hall, at East Boston, for Pierce & Hunnewell of Boston; 177 x 36 x 22; 1084 tons, old measurement; capacity for measurement cargo, about 1750 tons. The *John Gilpin*, launched a few months later from the Hall yard, for the owners of the *Polynesia*, is said to have been a sister ship, but through more fortunate conditions attending her various voyages she has the better record of the two. The whole life of the *Polynesia* appears to have been a continued series of adversities, mishaps, and accidents and her end was conformable to her previous experiences. While it was conceded that she was a capable and fast ship, always well kept up, yet in her record there is only one passage wherein she made a showing for speed and even on that particular trip she was partially dismasted.

On her maiden voyage the *Polynesia* arrived at San Francisco, Dec. 8, 1852, her captain, Jacob G. Homer, reporting a passage of 140 days from Boston. She had generally heavy weather throughout and her run was slower than that of other clippers about that time. From San Francisco she went to Singapore in 65 days; thence proceeding to Calcutta. Left the Sand Heads, June 20, 1853, and was 111 days to Boston. Loaded at New York and under command of Capt. Horace H. Watson, arrived at San Francisco, Apr. 10, 1854, after a passage of 104 days. While lying to in a heavy gale, two days after passing out by Sandy Hook, she was struck by a hurricane lasting three hours, losing two topgallant masts, the main-topsail yard and having the mainmast badly sprung. The bulwarks were stove and the binnacle carried away. In spite of this mishap, however, she passed Cape Horn on the 49th day out and had good prospects for making a very fast passage but Captain Watson was disappointed by finding very light winds in the Pacific. Was 34 days from the Cape to the equator and 21 days thence to destination. Completing the voyage she returned East with whale oil from Honolulu.

On her third voyage she arrived at San Francisco, July 16, 1855, in 125 days from Boston. Was 22 days to the line and 54 days to the Horn. Lost foretopmast. Crossed the equator 95 days out and was 18 days making the final 600 miles. Sailed from San Francisco, Nov. 11, 1855, and was 105 days to New York. Captain Perkins then assumed command and took her out to San Francisco arriving Aug. 28, 1856, after a passage of 132 days from New York, in light weather, except for 15 days of storms off the Horn. From San Francisco she went to Honolulu in 13 days; thence to Calcutta and back to New York. On her fifth voyage she had adverse weather throughout; was 26 days off the Horn and arrived at San Francisco, Dec. 15, 1857, in 139 days from Boston. Then went to Honolulu in 14 days and was 105 days thence to New Bedford. At Honolulu, Captain Perkins was superseded by Captain Scott, with the result that the crew refused duty and were put in prison by order of the consul.

At Boston, another change in captains was made, H. G. Morse, formerly in the clipper bark *Behring,* being put in command and the *Polynesia* sailed Sept. 9, 1858, for San Francisco. After getting to sea she was found to be leaking in topsides and on the 14th, with four feet of water in the hold and the pumps useless, Captain Morse put her about for Boston, where she arrived the 21st. After being re-caulked, having a new foremast stepped, and merchantable freight substituted for what had been damaged in the 'tween decks, she again proceeded on her voyage. Her usual bad fortune again attended her and what occurred is best told in the words of Captain Morse, who relates;—

"Everything being in readiness, we started again; fine weather; no use for pumps, ship perfectly dry. Heavy banks of clouds to the southeast and barometer falling; found ourselves in a stationary cyclone; it was five days veering from south by east to east-north-east, during which time the barometer never rose over 28: 30; ship on the port tack, with constant strain on the port rigging. The lee rail was constantly under water for three days, when I decided that the lower masts must be relieved from their burden, or the whole business would go by the board. Imagine yourself entombed within a dome or arch-shaped space, surrounded by a black, atmospheric mass surcharged with electricity, a huge cavern of darkness. This turbulent cauldron is constantly lighted by blinding flashes of lightning, while deafening peals of thunder appal the spectator. The sea, being relieved from pressure, rises frantically in confused masses of every conceivable shape and the ship is thrown from side to side, plunging and battling with the waves. Suddenly the gale bursts in tremendous fury from the opposite quarter; the roar of the elements has stunned all sense of hearing; the sight is dimmed by the intense flashes; the mariner, half paralyzed, lashed to the rail; waves threaten to engulf all. It was certain that something would have to go unless a remedy was found. We cut maintopgallant shrouds and slackened up the back-stays; over she came, sixty feet of topgallant, royal and skysail. This relieved the ship and lower masts. The rigging had stretched so much that the mainmast was jammed over in the upper deck; passed chains around the lower masthead, set up an end to the mainyard on deck, strapped the topmast back-stays to the mast seven feet below the cross-trees. Having secured the main, and cleared away the wreckage, found that the foremast required the same treatment. On the morning of the fifth day, we kept off for the south, wind four points on the port quarter, in order to carry sail enough to avoid heavy rolling, which would certainly have made a wreck of the *Polynesia*. A new topgallantmast was made and the mainmast head, which was found to be twisted, was fished with oak planks and chain lashings. Eventually everything was in good shape to stand a banging off the Horn."

The equator was crossed on the 40th day out from Boston and from the latitude of Rio until getting into the Pacific, had strong westerly gales and a head sea. Was 21 days from the equator to San Francisco, arriving Mar. 25, 1859, in 152 days from the time she had last left Boston.

The *Polynesia* sailed from San Francisco, Apr. 23, 1859, and was 11 days to Honolulu, thence eight days to Jarvis Island. Loaded a cargo of guano and was 101 days to Hampton Roads; thence proceeded to New York. Captain Morse described Jarvis Island as having an area of about one square mile, the highest point being some 20 feet above sea level. He first sighted the flag-pole, then the house and lastly the island. The ship was kept under commanding canvas, the six topsails, jib and spanker, and was made fast to the buoy less than 400 feet from the reef and in 90 fathoms of water. Captain Morse was anxious to leave a record day's loading behind and this was accomplished by the ship lading 215 tons one day. The guano was taken to the beach in flat cars running on a rude track made of joists with hoop iron nailed on top and thence to the ship in boats. The force employed consisted of one mule, some 60 Kanakas and the crew of the *Polynesia*, who did the stowing.

On her seventh voyage, the *Polynesia* arrived at San Francisco, June 28, 1860, from New York, in 138 days. She was 28 days to the line in very heavy weather; 64 days to the Horn, off which had storms for 20 days and was 29 days from the equator to destination. Four days before arrival, she was in collision, during the night, with the coasting bark *Ork*, losing the bowsprit and all head gear besides having a portion of the cutwater carried away. The bark was badly damaged but did not leak. A heavy sea was running and both vessels were under double reefed topsails at the time. After being repaired at San Francisco, the *Polynesia* sailed Aug. 3rd, and was 12 days to Honolulu, thence proceeding to Baker's Island where she loaded 1115 tons of guano and sailed about Oct. 1st, for Hamburg. Arrived at New York, May 29, 1861, in 33 days from Hamburg.

At New York, Captain Morse was succeeded by Captain Wood and the *Polynesia* sailed for San Francisco on what was to be her last passage. Arrived out Jan. 23, 1862, after a run of 140 days. Was 42 days to the line; 29 days thence to 50° South; 17 days rounding the Horn; 115 days to the equator and 21 days thence to inside the Farallons but was then detained four days in a dense fog.

On Mar. 1, 1862, the *Polynesia* was anchored in San Francisco harbor, cleared and ready to sail for Hong Kong, in ballast. Some of the crew deserted, intending to go to the Cariboo mines, but were rounded up and put back aboard by the police. At one o'clock in the morning of Mar. 3rd, she was discovered to be on fire. The hatches were put on allowing only sufficient space for lines of hose to enter. Assistance from the U. S. ship *St. Mary's*, in the form of fifty men with portable pumps, was received and for a time it was thought that the fire was under control. It, however, continued to gain the mastery and as the ship was surrounded by other vessels and in the fairway, an attempt was made to scuttle her but this was stopped by the harbor master. The anchor chain was finally cut through with saws, files and chisels and the blazing ship was taken in tow and beached on the mud flats at the South End. She proved a total loss and the hulk was sold for breaking up, realizing $2300. She was valued at about $50,000 and insured for $47,000. Her registered owner was James Hunnewell of Boston. The crew, who were supposed to have set her on fire, had been put in irons by Captain Woods and sent ashore to jail.

PRIDE OF AMERICA

BUILT at Richmond, Me., in 1853; 213 x 38 x 22; 1826 tons. Sold in March 1854 to go under the British flag. Renamed *Pride of the Ocean*. Reported foundered in 1883.

PRIDE OF THE OCEAN

BUILT by Daniel Foster, at Warren, R. I., in 1853; 197 x 42 x 24; 1525 tons; Cady, Aldrich & Reid of Providence, R. I., owners. Sold April 1854, to go under the British flag. Renamed *Belgravia*.

PRIDE OF THE SEA

BUILT by Foster & Boose at Baltimore, Md., in 1853; 218 x 41 x 23; 1600 tons; James Hooper & Co., of Baltimore, owners. On a voyage from New Orleans to Liverpool she stranded on St. Patrick's causeway, took fire and became a total loss.

PRIMA DONNA

MEDIUM clipper ship, built in 1858, by Greenman & Co., at Mystic, Conn.; 203:6 x 42 x 24; 1529 tons, new measurement. While her ends were reasonably sharp, she had a flat floor and was a good carrier. She crossed three skysail yards and having a lively sheer, she was prominent among handsome ships. A white and gilded eagle image of a female was her figurehead. She carried a mounted rifled cannon on the poop during the Civil War. Her first owner was John A. McGaw of New York. In 1875 she was reported as being purchased by C. H. Mallory & Co.

Between 1858 and 1877, the *Donna* made 14 passages from New York to San Francisco. Her cargoes were always delivered in first-class order and she was a favorite with shippers. She made no particularly fast run, her shortest round voyage being her maiden effort when she was 118 days from New York to San Francisco, returning to New York, in ballast, in 110 days. Outward bound, she was off the Platte in company with the *Neptune's Favorite* which sailed four days after her. She led the latter into San Francisco, three days, although her whole run was one day longer. On Feb. 14, 1867, she was towed to sea from New York in company with the *Governor Morton*, both ships making sail simultaneously. New York papers, referring to the "race," said—"both ships being of equal sailing capacity, and having charts marked out accurately, it is only an accident that can give one an advantage." Both passed through the Golden Gate the same day, the *Morton* three hours ahead, their passages being 123 days. On the same dates they had made both equatorial crossings, passed through the Straits of Le Maire and had the same time making the run around Cape Horn. On Apr. 10, 1869, the *Donna* passed out by Sandy Hook in company with the *Ocean Express*, said to be of about her model and sailing capacity. The *Express* led by 11 days to the Golden Gate, her advantage having been gained through having good trades in the North Pacific while the *Prima Donna* had light winds and calms and was 36 days on that portion of the run.

The average of the 14 westward passages of the *Prima Donna* is 137.7 days; fastest, 118 days; slowest, 155 days. Over the different portions of these runs, the fastest and slowest, no two of which items are of any one single passage, are:—from New York to the equator, —fastest, 24 days; slowest, 40 days; New York to 50° South, Atlantic,—51 days and 71 days; from 50° to 50°,—13 days and 34 days; New York to Pacific equator,—93 and 131 days; equator to the Golden Gate,—21 and 36 days. Of her homeward passages from San Francisco, seven were to New York; four to Liverpool or Queenstown; one to New Bedford; one to Callao and England and one to Callao, Mauritius and Havre. Average to New York, 114 days; fastest, 100 days, in 1862, when she was 15 days to the equator and 41 days to the Horn. On leaving San Francisco it was blowing a hard gale and she was unable to drop her pilot, Mr. Abbott, whom she carried to New York. Two of her runs over this course were made in 105 days each; her slowest run was 133 days. Fastest run to Liverpool, 118 days; slowest, 136 days; average, 126 days. Her run to New Bedford was 110 days.

In 1878 the *Donna* engaged in trade between New York, Japan, China and the Philippines. In March 1882 she arrived at Yokohama from New York; went thence to Manila and Hong Kong; left the latter port Oct. 18th, passed Java Head, Dec. 26th, the Cape of Good Hope, Jan. 26th, and arrived at New York, Mar. 27, 1883, in 160 days from Hong Kong and 91 days from Java Head,—a slow passage throughout. She was later sold and went under the Austrian flag, without change of name, her hailing port becoming Trieste.

Her first commander was Captain Pray who had superintended her construction. After two voyages, Captain Herriman took her over. In 1868, Capt. J. B. Miner succeeded. From 1869 until about 1880, Capt. William H. Lunt was in charge, and in 1881-1883, Captain Hatch.

QUEEN OF CLIPPERS

CLIPPER ship, built by Robert E. Jackson, at East Boston, Mass.; launched Mar. 26, 1853. Keel, 235 feet; deck, 245; over all, 258 x 44: 6 x 24: 6; 2361 tons, American measurement, old style; 2197 tons, foreign measurement. She had three complete decks; dead rise, 18 inches; sheer, four feet. Her lines were slightly concave below and convex above the water. Her entrance was quite long and sharp and her run easy but her model was not that of the extreme clipper type. The graceful carved figure of a queen ornamented her forward and her oval stern was particularly neat, having a semi-elliptical turn at the monkey rail. The cabin accommodations were as perfect as those of an ocean steamer of her day and as handsomely decorated. On deck her appearance was not as agreeable to the eye as many of her contemporaries nor was she as heavily sparred. Her fore and main masts were built sticks; the lower main mast was 92 feet long; the topmast, 54 feet; topgallant, 30; royal, 29; skysail mast, 14 feet. The corresponding yards were 90 feet; 70; 53; 44 and 31 feet long. Her original owners, Seccomb & Taylor of Boston, sold her soon after she was launched, to Zerega & Co., and D. Fowler of New York, for $135,000, and Capt. Reuben Snow, who was to have commanded her, relinquished the position to Capt. John Augustus Zerega, formerly of the packet ship *Arctic*. Great doings in the way of speed were expected of the *Queen* and her ability to make 18 to 20 knots was not questioned by enthusiastic admirers.

After proceeding to New York, the *Queen* loaded 3000 tons of general merchandise (freight list $65,000), and with 17 cabin passengers, took her departure, June 30, 1853, for San Francisco. Light winds and calms were experienced from the start. She was 34 days to the line; 62 days to 50° South; 12 days rounding the Horn; 19 days running up the South Pacific to the equator and 26 days thence to port; total passage, 119 days; but when 105 days out she was only 500 miles distant from the Golden Gate. Had 16 days of calms on the passage and for one stretch of 35 consecutive days had her three skysails set. Her best day's run was 276 miles in the S. E. trades in the Atlantic, when for several hours she logged 17 knots, but the breeze gradually died out and the day ended in a dead calm.

On arrival at San Francisco she was drawing 22 feet and was the largest ship to enter port up to that time. The copper had started from both sides of the bow causing a leak which required constant pumping for several weeks to keep the ship clear of water. From San Francisco she went to Callao, in 58 days, but being then found to be still leaking, she left there on Feb. 6, 1854, in ballast, for home. On Mar. 21st, when 42 days out from Callao, she was forced to put into Bahia to be hove down and caulked. She finally reached

New York, June 8, 1854. She subsequently crossed to Liverpool from whence she went to the Mediterranean and during the Crimean War was under charter to the French Government as a transport. In 1856 she was reported as having been sold at Marseilles, on French account, the consideration being 150,000 francs. She was renamed *Reina des Clippers*, hailed from Marseilles, and was registered as owned by Aquarora & Company. One report was that she met her end a few years later but particulars of her fate are not at hand.

QUEEN OF THE EAST

BUILT by Metcalf & Noriss, at Damariscotta, Me., in 1852; 184 x 38 x 23; 1275 tons; Crocker & Warren of New York, owners. Lost on a reef in the South Pacific, in April 1872, while on a voyage from San Francisco to Newcastle, N. S. W.

QUEEN OF THE PACIFIC

MEDIUM clipper ship, built at Pembroke, Me.; launched in November 1852; 1356 tons, old measurement. Owned by Reed, Wade & Co., of Boston. She had quite sharp lines and was called a fast sailer, but her short sea life was replete with mishaps and on three out of her five completed voyages she was forced to put into ports en route. She has no fast passages to her credit.

On her maiden voyage she left Boston, Jan. 26, 1853, for San Francisco, Capt. W. Reed in command. Through a portion of her ice cargo melting, she became very crank and could not carry much sail. Was 30 days off the Horn, losing a topmast, having the head started and developing a bad leak. Put into Valparaiso, June 6th, 131 days from Boston; sailed the 16th and was 53 days to San Francisco, being 31 days from the equator, in light winds and calms. Then went to Singapore in 64 days and from Calcutta to Boston in 119 days. Her second voyage was from Boston to Callao, returning from Callao to Hampton Roads in 72 days. She then took a cargo of coal to Nicaragua, for the steamship line; thence to Calcutta and home. In January 1857 she left New York for San Juan del Sur, with coal. In latitude 25° North, was dismasted in a hurricane and put into St. Thomas, in February, leaking badly. She was condemned and sold, the voyage being abandoned.

After being repaired by her new owners, she left New York, July 8, 1858, for San Francisco, under command of Captain Du Bois, formerly in the *Shooting Star*. When ten days out it was found that practically all her fresh water had been lost as the cargo in the lower hold had chafed holes in the large iron tank which reached to the main deck. In the face of light winds and no rain, all hands were put on an allowance of one pint daily until Pernambuco was reached, 37 days out. From Pernambuco she was 26 days to the Straits of Le Maire and was 14 days rounding the Horn. On the 77th day she was 600 miles from the Golden Gate, but took 12 days to cover that distance. Her passage was 89 days from Pernambuco and 126 sailing days from New York to San Francisco. She returned to New York direct in 107 days.

Sailed from New York, July 28, 1859, for San Francisco and was lost on a reef about 180 miles north of Pernambuco, on Sept. 19th. A portion of the cargo in the 'tween decks was saved but attempts to get her off were futile and she broke in two amidships.

QUEEN OF THE SEAS

THE clipper ship *Queen of the Seas*, was launched from the yard of Paul Curtis, at Medford, Mass., Sept. 18, 1852, for Glidden & Williams of Boston; 184 feet, keel; 195 feet from stem to stern post; 214 over all x 38: 8 x 22; 1356 tons. She had a dead rise of 20 inches; sheer, 2½ feet; height between decks, seven feet and ten inches; long and easy ends and was only 18 feet wide, 20 feet abaft the apron. She carried as a figurehead the representation of a queen in flowing white garments, crowned and holding a wand in her left hand. Each cat-head was ornamented with a gilded sun and her semi-elliptical stern had gilded fancy work. In materials and strength of construction she was not surpassed by any ship of her size and her interior finish was of the finest. She was sparred as follows:

MASTS

	Foremast	Main	Mizzen
	82	85	76
Top	46	48	39
Topgallant	25	26	21
Royal	16	17	10

YARDS

	70	78	58
Top	55	62	46
Topgallant	41	47	34
Royal	32	36	26

On her first voyage she arrived at San Francisco, Mar. 11, 1853, in 131 days from Boston and 42 days from Valparaiso. Had put into that port when 85 days out and was 3½ days there. She fell to leeward of St. Roque, losing thereby some 13 days and was under close-reefed topsails while doubling the Horn. Was drawing 21 feet of water and in bad trim on the voyage, being a foot by the head. From Valparaiso to port, encountered sharp head winds most of the way, particularly in the North Pacific; yet she went to the Golden Gate in 22 days from the line. On only one day did she have a chance to show her qualities as a fast sailer and then she made 315 miles in 24 hours. She sailed from San Francisco, Apr. 3, 1853, and arrived at Boston, July 16th, in a passage of 104 days. On arrival, Capt. Elias D. Knight, who had her on her maiden voyage, was succeeded by Capt. Benjamin Tay and she left Boston, Aug. 22, 1853, and arrived at Sydney, Dec. 6th, in a passage of 105 days. She sailed from Calcutta, Sept. 21, 1854; put into Newport, Jan. 10th, 111 days out and arrived at Boston, Jan. 21, 1855. She loaded at Boston for San Francisco, arriving out Aug. 2, 1855, Captain Tay reporting 136 days' run; 28 days to the line; 68 days to Cape Horn; crossing the equator in the Pacific, June 30th, and for the final 20 days of the passage, light winds and calms. Sailed from port Aug. 21st, and arrived at Shanghai, Oct. 17, 1855, via Honolulu. Left Shanghai, Nov. 9th, and arrived at New York, Mar. 22, 1856.

At New York she again changed commanders and under Captain Cobb left New York, June 3, 1856, and was 95 days to Melbourne. From Melbourne she went to Hong Kong and was reported at that port, Jan. 20, 1857, loading coolies for Melbourne. From Melbourne she returned to Hong Kong and was in port there Sept. 16, 1857. From Hong Kong she seems to have gone back to Australia and returned to Hong Kong, sailing from there, June 11, 1858, for Manila. From Manila she returned to Boston and under Captain Crowell arrived at San Francisco, May 17, 1859, in 139 days from Boston. Left June 19th, for Howland's Island. Probably conditions prevented her loading there for we have her arriving at Valparaiso, Aug. 24th, and sailing from Callao, under Captain Pearce, about Dec. 10, 1859, for Liverpool; passage reported as 84 days.

The *Queen of the Seas*, still under command of Captain Pearce, loaded with coal and sailed for Shanghai and is supposed to have foundered in the Formosa channel about Sept. 21, 1860. The last news of her comes from a letter written by Captain Hamilton of the ship *Lebanon:* "I was in company with the *Queen of the Seas* in the Formosa channel for eight days, from Sept. 13th-21st, in a severe gale; we could make no progress against the wind and current; on the morning of the 21st, the wind increased to a hurricane with a tremendous sea but eased up towards night but the *Queen* was no longer in sight." The *Queen* and freight money were valued at $73,000 and cargo at $15,000.

QUICKSTEP

BUILT at Freeport, Me., in 1853; 836 tons; for Dunham & Dimon of New York. Sold to go under the British flag in 1863.

R. B. FORBES

EXTREME clipper ship, built in 1851, by Samuel Hall, at East Boston and named after one of Boston's most prominent citizens, Robert Bennet Forbes, merchant and navigator. She was launched July 31st and was a fine specimen of the speedy and beautiful models from the Hall shipyards; 156 x 32 x 19½; 756 89/95 tons, capacity tonnage, 1000; 21 inches dead rise; two feet sheer. A gilded billet took the place of a figurehead. The stern was the exact duplicate of the *Game Cock's*, even to the gilded work. She was said to sit in the water as trim as a pilot boat. J. S. Coolidge & Co., of Boston, were her owners.

On her maiden voyage she left Boston, Sept. 27, 1851, under command of Capt. Justus Doane, and arrived at Honolulu, Jan. 5, 1852, in 99 days, anchor to anchor, and 96½ days from land to land. Captain Doane reported 30 days to the line and 60 days to the Horn; best day's run, 312 miles, on Dec. 29th; in three consecutive days made 900; on several occasions logged 14½ knots. This passage is the fastest on record for a merchant sailing vessel and very closely approaches the run of the crack sailing frigate, *Portsmouth*, in 1848, which made 97 sailing days from Norfolk to Hilo, via Rio, Valparaiso and Callao. In continuation of her voyage, the *Forbes* was 21 days and 13 hours, from Honolulu to Hong Kong, which is very close to record; distance logged, 5400 miles; daily average, 250.6. She left Whampoa, Apr. 3rd, and arrived at New York, July 16th, in 104 days, beating by six days the celebrated *Sea Witch* and completing a remarkably fast round voyage, one creditable to any of the flyers of double her tonnage.

The second voyage was 127 days from Boston to San Francisco with 24 days off the Horn in heavy gales and four days off the California coast. Thence was 16 days from San Francisco to Honolulu; 41 days thence to Singapore; thence 30 days to Calcutta and from there 101 days to New York, arriving Dec. 18, 1853. Her third voyage was 137 days from New York to San Francisco with light or contrary winds throughout. Had to go as far north as 43°, in 144° West, before she could get a slant into port, and then was two days off Point Reyes in the fog. Captain Ballard had taken command and he continued in the ship until she was sold. Completing this voyage she crossed to China and was 99 days from Whampoa to New York, 97 days from pilot to pilot. Was up with the Cape 51 days out and crossed the equator on the 73rd day. Beat the *Swordfish* one day from Anjer and arrived at New York, Feb. 17, 1855.

During the six years between April 1855 and May 1861, the *Forbes* was engaged in trade between New York or Boston and the East Indies. Among her outward passages were two to Batavia in 86 and 87 days respectively; one to Hong Kong in 98 days and one to Rangoon in 93 days. Of her homeward runs, one was from Shanghai in 110 days; one from Singapore in 96 days; two from Penang in 93 and 102 days, and one was from Padang in 78 days, 45 days from Cape of Good Hope and 35 from St. Helena. In December 1861 she was again at San Francisco in 127 days from Boston; thence 73 days to Calcutta and thence to Boston. Then went out to Batavia in 83 days; thence to Bangkok, via Singapore; thence to Hong Kong, where she was sold for the coolie traffic, the reported consideration being $17,000. Aug. 26, 1864, she put into Hong Kong, dismasted, and is said to have been condemned. In the Registers of 1865 to 1872, she appears as the ship *Donna Maria Pia*, owned in Macao by M. A. de Pont.

RACER

CLIPPER ship, launched from the yard of Currier & Townsend, at Newburyport, Mass., Feb. 8, 1851; 207 x 42: 8 x 28; 1669 tons, old measurement. Dead rise, ten inches. A beautiful gilded head of a race horse ornamented her stem, while a large spread eagle embellished her particularly neatly molded stern. Her foremast was 84 feet long by 31 inches in diameter; the foretopmast was 47 feet by 17 inches; topgallant and royal masts, 42 feet long. Foreyard, 74 feet; topsail yard, 60 feet; topgallant, 44 feet; and royal yard, 34 feet. She had no flying kites but spread 8152 yards of canvas in a single suit of sails. She had three decks and was equipped with an hospital, an ice house and all such other necessary accommodations as were essential to a first-class passenger ship of her time, she having been built to be operated as a regular packet in the "Red Cross Line" between New York and Liverpool, being one of the few ships of clipper model to be constructed for that class of trade. In every way she was a noble appearing vessel and exceeded in size anything previously put afloat on the Merrimac River. Her cost was reported as being something over $120,000, her construction being supervised by Capt. Henry W. Steele, who became her first commander.

On her first voyage, the *Racer* left New York, Aug. 20, 1851, with 80 passengers and had rather a long passage to Liverpool. On the return she reached New York, Nov. 27th, 33 days out, with 769 passengers. Again left New York, Jan. 10, 1852, and was 14 days to Liverpool. Captain Steele wrote home: "We went from land to land in 12 days but were delayed in the Channel 10 hours by fog." The return trip occupied 28 days and she had 785 passengers.

The demand for tonnage to California being very great about this time, the *Racer* was put up for San Francisco. Arriving out Oct. 19, 1852, Captain Steele reported a passage of 131 days from New York, in practically light and baffling winds throughout, with but one day on which she had an opportunity of making a showing and on that occasion she logged 394 miles in the 24 hours. She was within 200 miles of the Golden Gate for eight days. From San Francisco she crossed to Shanghai where the pilot ran her ashore on the river bank and she was put in dry dock for repairs. Sailed from Shanghai, June 11, 1853, and had a long passage down the China Sea against a strong monsoon, followed by very unfavorable weather in the Indian Ocean. Arrived at London, Dec. 13th, in 105 days from Anjer. Her reputation as a fast sailer had however already been well established in England and her agents were not long in negotiating one of the heaviest charters ever recorded in Europe up to that time, being £10,000, from London to Sydney and £8000 for the return from Calcutta to London. With Captain Ainsworth in command, she left London, Apr. 12, 1854; Portsmouth, the 14th; and arrived at Sydney, July 29th, in a passage called 106 days. Was 69 days from Sydney to Calcutta; sailed from that port Feb. 3, 1855, and was 101 days to London.

On May 5, 1856, the *Racer* left Liverpool for New York and on the night of the 6th, she struck on the Arklow Bank, near Wicklow, east coast of Ireland. She soon settled so that one side was under water and there being no prospect of her being saved, she was abandoned. The passengers and crew were returned to Liverpool. Arrangements were made to salve the cargo but the ship was found to be in possession of crowds of people from the neighborhood so intent on plundering that it was necessary to fire on them before they would desist. The value of the *Racer* at the time was placed at $90,-000.

The loss of the *Racer* left the *Dreadnought* and *Highflyer* as the sole members of the "Red Cross Line," which was owned and operated by E. D. Morgan, F. B. Cutting, David Ogden and associates of New York, Mr. Ogden being the agent. The *Highflyer* had been diverted to the California trade and about the time of the loss of the *Racer*, was reported as "missing" while on the passage from San Francisco to Hong Kong. This left the *Dreadnought* the solitary survivor of the line. The others, which had previously met their fate, all within a very short space of time, were: the *St. George*, burned; *St. Patrick*, wrecked; *Andrew Forster*, sunk after collision and the *Driver*, missing.

RADIANT

MEDIUM clipper ship, launched Jan. 24, 1853, by Paul Curtis, at East Boston, Mass., for Baker & Morrill of Boston; 197 x 37: 11 x 24: 4; 1318 47/95 tons. A golden billet head and gilded representations of the sun, on the cat-heads, were her only ornaments forward. She was a rakish, handsome ship, well and strongly built and her cabins were elegantly fitted up. She was a good carrier and showed good speed when reasonably favorable opportunity afforded her a fair chance. Lower masts, counting from foremast, were:—82, 86 and 76 feet; topmasts, 46, 48 and 39; royals, 16, 17 and 13; poles, 11, 12 and 10. Yards in proportion.

She sailed from Boston, Mar. 2, 1853, under Capt. Allen H. Bearse, deeply laden, drawing 23 feet; crossed the line, 24 days out; passed the latitude of Rio, 12 days later; made Staten Land, 61 days out; was off the Horn 18 days in very heavy weather, with much hail and snow and was driven to 59° South; had head knees carried away, forecastle stove in and received damage on deck; passed Juan Fernandez, May 29th, 84 days out and had light winds and calms thereafter to port; crossed the equator, 102 days out and arrived at San Francisco, July 14th, in 134 days from Boston. Had been within 700 miles of port for ten days. Best day's run, 260 miles; best week, 1575 miles. From San Francisco she went to the Chincha Islands for guano and was 73 days from Callao to New York.

The second voyage is said to have been from New York to Australia; thence to Peru and 80 days from Callao to Hampton Roads, arriving Apr. 3, 1855, and at New York, Apr. 11th. She then loaded for San Francisco, arriving there Oct. 12, 1855, in 137 days' passage. On July 31st, the foremast was struck by lightning, the topgallant and royal masts being damaged and the topgallantsail burned. In descending to the deck the bolt took out pieces about the masts. She was only eight days between the 50's; passed Cape Horn, Aug. 8th; crossed the equator, 103 days out, and was within 400 miles of destination for ten days. This voyage was completed by her going to Manila and thence to Queenstown where she arrived Jan. 24, 1856. Sailed from London, May 12th; from Deal, the 14th and arrived at Calcutta, Aug. 24th, in a voyage called 102 days. Was then 103 days from Calcutta to New York.

The *Radiant's* third visit to San Francisco was in September 1858, Captain Hallett, in command, in 143 days from New York, returning home via Manila. On Mar. 12, 1861, she reached San Francisco, Capt. Nathaniel Matthews in command, in 137 days from Boston. Went to Queenstown, in 110 days, with 1712 short tons of wheat and flour. On a voyage from London for Cardiff, Oct. 26, 1861, she was in collision, off Dungeness, with H. B. M. *Orion* and lost bowsprit and figurehead. She then crossed over to Boston and sailed thence Dec. 7, 1861. Was 26 days to the line; 60 days to the Horn, off which was only seven days; crossed the equator 91 days out and arrived at San Francisco, Mar. 28, 1862, in 111 days from Boston. Went to Callao in 49 days; loaded for London and was 97 days to Deal. Left London, Mar. 30, 1863, for Mauritius, Captain Matthews still in command. Went on to Calcutta where she was sold and in the register of 1868 she appears as the ship *Radiant* of that port.

Her old owners, Baker & Morrill, had a second *Radiant* built at Boston in 1868, of 1255 tons burden, Captain Chase in command. This ship was lost in 1871 on the Crocodile Reef, some 12 hours out from Singapore, while bound for Boston.

RADUGA

MEDIUM clipper ship, built by Currier & Townsend, at Newbury, Mass., in 1848, for H. Prince and others, of Boston. Sold at Boston by auction in 1851 for $32,500; 149 x 29 x 19; 587 tons, old measurement. She was of quite sharp model and has a number of fast passages to her credit.

On her maiden voyage the *Raduga* left Boston, May 12, 1848, under command of Capt. Thomas Leach and made the run to Liverpool in 18 days. Sailed from Liverpool, June 25th and was 31 days to the line, logging 4280 miles, with 232 miles as her best day's work. Ten days later, when in latitude 25° South, at 6 o'clock in the morning a squall came out of a clear sky without any warning whatever, accompanied with a rumbling noise. The sails on the mainmast were instantly taken aback and then immediately filled, resulting in the mainmast breaking short off square with the deck. Its fall brought down the mizzen topmast and the foretopgallant mast with the fore topsail yard, the spars falling overboard. Fearing damage to the hull these were reluctantly cut adrift and the ship was wore around for Rio, which port was reached Aug. 13th. Shore interests endeavored to force the discharge of the cargo, but Captain Leach demurred and making such repairs as he thought necessary, was able to get his ship away on Sept. 11th, and arrived safely at Hong Kong, 89 days later. The passage from Anjer to destination occupied 29 days, with much beating to windward and the ship rather crank. Sailed from Whampoa, Jan. 2, 1849; passed Anjer, nine days out; best day, 238 miles. Was off the Cape, 46 days from Hong Kong; best day, 260. Had very light S. E. trades and was 23 days from the Cape to the line with 234 miles as the best day. Arrived at New York, Apr. 4th, in 92 days from Whampoa; total distance logged 14,238 miles, an average of 115 miles daily.

On her second voyage she left New York, Apr. 24, 1849, and was 102 days to Manila. Sailed from Macao, Oct. 23rd, and was 104 days to New York. Then made a round voyage to Hong Kong, reaching New York on return after a passage of 101 days. Sailed from New York, Apr. 3, 1851, under command of Captain Cook and went to San Francisco in 140 days, with light winds throughout. Was 20 days thence to Honolulu and 32 days from there to Shanghai. Then went to Batavia; thence 97 days to Boston. Sailed from Boston, June 30, 1852, and crossed the line 35 days out. In the South Atlantic was run into by the ship *Crusader*, Boston for Valparaiso, and so badly damaged that Captain Cook put about for Rio, where the ship was one month repairing. Was 25 days from Rio to the Horn, off which had heavy gales for 18 days, losing some spars and sails. Was 27 days running up the South Pacific and was detained outside the San Francisco Heads nine days in a dense fog. Passed through the Golden Gate, Jan. 3, 1853, in 95 days from Rio. Thence crossed to China and was 112 days from Whampoa to New York, arriving Aug. 25, 1853.

The following voyage is said to have been made under command of Captain Lamson; Boston to Melbourne, Calcutta, Mauritius and back to Boston. Then, under command of Captain Green, she went to Valparaiso in 88 days; thence to Honolulu; thence 37 days to Manila and from that port was 111 days to Boston, arriving Sept. 21, 1856. On Mar. 12, 1857, she reached Honolulu, Capt. Green reporting his passage from Boston as 122 days. Thence to Manila and Boston. On Aug. 16, 1858, she was at San Francisco in 174 days from Boston, via Rio, 85 days, Capt. Burditt in command. Thence 15 days to Honolulu and 50 days from there to Manila; thence to Boston. Arrived at Honolulu, Sept. 3, 1859, in 119 days from Boston and for several years thereafter was mainly engaged in trade between these ports, the return cargoes being whale oil to New Bedford. Her outward runs were generally about 120 days with the homeward passages somewhat shorter, one of these being 103 days, arriving at Boston, Mar. 25, 1863. Oct. 15, 1861, was the date of her last arrival at San Francisco, she reaching port in 152 days from Boston, Captain Burditt in command. Went to Honolulu in 17 days and sailed thence Jan. 18, 1862, for New Bedford.

On her last voyage as an American ship, the *Raduga* sailed from Boston, May 15, 1863, and had a long run out to Honolulu,— about 155 days. After arrival she was sold to Charles Brewer & Co., of Honolulu, and was renamed *Iolani*, going under the flag of Hawaii. She was kept on the triangle run between Boston, the Islands and New Bedford and made consistently good average passages. Her masters were Captains Green, Ropes and Terwilliger. In the early '70's she was sold to C. H. Pendergast and renamed *Modesta*, with hailing port Barbados, she being rerigged as a bark. In 1890 she was reported as having been lost after collision.

"Queen of the Pacific," 1356 tons, built at Pembroke, Maine, in 1852

"R. B. FORBES," 757 TONS, BUILT AT EAST BOSTON, MASS, IN 1851
From a wood engraving in "Gleason's Pictorial"

"RACER," 1669 TONS, BUILT AT NEWBURYPORT, MASS., IN 1851

From a lithograph by N. Currier, 1854

"Radiant," 1318 tons, built at East Boston, Mass., in 1853. In the background, the
"John Land," 1054 tons, built at South Boston, in 1853

From a painting by Lane

RAINBOW

CLIPPER ship, launched Jan. 22, 1845, from the yard of Smith & Dimon, at New York, and built to the order of Howland & Aspinwall of that city; 159 x 31: 10 x 18: 4; 757 tons, old measurement. It is said that her model resembled in some respects, that of the *Ann McKim*, which was owned at the time by Howland & Aspinwall and which was conceded to be the fastest merchant ship then afloat. The *Rainbow* had long, hollow lines and was the first example of the improved model of China traders. She was rather a wet ship and at first was apparently oversparred. She carried skysails, set topgallant studdingsails and there were 500 yards of canvas in her main course. It is said that her lower masts were reduced three feet on her first arrival at Hong Kong. The command was given to Capt. John Land, a veteran navigator, particularly well known in connection with his command, the ship *Splendid*, engaged at different times in the China trade and again operating as a New York-Havre packet.

On her first voyage, the *Rainbow* sailed from New York, Feb. 1, 1845, and arrived at Hong Kong, May 14th, in 102 days' passage. Sailed from Whampoa, June 1st, and reached New York, Sept. 17th, in 108 days. A published narrative of this voyage contains the information that the ship lost all three topgallant masts when four days out from New York. Subsequently the crew considered that they were being over-worked and recalling the old "bucko" reputation of their captain, were on the point of mutiny when the passengers interceded and prevented serious trouble. Another incident of the voyage as related, was the speaking by the *Rainbow*, near Java Head, when outward bound, of the ship *Monument*, homeward bound from Canton. The *Rainbow* completed her passage to Hong Kong; was 18 days in port at Whampoa, discharging and loading, and arrived at New York ahead of the *Monument*. The *Rainbow's* best speed during this voyage was in the North Atlantic, homeward bound, when she sailed 14 knots in the northeast trades.

On her second voyage, the *Rainbow* left New York, Oct. 1, 1845, and was 99 days to Hong Kong, arriving Jan. 8, 1846. Sailed from Whampoa, Jan. 24th, and arrived at New York, Apr. 18th, in 84 days' passage. Her third homeward passage was 86 days, she having left Whampoa in December 1846 and reached New York in March 1847. She then crossed to Liverpool in 21 days, later going out to Hong Kong. Arrived at New York in February 1848, in 88 days from Whampoa. Captain Land was then succeeded by Captain Hayes and the *Rainbow* sailed from New York, Mar. 17, 1848, for Valparaiso and China, but was never thereafter heard from. The belief was that she foundered off Cape Horn.

During the period covered by the career of the *Rainbow*, particularly favorable conditions of wind and weather were encountered on the China run, outward and homeward, resulting in a remarkable series of fast passages. The captains achieving fame in this respect, included Josiah P. Cressy in the *Oneida*; Nathaniel B. Palmer and his brothers, Alexander and Theodore D., in the *Houqua*; Nathaniel B. Palmer in the *Samuel Russell*; Robert H. Waterman in the *Sea Witch* and the *Natchez*. The most noteworthy passage of all was that made by the last named ship, a vessel with no claim of being a clipper but whose time, in 1845, was 78 days and 6 hours from off Macao to the Barnegat pilot, with only 276 miles as the best day's work. In later years it was the opinion of old China clipper captains that the winds were, in a measure, dying out and the trades becoming unstable. While fast passages were made from time to time, a cycle of such did not recur.

RAMBLER

BUILT at Medford, Mass., by Hayden & Cudworth, in 1854; 182 x 37 x 23 x 1119; Baxter Bros., of Yarmouth, Mass., and Israel Nash of Boston, owners. Sold to go under the German flag, in 1863. Name changed to *Fanny*.

RAPID

CLIPPER ship, launched from the yard of Roosevelt & Joyce, at New York, Dec. 20, 1852; 179 x 36: 8 x 20; 1115 tons. Owned by James Bishop & Co., of New York. Called by Maury an "Out and Out clipper." Said to have been sold under the Danish flag in 1859. In 1866 was registered as owned by the Danish consul at Hong Kong, her hailing port being that city.

Arrived at San Francisco, Nov. 25, 1854, under Captain Willing, in 135 days from New York. Was 71 days to Cape Horn and off it ten days in alternate gales and calms; crossed the equator Nov. 1st and made land below Monterey, on the 20th. Had heavy weather in Atlantic and light in the Pacific. Sailed from San Francisco, under Captain Corning, Dec. 8, 1854, and arrived at Shanghai, Feb. 10th, in a passage of 64 days. Sailed thence for London, clearing Java Head, Apr. 3, 1855, thence 27 days to the Cape of Good Hope and reaching her destination, from London made a round voyage to China. Arrived at San Francisco, Jan. 5, 1857, Capt. Phineas Winsor (formerly of the packet ship *Angelique*) in command, in 220 days from New York. On Aug. 18th, in 60° South, 72° West, had very heavy weather with great cold; split sails, started cutwater and became leaky; lost ten men and ten more were disabled, leaving the captain, mates and carpenter to work the ship. Put back to Rio, arriving Sept. 25th. Repaired and sailed again and was off the Cape for 11 days in heavy gales, losing sails and sustaining other injuries. Crossed the equator, Dec. 16th; after which was becalmed three days. Her run from the equator to port was practically made in the fine time of 17 days. From San Francisco she went to Callao; thence to England and arrived at San Francisco, Aug. 4, 1858, in 128 days from Liverpool.

As the Danish ship *Rapid*, Captain Moller, she arrived at San Francisco, Mar. 30, 1861, 50 days from Hong Kong, beating the clipper *Lotus* three days on the passage. Besides the captains mentioned, the *Rapid*, while under the American flag, was commanded at various times by Captains Howe, Bulchen and Pike. Capt. Moses

Pike, besides the *Rapid*, had commanded the *Medora*, *Archer* and other vessels. He died Jan. 27, 1890, aged 78 years.

RATTLER

EXTREME clipper ship, launched by George Thomas, at Rockland, Me., on Oct. 15, 1852; 185 x 35 x 21; 1121 tons, old measurement; 909 tons, new, and 853 by foreign rules. She is described as being as sharp as a razor and, in a way, a small edition of the celebrated *Red Jacket*, a later production of the same builder. The *Rattler* has to her credit the record run from Callao to San Francisco Heads in 28 days, made in 1878, when she was known as the Costa Rican ship *Martha*. On this passage she carried a cargo of sugar and her run has never been approached by any except a vessel in ballast and of such she leads by a full two days. In 1858 she was seven days from 50° South, Atlantic, to 50° South, Pacific, which is one day longer than the record held by the *Young America*. Her run of 83 days from New York to Melbourne, in 1871-1872, was the fastest that had been made for some years previously.

Shortly after her launch, the *Rattler* was purchased for about $66,000 by William Whitlock, Jr., of New York, an independent ship owner, who, when freights were dull, had capital to invest in cargoes so as to load his ships quickly. Mr. Whitlock also operated a line of packets between New York and Havre. In 1873, the *Rattler* was sold and during the remainder of her career, was operated entirely in the Pacific Ocean, principally in the offshore lumber trade. She was under the Nicaraguan flag as the *Terecina Ferreira*, in 1874, later becoming the Costa Rican ship *Martha*. At her end she was the British bark *Martha*, of Shanghai. In November 1889 she put into San Francisco in distress while on a voyage from Puget Sound to Australia, and shortly after was sold for $2300 to the Johnson Wrecking Company, to be broken up.

On her maiden passage the *Rattler* left New York, Jan. 3, 1853, under command of Capt. Richard Brown and all predictions were that she would make a fast run to San Francisco, but except for 20 days of heavy gales, off the Horn, nothing but light winds were encountered, particularly in the Pacific, and her passage was 122 days. From San Francisco she went to Valparaiso and was 72 days thence to Boston, arriving Feb. 20, 1854. Her experience with light winds was similar to that on her outward run. Shortly after passing the Horn she was becalmed two days and from Valparaiso until being up with the Bermudas, she had occasion to reef topsails only once.

She proceeded to New York, after discharging, and was put on the run as a regular packet to Havre; took her departure Mar. 27, 1854, and from then until Aug. 14, 1855, completed four round voyages of which the fastest eastward is reported as 18 days and the fastest westward, as 26 days. In the autumn of 1855, after arrival at Havre, she was chartered by the French Government to take troops from Marseilles to the Crimea, after which voyage she returned to New York, Apr. 16, 1856, in 32 days from Havre. She then resumed her position as a regular Havre packet until January 1858, making better than average voyages. On Mar. 9, 1858, she sailed from New York under command of Captain Almy and was 115 days to San Francisco with generally light winds prevailing throughout. She was 59 days to Cape Horn and it was on this passage that she made the new record run of seven days between the parallels of 50° South. Completing this voyage she was 112 days from San Francisco to New York. Returning to San Francisco she was 162 days on the passage, under adverse weather conditions; 30 days to the line and did not clear Cape Horn until the 96th day out. She returned home via the west coast of Mexico, loading dye woods at Ypala, and arrived at New York, June 4, 1860. She then made a round to Liverpool and was thereafter, until March 1862, again employed as a Havre packet.

Sailed from New York, May 17, 1862, and arrived in San Francisco, Oct. 2nd, having experienced bad weather on the passage. Proceeded to Hong Kong in 49 sailing days, thence to Manila, returning to San Francisco and thence to Boston in 100 days. Was then 119 days from Boston to San Francisco, returning to New York via Manila. On the following voyage, Capt. B. F. Marsh in command, she was within 500 miles of San Francisco when 113 days out from New York but required 17 days to cover this distance in very light winds. Returned to New York via Hong Kong. Again went out to San Francisco, passage 114 days; loaded breadstuffs and $800,000 in treasure and on arriving at Hong Kong, Sept. 30, 1867, was caught in a typhoon and was run ashore to prevent being blown to sea; subsequently was gotten off with apparently but little resultant damage. However, on her arrival at New York, extensive repairs were made and she was reclassed A 1½ for three years. She then loaded a cargo of railroad iron and made the passage to San Francisco in 133 days. The clipper ship *Fearless,* similarly laden, arrived the same day, Jan. 11, 1869, in 161 days from New York. From San Francisco, the *Rattler* went to Manila in 51 days, and thereafter, for a period, was operated between Manila, Hong Kong and Australia. In the early part of 1870 she was 61 days from Newcastle, N. S. W., to Hong Kong, with coal. On Jan. 27, 1872, she reached Melbourne after the fine run of 83 days from New York, Captain Marsh being still in command.

The subject of this sketch must not be confused with two ships of the same name, built in Baltimore, and her contemporaries. The first, of 538 tons, built in 1842, was called a clipper and was in San Francisco in May 1853, in company with the Rockland-built *Rattler.* This Baltimore *Rattler* was lost in December 1853, while homeward bound from Callao. Her successor, built in 1854, of 794 tons, was never engaged in trade with California and in the early 60's was sold to Italian parties, continuing under her original name, hailing from Palermo. She was described as being a medium clipper.

RAVEN

EXTREME clipper ship, built by James M. Hood, at Somerset, Mass., and launched, fully rigged, July 1, 1851. She was built for the East India trade on the account of Crocker & Sturgis of Boston, but ownership soon passed to Crocker & Warren of New York; 158 x 32: 8 x 17; 711 tons, old measurement; 630 tons, new measurement. Dead rise, 24 inches; had no figurehead, simply a billet head and was in every way considered a little beauty and proved to be a very fast sailer. Capt. William W. Henry was commander for the first two voyages, being succeeded by Capt. Josiah Crocker. Later on, Captain Worth and Capt. Charles E. Jenkins had her for short periods, while Captain Nye was master for the final three years of her career under the American flag.

She first arrived at San Francisco, Nov. 19, 1851, in 106 days from Boston. The previous day, the *Typhoon*, a clipper of more than double her size, had reached port in 108 days from New York, while the day following, the celebrated *Sea Witch* put in an appearance in 111 days from New York. The *Raven* had lost her maintopmast three days before arrival, causing a delay of a full day. In continuation of the voyage the *Raven* had the satisfaction of beating the *Sea Witch* three days from San Francisco to Hong Kong and also three days thence to New York. The latter passage occupied 107 and 110 days respectively, being made in the unfavorable season.

The *Raven's* second voyage was 122 days from New York to San Francisco, with heavy weather off the Horn and continuous gales thence to destination. From San Francisco to Manila, she was 50 days and thence to New York in 102 days.

On her third outward passage she was one of six first-class clipper ships to reach San Francisco within a few hours of each other on Dec. 10 and 11, 1853. The *Witch of the Wave* was 117 days; *Raven*, 119; *Mandarin* and *Hurricane*, each 123; *Trade Wind*, 125 and *Comet*, 128. The best day's run made by any of the six, was the *Raven's* 310 miles, the *Witch of the Wave* being second with 289 miles. The *Witch* had the advantage in rounding the Horn, being but 13 days against *Raven's* 21 and *Comet's* 29 days. Completing her voyage the *Raven* was 54 days from San Francisco to Singapore; thence to Padang and was 92 days from there to New York.

The outward passage of the *Raven* on her fourth voyage, in 1854-1855, was her last Cape Horn run, having 124 sailing days from New York, 84 days from Rio to San Francisco. Had ten days off the Horn, in heavy gales, losing cutwater and head and sustaining other slight damage. Homeward bound, she was 55 days from the Golden Gate to Singapore and 83 days from Padang to New York. The following voyage was from Richmond, Va., to Sydney, in 103 days, made in the season for long passages; 37 days thence to Padang and 80 days from there home, arriving June 13, 1856. During the following three years she made four outward passages to Singapore, Batavia or Padang, the two fastest being 87 and 91 days. All returns were from Padang, of which three were in 89, 94 and 90 days. In 1859-1860 she was 118 days out to Hong Kong and 120 days home from Padang. She then went out to China, Japan and Siam and was 131 days home from Manila, arriving Nov. 9, 1862.

The next year she sailed for San Francisco but was obliged to put into Rio, leaky, and was condemned. The insurance paid amounted to $20,000 and her cargo was forwarded by the British ship *Oliver Cromwell*, arriving out April 1864. The *Raven*, which, some time previous to her arrival at Rio, had been rerigged as a bark, was sold and repaired and for some years was registered as the bark *Bessie*, hailing port, Rio; owned by J. De Costa Galvao of that city. In 1871 she appears in Lloyd's American Register as the bark *Don Antonia dos Santos*, Captain Pareira, owned by J. N. V. Carvalho of Lisbon and in 1875 she is registered as the bark *Mondego*, Captain Almeida, owned by A. S. Palminos of Lisbon.

RED GAUNTLET

CLIPPER ship, launched Dec. 1, 1853, from the yard of James W. Cox, at Robbinston, Me.; 178 x 35: 6 x 22; 1038 tons, old measurement; managing owners, F. Boyd & Co., of Boston. Her builder had an interest.

The first voyage of the *Red Gauntlet* was a round between Boston and Liverpool, Capt. Thomas Andrews in command, arriving out Feb. 20, 1854. On the return passage she reached Boston, May 15th, in 35 days from Liverpool. She then loaded for San Francisco and sailed from Boston, Aug. 12th and was 34 days to the line; thence, 26 days to 50° South; 15 days to 50° South, Pacific; thence 21 days to the equator and from there had the excellent run of 17 days to within 50 miles of the Golden Gate, but five days of calms, then experienced, prolonged her whole passage to 118 days. She crossed to Shanghai in 52 days and was 111 days thence to New York. On the following voyage she reached San Francisco, Mar. 1, 1856, in 194 days from New York, via Valparaiso, 49 days. She was 51 days to the line and was not up to 50° South, Atlantic, until the 80th day out. During the 29 days she was rounding Cape Horn, very heavy gales were encountered; the rudderhead was broken; cutwater and stem started; an entire suit of sails and some spars were lost and for a time she made some water and for 24 hours had five feet in the hold. The officers and crew suffered terribly from cold and exposure. The wife of Captain Andrews was unceasing in her efforts to increase the comforts of the crew by making hot tea, attending the sick, etc. The ship was headed for Valparaiso, arriving Dec. 17th, 120 days out and was in port, repairing, 25 days. Was thence, 20 days to the equator and 29 days from there to San Francisco. Sailed thence Apr. 2, 1856, and arrived at Honolulu on the 19th, under 17 days out. Sailed the 24th and arrived at Hong Kong, May 14th, in 19 days from Honolulu, a remarkably fast run. Sailed from Whampoa, Aug. 9th, and had a tedious time beating down the China Sea, being 53 days to Anjer. Stopped at St. Helena, Nov. 13th,

96 days out; sailed 15th and was 47 days to New York; arriving Jan. 1, 1857, in 143 sailing days from Whampoa and 90 from Anjer.

Sailed from New York, Mar. 28, 1857, and was 92 days to Melbourne; thence 34 days to Batavia. Left there Nov. 15th and was at St. Helena, Jan. 9, 1858, 55 days out. Proceeded on the 16th and made the Needles Light, Feb. 21st, 36 days from St. Helena, but the wind shifting she lay to; received the Cowes pilot 27th and anchored but was driven out to sea by a gale, losing foretopmast, jib, staysail and spencer. Finally got to anchor at Cowes, Mar. 8th and went to Bremen. On June 9th, arrived at Cardiff; thence to Manila, arriving out Oct. 31st; sailed Mar. 12, 1859, and arrived at New York, June 23rd, in 103 days' passage. Captain Andrews was succeeded by Capt. A. H. Lucas. Sailed from New York, Sept. 27th, and arrived at Shanghai, Feb. 7, 1860, in 133 days. Sailed from Woosung, Mar. 27th, and arrived at New York, July 25th, in 120 days' passage, 95 days from Anjer and 60 from the Cape. Left New York, Aug. 29th, and between that date and Feb. 26, 1861, made two round voyages to Liverpool. Then made a passage to Havana, arriving at New York on return, Apr. 14th, in ballast, a seven days' run. Loaded for San Francisco and arrived out Dec. 30, 1861, after a passage of 144 days. Was 38 days to the line; 76 to the Horn, off which had 25 days of heavy gales. Sailed from San Francisco, Feb. 10, 1862, for Hong Kong. Went to Yokohama and Shanghai; left the latter port July 19th and was 55 days to Anjer; thence 32 days to the Cape, off which had very heavy gales; arrived at New York, Dec. 14th, 148 days out, a very long passage but all other vessels making the run about that time reported the same experiences. From New York she then made a round voyage to New Orleans, as a Government transport, arriving on return, Mar. 23, 1863, 18 days from the southern port, in ballast, but with passengers. Left New York, Apr. 10th and arrived at Boston the 12th.

The *Red Gauntlet* loaded at Boston with coal, ice, musical instruments, etc., for Hong Kong, and sailed May 22, 1863. On June 14th, in about 8° North, 34° West, she was captured by the Confederate privateer *Florida*. The latter kept in company many days until she had transferred all the *Gauntlet's* coal into her bunkers when the torch was applied to the prize and she was destroyed. Claims filed with the Geneva Awards Commission totaled $124,-474.94, of which $60,851 was value of ship; $32,678, cargo; $15,-188, freight money; $5675, wages of 38 men for seven months, the expected period of the voyage. Five of the crew volunteered to serve on the *Florida*. She was insured in Boston for $41,000.

RED JACKET

THE extreme clipper ship *Red Jacket* was justly celebrated for the delicate beauty of her graceful lines throughout. Her arched stem was as pleasing to the eye as was her powerful but exquisitely modeled stern, while her spars and rigging were perfectly proportioned. To the end of her days as a sailing ship she was everywhere considered as the handsomest of the large clipper ships put afloat by American builders. Her entrance lines were hollow and her ends long and very sharp. She had three decks and her dimensions, according to Lloyd's Register were, 251:2 x 44 x 31 feet; tonnage, 2305. She was modeled by Samuel H. Pook and built by George Thomas, at Rockland, Me., and was owned by Seacomb & Taylor of Boston. She was launched Nov. 2, 1853, and a week thereafter was towed to New York to receive her spars and rigging.

The command of the *Red Jacket* was given to Capt. Asa Eldridge, formerly master of the "Collins Line" packet ship *Roscius*, a seaman and navigator of international reputation. Uncoppered and manned by a very indifferent crew, she left New York, Jan. 11, 1854, and with snow, hail or rain almost every day of the run, she arrived at Liverpool on the 23rd, her elapsed time from dock to dock being 13 days, 1 hour and 25 minutes, a record passage which stands to the present day. Her three poorest days were 106, 119 and 150 miles and her three best days, 413, 374 and 371 miles respectively. Some of the English papers questioned the correctness of the figures of her run and Captain Eldridge came out with a letter to the Editor of the "Times," offering his log book for exhibition and adding: "I took pilot off Point Lynas at noon of the 23rd inst; thence to the Bell Buoy was 2 hours and 20 minutes, the weather being thick and squally; no steam tug was to be found and the pilot refused to take the ship up the river."

The *Red Jacket* was the subject of much favorable comment at Liverpool and was immediately chartered by the "White Star Line" for a round voyage to Melbourne. Under command of Capt. Samuel Reid she sailed May 4, 1854, and arrived out July 12th, her time from the Rock Light to Port Philip Heads being 69 days, 11 hours and 15 minutes; time under sail, 67 days and 13 hours; total distance sailed, 13,880 miles. From Liverpool to the Cape she had light winds and poor trades, being 25 days to the line and on the meridian of the Cape, in latitude 45° South, on the 51st day out. In running her easting down she went to 52° South, and had much cold weather with snow, hail and sleet. At times the entire forward part of the ship was covered with ice. Frequent entries are made in the log of high or cross seas, heavy gales and strong gales and squalls. However, she braved them all without mishap and her time of 19 days from the meridian of the Cape to Melbourne is believed never to have been equaled, much less surpassed.

The *Red Jacket* sailed from Melbourne, Aug. 3, 1854, with passengers and gold dust to the value of about £200,000, sterling. She rounded the Horn, 20 days out, and on the 42nd day crossed the line, having run 10,423 miles thus far. Thereafter, nothing but calms and light winds were encountered and she was 31 days to Liverpool making her passage in 73 days. Total distance sailed, 14,863 miles; average, 202¼ miles daily; best day, 376; best speed, 18 knots; made 14 and 15 knots, close hauled. The round voyage was made in 5 months, 10 days and 22½ hours, including detentions, and excited considerable interest not only for its unprecedented rapidity but also on account of the dangerous position in which the vessel was placed in the ice off Cape Horn, when homeward bound, and the "London News" published some views showing her entirely surrounded with field ice. Many icebergs were also met with, one being estimated as two miles in circumference and some fully 200 feet high.

On arrival at Liverpool, the *Red Jacket* was purchased by Pilkington & Wilson for continued operation in their "White Star Line" of Australian passenger ships the reported price being £30,000, sterling. Other ships employed in this line included the *Empress of the Seas* and *Chariot of Fame* and the Colonial-built ships *White Star*, *Shalimar* and *Mermaid*. The *Red Jacket* was always a favorite with the traveling public and was acknowledged to be the handsomest, if not the fastest vessel in the British merchant service. In the fall of 1855 her passage to Melbourne was faster than that of any other ship including the *James Baines*, the New York clipper *Invincible* and the *Lightning*, although it must be admitted that the latter was handicapped to some extent by a damaged bow. Homeward bound, this voyage, both the *Red Jacket* and *Lightning* made slow time,—86 days. Captain Milward was then in command of the *Jacket*.

After the decline of the passenger traffic to Australia, in sailing ships, the *Red Jacket* made some trips to other ports and in 1865 she was at Calcutta. In 1868 she is listed as owned by Wilson & Chambers of Liverpool, but shortly thereafter she was sold and went into the timber trade between Quebec and London, being so engaged as late as 1882. On Jan. 20, 1871, while coming to an anchorage in the Downs, she fouled a bark and lost her jibboom. On her passage across the Atlantic she had had the foretopmast carried away and the mainmast sprung. In 1878 she collided with and sunk the *Eliza Walker* but fortunately was able to save all her crew.

Eventually the *Red Jacket* went to Cape Verde as a coal hulk. She was named after a noted Seneca chief of the Wolf clan, who, during the American Revolution, espoused the cause of Great Britain. The chief Sagoyewatha (he that keeps them awake) was conspicuous from the brilliant red jacket that he wore, a present from a British officer, hence the name.

An Anecdote of the Red Jacket

On July 12, 1854, the former packet ship *Bavaria* arrived off Port Philip Heads after a passage of 92 days from New York. Among her passengers was George Francis Train who had previously been connected with the prominent Boston shipping firm of Enoch Train & Co. Mr. Train was accompanied with a force of clerks and also had on board complete fixtures for the establishment in Melbourne of a shipping and commission house which was to be later known as Caldwell, Train & Co. This firm had many important agencies among which was that of the "White Star Line" of passenger packets running between Melbourne and the mother country. Mr. Train had been appointed by Duncan Sherman & Co., as their agent for the purchase of gold for shipment to London or New York. He was also the representative of the Boston Underwriters. At the time the following incident occurred, the firm of Caldwell, Train & Co., had been dissolved and Captain Caldwell, the retiring partner, was to go to England in the *Red Jacket*. To quote Train's story:—

"It was of course customary to have all bills of lading signed by the ship's captain. But Captain Reid had been arrested at the instance of one of the passengers, and the ship was libeled on account of a claim. For this reason Captain Reid had not been present to sign the bills of lading. In Boston, I had often signed bills of lading in the absence of the captain, so I had no hesitancy as to my course in this emergency. I considered that I had a perfect right to sign the bills and so I did sign them for the $1,000,000, putting it 'George Francis Train, for the captain.'

"Now the English are a conservative people. When they see anything new it 'frights' them. They cannot understand why there should ever be occasion for anything new under the sun. When the Melbourne banks saw that I had signed the papers, they were scared nearly out of their boots. They had never heard of such a procedure and thought their insurance was gone.

"But this was not all. The *Red Jacket* was the fastest clipper that had then visited Melbourne and it occurred to these bankers that I was going to run off with this gold and become a Captain Kidd or a buccaneering Morgan. They grounded their fears upon the facts that my wife was aboard; that Captain Caldwell, my partner and friend, was also a passenger, and they believed that Captain Reid was on board, although under arrest. To suspicious bankers here was a really strong case against me.

"In the meantime the *Red Jacket*, with her trim sails bellied with the wind and sweeping along in a way of her own that nothing in the South Seas could imitate or approach, was passing down Hobson's Bay. The Government and the Melbourne authorities despatched two men-of-war after her. There was no possibility of her being overhauled by these craft and I gave orders to make for Point Nepean. The sheriffs from Melbourne, who thought Captain Reid was aboard, stayed on the ship but I ordered them put off at the Point. They were furious but could do nothing since they could not act for Melbourne, at sea, under the Stars and Stripes. Accordingly they were put on a tug and taken back to Melbourne. Immediately after the sheriffs left the ship, a little yacht, the *Flying Eagle*, with Captain Reid aboard, came alongside and the Captain was put on the *Red Jacket* just outside the jurisdiction of Australia.

"The *Red Jacket* caught the wind again and showed her clean heels to the slow-sailing men-of-war.

"The authorities and the bankers did not like the proceedings at all, but saw that they could do nothing. There was great anxiety in Australia for some months. When it was learned that the $1,000,-000 was landed in Liverpool without the loss of a farthing, I was heartily congratulated although the British spirit never forgave the taking of matters into my own hands and making the best of a bad situation. Their conservatism had received a bad shock."

RED ROVER

CLIPPER ship, launched from the yard of Fernald & Petti-grew, at Portsmouth, N. H., in November 1852; 172 x 35 x 23; 1021 tons by old measurement and 766 by new; owned by R. L. Taylor of New York. She was a very sharp ship and has an enviable record for speedy passages. Her first commander was Capt. W. O. Putnam, who, after two voyages, was succeeded by Captain Logan. In 1858 Captain Cumming took her.

The *Red Rover* sailed from New York in December 1852 and arrived at San Francisco, Apr. 19, 1853, a passage of 117 days. When 36 hours out, in a severe gale, she lost maintopmast and two topgallant masts with all yards attached. Was off the Horn 19 days; put into Juan Fernandez for water, when 79 days out, and was there two days; was 19 days from the equator to destination, being off the Golden Gate three days in heavy gales during which she lost a number of sails. From San Francisco she went to Callao, in 43 days, and was 70 days thence to New York, arriving Nov. 17, 1853.

While loading at New York for her second voyage she was damaged to some extent on Dec. 26th by the fire which necessitated the scuttling of the *Great Republic*. Arrived at San Francisco, May 24, 1854, in 120 days from New York. Was 22 days to the line and 19 days off the Horn. On approaching the Golden Gate she again experienced heavy gales, having a boat stove, the cabin filled with water and receiving some damage on deck. Had been 98 days to the Pacific equator crossing. From San Francisco she went to Callao, in 44 days, thence 84 days to New York, arriving Dec. 9, 1854, via Hampton Roads. On her third voyage she was 20 days from New York to the line; 48 days to 50° South; eight days making the Cape Horn passage; 80 days to the Pacific equator crossing and on the 92nd day was 900 miles from the Golden Gate with every prospect of getting into San Francisco in less than 100 days from New York. She then, however, got into a belt of light winds and calms and was 16 days covering this remaining short distance. Passed through the Golden Gate, June 13, 1855, 108 days out. From San

"RADUGA," 587 TONS, BUILT AT NEWBURY, MASS, IN 1848

From a drawing made in 1863, by A. M. Rogers

"Red Jacket," 2305 tons, built at Rockland, Maine, in 1853

"RED JACKET," 2305 TONS, BUILT AT ROCKLAND, MAINE, IN 1853

From a lithograph in the Macpherson Collection, showing her under the British flag

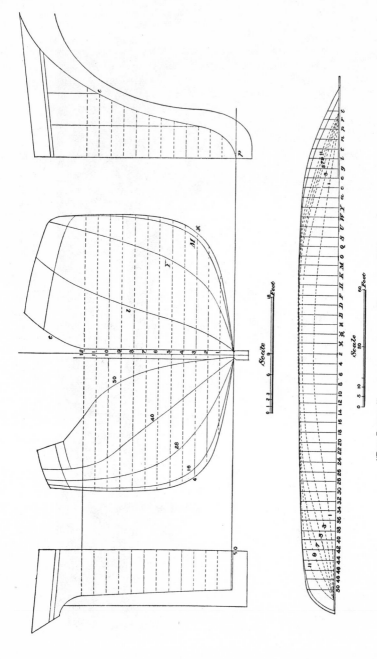

"RED JACKET," 2305 TONS, BUILT AT ROCKLAND, MAINE, IN 1853
Lines from Hall's *Ship-Building Industry of the United States*, 1884

Francisco she returned to New York direct, arriving Oct. 21st, 98 days out.

When three days out from New York on her fourth voyage, the *Red Rover* was thrown on her beam ends in a very heavy gale. The mainyard was carried away and sails were torn into shreds from the bolt ropes. The cargo shifted and thereafter she had a list of three strakes which materially lessened her speed when sailing with starboard tacks aboard. Was 27 days to the line; 50 days to 50° South; 13 days rounding the Horn; had the mainyard sprung; was 26 days in the South Pacific and 23 days from the equator to San Francisco. From Cape Horn to destination had no occasion to furl the mizzen royal. Arrived Apr. 7, 1856, her passage of 112 days from New York being very fast under the circumstances. From San Francisco she went to Havre, via Callao. On her fifth voyage she was in 50° South, Pacific, when 60 days out from New York; then had very light winds and was 38 days to the line, crossing on the 98th day. Was becalmed close to the Golden Gate for seven days and arrived at San Francisco, July 4, 1857, in 123 days from New York. She thence went to Valparaiso in 52 days, later proceeding to Iquique. Arrived at London, Feb. 4, 1858, after the fine passage of 65 days from Iquique and while riding at anchor at the entrance to the East India dock, she went adrift and stranded. Soon after she was run into by a German steamer, receiving considerable damage which necessitated her going on Victoria dock for repairs.

From London, the *Red Rover* went out to Victoria, B. C.; thence to Hong Kong, with lumber, and from there she went to Melbourne. Sailed from that port, Aug. 27, 1859, with Chinese passengers and arrived at Hong Kong, Oct. 6th, a fast passage of 40 days. She then loaded at Hong Kong for Victoria, B. C., and on May 27, 1860, reached San Francisco, 11 days from Victoria, in ballast. Then went to Baker's Island where she loaded 950 tons of guano for Hampton Roads and arrived out Dec. 5, 1860, after a passage of 99 days. After arrival at New York she underwent an overhauling, also receiving new masts. Shortly thereafter she was sold for $25,000 to

James Baines & Co., of Liverpool and was operated in their "Black Ball Line" of Australia packets. The following copy of a letter from one of her former captains shows that she well sustained the reputation she had acquired while under the American flag.

"Newcastle-on-Tyne, 10th October, 1892

"My dear Mr. Matthews.

"I had the honor of being chief officer of the *Cairngorm* in 1860-1861 and left her to take command of the American-built clipper ship *Young Australia*. In 1862, the *Stornoway* left Sydney for London and about one day later I left Melbourne with the *Young Australia*, also for London, via Cape Horn. Both these vessels belonged to the same employ, viz, The Liverpool Black Ball Line. In the South Atlantic, I overtook the *Stornoway* and on actual recognition we both did our utmost to outstrip one another. This lasted (within sight of each other) for about ten days when we parted company in the night and I had the satisfaction of arriving at destination (London) about two days earlier than the *Stornoway*. The *Young Australia* above referred to was previously named *Red Rover*.

"Yours respectfully,

"Wm. Lowrie."

The "American Record" of 1869, gives the hailing port of the *Young Australia* as Liverpool and J. P. Foulks as owner. She was wrecked on Moreton Island, May 31, 1872, four and a half hours after leaving her anchorage at Brisbane, homeward bound. While in the act of going about the wind fell calm and the anchor being let go too late she was hove on the rocks by the heavy swell. Passengers and crew were got ashore with some difficulty. By June 6th, the hull had broken in half and on the 7th, the wreck was sold at auction in Brisbane.

REINDEER

BUILT by Donald McKay, at East Boston, in 1849, 806 tons; George B. Upton, John M. Forbes and Sampson & Tappan, owners. Her first voyage was to San Francisco in 130 days, arriving Apr. 2, 1850. Remained in the California and Manila trade and was wrecked on a coral reef near the village of Iba, on the coast of Zambales, P. I., Feb. 12, 1859, while bound for San Francisco from Manila, with a valuable cargo.

REPORTER

MEDIUM clipper ship, launched from the yard of Paul Curtis, at East Boston, Mass., Sept. 3, 1853, for the account of David Snow and others of Boston. She was designed for the cotton trade and was the first clipper built vessel to cross the bar at the mouth of the Mississippi. Her construction was superintended by Capt. Octavius Howe who owned an eighth interest and became her first commander. In model, the *Reporter* was somewhat sharper than the general run of medium clippers and she had 15 inches dead rise at the half floor. She was narrow for her length, her dimensions being: length of deck, 207: 5; beam, 39; depth of hold, 24: 6; tonnage, 1474, American old style, 1431 tons by British measurement. She had single topsails and crossed but one skysail yard, that on the main. The spars of the mainmast measured: lower mast, 88 feet; those above, in order, 48, 27, 18 and 15 feet; corresponding yards were, 78, 60, 46 and 36 feet, length of skysail yard not given. Her cost of construction was $80,750. For a figurehead she carried a full-length representation of a reporter taking notes, but it was not considered very artistic and one critic wrote "It looks like Col. Green of the Boston Post, before he lost his hair and got religion."

The *Reporter* left Boston on her maiden voyage, Oct. 13, 1853, with a full cargo, for New Orleans and was 15 days on the run. Her large tonnage was against her securing a cargo quickly as shippers had been embarrassed by having smaller ships detained for long periods at the bar. She finally got away Dec. 10th, with 3000 barrels of flour, 6000 staves, 3239 bales of cotton under deck, 50 on deck and ten bales in the cabin. She reached Liverpool, Jan. 9, 1854, after a rough passage. She was drawing on arrival only 16: 10 aft, was down by the head five inches and was not coppered and yet her passage of 30 days was the fastest made about that time. The day after his arrival at Liverpool, Captain Howe wrote David Snow: "Our passage was not a clipper's, according to my ideas, but taking into consideration that of other ships, it is certainly an extraordinary one. In something short of 31 days we were at anchor in the river and a portion of the night previous we were lying off the light ship waiting for day-light. You can see by referring to the papers that we have given the whole fleet from the north, south and west, an AWFUL WHIPPING." The *Reporter* lost on the passage a portion of the carved work on her head and her captain expresses the belief (perhaps hope) that the rest will follow before he reaches Boston.

At Liverpool she was offered for sale for $100,000, but the market for clippers being glutted, no sale was made. At Liverpool she loaded salt and taking on cabin and steerage passengers crossed to Boston in 29 days; freight list, £2156. At Boston she was chartered by Gage, Hittenger & Co., to carry ice to New Orleans and had a long and tedious passage of 21 days. Was three days at the bar, over which four tugs were required to drag her. At New Orleans she loaded cotton at 15/16 pence, the highest price paid that season, and sailed for Liverpool on June 16, 1854. Had light winds to the chops of the Channel where she was detained eight days by adverse winds. In the Gulf Stream she was struck by lightning, the fore royalmast being splintered and a large piece being torn out of the planking. Several of the watch on deck were knocked down but not seriously injured. She left Liverpool, Aug. 29th, under charter to the "Enoch Train Line," with a full cargo and 371 passengers and was 27 days to Boston. From Boston she went to New Orleans and found cotton freights very dull, ⅜ pence to Liverpool, being hardly sufficient to pay a vessel's expenses. After some delay the *Reporter* took on 3768 bales of cotton and some heavy freight for ballast and sailed for Liverpool; freight list only $12,485. In common with others making the run about this time she had a most extraordinary spell of easterly winds. During 17 days made only 500 miles, having on some days lost as much ground as had taken several days to gain. From Liverpool she crossed to Mobile in 42 days and after a tedious delay took cotton at ¼ pence and went back to Liverpool in 34 days where she was chartered for £1450 by the "Enoch Train Line" and was 25 days to Boston with 382 passengers. This passage ended her trans-Atlantic work. During her first year of service she had earned net for her owners $53,600 but her second year showed a net loss of $10,000.

The *Reporter* had proved ability to sail fast, particularly with strong winds in a rough sea. She worked easily and was in every way a perfect ship but was not as well adapted for light cargoes, such as cotton, as were fuller models. She was therefore offered for sale and in November 1855 she was purchased for $76,000 by W. F. Weld & Co., of Boston, to be tried out in the Cape Horn run wherein it was believed she was eminently fitted. This opinion proved to have been justified and she was successful from her advent.

The *Reporter* sailed from New York, Dec. 10, 1855, under command of Captain Howes, and was 107 days to San Francisco, reaching port in company with the clipper *Tornado,* whose run was 110 days, due to having met lighter winds in the South Pacific. From San Francisco, the *Reporter* was 58 days to Manila and leaving there July 16th, was 108 days to Boston. Her freight list to San Francisco was $42,000 and her round-the-world voyage was eminently satisfactory to her new owners. She then returned to San Francisco from New York, in 114 days, arriving Apr. 17, 1857. Was in latitude 27° North, Pacific, on her 98th day out. From San Francisco she went to Callao, thence to France and arrived at New York, Apr. 11, 1858, in 30 days from Havre. On Oct. 14, 1858, she was again at San Francisco in 132 days from New York, with light weather throughout. She then went to Manila in 49 days; thence 109 days to

Liverpool, arriving at New York, Sept. 14, 1859, from Liverpool. Again loaded for San Francisco, now under command of Captain Holt, and arrived out May 17, 1860, in 116 days. The features of this passage were her ten days between the two 50's and her 17 days from the equator crossing to port. She completed the voyage by going to Callao in 48 days, thence 72 days to Hampton Roads.

On her last passage from New York to San Francisco, the *Reporter* reached destination May 5, 1861, Captain Howes reporting his run as 103 days. She was 20 days to the line; thence 27 days to 50° South; was eight days rounding the Horn, being in 50° South, Pacific, on the 55th day; six days later, then being 61 days out, she was on the parallel of Valparaiso, remarkably fast time thus far; then had light trades and baffling winds or calms to the line, crossing on the 83rd day out; thence 20 days to port. Her passage was equalled a month later by the *Andrew Jackson*, these being the two fastest runs over the course during 1861. The *Reporter* arrived at Queenstown, Jan. 10, 1862, from San Francisco, via the west coast of Mexico.

She left New York, June 3, 1862, commanded by Capt. William H. White, for San Francisco. On Aug. 16th, off Cape Horn, she started to leak in a severe gale. The next day a tremendous sea demolished all the boats and dissipated any hope of saving the ship. All hands embarked on two rafts, hastily constructed, one of which was fallen in with by the British bark *Enchantress*, but only four of its occupants were alive the rest having died of cold and exposure. These were landed at Caldera. The four saved were William Townes, the second mate, William Bacon, steward, and Charles Steele and George Miller, seamen. The other raft was never heard from, bringing the total loss to 32 souls. The insurance paid on vessel, cargo and freight money was $437,664.

RESOLUTE

C LIPPER ship, launched Jan. 15, 1853, by Westervelt & Sons, at New York. At the time it was stated that she was the first ship to be built in the United States for English owners, her construction having been ordered by a Mr. Miller of London, but such arrangement could not have been fully consummated as she was an American ship during her early career. She was of a fine model and was a handsome little ship; 151 x 34: 2 x 19: 4; 786 tons, old measurement; 622 tons, new measurement.

While under the American flag the *Resolute* was operated principally in the China trade, making but one passage from New York to San Francisco. This was in 1856, her passage being 145 days. Captain McKenzie, in command, reported being 35 days to the line; 62 days to the Horn, off which was 15 days; was 110 days to the equator and seven days outside the Golden Gate, in calm weather with a dense fog.

Her maiden voyage was from New York, sailing Feb. 15, 1853, and going out to Melbourne in 98 days, Captain Perry, formerly in the steamship *Franklin*, in command. She then went to China and sailed from Whampoa, Dec. 8, 1853, for London. Arrived out Apr. 3, 1854, in a passage of 116 days. Capt. Daniel McKenzie then succeeded to the command and left London, June 3rd, passing the Lizard, June 6th. Was 25 days to the line, 54 days to the Cape and 90 days to Anjer. Went to Hong Kong and Foo Chow, at which latter port she loaded for New York. Sailed thence Apr. 24, 1855, and arrived home, Aug. 28th, in a passage of 126 days; 88 days from Anjer. Her next voyage was her run out to San Francisco, thence 50 days to Hong Kong. Again loaded at Foo Chow and sailed thence, Oct. 22, 1857, arriving at New York, Feb. 20, 1858, 121 days out and 86 days from Anjer. She then went back to China and returned to New York in 105 days from Penang. The following voyage was to China, the return being to England, where she was sold, after arrival, to J. Moorewood & Co., of Bristol. Captain McGilvery was placed in command and the *Resolute* went from Cardiff to Shanghai, arriving Feb. 6, 1863. Left Shanghai, Mar. 28, 1863, and arrived at New York, July 18th, a passage of 112 days and 85 days from Anjer. Sailed from New York, Aug. 30, 1863, for Hong Kong and arrived back at New York, June 15, 1864, in 105 days from Whampoa, 92 days from Anjer and 52 days from the Cape.

For a number of years the *Resolute* continued in trade between China and New York, under Captain McGilvery and his successor, Captain Holt. In 1871 she was sold by Moorewood & Co., to parties in Barcelona, Spain, who altered her name to *Resoluda*. In 1875 she was so listed, her owner being given as J. Escoffet.

REYNARD

MEDIUM clipper ship, built in 1856, by George W. Jackman, at Newburyport, Mass.; 182: 6 x 37 x 23; 1051 tons, old measurement; 1029 tons, new measurement. An image of a fox was her figurehead. She was owned by Bush & Comstock of Boston. She was a good carrier, being able to stow 1900 weight and measurement tons and on one occasion loaded 1400 tons of guano. She was well built of first class materials which is evidenced by the fact that she classed A 1½ when over 25 years old.

Her maiden voyage was from Boston to San Francisco, arriving out Jan. 22, 1857, in 139 days. Captain Drew reported a week of very heavy weather in the North Atlantic, it blowing a perfect hurricane at times; thence, until getting into the Pacific, had nearly all light winds; from 50° South, Pacific, to making the Farallon Rocks, had the good run of 39 days. From San Francisco she crossed to China and thence to Bangkok, for rice, and then from Shanghai home. On her second voyage she was 132 days from Boston to San Francisco, arriving Sept. 24, 1858, Captain Freeman in command. Was 20 days rounding the Horn; shipped a sea which carried the mate overboard and killed a seaman; crossed the equator 104 days out and was within 800 miles of the Golden Gate for two weeks. Returned East via Jarvis Island, with guano. Loaded at New

York and sailed Sept. 30, 1859. Six days later, in a hurricane, lost everything on the mainmast except the lower mast, also lost mizzen topgallantmast and nearly an entire suit of sails; put about for repairs and was towed into Boston, Oct. 17th. Sailed again, Nov. 4th, and was 130 days to San Francisco. Thence went to Callao in 60 days and returned East in ballast.

The *Reynard* was then withdrawn from the California run and made a number of voyages between New York and England with Captain Seymour in command. On Aug. 22, 1861, bound from London to Cardiff, she was in collision, off Dover, with the British ship *Westburn*, for Melbourne, the latter being obliged to return to port for repairs. The *Reynard* went out to Hong Kong from Cardiff and thence to Manila where she loaded for New York. Sailed May 20, 1862, and was 146 days on the passage, being 104 days from Anjer. From New York she crossed to London, thence to Cardiff to load for Calcutta. While in the East Dock at Cardiff, the sea washed away a portion of the dock gates causing the *Reynard* to break adrift, her stern being damaged. She left Cardiff, February 18th, and was 109 days to Calcutta.

After returning East she was put back in the California trade and arrived at San Francisco, June 9, 1865, in 141 days from New York, Captain Crosby in command. Had generally light winds and was becalmed ten days in the North Pacific. Completing this voyage she went to New London via Honolulu and Baker's Island. On Dec. 11, 1866, she was again at San Francisco, after another light-weather passage of 140 days from New York, Captain Gallaghan then in command. Returned direct to New York, in 118 days. Under Captain Emery left New York, Sept. 8, 1867, and was 150 days to San Francisco, with practically nothing but light and variable winds and calms throughout the trip. She then crossed to Hong Kong in 42 days and returned to the Golden Gate in 46 days. Then went to McKean's Island for guano and left there Oct. 12th for Savannah. Sailed from Boston, May 18, 1870, under Capt. H. R. Arbecam. Was 23 days to the line; 52 days to the Horn and crossed the equator

79 days out, very good time thus far; light winds, however, were met with and she was 31 days to San Francisco; 110 days from Boston. Then went to Honolulu in 11 days, thence to Baker's Island to load guano for England. While at the Island, a heavy gale came up and she was forced to slip moorings and put to sea. After ten days she returned, completed her lading and sailed Jan. 3, 1871, reaching Queenstown in 108 days.

About this time she was sold to D. D. Kelly of Boston and was operated on the Atlantic, her rig being changed to that of a bark. On Oct. 21, 1877, she made her final appearance at San Francisco, 153 days from Boston. Captain Kingman, in command, reported being in sight of the Horn the 67th day and then experienced a series of heavy gales lasting 20 days. He had never experienced such boisterous weather on any of his previous 23 Cape Horn passages. The *Reynard* sailed from San Francisco, Nov. 29, 1877, for Cork, via one of the guano islands. The *Reynard* was subsequently sold to D. & J. Maguire of Quebec and went under British colors without change of name. She was operating in the Atlantic as late as 1886.

RINGLEADER

CLIPPER ship, built by Hayden & Cudworth, at Medford, Mass., in 1853, for Howes & Crowell of Boston. She was placed in command of Capt. Richard Matthews who continued in her until the fall of 1861, after which Captain White was master until her loss. Tonnage, 1153 51/95.

The *Ringleader* was a fast sailer and has a fine record in spite of the fact that she encountered a great proportion of fine and light weather on each of her six passages from Boston or New York to San Francisco. Her average figures out 116 days, port to port. On the first trip, 110 days, she was within 400 miles of destination when 100 days out. On the fourth trip, 114 days, she was 700 miles from the Golden Gate when 98 days out; on both of which runs, she had crossed the equator in the Pacific when 85 days out. On the third run out she crossed on the 84th day, although she had been up with 50° South, Atlantic, 41 days from Boston and 23 days from the line, having been 18 days to the line. Her passage of 78 days from Boston to Melbourne was also very fast.

Leaving Boston on her maiden passage, Oct. 20, 1853, she arrived at San Francisco in 110 days; thence to Manila in 47 days and thence to Boston in 112 days. Left Boston, Oct. 18, 1854, touched at Pernambuco, Nov. 19th, and arrived at Melbourne, Jan. 5, 1855, 78 days out; thence 53 days to Calcutta; thence 102 days to London; thence to Boston, being 22 days from Land's End and arriving Sept. 23, 1855. Sailed from Boston, Oct. 28, 1855, and was 107 days to San Francisco and thence 48 days to Shanghai. Loaded at Foo Chow, sailing thence June 17, 1856, and had a tedious run of 53 days to the Straits of Sunda, clearing them Aug. 9th. Arrived at Gravesend, Oct. 31st, 136 days out and reached London, Nov. 4th; then crossed to Boston, being 22 days from the Lizard Light. Left Boston Feb. 17, 1857, and was 124 days to San Francisco. Returned direct to New York in 124 days. Sailed from New York, Apr. 3, 1858, and was 114 days to San Francisco. Off the Horn and again in the South Pacific, spoke the *John Land,* but the latter arrived in San Francisco three days ahead, the *Ringleader* taking 16 days to make the final 700 miles. The *Ringleader* was 55 days from the Golden Gate to Shanghai; again loaded at Foo Chow for London; sailed Feb. 24, 1859, and arrived out in 109 days. Sailed from London, Sept. 26th, and arrived at Hong Kong, Feb. 21, 1860, in 148 days' passage. Loaded at Manila for New York; sailed Mar. 31st; passed Anjer, Apr. 19th; Cape of Good Hope, May 26th; crossed the line, July 3rd; arrived at destination Aug. 2nd, in 124 days from Manila, 105 days from Anjer and 68 days from the Cape. Loaded at Boston for San Francisco; sailed Sept. 10, 1860; had 39 days to the line; when 19 days out, stove bulwarks and lost sails in a hurricane; had no trades in the North Atlantic; had to cross the equator three times; passed through the Straits of Le Maire, 66 days out; was in 51° South, 83° West, on the 78th day;

crossed the line, 98 days out; was off the Horn in company with the *Flying Childers* and led her into San Francisco two days, although both had the same passage from Boston,—115 days. The *Ringleader* then went to Ypala, west coast of Mexico, where she loaded dye woods for England. Was off Cape Horn about May 10th and arrived at Falmouth, July 5th. Proceeded to London and thence to Boston, arriving Sept. 9th, in ballast.

Captain White assumed command and arrived at San Francisco, Feb. 17, 1862, after a passage of 130 days; thence went to Yokohama via Honolulu; arrived at Shanghai, Oct. 14th; was at Foo Chow, Nov. 11th; thence back to Shanghai and from there to Hong Kong. Left Hong Kong, May 3, 1863, for San Francisco, without any cargo but with several hundred Chinese coolies; also had some white cabin passengers. On May 9th she struck on the Formosa Banks. One account says that as soon as she struck she was surrounded by piratical Chinese fishing boats, the crews of which drove the coolies ashore and began pillaging the ship. Captain White with the ship's crew got away in the boats, but two seamen were drowned. The captain ultimately reached San Francisco on the bark *Emily Banning*, while some 200 of the coolies arrived there Sept. 15th, on the *Don Quixote*, which ship had also on board 400 additional coolies picked up at Simoda, *ex* the clipper *Viking*, lost on the Japanese coast.

RIVAL

BUILT by Hayden & Cudworth, at Medford, Mass., in 1855; 983 tons; Howes & Crowell of Boston, owners. Sailed from Rangoon, Burmah, Mar. 27, 1872, for Falmouth, Eng., and was never heard from.

ROBIN HOOD

EXTREME clipper ship, built in 1854, at Medford, Mass., by Hayden & Cudworth, for Howes & Crowell of Boston, who were the owners during the whole career of the ship; 186 x 37 x 23; 1181 tons, old measurement; 981 tons, new measurement. The figurehead was a life-size image of *Robin Hood* showing his bended bow.

The maiden passage of the *Robin Hood* was from Boston to San Francisco in 127 days. Thereafter she made 11 runs from New York to the Pacific coast port, two of which were made in 107 days each. Her two longest runs were 134 and 140 days, on which occasions she was detained off Cape Horn 20 and 21 days, respectively, in heavy westerly gales. Her average for the whole 12 passages is 125 days. From San Francisco she made five direct runs to New York, the fastest being 88 days, in 1862. Her time on the others was, 107, 108, 117 and 117 days. In 1863 she was 112 days from the Golden Gate to Liverpool.

Her fastest homeward passage from China was in 1854-1855, when she left Shanghai during the favorable monsoon and reached New York, Mar. 16th, 95 days out; 75 days from Java Head and 43 days from the Cape of Good Hope. The following year she was 103 days on the same run. On Feb. 10, 1865, she put into New York for orders, being 107 days from Rangoon, and was thence towed to Boston. In 1860 she was 47 days from San Francisco to Callao, going thence to New York, in ballast, in 77 days. In 1864 she made the run from San Francisco to Honolulu in 11 days and two years later was 30 days from the Island port to Shanghai. In 1859 she was 23 days from 50° South, Pacific, to the equator and 17 days thence to San Francisco; fast time.

In June 1861, shortly after leaving Melbourne for Singapore, she was in collision with the ship *Herbert*, of Boston, but was not seriously damaged and arrived at destination after a passage of 52 days.

She sailed from San Francisco, July 20, 1869, for Baker's Island, to load guano for Hampton Roads. At the Island, on Aug. 20th, having 400 tons of her cargo on board, she was totally destroyed by fire. The rigging was cut away and some of the spars and sails were saved but the hull was burned right through. The weather being fine, Captain Taylor was ashore at the time, intending to stay over night. The ship's complement arrived at Honolulu in December, when the captain had some of the crew put in jail on the charge of having set fire to the ship.

The first commander of the *Robin Hood* was Capt. Richard Bearse; subsequently Captains Matthews, Crowell, David, Kelley and Taylor were in charge.

ROEBUCK

BUILT by Bourne & Kingsbury, at Kennebunk, Me., in 1851; 170 x 33 x 22; 815 tons; Thaddeus Nichols and Thomas Curtis of Boston, owners. Her first voyage was from Boston to San Francisco arriving July 3, 1852, in 152 days. Lost on the Willie's rocks, Cohasset, Jan. 28, 1859, while bound from Boston for Philadelphia.

ROMANCE OF THE SEAS

EXTREME clipper ship, launched Oct. 23, 1853, from the yard of Donald McKay, at East Boston, Mass.; 240: 9 x 39: 6 x 20; 1782 tons, old measurement. Dead rise, 15 inches; sheer, 4½ feet. She was designed by her owner, George B. Upton of Boston, and was the sharpest ship built in that city up to that time. Her lines were concave below and convex above and her long, sharp bow was ornamented with a female figure intended to represent "Romance," with the name of "Scott" on one side and "Cooper" on the other. She had elegant accommodations for passengers and her officers and crew were well provided for. She crossed but one skysail yard, that on the main. The fore, foretop, topgallant and royalmasts were in length respectively: 78, 45, 20 and 15 feet; the corresponding masts of the main were: 81½, 47, 25, 16½ and 12½; the mizzen: 76, 38, 18 and 12½. The corresponding yards were: 72, 55, 33 and 28 on the foremast; 83, 63, 45½, 34 and 28 on the mainmast; and 57, 45, 33 and 24 on the mizzenmast. Capt. Philip Dumaresq was appointed to the command.

The *Romance* loaded some 2000 tons of cargo on a draft of 18½ feet and left Boston, Dec. 16, 1853, for San Francisco. Three days previously the New York-built and owned clipper *David Brown*, had taken her departure from that port, also on her maiden passage and for the same destination. Considerable money was wagered on the result of the runs of the two ships, both of which were the masterpieces of their respective builders. The *Romance* arrived out Mar. 23, 1854, after a passage of 96 days and 18 hours, entering port a few hours ahead of the *Brown* whose time was 99 days. In the North Atlantic the *Brown* had increased her lead over the *Romance* by one day, crossing the line four days ahead, but in the South Atlantic the *Romance* gained three days and continued one day behind until at the end of her 89th day when she was abreast of her rival in latitude 30° North, Pacific, being also then three degrees of longitude to the good and 540 miles in a direct line from the Golden Gate. She had crossed the equator 78 days out from Boston and 56 days from the Atlantic crossing and on the whole passage to San Francisco logged 15,154 miles, an average of 156.6 daily, with 322 as her best day.*

The *Romance* and the *Brown* sailed from San Francisco, in company, on Mar. 31st and arrived at Hong Kong, May 16th, the *Romance* one hour ahead. She had set her skysail and three royal studding sails just outside of the Golden Gate and they were not taken in until entering Hong Kong harbor. The *Romance* loaded at Whampoa, for London, and was 103 days on the passage, 80 days from Anjer, while the *Brown* was 111 days from Shanghai to London, but 72 days only, from Anjer. The *Romance* is said to have made

* For further details of this race, see account of the *David Brown*.

4172 miles in 16 consecutive days, on seven of which her daily average was 307. Although no further opportunity ever occurred for the two ships to sail together, it is apparent that neither had an advantage over the other in sailing ability and both are considered as ranking among the fastest sailing ships ever built.

The second voyage of the *Romance* was a round between London and China. Under command of Capt. William W. Henry she went out to Hong Kong, being 99 days from Deal. Sailed from Shanghai, Nov. 1, 1855; passed Anjer, the 29th; was 40 days from there to the Cape and reached Deal, Mar. 7, 1856, having had light winds during the passage of 126 days. She arrived at Boston, Aug. 15th, from London, being 22 days from the Lizard.

On her third voyage, the *Romance* sailed from New York, July 3, 1856, and was 29 days to the line. Passed through the Straits of Le Maire, 56 days out, and was off the Cape on the following day. Very heavy gales were then experienced, the decks being often flooded. The figurehead was carried away, one boat smashed, the steering apparatus broken and other damage received. Crossed the equator 90 days out and 20 days later made land off Monterey, but had to stand offshore and beat up to the Golden Gate, taking over two days. Arrived at San Francisco, Oct. 24th, in 113 days' passage. Her log shows a continuation of light and baffling winds with poor trades. There were 26 days on each of which less than 100 miles were made; poorest days, 27 and 30 miles; best day, only 244 and best ten consecutive days, 2006 miles, this being in the South Atlantic. Sailed from San Francisco, Nov. 17th, and arrived at Shanghai, Dec. 22nd, a passage of 34 days and 4 hours, which has been beaten only by the record run of the *Sword Fish* (32 days and 9 hours), in 1853. Sailed from Shanghai, Feb. 16, 1857; passed Anjer, Mar. 5th, and arrived at New York, May 27th, in 100 days' passage; 83 days from Anjer.

Commencing her fourth voyage, the *Romance* sailed from New York, July 3, 1857, under command of Captain Caldwell and arrived at Batavia, Sept. 28th, in 88 days. During the following 12

"Reporter," 1474 tons, built at East Boston, Mass., in 1853

From a painting made in 1854 by D. McFarlane

"RINGLEADER," 1153 TONS, BUILT AT MEDFORD, MASS, IN 1853

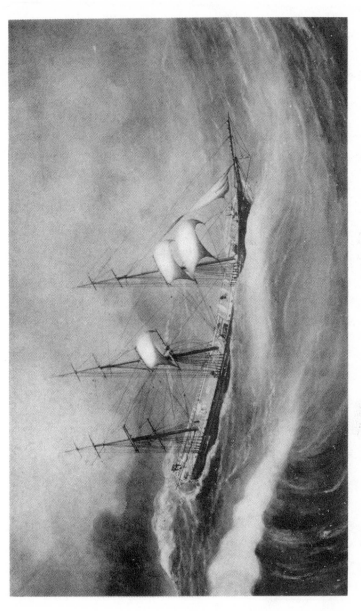

"RINGLEADER," 1153 TONS, BUILT AT MEDFORD, MASS, IN 1853

From a painting by A. V. Gregory, showing the ship in the South Atlantic, riding her easting down

"SEA WITCH," 907 TONS, BUILT AT NEW YORK, IN 1846

From the oil painting by Charles R. Patterson

months she was engaged in trading between Hong Kong, Bangkok and Shanghai. Sailed from Shanghai, Mar. 20, 1859; passed Anjer, Apr. 9th; the Cape, May 7th; and arrived at New York, June 22nd, in 94 days from Shanghai and 74 from Anjer. She again left New York, Aug. 11th; passed Anjer, Nov. 4th, 84 days out; and arrived at Hong Kong, Dec. 6th, in 116 days from New York. Had very heavy weather in the China Sea, losing the crossjack and the maintopsail yard and having the rudder carried away. Loaded at Manila from whence she took her departure June 23, 1860, and was 109 days to Boston.

In prosecution of her sixth voyage she left Boston, Dec. 28, 1860, under command of Capt. Ashman J. Clough; crossed the line 25 days out; passed the Horn on the 50th day and crossed the equator 80 days out; had fine trades to latitude 26° North and when 93 days out was three days' sail from the Golden Gate; then had light winds and did not arrive at San Francisco until Apr. 13, 1861, being some hours under 106 days from Boston. Her time of 55 days between the two equator crossings was very fast. Sailed from San Francisco, May 12th, and arrived at Queenstown, Aug. 13th,—a passage of 93 days. At that date this was the fastest passage that had been made from San Francisco to Great Britain except that of the clipper ship *Panama* (86 days and 17 hours), to Liverpool in 1860. Since then thousands of passages have been made by first-class ships over this course but the time made by the *Romance* has been equalled or excelled in only six instances, the fastest being 89 days. The *Romance* discharged her grain cargo at Liverpool, thence crossing to Boston and there being ordered to New York, arrived at the latter port, Oct. 27, 1861, her total passage being reported as 34 days.

On her last Cape Horn run, the *Romance* sailed from New York, Feb. 7, 1862; was 20 days to the line; 53 days to 50° South and 18 days rounding the Horn; crossed the equator 86 days out and arrived at San Francisco, May 24th, in 106 days' passage. Had been off the entrance to the Golden Gate for four days. Sailed from San Francisco, June 7th, and arrived at Hong Kong, July 24th, in 46 days. She then made a round voyage to Bangkok, finally loading at Hong Kong for San Francisco. Sailed Dec. 31, 1862, and in April 1863 was officially posted as missing. Thirty-five lives were lost with her. Insurance on ship and cargo was $266,000. Her old time rival, the *David Brown,* had met her fate two years previously, in the North Atlantic, while on a passage from San Francisco to Liverpool.

Some ten years ago there was printed in the "Boston Herald" what claimed to be a description of the sailing of the *Romance of the Seas* on her first voyage. We cannot vouch for its authenticity but the scene is pictured true to life and applies equally well to any clipper of the period:

"Full over the din rings the voice of the mate; 'Now then boys, heave away on the windlass; strike a light; its duller than an old graveyard.' The chanteyman begins with a song, 'Paddy works on the railway' which continues through various verses, with but little variation, until the mate calls out, 'Vast heaving,' lifts his hand and reports to the captain 'The anchor's apeak, sir.' 'Very good, sir; loose sails fore and aft,' is the order from the 'old man.' Now the mate's voice roars through the ship and across the wharf, 'Aloft there and loose sails. One hand stop in the tops and crosstrees to overhaul the gear.' 'Aye! aye! sir; royals and skysails?' 'Yes, royals and skysails; leave the staysails fast. Lay out there, four or five of you and loose the headsails. Here, you in the green spotted shirt, lay down out of that; there's men enough up there now to eat those sails.'

"And so the orders crowd upon each other as the ship gets under way. 'Mr. Coffin, take some of your men aft and look after the main and mizzen; put a hand at the wheel; have the ensign halliards clear; lay the accommodation ladder in on deck. Let that spanker alone. Hi! there! on the foretopsail yard, there; if you cut that gasket, I'll split your skull; you lubber, cast it adrift. Bo'sun, get your watch tackles along to the topsail sheets. Here, some of you genteel shipmates, get that fish-davit out and hook on.'

"And then, as the ship feels the breath of life in her sails:—

'Sheet home the topsails. Look out for those clewlines at the main, bo'sun; ease down handsome as the sheets come home.' And having infused a little ginger into the crew and longshoremen, the mate has the satisfaction of seeing them walk away with the three topsail halliards, singing, 'Away, 'way, 'way, yar; we'll kill Paddy Doyle for his boots.' And the ship pays off and gathers way, the crowds at the wharf giving three rousing cheers. The ensign is dipped and the clipper is on her way past Boston Light to Cape Horn."

ROVER'S BRIDE

EXTREME clipper, built at Baltimore, Md., in 1853; 383 tons; J. D. Nason of San Francisco, owners. Sold in Australia in 1854.

S. S. BISHOP

THE clipper ship *Stilwell S. Bishop*, generally known as the *S. S. Bishop*, was launched from the yard of William Cramp, at Kensington, Pa., Oct. 21, 1851, and was a handsome model with very sharp lines; 140: 1 x 31: 4 x 15; 595 tons, old measurement. She was a fast sailer, credited with often doing 14 knots, though she was said to be rather a wet ship, going through seas rather than over them. Her original owner was Henry Simon, Jr.

On her first Cape Horn passage she left Philadelphia, May 31, 1852, under command of Captain Tirley, and arrived at San Francisco in 121 days and this was also the length of her run over the same course in 1853, under Captain Josiah Sherman. In 1854 she was 112 days from Baltimore to San Diego, Cal., thence going to San Francisco. The fourth run was in 1855, under Captain Shankland, in 127 days from Philadelphia to San Francisco and the fifth and last, in 1856, under Captain Lindsay, was over the same course, in 117 days according to dates, but 113 days, per published reports. On two occasions she crossed the line in the Atlantic when 22 days out; from port of departure to the equator crossing in the Pacific, her average is 96 days; fastest run, 91 days and slowest, 104 days. From the Pacific equator to the Golden Gate her average is 23 days; fastest, 19 days to San Francisco and 21 days to San Diego; slowest, 28 days. Her fastest run from 50° to 50°, was 12 days. In 1852 she had decks swept repeatedly, off Cape Horn, and lost her deck load, and in 1855 she was forced to jettison a quantity of cargo.

Homeward bound her first passages were to Philadelphia, in 114 days from San Francisco, via Rio, and 72 days from Callao, respectively. Her last three returns were to New York, in 101 days direct and 118 days via Rio and 104 days from Honolulu.

Shortly after her arrival east, in 1856, the *Bishop* was sold to Rutter, Newell & Co., of Baltimore and was renamed *Grey Eagle*. For many years she was operated in trade principally with Rio and was always famous for the rapidity of her passages. Among fast runs credited to her are a round trip, Baltimore to Rio, in 59 days, including time at the Brazilian port. She was 29 days from Rio to the Capes, in June 1882, while other vessels were 35 to 40 days and on one occasion she is said to have made the run from Cape Henry to the line, in 14 days and 20 hours. During the late '60's she was owned by Whitridge & Co., of Baltimore. In 1870 she was rebuilt at Noank, Conn. About 1878 she appears rigged as a bark. As late as 1886 she was still engaged in trade, being owned by Bendell & Bro. Her name does not appear in the registers of 1889.

SAMUEL RUSSELL

CLIPPER ship, built in 1847, by Brown & Bell, at New York, for A. A. Low & Brother. She was named after the senior member of the prominent American firm of Russell & Co., operating in China, in which the Messrs. Low had a partnership at one time. Dimensions: 173 x 34: 6 x 19: 11; 957 tons, old measurement; 752, new measurement. She was slightly larger than the celebrated *Sea Witch*. Although she was not of the extreme model of the clippers later brought out to meet the necessities of the California trade, her masters were always ambitious to have her classed with them and on the occasion of her making 14 knots and covering 328 miles in 24 hours, in a "Cape wester," while bound to China in 1851, her captain wrote:—"Now sir, I humbly submit if this is not a feat to boast of; if it is not an achievement to entitle a ship to be classed among clippers." On another occasion she is said to have made 6722 miles in the 30 days between Nov. 8th and Dec. 7th; best day, 318 miles.

On her maiden voyage the *Russell* sailed from New York, Sept. 14, 1847, under command of Capt. N. B. Palmer who had superintended her construction and embodied in her model many ideas gained in his long experience as master in the China trade. On the 87th day out she passed through Allass Strait, between Lombok and Sumbawa, and taking the eastern passage, arrived at Hong Kong in 114 days. The voyage was completed by her passage from Whampoa to New York, in 83 days. Captain Palmer was then succeeded by his brother, Theodore D., who, after making two round voyages between New York and China, turned the command over to Capt. Charles Porter Low who had been in the *Houqua*, also belonging to the Messrs Low. The *Russell* then loaded for San Francisco and sailed from New York, Jan. 15, 1850. On account of the high freight rates prevailing, she was loaded as deeply as a sand barge, her freight list being some $75,000 on the 1200 measurement tons of general cargo she had aboard. In the Gulf Stream she shipped much water and lost the binnacle and her two large compasses, being forced to use a boat's small compass until she was off Rio, 29 days out, when she fortunately fell in with a ship bound to California with passengers from whom she was able to borrow two fine instruments. She had crossed the line 20 days out; was thence 24 days to 50° South, and then 17 days rounding the Horn. High seas flooded the decks, day after day, and at times the ship would go under water so that Captain Low thought she would never come up. This being the captain's first experience of Cape Horn, he lost several days through taking in sail preparatory to expected gales which failed to develop. In the South Pacific either light or head winds were experienced and her time was 29 days from 50° South to the line, which was crossed on the 90th day out. On May 6th she anchored in San Francisco bay, her passage, given as 109 days, being the shortest up to that time although it must be admitted that no real clippers had theretofore been over the course. This run has been the subject of comparison with that of the *Sea Witch* (97 days) and other clippers, in what has been called "the race of 1850," in spite of the fact that the *Russell's* competitors took their departures from New York at different seasons, the dates varying from two to six months after her.

Completing her voyage, the *Russell* was 14 days from San Francisco to Honolulu and thence, 37 days to Hong Kong. Sailed from Whampoa, Oct. 29, 1850, and was 89 days to New York. Captain Low then took command of the new clipper *N. B. Palmer*, belonging to the same owners as the *Russell*, his former mate, Mr. Limeburner, succeeding him in the latter. After making two round voyages between New York and China, on the second of which her time to Hong Kong was 92 days and return 95 days, the *Russell* was again put on the San Francisco run and made three consecutive passages. On the first, arriving out Dec. 9, 1852, in 118 days, she had much heavy weather. When ten days out lost the fore and main yards and off the Platte again lost the mainyard and had rudderhead damaged. From San Francisco she was 50 days to Shanghai. Sailed from Whampoa, Apr. 10, 1853, and was 103 days to New York. Sailed thence, Oct. 5th, and arrived at San Francisco, Jan. 21, 1854, in 106 days' passage. For four days was within 200 miles of the Golden Gate, in the fog. Crossed to Hong Kong; loaded at Foo Chow, sailing towards the end of August, and arrived at New York, Dec. 7, 1854, in 105 days. Her last arrival at San Francisco was June 13, 1855, in 116 days from New York. Went to Hong Kong via Honolulu; loaded at Foo Chow, sailing in August. Had the long and tedious passage of 43 days down the China Sea to Anjer, against a strong adverse monsoon, during which she sprung a leak. Under the most trying circumstances, including a shortage of provisions, her captain, Samuel Yeaton, with his mates Osborne and Taylor, success-fully completed the passage to New York without having put into any port en route, arriving Jan. 12, 1856, 123 days out. In recognition of their self-sacrificing and untiring efforts on behalf of owners and underwriters, the captain and his officers were presented with a purse of $1525.

After this voyage the *Russell* was engaged in trade between New York and China or Japan. Among some of her voyages may be mentioned the following:—in 1857, New York to Hong Kong in 96 days; returning, left Foo Chow in August and was 49 days to Anjer and thence 78 days to New York; in 1858, 101 days out to Hong Kong and 95 days home from Foo Chow; the next year she was also 95 days from Foo Chow home; in 1861 her homeward passage was from Hong Kong, 94 days; in 1863 it was 89 days from Foo Chow. On these four last passages she had left the China coast during the favorable monsoon season. Leaving Yokohama in November 1865, she was 23 days to Anjer and 80 days thence to New York. In 1850 and in 1852 her runs home from Anjer were 70 days each. On her passage from New York to Hong Kong, in 1851-1852, she crossed the line 19 days and 20 hours out and passed through Allass Straits on the 68th day,—a very fast run. When bound to San Francisco in 1853, she was only 16 days from Cape St. Roque to latitude 50° South, which time is believed to have never been beaten and to have been equalled in only a few instances.

About 1860, Captain Winchell succeeded to the command of the *Russell* and several years later Capt. Frederic G. Lucas became her master and so continued until her end. On Nov. 23, 1870, she was wrecked on a reef in the Gaspar Straits. All hands landed on Gaspar Island but their provisions giving out, they again took to their boats and were subsequently picked up by the ship *Mogul*. The wreck of the *Russell* was sold for $370 and the cargo brought about $1800. She was still owned by the Messrs Low and during her whole career had been a very successful vessel.

SANCHO PANZA

MEDIUM clipper ship, launched from the yard of Samuel Lapham, at Medford, Mass., Aug. 5, 1855, for John Ellerton Lodge of Boston; 152: 6 x 34 x 21: 5; 876 tons, old measurement; 736 tons, new measurement. A very neat and pretty little ship.

On her first voyage she left Boston, Oct. 13, 1855, and reached San Francisco, Mar. 8, 1856, in 147 days' passage. Capt. J. B. Hildreth was so disgusted with the passage that he entered on the log, "The devil take *Sancho Panza*; she is as bad as her namesake." On the other hand, Lieutenant Maury, after analyzing her log, put the blame on the captain instead of the ship, saying that she had not been properly handled. It appears, however, that neither critic was fully justified, for practically all vessels taking their departure at about the same time, from New York and Boston, had the same weather, particularly in the North Atlantic, as was experienced by the *Sancho*, and a number, including the *Charmer*, fell, like her, to leeward of St. Roque, not clearing that bugbear of navigation until 45 to 53 days after sailing. The *Sancho*, in a most vexatious series of calms, had for nearly her whole passage the royals and studdingsails set. Through the tropics she had barely steerage way and in both oceans the trades were very light. Her log showed a woeful record of poor daily work with only an occasional run of 300 miles to show what she could do. She was four days at Juan Fernandez replenishing her water supply and was within three days sail of the Golden Gate for 12 days. The *Charmer* arrived a few hours before her, 140 days from New York, her captain reporting nearly identical weather conditions throughout the whole run.

In continuation of this voyage the *Sancho* went to Hong Kong in 53 days; proceeded to Foo Chow and loaded for Boston. Sailed Dec. 10th; passed Java Head the 29th and thence had 40½ days to the Cape, this being four to eight days longer than other clippers did the course in at the same period. She arrived at Boston, in 110 days from Foo Chow, 89 days from Java Head and 48 from the Cape.

On her second voyage she left New York, June 28, 1857, under command of Captain Bird and arrived at San Francisco, Nov. 16th, in 141 days' passage. She was 33 days off the Horn and was within 400 miles of the Golden Gate for ten days. Sailed from San Francisco, Dec. 8th, and reached Hong Kong, Jan. 20, 1858,—42 days out. Proceeded to Shanghai and sailed from Woosung, Nov. 13th; passed Anjer, Dec. 3rd; was off Cape Hatteras ten days in heavy gales and had her pilot aboard three days before being able to enter New York harbor; passage from Woosung, 101 days. Sailed from New York, Apr. 24, 1859, and went out to Hong Kong in 100 days. Loaded at Shanghai; left Woosung, Dec. 28, 1859, and arrived at New York in 102 days; 81 days from Anjer. Loaded at Boston for Hong Kong and sailed May 25, 1860, going out in 119 days. Sailed from Foo Chow, Jan. 1, 1861; was 22 days to Anjer and two days clearing the straits, arriving at New York, Apr. 13th, 102 days out, 78 days from Java Head, 48 days from the Cape and 25 days from the line. Had been ten days in North latitude 30°, in strong northerly gales and a heavy sea. Four days before entering port, shipped a sea while running and had forward house stove and cabin filled. When three days out from Foo Chow had a typhoon of 12 hours duration; lost nearly an entire suit of sails; ship almost on beam ends, with the upper dead eyes in the water, losing everything off the starboard side, bulwarks, firewood, martingale and every thing about the jibboom; had bowsprit sprung, rudderhead split, cabin house stove and cabin filled.

Sailed from New York, July 13, 1861, and was 96 days to Melbourne. Sailed thence, Nov. 14th, and arrived at Singapore, Jan. 7, 1862, in a leaky condition. Was caulked and proceeded to Shanghai, thence to Hong Kong and finally loaded at Foo Chow for London. Arrived out, Jan. 3, 1863, 105 days from Anjer and 72 days from the Cape. Capt. Nathaniel Hale, who had been in command for a number of years and who had previously been master of the *Argo-*

naut, also owned by Mr. Lodge, died at London, three days after her arrival, aged 40 years. The *Sancho Panza* was then sold, going under the British flag as the *Nimrod* of London, owned by J. Pearce & Co., and commanded by Captain Pearce. She remained under this ownership until 1868 when she is registered as owned by Clark and others; hailing port, London, Eng. In 1874 she was owned by J. P. Rogers; hailing port, Plymouth, Eng. In 1875 she appears as the bark *Nimrod*, under the same ownership. In 1890 she is listed as the German bark *Nimrod* of Elsfleth.

SAN FRANCISCO

EXTREME clipper ship, built in 1853, by Abraham C. Bell, at New York; launched Aug. 25th; 198 feet on deck; 190 keel x 38 x 22; 1307 tons. Owned by Rich & Elam and Thomas Wardle of New York. On her first and only passage she left New York under command of Captain Sitzer, Oct. 25, 1853, and arrived at San Francisco, Feb. 8, 1854, 106 days out; had taken pilot off the Farallons the day previous and on Jan. 29th, 96 days out, was 450 miles off port. Near the Horn spoke ship *Ringleader*, from Boston, Oct. 21st, and ship *Morning Light* and led the former into San Francisco, six hours and the latter, 20 hours. There also arrived in port the same day the clipper ships *Matchless*, in 110 days from Boston, and the *Golden City*, in 106 days from New York. The story of the run of the *San Francisco* can best be told by extracts from her log, as follows:—

Sailed from New York, Oct. 25, 1853; discharged pilot off Sandy Hook, at noon, and proceeded to sea with fresh breeze. Moderate winds to Nov. 4th, when experienced a heavy gale from E. S. E., which lasted 21 hours, after which winds prevailed from S. E. and continued until the N. E. trades were met. Crossed the line 27 days out. On Dec. 14th, passed to the westward of the Falkland Islands; 15th, made Staten Island, wind ahead. Signaled a clipper and passed her; 16th, passed through the Straits of Le Maire; 18th, 54 days out, passed Cape Horn, ten miles distant, with all sail set; 21st, wind shifted to S. W., tacked ship to northward. Dec. 28th, spoke clipper ship *Ringleader* of Boston; next day, passed several ships among them the clipper *Morning Light,* and exchanged signals. Took the N. E. trades in 6° North, and had ship braced by the wind until Jan. 29th, when San Francisco bore N. E. by N., half N., 450 miles distant. Were then becalmed three days and had foggy weather until Feb. 6th, when wind hauled to N. W., and we got good observation, Farallon Islands being distant about half a mile. Took pilot, which ends our voyage of 105 days. Have not reefed topsails during passage except in gale of Nov. 4th, and have not had one good day's run, although experienced very fine weather.

On entering the Golden Gate, Feb. 8th, the pilot being in charge, the *San Francisco* missed stays, and went on the rocks at Rialto Cove, on the north shore, just within Point Bonita, the North Head. As soon as the news of the occurrence reached the city, a multitude of plunderers hastened to the wreck and proceeded to help themselves, owner's and agent's representatives vainly attempting to drive them away. Many of them were armed and defied opposition, fought among themselves and frequently stole each others' booty. It was reported that soldiers from the Presidio, across the Golden Gate, were among the crowd. Finally a storm came up and many of the boats, with their stolen contents, were swamped and some 12 of the wreckers were drowned. The ship was then sold, as she lay, to Capt. Robert H. Waterman, for $12,000 and he had removed $20,000 worth of cargo before she broke up. She was valued at $103,000; freight money, $50,000; both being fully covered by insurance; cargo was valued at $400,000 and insured for $365,000.

SANTA CLAUS

MEDIUM clipper ship, built by Donald McKay, at East Boston, Mass.; launched Sept. 5, 1854. Keel, 184 feet; length over all, 194 x 38: 6 x 22: 11; 1256 tons, old measurement. She was built for account of Joseph Nickerson & Co., of Boston, under the superintendence of Capt. Alden Gifford. While capacity for cargo was a principal feature in her model, she had good lines and was called a handsome ship. Her lower masts were 80, 84 and 75 feet long, respectively and the corresponding yards, 68, 76 and 56 feet. She had as a figurehead a representation of Santa Claus. Capt. Bailey Foster of Brewster, was appointed her commander.

On her maiden voyage she left Boston, Nov. 15, 1854, and arrived back at her home port, Aug. 15, 1855, having made the voyage to Calcutta and return in nine months. The homeward passage was 114 days from the Sand Heads. On Sept. 21, 1856, she arrived at San Francisco in 140 days from Boston, with light winds all the run excepting 27 days off the Horn in heavy weather and much ice. The *John Gilpin* reached San Francisco the day after her, having had the same length of passage and reporting similar weather. The two ships had met near the Platte. Completing this voyage, the *Santa* took guano from the Chincha Islands to Hampton Roads. She then loaded at New York for San Francisco and made the passage out in 128 days. She was up with the line when 27 days out but fell to leeward of Cape St. Roque and was 14 days beating around, having to cross the line a second time, the 40th day out. Passed through the Straits of Le Maire on the 67th day; had fine weather off the Horn and very light winds and poor trades in the South Pacific. Near the Cape, spoke the clipper ship *Challenger,* also bound for San Francisco. The latter led her five days to the equator and also into port. The *Santa* then made two round voyages between San Francisco and Hong Kong, the first being 41 days outward and 40 days returning; the second, 51 days outward and 50 days returning. She then went back to Hong Kong in 48 days; thence 88 days to Callao, arriving Feb. 2, 1860; thence to Hampton Roads, with guano from the Chincha Islands.

The last visit of the *Santa Claus* to San Francisco was in Sept. 1861, when she arrived in 140 days from Boston. Capt. Charles Hopkins of Brewster, who had been in the *Kingfisher*, was in command and reported being 22 days to the line; thence 36 days to 50° South; 21 days rounding the Cape in very heavy weather, having sails split, bulwarks stove and steering apparatus broken; crossed the equator 105 days out and in latitude 16° North, lost nearly an entire suit of sails in a hurricane. From San Francisco went to Callao in 60 days; thence with guano to Browershaven, in 101 days, arriving July 21, 1862.

In January 1863, the *Santa Claus* arrived at Panama with a cargo of coal for the Pacific Mail Steamship Company. Later she proceeded to Callao and loaded guano at the Chincha's for Hamburg. Sailed from Callao, May 30, 1863, and on July 18th, in latitude 37° South, longitude 31° West, reported to a passing ship that she was leaking badly but could make port. On Aug. 9th, when in 5° North, 45° West, and attempting to reach St. Thomas, she was abandoned in a sinking condition. All hands reached Cayenne in the ship's boats. Captain Hopkins was subsequently in command of the *Mountain Wave*.

SEAMAN

A PERFECT type of the celebrated Baltimore clipper ship, the *Seaman* was built by R. & E. Bell of that place and was launched Sept. 7, 1850; 136 x 23: 10 x 15 feet; 546 tons; original owner, Thomas Handy of New York. She was described as a perfect little beauty, reminding one of a yacht, ship rigged.

Under Captain Myrick she sailed from New York, Nov. 23, 1850, and was 21½ days to the line and 46 days to 50° South. On the 66th day out was north-bound in the Pacific; crossed the equator 89 days out and had a magnificent run of 18 days to San Francisco; total, 107 days from New York. Captain Myrick reported being only

30 days from the latitude of Valparaiso to the Golden Gate,—remarkable time. She left San Francisco, in ballast,* Apr. 18, 1851; was 35 days to Valparaiso; stayed in port several days; was thence 28 days to Rio and 31 days from that port to Baltimore. Actual sailing time from San Francisco, 94 days.

On her second Cape Horn voyage the *Seaman* left New York, Aug. 3, 1852, commanded by Captain Daniel, and arrived at San Francisco, Dec. 9th, 128 days out. She had made the good time of 20 days from the line in the Atlantic to 50° South; otherwise had light and baffling winds, except off Cape Horn where heavy gales were met for 24 days. Crossed the Pacific equator, 102 days out. Left San Francisco, Dec. 25th; reported at Rio, Mar. 4, 1853, making 69 days; arrived at New Orleans, Apr. 2nd, in 98 days gross, after leaving the Pacific port. Thereafter went to New York in 15 days.

On Feb. 6, 1855, in latitude 36° North, longitude 63° West, the *Seaman* was struck by lightning and burned to the water's edge. She was bound from New Orleans to Marseilles. Captain Daniel and the officers and crew were rescued by the brig *Marion* and later sent home by the *Black Warrior*.

SEAMAN'S BRIDE

EXTREME clipper ship, built in Baltimore, by R. & E. Bell, in 1851; launched June 25th; 152 x 31 x 19; 668 tons, old measurement. She was of the same model as the slightly smaller clipper *Seaman*, a product of the same yard, the previous year. Her original owner was Thomas J. Handy of New York, and she was placed under command of Captain Myrick, who had made one round voyage from New York to San Francisco in the *Seaman*.

The *Seaman's Bride* left New York, Dec. 12, 1851; was 28 days to the line; 30 days thence to 50° South, and 16 days rounding the Horn. Off the Cape she had the foremast carried away in a heavy

---

* The Baltimore papers say on her return voyage that she had a full cargo.

squall during the night of Feb. 19th, and was forced to put into Valparaiso. Spars were found to be very scarce there and she was detained about a month refitting. On proceeding she encountered very unfavorable winds and trades and was 42 days from the Chilian port to San Francisco, arriving May 20, 1852. Then crossed to Shanghai in 57 days. Sailed from that port Oct. 6th and reached New York, Jan. 31, 1853, 117 days out, 90 from Java Head and 57 days from the Cape. She then returned to San Francisco, arriving July 28, 1853, after a passage of 120 days. Was 14 days off the Cape in heavy weather and 29 days from the equator to the Golden Gate, being becalmed near the Heads for seven days. Captain Myrick was succeeded by Captain Mayo who took the *Seaman's Bride* from San Francisco to New York, in 110 days, including a short stop at Rio. Sailed from New York, Jan. 24, 1854, and was 119 days to San Francisco. Was 27 days to the line; had very heavy weather between the Platte and the Horn, but fine weather in coming around. Was 19 days from the equator to destination.

The passage quoted was the last Cape Horn run made by the *Seaman's Bride*, at least as an American ship. From San Francisco she went to Manila; sailed thence Sept. 12, 1854, and arrived at New York, Jan. 6, 1855, in 116 days' passage; 81 from Java Head and 51 days from the Cape. On Mar. 13, 1855, she sailed from New York and was 26 days to Hamburg. She was subsequently sold to merchants of that city who had her name changed to *Carl Staegoman*.

In 1856, there was built at Belfast, Me., a medium clipper ship called *Seaman's Bride*, which was owned in, and hailed from Boston. This ship was lost at Baker's Island in 1865.

SEA NYMPH, OF BALTIMORE

CLIPPER ship, built in 1850, at Baltimore; 537 tons; described as a little beauty. Her first passage was from Baltimore to New York and she made the distance from the wharf to Cape Henry, 170 miles, in 12½ hours, an average of 13.6 miles per hour. Her whole passage to New York was 74 hours. Loading for San Francisco, she took her departure on Dec. 15, 1850, and arrived out May 21, 1851, after a long run of 157 days. Her captain, Philip M. Hale, did not make public any memorandum of the passage, which was a disappointment to the backers of the ship and which was 61 days longer than the run of the *Surprise* which had left Boston, Dec. 13th. The *Sea Nymph* went to Hong Kong from San Francisco, stopping off Honolulu, July 24th, 12 days from the Golden Gate. From Whampoa she went to New York in 110 days.

She arrived at San Francisco, July 4, 1852, in company with the clipper ship *Stag Hound,* both reporting 124 days from New York, with much light weather and calms on the way. The *Argonaut* also reached port the same day in 134 days. The *Sea Nymph* crossed to Shanghai, in 58 days and sailed thence, Oct. 26th; passed Anjer, Nov. 16th; arrived off the Highlands, Feb. 5, 1853, 102 days from Shanghai; took pilot the 7th and anchored in New York the 8th, in 105 days. She had been offered for sale while in port at San Francisco, but there were no purchasers. She was, however, ultimately sold and for a time operated on the coast of Asia, carrying rice from Siam to China. In the late 50's she took lumber from Puget Sound to China and was reported as being under the North German flag, bark rigged. On Nov. 30, 1860, she was reported as reaching Hong Kong, totally dismasted, after crossing the Pacific from Victoria, B. C., and was condemned.

"SHOOTING STAR," 903 TONS, BUILT AT MEDFORD, MASS., IN 1851

"SOUTHERN CROSS," 938 TONS, BUILT AT EAST BOSTON, MASS., IN 1851

"ESTHER MAY," 499 TONS, BUILT AT BRISTOL, R. I., IN 1847, AND THE "SOUTHERN CROSS," BUILT AT EAST BOSTON, MASS, IN 1851

From a painting by Lane

"Sovereign of the Seas," 2421 Tons, Built at East Boston, Mass., in 1852

SEA NYMPH, OF NEW BEDFORD

MEDIUM clipper ship of 1215 tons, built in 1853, at Fairhaven, Mass., by Reuben Fiske & Co., for Edward Mott Robinson of New Bedford. Her model was quite up to the standard of medium clippers turned out by more prominent builders and she proved to be a fast sailer and a successful merchant ship. On her first passage, however, she narrowly escaped disaster. While bound from New Bedford to New Orleans, she developed a leak of some 400 strokes per hour and it was found that an inch and a half auger hole had been bored in her bottom and lightly plugged by a bung.

The *Sea Nymph* arrived at San Francisco, Apr. 12, 1855, in 145 days from New York. Captain Fraser reported having very unfavorable weather in the Atlantic and was not well clear of the Cape until the 89th day out. Put into Valparaiso and was only 38 days thence to the Golden Gate, in spite of the fact that he was within 600 miles for ten days. At San Francisco, Capt. Charles D. Harding assumed command and returned to New York with guano from the Chincha Islands. The following year, 1856, the run to San Francisco was made in 113 days, with good weather throughout. Crossed the equator, 19½ days from New York; had no storms off the Cape and on the 88th day out was on the line in the Pacific. Again returned home with guano. In 1858-1859, with Captain Whiting, Jr., in command, the passage to San Francisco was made in 137 days and the return in ballast to New York, direct, in 104 days. The memoranda of the subsequent voyage on which she arrived at San Francisco, Apr. 24, 1860, 126 days from New York, is interesting;—"Sailed from New York, Dec. 19, 1859; 22 days to the line; was off the Horn 55 days out; then had heavy gales and strong easterly currents for 18 days and made little or no westing. On Mar. 1, 1860, in 60° South, 70° West, took a southerly wind and had little or no variation in a run of over 4000 miles to near the equator, which was crossed in 106°, 20 days from 50° South. Took the northeast trades in 3° South, and carried them to 32° North, 135° West. Have had a remarkably pleasant passage and weather." Completing the voyage the *Sea*

Nymph went to Mazatlan, Mexico, and sailed thence June 19, 1860. Off Acapulco, on July 5th, in a hurricane, carried away fore yard and twisted rudderhead and was 74 days from Mazatlan to Cape Horn, arriving at New York, Oct. 31, 1860.

On May 4, 1861, when 120 days out from New York, for San Francisco, the *Sea Nymph* went ashore in the fog, just north of Point Reyes and about 35 miles northwest of the Golden Gate entrance. A life boat being capsized, communication with the shore was finally made by means of a kite landing a small line attached to a hawser. The crew were landed with the loss of but one man. The cargo was 1778 tons of general merchandise valued at $250,000. Vessel and cargo were sold May 9th, to a Mr. Benjamin, for $9700 and Capt. Edgar Wakeman, a prominent shipmaster, superintended the wrecking of the ship, living on the beach near by for 85 days. When the ship finally went to pieces it was flood tide and what cargo was still aboard was washed ashore. Only a few days before Wakeman had bought the wreck for a small sum as it was supposed that further salvage would be nominal, while, as it turned out there was enough saved to load two schooners and the captain made a profit of several thousand dollars.

SARACEN

BUILT by E. & H. O. Briggs, at East Boston, in 1854; 192 x 36 x 23; 1266 tons; Curtis & Peabody of Boston, owners. Sold at San Francisco, in December 1865 to go under the Italian flag and renamed *Teresa*.

SEA SERPENT

EXTREME clipper ship, built by George Raynes, at Portsmouth, N. H., and launched in December 1850. Length between perpendiculars, 194: 6; over all, 212; extreme beam outside, 39: 3; depth of hold, 20: 8; 1337 tons, old measurement; 975 tons, new measurement. Dead rise, 40 inches; swell of sides, four inches; sheer, two feet. An eagle was the figurehead while a serpent in green and gold ornamented the stern. Her lower masts were 83, 87 and 78 feet long, respectively, being fully equal to those of the *Flying Cloud*, a larger vessel by nearly 400 tons, and she was otherwise heavily sparred. The masts raked 1 inch, 1¼ and 1½ inches to the foot. Her owners, Grinnell, Minturn & Co., of New York, were so well pleased with her general appearance that they paid her builder a bonus and distributed a sum of money among the mechanics employed in her construction. As an evidence of the fine workmanship done and material used it is stated that underwriters were never called upon to pay any claims for damage to her cargoes. While very sharp, with a bow like a wedge, she was dry and an excellent sea boat in every way, proving as well to be a very fast sailer and in light winds slipping through the water on her course, while other ships nearby would not have steerage way. Frequently 15 knots had been taken off the reel.

On her maiden voyage the *Sea Serpent* left New York, Jan. 11, 1851, and it was expected that her passage to San Francisco would be 100 days or less. Weather conditions, however, proved unfavorable; light or adverse winds prevailed; the bowsprit was sprung four days out from New York and in two weeks of very heavy gales off Cape Horn, a number of spars were carried away and sails split. When 72 days out she put into Valparaiso for repairs and was in port eight days. Thence to San Francisco light winds were experienced prolonging that portion of the passage to 45 days. Total time of the passage, 125 days; actual sailing time, 117 days; very good considering the circumstances. From San Francisco she was 42 days to Hong Kong and leaving Whampoa, Oct. 16, 1851, was 100 days to New York and 82 days from Anjer. On her second voyage she was 18 days from New York to the line; thence 70 days to the equator in the Pacific and 24 days thereafter was at San Francisco; passage 112 days. Was then 12 days from the Golden Gate to Honolulu and 37 days thence to Hong Kong and, leaving Whampoa, Oct. 4, 1852, was 88 days to New York, being within 50 miles of Sandy Hook on 86th day. This was the fastest passage of the year and a remarkable one considering the season. Her around-the-world voyage had occupied 9 months and 25 days, including time in ports. On her third voyage she left New York, Feb. 11, 1853, crossed the line in 19 days and 16 hours from Sandy Hook; sighted Cape Horn, Apr. 1st at noon, 48 days out; was 18 days between the 50's; crossed the equator in the Pacific, May 5th, 82 days out, and when in 20° North, had excellent prospects for making the passage in under 100 days, but there encountered 12 days of calms and head winds; passed through the Golden Gate, June 1st, 110 days from New York. Crossed from San Francisco to Hong Kong in 38 days. Left Whampoa, Sept. 10, 1853; went to Anjer by the Eastern passage, being 29 days, the fastest time of any made that season, and arrived at New York, Dec. 20th, in 101 days from Whampoa and 72 from Anjer. The fourth voyage was 116 days from New York to San Francisco. Crossed the equator in the Pacific, 91 days out, but then had nothing but light winds and calms to port. Sailed from San Francisco, July 5, 1854, and was 47 days to Hong Kong. Loaded at Shanghai for New York; sailed Nov. 5th; had a good run for the season of 16 days to Anjer and arrived at destination, Feb. 15, 1855, in 102 days from Shanghai and 86 from Anjer. In a sudden squall off the Platte lost maintopmast.

Capt. J. D. Whitmore took command and left New York, Apr. 11, 1855, for San Francisco. On May 16th, in 8° 26' South, 33° 30' West, Captain Whitmore wrote:—"Since leaving 38° North, have had the wind dead ahead, it not being to the eastward of southeast all that time and to get thus far the ship has sailed 5531 miles, averaging on a bowline 158 miles daily for 35 days; pretty good work. Take also into account the spars and rigging of the ship rather shaky at the time." In the South Atlantic she lost the main-topmast, split a number of sails and received other damage which caused Captain Whitmore to put about for Rio. She was thence 81 days to San Francisco but on the 66th day was within 500 miles of the Golden Gate. Her time from the equator to port was 30 days, in very light winds and calms. Left San Francisco, Oct. 17th; arrived at Honolulu in 11 days and reported at Hong Kong, Dec. 8th. Left Whampoa, Jan. 3, 1856, in the full strength of the northeast monsoon; was eight days to Anjer and two days later cleared the Straits and arrived at New York, Mar. 22, 1856, in 79 days from Whampoa, 69 from Java Head and 39 from the Cape of Good Hope. Her time from China has been beaten by only two ships, the *Sea Witch* and the *Natchez*, the run of the latter being in the nature of a lucky freak, 78 days and 6 hours, Macao to pilot off Barnegat, in 1845.

On arrival at San Francisco, Sept. 6, 1856, Captain Whitmore reported having had bad luck all the passage of 130 days; was 22 days off the Horn and 26 days from the equator to port. Went to Hong Kong via Honolulu and was on the coast trading between Hong Kong, Bangkok and Shanghai until the fall of 1858 when she loaded for San Francisco. Arrived at that port, Jan. 16, 1859, in 45 days from Hong Kong, encountering strong southeast winds from longitude 140° West, making the land near Port Orford, Southern Oregon, when 38 days out; then had light winds and calms to destination. Left San Francisco, Feb. 22nd; was 12 days to Honolulu and in port there five days; thence 25 days to Hong Kong or 37 sailing days from the Golden Gate. Sailed from Foo Chow, June 19th, and was 47 days to Anjer in the height of the adverse monsoon; arrived at London in 130 days from Foo Chow. Beat the *Fiery Cross*, nine days, the *Ellen Rodger*, six days, the *Crest of the Wave*, 17 days and the *Ziba*, four days, all of which British tea clippers had left Foo Chow between June 9th and 19th.

The *Sea Serpent* sailed from London, Nov. 29, 1859, for Hong Kong and put into Rio, Jan. 9, 1860, leaking, having struck a reef just north of the line while going 11 knots. Repaired and sailed Apr. 9th and arrived at Hong Kong, June 22nd, in 74 days from Rio. Arrived at New York, Feb. 11, 1861, in 102 days from Hong Kong and 79 days from Anjer. Left New York, May 19th, under Captain Pike; in the South Atlantic lost foretopmast; passed the Horn, 54 days out; had very light winds in the North Pacific and was four days off San Francisco Heads, in a dense fog; total passage, 120 days. Went to Hong Kong in 47 days and thence to New York in 107 days. The following voyage, Captain Thorndike in command, was 119 days from New York to San Francisco; thence 41 days to Hong Kong; thence 12 days to Singapore; thence to Shanghai and from there to Manila. Arrived at New York, Aug. 2, 1864; 106 days from Manila, 49 from the Cape and 20 days from the equator crossing. Captain Winsor now took command, leaving New York, Nov. 5, 1865; was 27 days to the line; passed the Horn 53 days out and was on the equator in the Pacific on the 79th day; thence had 22 days, making her passage 101 days, which had not been beaten for the previous five years and equaled during that period only by the *Panama*. Went to Hong Kong in 41 days; sailed from Whampoa, Oct. 21st; passed Macao, the 22nd; Anjer, Nov. 16th and arrived at New York, Jan. 24, 1866, in 95 days from Whampoa, 69 from Anjer, 44 from the Cape and 22 from the equator; was five days north of Cape Hatteras in heavy westerly gales, and seven days in a dense fog. Sailed from New York, Aug. 4, 1866, and was 115 days to San Francisco with moderate winds and fair weather except for 12 days of heavy gales between the two 50's. Was 29 days from the equator crossing to the Golden Gate. From San Francisco she was 44 sailing days to Hong Kong, via Honolulu, and from China went back to New York. Sailed from New York, June 15, 1867, and was 126 days to San Francisco. Captain Winsor reported nothing but light winds or calms except for the 23 days of heavy weather while rounding the Horn.

Was off the Golden Gate eight days in a dense fog. Captain White assumed command and had the passage of 96 days back to New York, direct. Returned to San Francisco, arriving Oct. 14, 1868, after a tedious passage of 146 days of which 126 were of head winds. Had no trades whatever in either ocean; was within 400 miles of destination for 15 days, a dense fog preventing any observation being taken. She then went to Hong Kong, via Honolulu, in 42 sailing days and thence to New York.

In 1870 the *Sea Serpent* was 135 days from New York to San Francisco, having very light and baffling winds all the passage. Went home via Hong Kong. Her next and last Cape Horn passage was in 1871-1872, in 108 days from New York to San Francisco on which occasion she made the exceedingly fast time of 39 days from 50° South, Pacific, to destination, being but 17 days from the line. From San Francisco she went to Newcastle, N. S. W., in 55 days. She went thence to Hong Kong and her reported time, 30 days, is exceptionally good, nearly equal to record. She completed this voyage by going to New York, whence she returned to China, direct, arriving at Hong Kong, June 28, 1873, and the following month, proceeding on to Shanghai. Sailed from the latter port, Nov. 17, 1873, and arrived at New York, Feb. 19, 1874, in a passage of 95 days. In May, following, she was sold by Grinnell, Minturn & Co., for $22,500 to sail under Norwegian colors and was renamed *Progress;* hailing port Tonsberg. For a number of years she was engaged in the North Atlantic trade and in 1879 under Capt. P. A. Hall, left New York, June 24th, for London, passing Gravesend, July 11th, in 17 days. In July 1886 she was surveyed at Greenock but was not classed and as late as 1890 was still listed in registers.

Her first captain, William Howland, was well known as commander, for some ten years, of the *Horatio,* one of the most famous old time China traders, and after leaving her he commanded various packet ships. His successor in the *Sea Serpent,* Capt. J. D. Whitmore, had been in the *Tingqua.* He died in December 1860, while the *Sea Serpent* was in the Indian Ocean, homeward bound from Hong

Kong. The mate, Mr. Williams, finished the voyage. Capt. Samuel W. Pike, who had just arrived home in the *Mameluke*, then took charge, making one round voyage after which he was succeeded by Captain Thorndike, formerly of the *Live Yankee*, who also made one voyage. Captain Winsor took command in the fall of 1864, continuing for about three years when he was succeeded by Capt. Jeremiah D. White who remained in the ship until she was sold.

The following account of life on board the clipper ship *Sea Serpent* is taken from Bayard Taylor's "Visit to India, China and Japan in 1853," New York, 1875:—

I desired to return by way of San Francisco, but as no vessel was then up for that port, I changed my plans and took passage for New York in the clipper ship *Sea Serpent*, Captain Howland, which was announced to sail from Whampoa on the 9th of September, 1853. On the morning of the 9th we left Canton in the Macao steamer, which had been chartered to tow the *Sea Serpent* out to sea. We went swiftly down the crowded stream and soon reached the long stretch of green paddy-fields extending to Whampoa.

Near the mouth of Lob Creek we passed a tall pagoda, and another within a mile or two of Whampoa, crowning the top of a verdant knoll. The latter was built of dark-red stone, and with the ivy and wild shrubs waving from the horned roofs of its nine stories, was really a picturesque object. The shipping of Whampoa was now visible, and in less than half an hour we lay alongside of the good clipper which was thenceforth to be our ocean home. Whampoa is a long, scattering Chinese town, on the southern bank of the river. The foreign vessels anchored in the reach, for a distance of more than a mile, give the place a lively air, and the low, conical hills which rise from the shore, crowned here and there with Chinese buildings, relieve the tameness of the swampy soil on which the town is built. We were obliged to wait for the flood-tide, which detained us two hours.

The anchor was cheerily lifted at last, and we got under way for New York. In going down the river we had a fair view of all the vessels of war anchored in Blenheim Reach, which was only half a mile distant, on our right.

The river now became broader and frequently expanded on either side into great arms, some of which extended for many miles into the country. We passed the first bar, which was created by the Chinese sinking junks to prevent the English from reaching Canton. A high hill on the southern shore, near the second bar, which we reached about 5 P.M., is crowned with a pagoda 150 feet high, which is visible at a great distance. Beyond this, the river again expands, to be finally contracted into a narrow pass, at the Bocca Tigris, which we fortunately reached before dusk. It is a fine, bold gateway formed by two mountainous islands, which leave a passage of about half a mile between them. There are several Chinese batteries on either hand, but they are more formidable in appearance than in reality.

By the time we had passed the Bogue, it was dark. The tide was now in our favor, and we stood away towards Lintin. We had a large number of friends, including Messrs. Nye and Tuckerman of Canton, at dinner in the cabin, but about 10 P.M. they all bade us good-bye and returned aboard the steamer. We were cast off a little after midnight, and taking a northeast wind ran down past the Ladrones at the rate of ten knots an hour. When I went on deck in the morning, China was no longer visible. The weather was dull and rainy, but we continued to make good progress. On the afternoon of the 12th, by which time we had made 300 miles, a violent squall came on tearing our maintop-gallant sail and jib into ribbons. Heavy showers of rain succeeded and during the night the wind gradually settled into the regular south-west monsoon. By noon the following day, we were in Lat. 14° 54′ N.—consequently south of the Paracel Reefs, and beyond the latitude of violent typhoons. As the wind still blew steadily from the southwest, Captain Howland determined to change his course and make for the Straits of Mindoro, Basilan and Macassar, hoping to get the south-east trade wind in the Java Sea and thus make a better run to Angier than by slowly beating down the China Sea.

I found the *Sea Serpent* an excellent sea-boat, in every respect. She behaved admirably on a wind, slipping through the water so softly that we would not have suspected the speed she made. Although so sharp in the bows, she was very dry, scarcely a spray flying over the forecastle. In addition to Lieut. Contee and myself, there was but one other passenger, Mr. Parkman of Boston. Capt Howland was accompanied by his wife and child. The officers were intelligent and obliging, and our party, though small, was large enough to be agreeable. We were all well satisfied with the prospect of a cruise among the Indian Isles, and therefore welcomed the Captain's decision.

At sunset, on the 14th, we made land ahead, at a considerable distance. As the passage required careful navigation, on account of its abundant reefs, we stood off and on until the next morning.

Busvagon stretched along, point beyond point, for a distance of forty or fifty miles. The land rose with a long, gentle slope from the beaches of white sand, and in the distance stood the vapory peaks of high mountains. We sailed slowly along the outer edge of the islets, to which the larger island made a warm, rich background. The air was deliciously mild and pure, the sea smooth as glass, and the sky as fair as if it had never been darkened by a storm.

Towards noon the gentle south-east breeze died away; and we lay with motionless sails upon the gleaming sea. The sun hung over the mast-head and poured down a warm tropical langour, which seemed to melt the very marrow in one's bones. For four hours we lay becalmed, when a light ripple stole along from the horizon, and we saw the footsteps of the welcome breeze long before we felt it. Gradually increasing, it bore us smoothly and noiselessly away from Busvagon and the rocky towers and obelisks, and at sunset we saw the phantomlike hills of the southern point of the island of Mindoro, forty miles distant.

Our voyage the next day was still more delightful. From dawn until dark we went slowly loitering past the lovely islands that gem those remote seas, until the last of them sank astern in the flush of sunset.

The next day was most taken up with calms. The captain and mates spent much of their time in shifting the sails so as to get the most of the faint wind-flaws that reached us, watching for distant ripple-lines on the ocean, or whistling over the rail. In the afternoon land was descried ahead—the Cagayanes Islands, a little group in the middle of the Sooloo Sea. We saw great quantities of drift-wood, upon which boobies and cormorants perched in companies of two and three, and watched for fish as they drifted lazily along. In the neighborhood of the islands we frequently saw striped snakes, four or five feet in length.

The lofty coast of Mindanao, one of the largest of the Philippine Islands, was visible at sunrise, on the 19th. Before long Basilan appeared in the south-east, and by noon we were in the mouth of the strait. The observation gave Lat. 7° 3′ N., Long. 121° E. Two vessels were descried ahead, a ship and a brig, both lying close in to Mindanao, and apparently becalmed. In fact, we could easily trace a belt of calm water near the shore, caused by the high hills of the island, which prevented the southern breeze from "blowing home." We had a light westerly wind, with the tide in our favor, and just as the moon arose like a globe of gold, passed the eastern mouth of the strait and entered the Sea of Celebes.

We now experienced a succession of calms and baffling winds for five days, as we stood south by west across the Sea of Celebes, making for the Straits of Macassar. There was an occasional squall of an hour or two, which gave us a "slant" in the right direction. The wind at last shifted, so that we were able to run upon our course close-hauled, and on the afternoon of the 25th we caught a distant and misty view of the Haring Islands. The next morning at sunrise, we saw the lofty headland of Point Kaneoogan, in Borneo, at the western entrance of the straits. Cape Donda, in Celebes, thirty miles distant, appeared for a short time, but was soon hidden by showers.

On the 27th, at noon, we were in 0° 5′ S., having crossed the Equator about 11 A.M., and thenceforth, for four days, we slowly loitered along through the Straits of Macassar, with light, variable winds, and seasons of dead, sultry calm. The mercury stood at 88° in the coolest part of the ship. The sea was as smooth as a mirror, and as glossy and oily in its dark-blue gleam, as if the neighboring shores of Macassar had poured upon it libations of their far-famed unguent. Occasionally we saw the shores of Celebes, but so distant and dim that it was rather like a dream of land than land itself. We walked the deck languidly, morning and evening, sat under the awning by day, alternately dozing and smoking and reading, watched the drift-wood floating by—mangrove logs, with companies of seafowl making their fishing excursions—ate for occupation, and slept with difficulty: and thus the days passed.

On the 2d of October a light south wind reached us, and we left the dim, far-off headlands of Celebes—the land of sandal-wood groves and birds of Paradise. We made the twin rocks called "The Brothers," off the southern point of Borneo, and about noon passed between the islands of Moresses and Little Pulo Laut. The latter are noble piles of verdure, rising a thousand feet from the water, in long undulating outlines. The Java Sea is a beautiful piece of water, comparatively free from reefs and shoals, and rarely exceeding forty fathoms in depth, so that vessels may anchor in any part of it. Its surface is as smooth as a lake, and even when making eight or nine knots, there was scarcely any perceptible motion in the vessel. The temperature was delicious, and the south wind so bland, sweet and elastic, after the sultry, surcharged atmosphere of Macassar Straits, that the change was perceptible in the temper and spirits of all on board.

We had light but favorable winds, and for four days more stood across the Java Sea, averaging about 100 miles a day. The water was alive with snakes and flying-fish. Passing the Lubeck Islands and Carimon Java, we approached so near the Javanese shores that on the evening of the 6th the delicious land-breeze came off to us, bringing an odor of moist earth and vegetable exhalations. We expected to have a glimpse of Batavia, but made considerable northing, so that we lost sight of the low Java coast before morning. At noon we made the Thousand Islands, and as they have been but very imperfectly explored, we were obliged to go completely to the northward of them, instead of taking one of the numerous channels between. They are small and low, but thickly covered with trees, among which the cocoa-palm predominates. I counted thirty-three islands within a sweep of a hundred degrees. The wind being dead ahead, we stood on the northern tack until we made the North Watcher, and then fetched a S. by E. course, the current setting us to windward. The same evening, however, the wind changed, and before I turned into my berth, we were thirty miles off Angier Point, the last gateway intervening between us and the Indian Ocean. We had been twenty-eight days in making the voyage from Whampoa—a distance, as we sailed, of 2,613 miles.

I arose at sunrise on the morning of the 8th of October, in time to see the *Sea Serpent* enter the Straits of Sunda. On our left, five or six miles distant, arose the lofty headland of Point St. Nicholas; in front was the rock called "The Cap," and the island of "'Thwart-the-Way," while the mountains of Sumatra were barely visible far to the west. We were scarcely abreast of the headland when two native *prahus,* or boats, were seen coming off to us, the boatmen laboring at their sweeps with a sharp, quick cry, peculiar to semi-barbarous people. One of the boats was soon alongside, with a cargo of yams, plantains, and fowls, with such fancy articles as shells, monkeys, parroquets and Java sparrows. The captain and crew were Malays, and nearly all spoke English more or less fluently. The former had an account-book, showing his dealings with ships, and a printed register from the Dutch Government, containing notices of the vessels called upon in the straits. We were gratified to find that we had not been beaten, the shortest passage from Whampoa, previous to our own, being thirty days.

The second boat soon arrived, and between the two Capt. Howland managed to procure about fifteen cwt. of yams, with abundant supplies of potatoes, fowls, and paddy. The fruits they brought off were plantains, cocoa-nuts, ripe and green, and a few *mangosteens*, which were then going out of season.

At last, all the fresh stores were shipped, and we ran off before a spanking breeze. Point St. Nicholas, Button Rock, Angier and 'Thwart-the-Way soon disappeared, and the superb conical peak of the island of Crockatoa rose on our lee bow. We saw Prince's island at dusk, on the weather bow, and entered the Indian Ocean before the twilight had wholly faded—having made the passage through the straits under unusually favorable auspices.

At midnight a man who had been shipped by the Consul at Canton, died on board. He was an old sailor, who had fallen ill at Manilla, whence he had been sent to China, and there, by a blind course of drunkenness and harlotry, sealed his own doom. There was no hope of his recovery, for he had himself cut it off. It was a case of deliberate suicide. But he had probably survived all his friends, all associations of home, all manly energy and virtue, all pleasure in even mere animal enjoyment, all hope of any thing better in life, and accepted death with a reckless insensibility which disarmed it of fear. He was buried at noon the next day, Capt. Howland reading the funeral service.

The next morning the change from the island seas of the Indies, to the open ocean, was at once manifest in the dark-blue of the water, the paleness of the sky, the clearness and bracing freshness of the air, the wider stretch of the horizon, and the long, deliberate undulations of the sea, which gave our vessel a motion we had not felt for weeks before. Towards noon the wind abated, leaving us swaying uneasily to and fro, with the sails flapping heavily against the masts.

On Monday evening, the 10th of October, an unusual incident happened to us. The night was clear, and cooler than usual, with a light breeze, not more than three knots at most, and the same heavy swell which we had had for two days previous. I was walking the quarter-deck with Mr. Cornell, the second mate, about a quarter past eleven o'clock, when the ship suddenly stopped, and shook so violently from stem to stern that every timber vibrated. This motion was accompanied by a dull rumbling, or rather humming noise, which seemed to come from under the stern. We were at first completely puzzled and bewildered by this unexpected circumstance, but a moment's reflection convinced us that it proceeded from an earthquake. Capt. Howland and Mr. Contee came on deck just in time to feel a second shock, nearly as violent as the first. Those who were below heard a strong hissing noise at the vessel's side. There did not appear to be any unusual agitation of the water, notwithstanding the vessel was so violently shaken. The length of time which elapsed, from first to last, was about a minute and a half. The breeze fell immediately afterwards, and we had barely steerage way until morning.

There was a dead calm the following night, and at noon the reckoning showed a progress of twenty-eight miles in twenty-four hours. The swell was worse than ever, and the sails seemed to be slowly beating themselves to pieces against the masts.

The afternoon of the 14th was cloudy, with frequent squalls, but about midnight the wind came up out of the south and increased at such a rate, that by daylight we were making twelve knots an hour. The swell was still heavy, the sea covered with sparkling foam-caps, and the sky streaked with flying masses of cloud. The air had a bracing, exhilarating freshness and steadiness, which led us to hope that we had at last caught the long-desired "trades."

Our hopes were entirely fulfilled. My log of the voyage showed the consecutive days' runs of 269, 235, 227, 261, and 247 miles, during which time the ship kept on her course, scarce shifting a sail. The weather was gloriously clear and brilliant, with an elastic and bracing air, and a temperature ranging from 70° to 77°. The sunsets were magnificent; and at night the new Southern constellations united themselves to the superb array of Northern stars, reaching from Taurus to Gemini, and formed one sublime and glittering band across the heavens. On the 21st, the wind abated, and we made but 148 miles, but it freshened the next day, and so held until the 29th, when we achieved 268 miles, passed the latitude of Madagascar, and entered the Mozambique Channel. Here we encountered a heavy cross-sea and head current, but were cheered by the sight of the Cape pigeon and albatross, which wheeled and swooped across our wake, in lines as perfectly rhythmical and harmonious as strains of music.

On the 1st of November, the wind shifted to the south-west, obliging us to run close-hauled. In the evening the sea became very rough, rolling in long, heavy swells, which indicated that we had entered the ocean current setting westward around the Cape. The ship plunged so violently that we came down to double-reefed top-sails, and logged less than five knots. About four o'clock the next morning, while it was yet perfectly dark, the air was so pervaded with a fresh earthy smell, that the Captain tacked and stood off on a south-east course. Daylight showed us the bold, bleak coast of Africa, about five miles distant. We had made the land about fifty miles south of Port Natal.

The next morning, November 3d, found us becalmed off the Eastern headland of Algoa Bay. It was a warm, cloudless third of May in the lower hemisphere. We sounded, and finding fifty-five fathoms, endeavored to turn the calm to account by fishing for cod; but after sending down the line four times and having two hooks bitten off, a breeze came out of the east and began moving us forward too fast for the sport. The east wind nobly befriended us. At noon on the 4th we reached our Southern Ultima Thule (Lat. 35° 17′ S.), and headed westward for the Atlantic, fifty miles from the African coast. Cape Lagulhas, the southern extremity of the Continent, was 97 miles distant. The sky was cloudless, the sun warm, the air deliciously pure, and just cool enough to make walking on the quarter-deck enjoyable. The sea was smooth, and no sign in air or ocean betokened that we were in the vicinity of the dreaded Cape of Storms.

Now, at last, I felt that our prow was turned homewards—that our keel ploughed the Atlantic, and the old far-off Asian world lay behind me. There was a prophecy of America in the very air, and I invoked a threefold benediction on the cold south wind, which filled every inch of our towering piles of canvas, and carried us through the night at twelve knots an hour, dashing the ocean into phosphoric foam.

After making 532 miles in two days, the wind abated, and we dragged along slowly for three days more, through the variable latitudes, before taking the trade-winds again. The albatross and Cape pigeon followed us, past their usual latitudes, until the increase of temperature, in the neighborhood of the Tropics, warned them to return. The trade-wind, which we took on the 10th of November, was rather sluggish, and even with the addition of sky-sails and royal studding-sails, our pace was languid. The sea was unusually calm, and the swells over which we expected to be "rolling down to St. Helena," according to the sailor's ditty, did not make their appearance. No voyaging could be calmer and more agreeable, and our routine of life had come to be so settled and unvarying, that the day slipped by unawares.

On the morning of the 11th we passed the meridian of Greenwich, and began to count western longitude. The only other incident was the sight of a rakish-looking brig, which passed several miles astern. Mr. Contee, who had made a cruise in the African Squadron, at once pronounced her to be a slaver. Her movements betrayed an evident anxiety to avoid us. . . .

For three days after leaving St. Helena we had calm, sluggish weather, but on the 17th took the trade-wind again, and for five days thereafter averaged 200 miles a day. The wind was steady, dead astern, and the sea calm, with very little swell. The sky was overcast, and the atmosphere sultry, with a temperature ranging from 80° to 85°. Flying fish appeared in greater quantities than I ever noticed before. The phosphorescence of the sea was wonderful.

At midnight, on the 24th of November, we crossed the Equator in Long. 30° West., having been fifty-nine days in the Southern Hemisphere. We hoped to have taken the northeast trades soon afterwards, but were tantalized for a week with calms, and light, variable winds, during which we did not average more than 125 miles a day. On the 1st of December, in Lat. 12° N. a large butterfly and two dragon-flies came on board. The nearest land, the coast of Guiana, was more than 900 miles distant. I have never seen it stated that these insects are capable of such long flights.

We had been on board the *Sea Serpent* eighty-one days, and our hopes of spending Christmas at home were rapidly diminishing, when the long-desired trade-wind struck us. On the 2d of December we made 216 miles; on the 3d, 265 miles; and on the 4th, *three hundred* miles, which was our best day's run during the voyage. Our good ship fairly whistled through the water, cutting her way so smoothly that there was scarcely foam enough before her bows to throw a scud over the forecastle, or wake enough behind her stern to tell that she had passed. The beautiful wave-lines of her counter allowed the dead water to close as passively as if the ocean had not been disturbed.

On the morning of December the 11th, in Lat. 32° N. and off the lee of the Bermudas, the wind hauled round to the north-west and blew half a gale for the two following days, during which we ran westward under close-reefed topsails. So it came to pass that on the 14th we were two degrees *west* of New York, and somewhere off Darien, in Georgia. The wind then shifted more to the westward, and by noon on the 16th, we were in the edge of the Gulf Stream, about 75 miles to the southeast of Cape Fear. Three or four vessels bound north, were in sight, apparently driven under the lee of Cape Hatteras, like ourselves, by the violence of the northern gale. In the afternoon, an hermaphrodite brig, which had risen on the weather bow, stood down towards us and we saw a boat put off from her. We suspected at first that the brig might be a relief vessel, but were soon undeceived by the boat coming alongside. A raw, rough fellow, in a flannel shirt and red cap, came over the side, and stated that the brig was a Nova Scotian, bound from Magua to Cape Breton, had been out twenty days, and had but four days' provisions on board. He was on a begging errand, and was successful enough to get a barrel each of flour, bread, pork and beef. The brig had encountered strong northerly and northeasterly winds for the previous eight days. The boat's crew were hale, athletic Nova Scotians and it was refreshing to see such well-knit, sinewy frames, such bold, hearty features, and such ruddiness of warm and healthy blood. As the Bermudas had not suffered us to pass, I hoped that the sailor's couplet would apply both ways, and that Cape Hatteras would let us off easily. On Saturday morning, the 17th, a breeze sprang up from the southeast. Gradually increasing, it hauled to the northward and westward, and by noon we were dashing on our course at the rate of ten knots. The sky was too overcast to obtain an observation, but according to the reckoning we were in Lat. 35° 16′ N. and Long. 75° 17′ W. At 2 P.M. we ran across the inner edge of the Gulf Stream, and came at once upon soundings. The line of junction between the dark-blue water of the Gulf, and the pale-green of the shoals was marked with wonderful distinctness. The stern of our vessel was in the former, while the latter reached to her waist. Within the distance of a ship's length, the temperature of the sea changed from 72° to 62°. The water immediately became of a paler green, and we felt an ugly ground swell. At the same instant Mr. Cornell discerned land off the port beam, and a single glance sufficed to show that it was Cape Hatteras, which, according to our reckoning, should have been weathered two hours before. The current of the Gulf Stream had evidently been much retarded by the strong northeastern gales.

It blew hard during the night, and there was a very heavy sea in the stream, but on soundings the water was smoother. We ran the whole night with no other sail than close-reefed fore and main topsails, and reefed foresail. In the morning the sky was clear and cold, and the air for the first time biting and wintry, rendering our heaviest clothing necessary to support the sudden change from the Tropics. The wind gradually veered to W.N.W., but by noon we were off Cape Henlopen. We ran close-hauled all day, striving to get to windward in order to make Sandy Hook the next morning, but found ourselves at sunrise about 40 miles to the eastward of it. The transition to a winter climate was like a cold plunge bath. The thermometer sank to 25°, and water froze on deck. At noon a pilot-boat hove in sight, running down towards us. The ship was put about, in order to meet her, but this movement gradually brought a bark, which was to windward of us, between us and the boat, and as the latter hoisted signal, the boat was obliged to give her the only pilot aboard.

We had a tedious night, of alternate calms and snow-squalls, and I slept very little, out of anxiety lest a stiff nor'wester should spring up and blow us out to sea again. But by morning we had a pilot aboard, and taking advantage of a shift of the wind, made a tack which brought us in sight of Sandy Hook and of two steam-tugs. At ten o'clock the *Leviathan* had grappled us; the useless sails were furled, and we sped surely and swiftly in the clear winter sunshine, up the outer bay, through the Narrows and into the noble harbor of New York. The hills of Staten Island glittered with snow; the trees had long been bare and the grass dead; and for the first time in nearly three years, I looked upon a winter landscape. It was the 20th of December, and 101 days since our departure from Whampoa. We rapidly approached the familiar and beloved city, and at 2 P.M. I landed on one of the East River piers.

SEA WITCH

CLIPPER ship, built in 1846, at New York; 170: 3 x 33: 11 x 19; 907 53/95 tons, old measurement; capacity for cargo, 1100 tons. She was built to the order of Howland & Aspinwall of New York, who had been greatly pleased with the performances of their earlier clipper *Rainbow*, both ships being modeled by John W. Griffith and built by Smith & Dimon. While of sharp model she was not in the class of the extreme clippers brought out a few years later to take care of the California trade. Her figurehead was a Chinese dragon with open mouth and partly coiled tail, ending in a dart. She was a handsome ship, rakish and heavily sparred; her mainmast was 83 2/12 feet long and 33 inches in diameter at the heel. Her owners, important merchants and particularly prominent in trade with Mexico, the west coast of South America and China, gave the command to Capt. Robert H. Waterman who had been in their ship *Natchez*, a former New Orleans packet. In this ship, which had no reputation for speed, Captain Waterman had made the run from Canton to New York, in 1843, in 92 days, and two years later he eclipsed all records from China by doing the 13,955 miles from off Macao to the Barnegat pilot, in 78 days and 6 hours. On this remarkable passage his best day was only 276 miles, but he had good winds throughout and did not have to tack once. Was but 17½ days from the equator to pilot. In the *Sea Witch*, Captain Waterman made three voyages, after which he took the steamer *Northerner* out to San Francisco for the Pacific Mail Company and then retired. He was, however, later persuaded to take command of the clipper ship *Challenge*, on her maiden run to San Francisco. The captain was an exceptionally skilful seaman and a great "driver."

On her maiden voyage, the *Sea Witch* sailed from New York, Dec. 23, 1846, and was 104 days to Hong Kong; returning, she reached New York, July 25, 1847, in 82 days from Whampoa and 62 from Anjer. On her second voyage she arrived at Hong Kong, Nov. 17, 1847, in 105 days from New York; left Whampoa, Dec.

29th; passed Anjer, Jan. 8th; best day, 284 miles; passed the Cape, Feb. 3rd, 36½ days out; best day from Anjer, 289 miles; crossed the equator 55 days out; from 5° South, 32° West, to 21° 30′ North, 60° 30′ West, made 2200 miles in eight days, averaging 275 miles; arrived at New York, Mar. 15, 1848, in 77 days and odd hours, from Whampoa, the fastest run on record to the present time. On her third voyage she was 69 days from New York to Valparaiso, sailing by observation 10,568 miles, an average of 6 2/5 knots per hour. Went up the coast to Callao and was 52 days thence to Hong Kong, sailing 10,417 miles, a rate of 8⅜ knots throughout. Arrived at New York, Mar. 25, 1849, 79 days from Whampoa, sailing 14,255 miles, an average of 7½ knots. Her best consecutive ten day's run was 2664 miles, averaging 11 1/10 knots per hour. Her best day on either of these three passages was 358 miles.

On her fourth voyage she was 118 sailing days from New York to Hong Kong, via Valparaiso and Callao. Her former mate, George W. Fraser, a Scotchman and also a great driver, was in command. On the return she reached New York, Mar. 7, 1850, in 85 days from Whampoa and 73 from Anjer. She then loaded for San Francisco and sailed Apr. 14th; arrived out July 25th, in 101 days' passage less four days in port at Valparaiso, or 97 sailing days. From San Francisco she crossed to Hong Kong in 46 days; sailed from Whampoa, Mar. 15, 1851, and reached New York in 102 days and 83 days from Anjer. On her sixth voyage she left New York, Aug. 1, 1851, and was at San Francisco, Nov. 20th, in 111 days' passage. She was in a race with the *Raven*, 630 tons, and the *Typhoon*, 1611 tons, whose time was 106 and 108 days respectively. In continuation of their voyages, both the *Raven* and the *Sea Witch* crossed from San Francisco to Hong Kong and from Whampoa went to New York. In both of these instances the *Raven* had the best of it by three days. From Whampoa home their runs were 107 and 110 days respectively, they having left China in the unfavorable season.

On her seventh voyage the *Sea Witch* left New York, Aug. 22, 1852, and arrived at San Francisco, Dec. 9th, in 109 days' passage.

Was 30 days to the line; 53 days to 50° South; 18 days rounding the Horn; 92 days to the equator and only 17 days thence to port. Then went to Shanghai in 41 days; left Woosung, Mar. 11, 1853; was 57 days to the Cape and arrived at New York, 106 days out and 87 days from Anjer. Sailed from New York, Aug. 9, 1853; was 31 days to the line; off the Cape of Good Hope the foremast was struck by lightning, the royal and topgallant being shivered and much iron-work broken. On Nov. 6th, she touched at Ampanam, Island of Lomboc; was 12 days getting through the Straits of Macassar; arrived at Hong Kong, Dec. 9th, in 122 days' passage, the slowest run she ever made. Captain Fraser, however, reported experiencing light winds and calms nearly all the way. From China she crossed to the west coast of South America and loaded at Coquimbo; on June 25, 1854, put into Valparaiso in a leaky condition and it was believed that some one had bored holes in her bottom. Repaired and sailed and arrived at New York in January 1855, 64 days from Valparaiso.

On her ninth voyage, which was destined not to be completed, she left New York, Apr. 5, 1855, and put into Rio with the body of Captain Fraser who had been murdered by his mate. Captain Lang was put in command and completed the passage to Hong Kong. Sailed from Amoy, Dec. 1, 1855, with 500 coolies for Havana and passed Anjer, Jan. 7, 1856. On Mar. 28th, when 118 days out, she struck on a reef about 12 miles from Havana, bilged and became a total loss. Was insured for $40,000.

SHOOTING STAR

EXTREME clipper ship, built by James O. Curtis, at Medford, Mass., and was the first real clipper to be built there. Launched Feb. 8, 1851, for Reed, Wade & Co., of Boston, after plans designed by Capt. John Wade. Keel, 154; deck, 164, and length over all, 171; beam, 35; depth of hold, 18:6. Tonnage, 903, old measurement. She had 24 inches dead rise and her long, sharp bow was ornamented with a female figure clothed in white garments, the waist encircled by a girdle of stars. She proved to be one of the fastest of the small clippers.

On her maiden voyage she sailed from Boston, Mar. 22, 1851, under command of Capt. Judah P. Baker and was 25 days to the line. In the South Atlantic she was partially dismasted and put into Rio. Was 90 days thence to San Francisco, being 124 sailing days from Boston. On her second outward voyage she was 105 days to San Francisco from Boston. In six working days, discharged her cargo and had all accounts and freight money settled and forwarded to her owners. In 1853 and in 1855 she made passages from New York to San Francisco in 123 and 116 days respectively. On the last mentioned trip she experienced strong southwest gales off the Platte which forced her to the eastward of the Falkland Islands, from which she was 20 days to latitude 50° in the Pacific; crossed the equator 92 days out. She made two passages from New York to Hong Kong, going out in 110 days in 1854 and in 98 days in 1856. These six passages constitute her outward runs from Eastern ports.

Of her homeward passages, the first was her fastest from China and was also the most notable run in her career. Leaving Whampoa in the full strength of the northeast monsoon, she made the run from Macao to Boston in 86 days. She made two other passages from China: in 1852, Woosung to New York in 106 days; in 1854, Whampoa to New York in 106 days, the first being in the poor season. Her two other return passages were from Honolulu, the first being in 1853 in 89 days to New London. On the second she put into Pernambuco when 87 days out, short of provisions. After sailing, she struck some rocks about 40 miles to the northward and had to lighter part of her cargo; got off slightly hogged and returned to Pernambuco; arrived at New York, Mar. 22, 1856. Sailed from New York, May 24th and was 98 days to Hong Kong. She then engaged in trade on the Asiatic coast and on one trip, being considerably damaged by a typhoon, she put into Singapore for repairs. Captain Du Bois paid off his crew and the ship was sold to a merchant of Bangkok the reported price being $40,000. She then went under the Siamese flag, continuing on the coast. In 1867 she was reported wrecked on the coast of Formosa.

The fastest round voyage made by the *Shooting Star* was her second. Leaving Boston, May 3, 1852, she was back at New York, Feb. 27, 1853, having circumnavigated the globe in 9 months and 24 days. Details of this run were: Boston to San Francisco, 105 days; thence to Hong Kong, 41 days; thence to Shanghai, 12 days; and thence to New York, 106 days. Total days at sea, 264; stays in ports, 36. On her passage out to San Francisco in 1855, Captain Kingman reported her best day's run as 305 miles, in the South Atlantic.

In 1859, Reed, Wade & Co., had a second *Shooting Star* built, a medium clipper of 947 tons. On Oct. 31, 1864, this ship, while on a voyage from New York to Panama, was captured and burned by the Confederate privateer *Chickamauga*. In 1867, the extreme clipper ship *Ino*, built at New York in 1851, was sold and renamed *Shooting Star*, subsequently being re-rigged as a bark.

SIERRA NEVADA

CLIPPER ship, launched from the yard of Tobey & Little-field, at Portsmouth, N. H., May 29, 1854, for Glidden & Williams of Boston, and was the largest ship that had been built on the Piscataqua River up to that time. Her construction was superintended by Captain Penhallow, who was her commander for the first four years. Deck, 222: 2; over all, 230; beam, 44: 4; depth of hold, 26: 4; draft, 23 feet. Three laid decks; dead rise, 20 inches; rounding of sides, 12 inches; sheer, 4½ feet. Old measurement tonnage, 1942; British, 1616; on one occasion she carried from New York to San Francisco 800 tons of heavy and 2600 tons of measurement cargo. Her ends were long and sharp, the lines being slightly concave up to light load line. Her nearly upright stem carried as a figurehead an Indian warrior. The oval stern was ornamented with an eagle on the wing, bearing in its beak a scroll on which were the ship's name and hailing port. She had a spacious cabin built into a half poop deck for officers and passengers which was furnished with every convenience of the day. She had very square yards but no flying kites, crossing nothing above royals. The main yard was 89 feet long; lower maintopsail yard, 77 feet; upper, 70 feet; topgallant yard, 53 feet and royal, 42 feet. The yards on the fore were but slightly smaller: mainmast, 91 feet long; topmast, 52; topgallant, 28; and royal, 18 feet. Bowsprit, 20 feet outboard; jibboom, 41 feet long; spanker boom, 58, and gaff 46 feet. She was easy in motion, stiff, and an excellent carrier of sail and when employed as an Australian passenger packet was a popular ship. On a passage from London to Rockhampton, in 1870, she had 497 passengers in cabins and steerage.

On her first voyage the *Sierra Nevada* left Boston, July 9, 1854, and was 97 days to Callao; loaded at the Chincha Islands and arrived at Hampton Roads, Mar. 16, 1855, being ordered thence to Liverpool, which port she reached Apr. 12th. On the passage she collided with the *Jane Leach*, losing her figurehead and bowsprit. On attempting to enter Wellington Dock at Liverpool, she grounded on the sill and was not floated for a week. Her back was broken and the dock owners denying responsibility, suit was brought by her owners who won on every point after years of litigation during which the defendants had appealed twice. The ship was sold, after her injury, for £9000 and was repaired and sailed from Liverpool, Nov. 25, 1855, reaching New York in 25 days. From the Lizard to the Grand Bank she was six days.

On her second voyage the *Sierra Nevada* reached San Francisco, July 15, 1856, Captain Penhallow reporting 128 days from New York. Was off the Horn 21 days during which lost foretopgallant mast and jibboom and had cutwater and headgear carried away. From San Francisco went to Callao in 53 days and thence to Hampton Roads in 69 days. The third voyage was 140 days from Boston to San Francisco; had no trades whatever; was becalmed ten days in the North Pacific and was off the Golden Gate three days; best day's run, 270 miles. Homeward bound, loaded guano at Elide Island, Lower California, and was 95 days thence to New York. Captain Blaney now assumed command and had a passage of 105 days from New York to Melbourne, arriving Nov. 20, 1858; thence 53 days to Hong Kong; thence in ballast to New York in something under 100 days; 79 days from Anjer. Capt. James G. Foster took command and had the remarkably fast runs of 97 days from Boston to San Francisco and 98 days on the return trip to New York. The peculiar feature of the fast outward passage was that it was entirely due to the time made in the North Atlantic and the North Pacific: 17 days and 16 hours from Sandy Hook to the line and 15 days from the equator in Pacific to destination. The rather long interim between the two equatorial crossings, 64 days, was due to very light winds in the South Pacific and detention off Cape Horn. In strong gales off the Cape, the chain bobstays parted and for ten days the jibboom was in jeopardy, not permitting any head sail to be carried. Captain Foster and the carpenter got under the bows but after several days of ineffectual effort to shackle the chain while they were being plunged out of sight intermittently, it was found necessary to run the ship into smooth water, near the land, before repairs could be made.

In 1861, Captain Foster reported his passage from New York to San Francisco as 114 days and the return to New York as 101 days. On the homeward run very light winds were encountered throughout, the royals not being clewed up during the final 50 days. The following voyage was made under command of Captain Horton and was the last made by the *Nevada* as an American ship. She arrived at San Francisco, Mar. 25, 1862, in 105 days from New York; went to Callao in 52 days and from there to London, with guano, in 80 days, arriving out Dec. 31st. While in port at San Francisco she had two mishaps, the first being nearly her end. While beating out through the Golden Gate, in ballast, for Callao, on Apr. 29th, she missed stays and went ashore on Fort Point. A dense fog prevailed but the revenue cutter *Shubrick* was able to get lines aboard and pull her off. She was put in dock at Mare Island Navy Yard and repairs cost $22,000. When again ready for sea and at anchor in the stream, she dragged on to the clipper ship *Phantom* and suffered damage amounting to $3000 to spars and rigging.

In March 1863, the *Sierra Nevada* was sold at London, to Mackay & Baines, for £10,750, becoming the British ship *Royal Dane*, of Liverpool, and being operated between that port and Australia by the "Black Ball Line." Some years later she was sold to J. P. Foulkes and hailed from London. In 1875 she was registered as owned by John Harris, hailing port still London. She was wrecked on the coast of Chile, in 1877, while on a voyage from Callao for Liverpool, with guano.

SILVER STAR

BUILT by J. O. Curtis, at Medford, Mass., in 1856; 1195 tons. Reed & Wade and later S. G. Reed & Co., of Boston, owners. Wrecked at Jarvis Island, Nov. 10, 1860, while loading guano.

SIMOON

EXTREME clipper ship, launched from the yards of Jabez Williams, at Williamsburg, L. I., Dec. 4, 1852, for Benjamin A. Mumford & Co., of New York; 205: 7 x 38: 8 x 22: 6; 1436 tons. She was to have been named *Sirocco*, but finding that name had been used on a Baltimore clipper, *Simoon* was substituted. She was of a very sharp model and proved to be a fast sailer.

She sailed from New York, Jan. 20, 1853, under Capt. Martin Smith and had a passage of 132 days to San Francisco, with adverse conditions prevailing throughout. On the third and fourth days out, near the Bermudas, carried away maintopgallant mast, swinging booms, etc., in heavy gales; fell to leeward of St. Roque and had only seven days of fair winds up to crossing the equator in the Pacific, 105 days out. The following from the log shows Captain

Smith's experiences in extricating his ship from a difficult "jam" near St. Roque:

"Feb. 18th; 1° 15' S.; 35° 03' W.; fresh and squally, ends light; crossed the line 29 days out, during 26 days of which had constant head winds. 19th; 0° 11' S.; 34° 07' W.; moderate winds. 20th; 3° 31' S.; 35° 48' W.; fresh, going 10½ to 11½ knots during night; yards very sharp up; are 70 miles from land. 21st; 4° 50'; 36° 15'; fresh winds; to leeward of Point Tairo and close to breakers there; tacked to north. 22nd; 3° 38'; 35° 48'; fresh; working ahead slowly along the land. 23rd; 3° 05'; 34° 36'; fresh; working to east. 24th; 2° 07'; 33° 31'; moderate—light—squally. 25th; 5° 11'; 34° 39'; moderate and pleasant; weathered St. Roque after four days hard beating. 26th; 6° 40'; 34° 29'; fresh and pleasant. 27th; 7° 06'; 34° 27'; light winds; first time in 35 days we've had a fair wind; made 350 miles on our course in the past nine days."

From St. Roque to 50° South she was 29 days, thence 17 days to 50° in the Pacific; thence 26 days to port.

The *Simoon* went from San Francisco to Callao in 46 days, taking the Eastern passage, crossing the equator in 84° West; the *Adelaide*, over the same course at about the same time, was 61 days. The *Simoon* also beat other clippers taking the Western route, the most traveled one. Sailed from Callao, Nov. 28th; passed Cape Horn, Dec. 18th; off the Falklands, took northeast winds which continued through the limits of the southeast trades; experienced a pampero which lasted one day; had three heavy gales after passing the Bermudas; arrived at New York, Feb. 10, 1854, in 74 days from Callao. Her second voyage was to Melbourne; thence to Peru for guano and arrived at New York, Feb. 5, 1855, in 65 days from Callao. Sailed from New York, Mar. 25th, and was 18 days to London; thence went to the Mediterranean and made a voyage to the Crimea as a French transport. Left Marseilles, Oct. 29th, and Gibraltar, Nov. 6th; arrived at Akyab, Feb. 8, 1856. After returning home she engaged in general trade, her maiden voyage being the only one she made to California.

In 1857 she left Callao, July 20th, and was 85 days to Antwerp. Sailed from New Orleans, June 5, 1858, and went to Liverpool in 35 days. Sailed from Liverpool, Oct. 13th, and arrived at Bombay, Jan. 21, 1859, in 100 days' passage. Thence to Liverpool in 101 days. Then went out to China and arrived at Valparaiso, Nov. 17, 1860, from Hong Kong. On Mar. 20, 1861, being inward bound to Baltimore from the West Coast, she struck a shoal in 24 feet of water, 18 miles south of Cape Henry, but three seas carried her over into deep water and no material damage resulted. On Jan. 3, 1862, Captain Langley in command, she arrived at Port Chalmers, N. Z., in 72 days from Glasgow and the "Otago Daily News," of the fourth had the following:—

"The clipper ship *Simoon* of New York, arrived at Port Chalmers early yesterday morning after an excellent passage of only 72 days from Glasgow. This is by far the quickest passage ever made to the Province and we trust, before the ship leaves, some public ovation will be paid the captain in recognition of his having shown how much the duration of the voyage between the Mother Country and Otago can be lessened. On entering port the *Simoon* fired a salute of 21 guns."

The "Sydney Empire," in commenting on the unprecedented fast passage, said that she was very fortunate with her shipment of 1000 prime Leicester sheep, losing less than five per cent on the voyage. Continuing her voyage the *Simoon* left Port Chalmers, Jan. 26th, and arrived at Valparaiso, Feb. 16th, another record passage of under 21 days. She returned to England from Caldera.

In October 1862, she left Liverpool for Aden and Ceylon and ports in India, Captain Smith in command. In October 1863, shortly after her return to Liverpool, she was sold to Lamport & Holt and for a time continued in trade with India, under the British flag, without change of name. About 1874 she was sold to Norwegian parties, who changed her name to *Hovding*, and as such, bark rigged in later years, she appears in registers as late as 1912. Her hailing ports at different times were Moss, Drobak and Christiania. Under foreign rules of measurement her registered tonnage was 1123, this reduction of 22 per cent from her American register being evidence of her very sharp model.

SIROCCO

CLIPPER ship, built in 1852, at Baltimore, by William & George Gardner; owned by Damon & Hancock of Philadelphia; 189 x 37 x 22:6; 1130 tons, old measurement. Registers describe her as being of sharp model. Most of her operations are said to have been in the Atlantic Ocean.

The *Sirocco* arrived at San Francisco, July 10, 1853, under command of Captain Sanford, in 139 days from New York. She was off Cape Horn for 22 days, receiving considerable damage in heavy gales. Had light winds in the Pacific and was 30 days from the equator to port. Then had a passage of 60 days to Callao, being 26 days to the line and 39 days to latitude 34° South. Arrived at Philadelphia, Mar. 13, 1854, from Callao.

In 1855 she loaded at Philadelphia for San Francisco and arrived out Nov. 23rd, in 125 days' passage. Captain West, then in command, reported that after having a good run of 20½ days to the line, he had to beat around Cape St. Roque which was not cleared until the 27th day; then, with unfavorable weather in the South Atlantic and having 24 days of heavy gales off the Cape, he was not up to 50° South in the Pacific until 80 days out. However, she then retrieved herself having from that point but 19 days to the line and 20 days later, or 39 days from 50° South, being within 200 miles of the Golden Gate,—very fast time for any season but particularly so for that time of the year. She then went to Hong Kong in 53 days and returned to San Francisco in 54 days, arriving June 27, 1856; was 11 days in the China Seas and had generally light winds throughout the whole run. This voyage was completed by her return East via Valparaiso.

Several years later the *Sirocco* was sold to go under the British flag without change of name and in 1862 she appears as hailing from Liverpool and owned by W. Rome & Co. She was reported as being lost at sea in 1873.

SKYLARK

EXTREME clipper ship, launched Aug. 4, 1853, at Somerset, Mass., from the yards of James M. Hood, for account of Crocker & Warren of New York, owners of the *Raven* and *Archer*, productions of the same builder; 193 x 36 x 22; 1209 tons, old measurement. Both in model and build she was a first-class ship and delivered her cargoes in fine order. On her sixth and last passage out to San Francisco, which was in 1864 and 138 days from New York, it was specially noted that all packages were bright and new and that no rust appeared on the iron castings stowed in lower hold. She had the name of being a fast sailer and frequently logged 15 knots under royals and topmast stu'nsails.

The *Skylark* made six passages from New York to San Francisco, as follows: 117, 146, 116, 142, 145 and 138 days. The memoranda of the different runs show a record of light or contrary winds in each instance. On the first passage, arriving at San Francisco, Jan. 15, 1854, in 117 days from New York, she had, aside from 15 days of heavy gales off Cape Horn during which she lost the head, cutwater, etc., nothing but light breezes and 28 days were practically calms. She made three passages from New York to China of which two were to Hong Kong in 91 days each and one to Amoy in 127 days.

Of her homeward passages, one was from San Francisco to New York in 1861 in 93 days, with light winds throughout; never reefed topsails. In 1854 she was 102 days from Calcutta to New York and in 1856, 134 days from Calcutta to Boston. From Shanghai she had two trips to New York; 123 days in 1857 and 106 days in 1860. In 1855 she went from China to Havana, arriving July 24th and reporting 88 days from Anjer. From Havana was 11 days to New York. Sailed from Manila, Dec. 10, 1862, passed Anjer the 29th and arrived at St. Helena, Mar. 6, 1863, and sailed the next day. Arrived at Liverpool, Apr. 25th, in 136 days from Manila. Discharged and loaded and reached New York, July 13th, 39 days from Liverpool.

Sailed from San Francisco, Sept. 1, 1858, in company with the *Raduga* and the *Elizabeth F. Willets,* all crossing the bar within a half hour of each other. At 2 P.M. of the 16th, the *Willets* rounded Diamond Head, being followed one hour later by *Skylark.* At 4 o'clock the *Raduga* appeared and at 5 o'clock the *West Wind,* which had left San Francisco two days after the others, also showed up. According to advices from Honolulu, the scene was one of the prettiest in the marine line ever witnessed there. The *Skylark* then loaded with whale oil and bone and arrived at New Bedford, Mar. 9, 1859, in 104 days from Honolulu. The *Skylark,* Captain Bursley in command, arrived at New York, July 11, 1861, from San Francisco, Francis Weeks, her second officer, having died on the passage.

On her last passage as an American ship, the *Skylark* left San Francisco, Mar. 22, 1864, for Baker's Island, to load guano for Falmouth, for orders. After arrival at the Island she had to slip moorings and put to sea on five occasions on account of shifting winds causing swell sufficient to endanger the safety of the ship. However, she was eventually loaded and made the passage to Europe. In 1864, the *Skylark* is registered as owned by H. P. Sturgis, hailing port, New York. In 1866 her owner is given as Chandler Robins and hailing port, Hamburg. In both years Captain Bursley in command. About this time she was sold to A. J. Schon of Hamburg, and was renamed *Albertine.*

Capt. William W. Henry, formerly of the *Raven,* was the first commander of the *Skylark;* on the second and third voyages Captain Dow was in charge; from 1857 to 1860, Capt. B. A. Follansbee was master, being succeeded by Capt. Francis Bursley.

SNOW SQUALL

EXTREME clipper ship, built in 1851, by Alfred Butler, at
Cape Elizabeth, Me. A small, very sharp ship with fine lines,
her actual carrying capacity being but 800 tons, against her register
of 742. She is said to have cost $30,410 and to have been purchased,
when just off the stocks, by Charles R. Green of New York, he being her owner during her whole career. Although at the outset her
record for speed was disappointing, she later demonstrated ability
to hold her own with much larger clippers and ranked among the
fastest of the fleet.

The *Snow Squall* was engaged in trade principally between New
York and the Far East. She made only three passages around Cape
Horn to the westward, all in the face of more or less difficulties or
mishaps. On the fourth, which was in 1864, she met her fate. Her
maiden voyage, in 1852, was from Boston to Honolulu in 135
days with adverse wind and weather conditions throughout. She then
crossed to China and went to New York from Shanghai in 97 days.
On Aug. 2, 1853, she reached San Francisco after a passage of 155
days from New York, in very severe weather. Was off the pitch of
the Cape when 62 days out, after which had 25 days of very heavy
gales and was driven backward and as far south as latitude 60°.
Had all the iron work of the bowsprit carried away, lost the steering
apparatus, started channels and received other damage. Was 40 days
from the equator crossing to San Francisco, being inside of Point
Reyes in a dense fog for four days. She then crossed to Shanghai in
46 days and was 110 days thence to London. Her next outward run
to San Francisco, arriving Jan. 30, 1857, was in 206 days from New
York, via Montevideo, 65 days. Had left New York, July 5, 1856,
and crossed the line 33 days out. On Sept. 5th, in 46° South, 60°
West, in a sudden squall lost all three topmasts with everything
attached. Bore up for Montevideo where repairs occupied 49 days.
When ready for sea a sudden pampero carried the Spanish brig
Cairo across her bows, taking out her jibboom, bringing down the

foretopgallant mast which twisted the mainmast-head and did other damage, all requiring a further delay of 21 days for repairs. From the Pacific equator crossing to San Francisco she was 22 days but covered all of the distance except the final 300 miles in 15 days. She then had a good run to Manila,—42 days from the Golden Gate. Was thence 111 days to New York, having taken her departure during the season of unfavorable monsoons. In 1856 she was 28 days from New York to Rio. Remained in port 17 days and returned to New York in 34 days.

Aside from the voyages quoted, the *Snow Squall's* outward passages were from New York (except one from Boston, in 1858) to China or Singapore, either direct or via Australia. A résumé of these passages shows the following as noteworthy, some, indeed, being very close to record. In 1854-1855: New York to Sydney, 85 days; Anjer to New York, 78 days. In 1859 and in 1860: Shanghai to New York, 91 and 92 days respectively. In 1861: Amoy to New York, 82 days; 70 days from Anjer and 38 from the Cape of Good Hope. In 1861-1862: New York to Melbourne, 82 days—81 days from pilot to pilot—the fastest passage over that route for three years; beat the *Jack Frost* from New York, 25 days, and the *Dirigo*, from Boston, 14 days. Went from Melbourne to Singapore in 30 days; thence to Penang and from there was 100 days to New York, arriving Sept. 5, 1862. She was off the Cape, July 7th, and in that vicinity for nine days, in company with a fleet of over 20 ships, in very violent westerly gales with a high, irregular sea, the ship laboring heavily. Was 36 days from St. Helena, 22 days from the line and three days between the Delaware Capes and Sandy Hook. She then went out from New York to Melbourne in 75 days, arriving Feb. 15, 1863; went to Singapore in 35 days; loaded part cargo; thence to Penang and completed lading. Arrived at New York, Sept. 15, 1863, in 94 days from Penang. On this passage she narrowly escaped capture by the Confederate privateer *Tuscaloosa*, the following particulars being from Captain Dillingham's account.

"For six months we had received no news relating to the operations of the privateers and did not know that a sailing vessel was used for that purpose. After a very quick and pleasant passage to the Cape of Good Hope, one noon a sail was seen by the man at the wheel, low down on the horizon, looking just a speck; but she was watched, of course, with interest by all on board. She gradually approached and thinking she needed assistance in some way, the American flag was hoisted on the *Snow Squall*. At once the stars and stripes were flying on the stranger. After a while it was discovered that the newcomer had portholes in her side. Coming to windward of us, she took the wind from our sails, being so near that speaking trumpets were not required in order to converse. The stranger asked, 'What ship is that?' to which the reply was given, 'The *Snow Squall*, from Penang for New York. What ship is that?' 'You heave to and I'll send some one on board to tell you,' the stranger replied and in an instant open flew his portholes and the after gun was fired at us, the stars and stripes were hauled down and the Confederate flag hoisted in its place.

"Presumably visions of their good luck filled the minds of the officers of the *Tuscaloosa*, for such she proved to be, but they were to be disappointed. 'Aye, Aye,' was the reply of the *Snow Squall*, as if she was going to comply with the request or order, and through the apparent small commotion on board the clipper, the would-be captors probably thought that soon they would be on her decks. In the meantime the *Snow Squall* had moved a little ahead and got a portion of the breeze in her sails. When the *Tuscaloosa* people saw this they fired another gun but as the sea was a rolling one, the guns did no damage and were doubtless fired to intimidate. We were not, however, so easily frightened and knew that our clipper could beat almost anything in sailing close to the wind. The chase began and lasted until four o'clock in the afternoon when the *Tuscaloosa* fired a broadside and gave up."

Captain Dillingham remained on deck all night to watch the steering of his ship and to look out for the approach of another privateer, should one come that way, and he used to say that he was not looking for any other vessels all the way to New York. A plucky man and a fine, sharp sailing vessel saved the *Snow Squall* and its valuable cargo. Captain Dillingham was awarded by underwriters a purse of $1375.14 "as a token of their appreciation of his prompt action by which he saved his ship and cargo from capture."

The *Snow Squall* sailed from New York, Jan. 2, 1864, for San Francisco. In the Straits of Le Maire she got ashore and on Mar. 1st, put into Port Stanley leaking badly. Her cargo was discharged and ultimately reached destination in the British bark *Orsini*. It being found impossible to make the necessary repairs at a moderate cost, the *Snow Squall* was condemned in July 1864 and was sold. Insurance companies took a loss of $65,000. Captain Dillingham reached Rio and took passage on the bark *Mondamin* for Baltimore; but his former escape from capture by privateers was not to be repeated, for the *Mondamin* fell into the hands of the *Florida*, in September, and was burned.

The captains who were in command of the *Snow Squall* were, Bursley, Girard, Lloyd and James S. Dillingham, Jr.

SOUTHERN CROSS

MEDIUM clipper ship, launched from the yard of E. & H. O. Briggs, at East Boston, Mass., Mar. 19, 1851, for Baker & Morrill of Boston. Keel, 164; deck, 170 x 36 x 21; 938 tons, old measurement. Dead rise, 20 inches; rounding of sides, six inches; sheer, 21 inches. Length of mainmast, 78 feet; maintopmast, 43; topgallant, royal and skysail masts, 50 feet, including pole. Main yard, 72 feet; topsail yard, 57; topgallant, 41; royal, 30; skysail yard, 19. Bowsprit, 27 feet outboard; jibboom and flying-jibboom, 28 feet. A gilded eagle on the wing was her figurehead. Her model was described as being a fair medium between that of the extremely sharp clippers then coming into vogue and the New York packet type, she being put in the class of such ships as the *Oriental, Samuel Russell* and *Sea Witch*. Authorities predicted that her maiden passage, which was to be from Boston to San Francisco, would be made in 110 days or under, but, as will appear, she was unfortunate in being twice partially dismasted on the run. As a matter of fact she never fully realized the anticipations of owners or builders as to speed and out of her ten passages from Boston or New York to San Francisco, her two fastest are 119 days in 1854-1855 and 120 days in 1855-1856. On this route her fastest time from port of departure to the line was 28 days, in 1862; to the Straits of Le Maire, 61 days, in 1859; rounding the Horn, 12 days, in 1856; from 50° South, Pacific, to the equator, 20 days, in 1859; to the Pacific equator crossing, 96 days, in 1856.

On her maiden passage she left Boston, May 8, 1851, and seven days later lost all three topgallant masts in a squall. Off the Platte, in a pampero of 45 hours' duration, she met with a similar mishap so that she was without topgallant sails nearly all the way from Boston until getting into the Pacific. On arrival at San Francisco, Sept. 22nd, in 136 days from Boston, Captain Stevens reported having encountered almost constant light or head winds; was becalmed ten days at one time; best day's work, 267 miles only. She sailed from San Francisco, Oct. 24th, and arrived at Singapore, Dec. 11th, which, less 3½ days in port at Honolulu, gives 43 days as actual sailing time,—an excellent run. She was at Calcutta in 56 sailing days from San Francisco and was thence 97 days to Boston, arriving May 21, 1852.

On her second voyage, the *Southern Cross* left Boston, June 25, 1852, and on Aug. 16th, the cargo in the lower hold was found to be on fire. A course was laid for Montevideo where she arrived 15 days later, her escape from complete destruction being by a very close margin. She arrived at San Francisco, Nov. 28th, in 75 days from Montevideo. From San Francisco she was 53 days to Manila and 105 days thence to New York, arriving June 3, 1853. Sailed from New York, Aug. 17th, and arrived at San Francisco, Jan. 11, 1854, a passage of 146 days with light winds predominating practically all the way. From San Francisco she went to Singapore in 56 days; thence 16 days to Calcutta; thence 119 days to Boston, arriving Sept. 17, 1854. Then went back to San Francisco, arriving Feb. 22, 1855, in 119 days from Boston. On Jan. 2nd, off Cape Horn, was in company with the *Phantom* and led her to their common destination one day. Continuing her voyage, the *Southern Cross* was 57 days to Manila and 116 days thence to Boston, arriving Oct. 13, 1855. Sailed from Boston, Nov. 8th, and arrived at San Francisco, Mar. 8, 1856, a 120 days' passage. Went to Batavia in 72 days; thence to Calcutta and from that port was 124 days to Boston, arriving Dec. 15, 1856.

On her sixth voyage the *Southern Cross* arrived at San Francisco, June 22, 1857, in 138 days from Boston. Then went to Batavia in 80 days; sailed thence Oct. 28th; passed Anjer, Nov. 1st and arrived at Boston, 78 days from Batavia. Arrived at San Francisco, July 4, 1858, in 140 days from Boston, to which port she returned via Calcutta. Arrived at San Francisco, Oct. 22, 1859, in 134 days from Boston. Captain Howes reported witnessing the Aurora Australis, one night off the Horn, there being a tremendous sea on and squalls of snow and hail, the spectacle being truly magnificent. From San Francisco the *Southern Cross* went to Hong Kong in 44 days, thence returning home. On her ninth voyage she reached San Francisco, Nov. 15, 1860, in 131 days from Boston. Then crossed to Hong Kong; made a round voyage to Saigon; then from Hong Kong to Bangkok and Falmouth, England, whence, on arrival Dec. 19, 1861, she was ordered to proceed to Boston, arriving at that port Jan. 20, 1862, 26 days from Falmouth. Loaded for San Francisco and arrived out June 27, 1862, in 128 days' passage. Sailed July 28th and hove to off Honolulu, 12 days out; proceeded the same day and 37 days later arrived at Hong Kong. Returned to San Francisco in 47 days, arriving Dec. 24, 1862. In heavy weather had the foremast sprung and the stem started which caused a bad leak. Sails and rigging were carried away and much damage was done on deck. Repairs costing some $20,000, were made when the ship was in dock at the Mare Island Navy Yard.

Being chartered to load dye woods on the west coast of Mexico for New York, the *Southern Cross* left San Francisco, Feb. 10, 1863, for Mazatlan. Thence proceeding to Buena Vista she loaded a full cargo of logwood and sailed Mar. 21, 1863. On June 6th, being 77 days out and just south of the line in the Atlantic, she was captured by the Confederate privateer *Florida* and burned. Captain Howes, his wife, the crew and passengers were taken on board the *Florida* and on June 27th were placed on board the whaling schooner *V. H. Hill* of Providence, which had been captured and bonded for $10,000. The *Hill* also received the ships' companies of the *Red Gauntlet* and *B. F. Hoxie* which had also fallen victims of the *Florida*. The claim filed by the owners of the *Southern Cross*, for the loss of their ship, was $55,000 for vessel and $10,000 for freight money.

The first master of the *Southern Cross* was Levi Stevens of Truro, Mass., who left her at San Francisco in December 1852 to engage in the shipping business as Stevens, Baker and Co. Captain Paine completed the voyage and made the following one. Capt. Thomas Prince Howes succeeded, continuing in the ship until he took the *Alarm* in 1859. Capt. Benjamin Perkins Howes then took the *Southern Cross* and was in her until her end. He then had the clipper brig *Lubra* built for trading in the South Seas. In September 1866 he was murdered in his cabin by Chinese pirates who had captured his brig. His wife who was a witness to his death, was not harmed. These two Captain Howes were natives of Dennis, Mass., but were not related. After the loss of the *Alarm*, Thomas Prince Howes was captain of the *Wild Hunter*. After giving up the sea he was prominent in the affairs of the Boston Marine Society, filling at different times every one of its offices. Afterwards, upon the nomination of that society, he served as Port Warden of Boston and as Pilot Commissioner for many years. He was considered a very capable navigator, yet he seldom made fast passages.

The following contemporaneous newspaper description of the

Southern Cross is reprinted through the courtesy of Mr. Ezra H. Baker of Boston.

"This beautiful vessel is a fair medium between the extreme sharpness of the clippers recently built here, and the New York packets, and may be classed with such ships as the *Sea Witch, Oriental,* and *Samuel Russell.* Her dead rise at half floor is 20 inches, with 29 inches depth of keel clear of the garboards. These afford her a good holding-on angle on the bottom, when by the wind, while her moderate dead rise gives her increased capacity, length of floor and buoyancy. Being, therefore, of a medium model—a model that has been often tested—there is nothing experimental about her. Possessing rounded lines, finely formed ends, good rise and length of floor, no doubt need be entertained of her success as a swift sailor, and what is more, of being a trust-worthy vessel in a heavy sea. Her bearings are such that she will endure driving, when, perhaps, a vessel of leaner ends might be compelled to shorten sail.

"Her length on the keel is 164 feet, between perpendiculars on deck 170, and over all 175. As her sternpost is at right-angles to the keel, the difference between her length on the keel and on deck, 6 feet, is the rake of her stem.

"Her extreme breadth of beam is 35 feet, depth of hold 21 feet, including 7 feet height of between-decks, and she registers 938 tons.

"She has 6 inches rounding of sides, and 21 inches sheer, but so truly graduated is the sheer, that she appears almost straight on the line of the planksheer; but her bow is carried up boldly, which imparts to her outline, end on, the easy and buoyant grace of the clipper. A gilded eagle on the wind forms the termination of the head, and descending from it, on the trail boards, is gilded carved work, which also encircles the hawseholes.

"The stern is light, and swells beautifully both from the line of the transom to the rail, and from the quarter timbers across. On the transom she is 26 feet wide, and on the rail 24. Her run is

clean, and owing to her light transom has an easy clearance up to
21 feet draught of water. She is sheathed with yellow metal up to
16½ feet forward, and to 17½ feet aft. Her name in gilded letters, ornaments the head and quarter boards, and her stern is also
ornamented with gilded carved work. Outside she is painted black,
and inside buff color, with blue waterways, &c. So far as appear-
ances are concerned, she is a noble looking vessel and gives promise
of being a swift sailer.

"Her frame hooks stanchions, and the hanging and lodging knees
in the lower hold are all of oak; the growth of Worcester county
in this State, and is considered equal to most of the live oak of
Florida.

"Her keel is of rock maple, moulded 32½ inches, and sides 16;
the floor timbers on the keel average from 16 to 17 moulded, and
from 10 to 12 sided; she has two depths of keelsons moulded 32,
and sided 16 inches, and these are bolted together with 1¼ inch
copper, driven through every floor timber and the keel, and rivetted,
and by iron of the same size driven through every navel timber blunt
into the keel. The ceiling on the floor is 4 inches thick, and in the
bilge she has two keelsons, each 12 by 8 inches, which extend the
whole length of the vessel, and are scarphed and square fastened.
The ceiling above is 6 inches thick, also square fastened. The beams
are 14 by 15 inches in the hold, and 9 by 15 in the between decks,
and the hanging knees in the hold are sided from 10 to 12 inches,
and moulded from 18 to 22 inches in the angles—have 5 feet bodies
and 3½ feet arms, and have from 16 to 19 bolts and 4 spikes in
each. The lodging knees meet and scarph in every berth, and are
closely bolted. She has three hooks forward and two aft (exclu-
sive of deck hooks), and they all extend diagonally along the skin,
and connect with the hanging knees under the beams. The hold
stanchions are kneed in the wake of the hatchways, and along the
intermediate spaces they are clasped with iron.

"The between decks waterways are 15 inches square, the strake over them 9 by 12, and that inside of them 8 by 12, all cross bolted. The deck plank is of Southern pine, 3½ inches thick. The clamp under the upper deckbeams is 6 inches thick, and the ceiling below 5 inches, all square fastened. The hanging and lodging knees are of hacmatac, and the lower ends of the former rest upon the standing strake over the waterways. These knees are finely finished and strongly bolted. The breasthook in this deck spans the bow completely, and is securely bolted from the outside. Her main transom is 18 inches square amidships, and the transom knees extend well along the sides, and almost meet across the stern.

"The upper deck waterways are 12 inches square, and the strake inside of them 5 inches thick, let into the beams below, and cross bolted. The upper deck is of clear white pine, 3½ inches thick. Her garboards are 7 inches thick, and the strakes outside of them are graduated to 4 inches, the substance of the planking on the bottom. She has 19 wales of 5 by 7 inches, and a beautiful narrow waist of 3 strakes, defined between the mouldings, of the upper wale and the planksheer.

"Her covering board and main rail are each 6 by 15 inches, and the latter in midships is 4 feet high, surmounted by a monkey rail. As already stated, she rises boldly forward, which makes the bulwarks higher there. The bulwark stanchions are of oak, and the bulwarks are of narrow boards, neatly tongued and grooved.

"We have already stated that her frame is entirely white oak; we may now add that she is very strongly fastened, and that more than usual care has been bestowed in driving her bilge and butt bolts and treenails. Her frame is seasoned with fine salt, and she is ventilated along the line of her planksheer, and through the bitts, and what is of more consequence, has Emerson's patent ventilators. These last are deservedly popular with all who have adopted them, and are now considered indispensable in almost every class of vessels. We have conversed with several intelligent ship masters about them and the verdict in their favor is unanimous.

"Her accommodations are excellent, both fore and aft. The crew have quarters in a large house, between the fore and main masts. This house is 37 feet long by 14 wide, and 6½ high, and also contains the galley and other useful apartments.

"The cabin is under a half poop deck, 26 feet long, and the entrance to it is protected by a house in front, which overlaps the deck aft, and contains two staterooms, two recesses, lockers, &c. The cabin descends from this house about three feet, and is beautifully wainscotted with plain branch mahogany, set off with enamelled pilasters, edged with gilding. The panels are oblong squares, and are finished in the first style of workmanship. The cabin contains four staterooms on the starboard side, and three and a water closet on the larboard side. Two of these staterooms, one on each side, overlook the main deck, and between them, clear of the staircase, is the pantry. The staterooms and cabin are splendidly furnished, well lighted and ventilated. She has two transom sofas, one above the other, and on the forward partition, a beautiful mirror, which gives a reflected view of the cabin abaft it. Nothing seems wanting to secure the comfort of those who may take passage in her.

"She has two handsome capstans, a patent windlass, a patent steering apparatus, an iron tank below, capable of holding 3000 gallons of water, good ground tackle and plenty of substantial boats. In a word, her outfits are all that they ought to be to ensure safety and success.

"She is a full rigged ship and looks splendidly aloft. The following are the dimensions of her masts and yards:

MASTS.

	Diameter, Inches	Length, Feet	Mast-heads, Feet
Fore	27	73	12
Top	14½	41½	7
Topgallant	10	23	0
Royal	8	15	0

Skysail	6½	11	pole	4
Main	28	78		12
Top	14½	43		7
Topgallant	10	23		0
Royal '	8	15		0
Skysail	6½	12	pole	5
Mizzen	21	70		10
Top	11	32		6
Topgallant	8	18		0
Royal	6	10		0
Skysail	4	7	pole	3

Yards.

Fore	19	66	yard arms	3¼
Top	14	53		4
Topgallant	9	38		2½
Royal	6	28		2
Skysail	5	18		1
Main	20	72		3¼
Top	16	57½		4
Topgallant	13	41		2½
Royal	9½	30		2
Skysail	7	20		1½
Crossjack	15	54		3
Mizzen topsail	10	39		3½
Topgallant	8	28		2
Royal	5	18		1½
Skysail	4	10		1

"Her bowsprit is 27 inches in diameter, and 27 feet outboard; jibboom, 14½ inches in diameter, and 28 feet outboard, including 3 feet end, and flying jibboom 15 feet outside of the wythe, with 3½ feet end, and the other spars in proportion. She is beautifully sparred, and well rigged. Her standing rigging is of four stranded patent rope, served over the ends, and snugly fitted aloft. It is enough to say that she was rigged by Capt. Brewster, of East Boston, to convince anyone conversant with nautical affairs in this vicinity, that she is well rigged. In the style of her rig, she is the same as the other clippers which we have described but we are free to confess that, so far as the eye is concerned, she appears a little heater aloft than any ship we have seen for some time.

"She is named after the most beautiful constellation of the Southern hemisphere.

"As a whole we consider her a ship of beautiful proportions, well built of good materials, handsomely finished, and liberally found. Messrs. E. & H. O. Briggs, of South Boston, built her, and so well satisfied were her owners of the faithful manner in which the builders had performed their contract, that they presented each of the builders with a handsome token of their approbation. She is owned by Messrs. Baker & Morrill, of this city, and will be commanded by Capt. Levi Stevens, an experienced and skilful sailor. She is now loading at Central wharf for San Francisco, and will be ready for sea in a few days. Success to her."

SOVEREIGN OF THE SEAS

THE *Sovereign of the Seas* shares with the *Flying Cloud* the honor of being the best known of the clipper ships of the fifties. She was built by Donald McKay, at East Boston, in 1852; built on speculation, not order; and it was predicted by many that she would prove an elephant on his hands. Dimensions; 258: 2 x 44 x 23: 6; tonnage, 2421. Her lines forward were concave but as they ascended became convex to correspond with her rail. She had 20 inches dead rise at the half floor and her widest point was 20 feet forward of her center. Her stem was plain, rose boldly and was ornamented with the figure of a sea god, half man, half fish, with a conch shell raised in the act of blowing. The hull was painted black and the figurehead bronze. All her lower masts were made, each mast in four pieces and hooped with iron. Her yards were all single sticks and she spread about 12,000 running yards of canvas. The bowsprit was 36 inches in diameter 20 feet outboard, and the jib-boom and flying jibboom were in one piece. The spanker boom was 55 and the gaff 45 feet in length. Her masts, counting from the foremast and including the skysail pole, were 185, 210 and 166 feet in length from heel to truck and raked ¾, ⅞ and 1⅛ inches to the foot. All her accommodations were on the upper deck leaving the between decks clear for cargo. She had two spacious cabins, elegantly furnished, built into a half poop deck; a large house abaft the foremast for part of the crew and a full topgallant forecastle the space under which was also fitted up for the accommodation of the crew. She drew 10¼ feet when launched and 21 when loaded. Soon after she was launched in June, she was bought by Andrew F. Meinke of the firm of Funch & Meinke, ship brokers, New York.

The *Sovereign* sailed from New York for San Francisco, Aug. 4, 1852, under command of Capt. Lauchlan McKay, brother of the builder. Besides being a master mariner, Captain McKay had served an apprenticeship with W. H. Webb, the well known shipbuilder and had also been carpenter on the U. S. frigate *Constellation* and was in every way fitted for the post. The *Sovereign*, on this voyage, had as crew, besides the captain,—four mates, two boatswains, two carpenters, two sailmakers, three stewards, two cooks, eighty able-bodied seamen and ten boys, a total of 105 hands. The crew were picked men and probably constituted the largest number of seamen ever shipped on a merchant sailing vessel. Why she carried so large a crew it is difficult to say, but, as will be seen, it turned out a fortunate circumstance. Captain McKay was furnished with wind and current charts by Lieut. M. F. Maury who predicted, if his directions were followed, a run of 83 days to the equator in the Pacific and a voyage of 103 days to San Francisco, a prediction which proved correct.

Twenty-five days from Sandy Hook, one of the best runs ever made by a sailing ship in August, the *Sovereign* crossed the line having had head winds all the way. Off the Falkland Islands she encountered a strong southwest gale with a tremendous sea but Captain McKay, under a press of sail, through squalls of rain and snow, drove his ship onward and beat his way from the Falklands to Cape Horn. "It was fearful," writes one who was aboard, "to see the topmasts bend and we hardly dared look aloft lest we should see the whole fabric blown away." The ship it is said behaved nobly during the long beat to windward and never once missed stays. Everything possible was done for the comfort of the crew; hot tea and coffee were provided for the men, day and night, while the ship's boys were kept busy at the forecastle stove drying the frozen and sodden garments. From the Cape, which was reached in 51 days, the *Sovereign* had head winds, calms and violent gales by turns. On Oct. 12th, in the latitude of Valparaiso, during a heavy gale, the maintopmast trestle trees settled, slacking the topmast backstays and away went the maintopmast over the side, taking with it the foretopsail yard, mizzen topgallant mast and every stitch of canvas off the foremast. The acting chief officer started to give orders to cut and clear away but Captain McKay insisted that everything should be saved and with a willing crew working day and night, by sunset of the next day had the ship under mainsail, crossjack and mizzen topsail, going 12 knots an hour. Well was it for the *Sovereign* that her captain had been a ship carpenter, for in 12 days, working day and night, the ship was as well rigged as when she left Sandy Hook and the captain could take his first night's rest. In recognition of his services on this occasion the underwriters of New York presented Captain McKay with a silver breakfast service of seven pieces and the Boston underwriters sent him a silver pitcher and his wife a gold bracelet.

The *Sovereign* crossed the equator in the Pacific 15 days after the accident, 83 days out from New York. Nineteen days later, Nov. 15, 1852, she arrived at San Francisco in 103 days from New York. As the ship neared the wharf thousands of people who had for some days been expecting her, crowded to the shore and greeted her with song and cheers. Although the time made on this passage does not seem fast compared with that made by the *Flying Cloud* and *Swordfish*, yet, considering the difficulties encountered and the month in which she sailed, it was a wonderful performance. Best day's run, 368 miles; best speed, 17 knots. The sailors received from the owners a bonus of $1000. The *Sovereign* was chartered to take a cargo of whale oil from Honolulu to New York, the first vessel to engage in this trade, which was useful as giving a cargo to the east instead of ships returning in ballast. She sailed from San Francisco, Dec. 22, 1852, and one of the officers writes home:—"We started out with 45 men. On the third day out down went the barometer and up went the wind. We were flying light and she heeled over until the lee rail was under water and we finally had to run before the wind; how she did fly; I have seen her sail away at the rate of 20 miles an hour when drawing 21 feet, but flying light, as she was, she must have been going at the rate of twenty-five." The run to Honolulu was rough and tedious and on reaching that port the crew, who had shipped for the passage only, left the ship and there was great difficulty in getting another. Finally, with only 34 men before the mast, the *Sovereign*, on Feb. 12, 1853, sailed for New York with a cargo of 8000 barrels of whale oil and a small amount of bone. With a crew much too small for a vessel of her tonnage and "the fore and main topmasts crippled; the fore topmast sprung in two places and the main topmast tender," it seemed hardly probable that the *Sovereign* would make a fast passage, but by following the sailing directions given by Lieut. Maury, on Mar. 9th she got a fine wind from the northwest and began the famous run during which she made 433 statute miles in 24 hours. One of the ship's officers writes to a friend in Boston:—"The day we ran 430 miles she had the wind on the larboard quarter and carried all drawing sail from the topsail down, but had the topmast been sound she could have borne the topmast-studding sail also. The sea was high and broken, the weather alternately clear and cloudy, with heavy showers, and at night we had occasional glimpses of moonlight. She ran about as fast as the sea and when struck by a squall would send the spray masthead high. Now and then she would fly up a point and heeling over skim along between the deep valleys of the waves, and then, brought to her course again, righten with majestic ease and as if taking a fresh start would seem to bound from wave to wave."

Lieut. Maury in his review of the voyage says:—"By following my route, having crossed the fortieth parallel, the *Sovereign* found herself with trade-like west winds. From March 9 to March 31, from 48° South in the Pacific to 35° South in the Atlantic, in 22 days she made 5391 nautical miles or 6245 statute miles, averaging 283 statute miles a day. From noon to noon she made 362 knots, equaling 419 statute miles; she made slightly better than this by figuring out the direction and time, 374 knots or 433 statute miles, a little better than the *Flying Cloud*." The highest rate of speed reported was 18 knots. The *Sovereign* reached New York in 82 days from Honolulu, called a record at that time. She received $98,000 freight money for the passage to San Francisco; $10,000 for her run to Honolulu and $30,000 for the voyage home, making her earning for the nine months, $138,000.

Freights to San Francisco were dull at this time and the *Sovereign* sailed from New York for Liverpool, June 18, 1853, with Mr. Donald McKay and his wife among the passengers. On this passage she drew 22½ feet and carried a crew of 44 men. She reached Liverpool, July 1, 1853, making the run in 13 days, 22 hours and 50 minutes, the best time ever made for the month of June. The steamer *Canada* left New York for Liverpool about the same time and beat her only two days on the passage, while at the end of the first five days the *Sovereign* was 325 miles in the lead. Her best 24 hours' run was 340 miles and the *Canada's* 306 miles. From the banks to Cape Clear the former averaged 12.75 knots an hour. On her arrival at Liverpool she was chartered by the "Black Ball Line" and her charterers boldly advertised:—"Freight seven pounds a ton for Melbourne; forty shillings a ton to be returned if the *Sovereign* does not make a faster passage than any steamer on the berth."

Captain McKay left the *Sovereign* at Liverpool and returned to Boston to superintend the construction of Donald McKay's new ship, the *Great Republic*. He was succeeded by his first mate, Mr. Warner, and under command of the latter the *Sovereign* sailed from Liverpool for Melbourne, on Sept. 7, 1853, with 64 passengers and a cargo valued at $1,000,000. On arrival at Melbourne, Captain Warner wrote to friends in Boston:—"We had a long passage of 78 days with light and baffling winds; 31 days to the line; set skysails on leaving Liverpool and never shortened for 35 days; the crew were insufficiently clothed and one half disabled." Although the passage was a slow one the *Sovereign* beat everything that sailed about the same time, including the British clipper *Gauntlet*. Captain Warner had two favorable runs, one of 1275 miles in four consecutive days, the other, 3315 miles in 12 consecutive days.

From Melbourne she returned to Liverpool in 68 days, beating the steamer *Harbinger* four days and all other vessels sailing about the same time from 15 to 20 days. She brought back a great deal of treasure and experienced a dangerous mutiny on the passage. Mar. 17, 1854, a quarrel broke out between one of the steerage passengers and a member of the crew. The mate interfered and was resisted by the sailor who was finally ironed. Fifteen or twenty of the crew then surrounded the mate and threatened to seize the ship if their comrade was not released. So serious did the situation become that not only the officers but the passengers, also, were armed and the mutineers driven forward at the mouths of their guns and pistols. Finally the ringleader, Hale, and two others, were ironed and confined between decks for the rest of the passage and the mutiny was quelled. On her arrival at Liverpool the *Sovereign* was sold to a Hamburg firm, J. C. Godeffroy and Son, and Captain Warner was succeeded by Captain Müller.

With the change in ownership the *Sovereign* seemed to lose her good luck and the rest of her sea life was a succession of misfortunes. From Liverpool she sailed for Sydney, N. S. W., and the 40th day out, near Cape Horn, carried away her topmasts in a squall. They were replaced and all damage repaired in six days but all chance of making a fast passage was gone and she reached Sydney in 84 days. It is stated, however, that on the passage she made the run of 410 miles in 24 hours and that her log proved her to have traveled occasionally at the rate of 22 knots an hour.

On her voyage by way of China, she ran aground near Woosung and had to discharge part of her cargo. She was finally floated and repaired and on the voyage from Shanghai for Liverpool she lost 11 of her crew from cholera; many others were sick and only 13 or 14 were left to run the ship. In 1859, on a voyage from Hamburg for China, she ran on the Pyramid Shoal in the Straits of Malacca and proved a total loss. According to one report she was said to have been under British colors at the time of her loss, having been sold in London in June 1858 for $40,000, after undergoing repairs to the amount of $12,000. There seems to be some doubt, however, as to her sailing under the British flag, as J. C. Godeffroy and Son of Hamburg, were, by all accounts, still her owners and are reported to have employed the American ship *Eloisa* to wreck her, thus recovering a portion of her cargo.

The following description of the *Sovereign of the Seas* was published in "The Boston Daily Atlas," at the time she was launched.

More than two centuries have passed away since this name was first applied to a ship. In 1637 that ship was built in Woolwich dockyard, her tonnage corresponding with the year. She was the first ship with "flushe deckes," and the largest of any vessel which had previously belonged to the British navy. Her keel measured 187 feet and 9 inches, her main breadth of beam was 48 feet 4 inches, and she had three decks, a poop and topgallant forecastle, and "bare five lanthorns, the biggest of which could hold ten persons upright." She was pierced for 126 guns, but probably only mounted 100.

How strangely this uncouth hulk would look alongside of her modern namesake. The difference between one of our clipper schooners and a Chinese junk would not be more marked; yet it is only by referring to the past that we can justly appreciate the improvements of the present.

Behold the modern *Sovereign of the Seas,* the longest, sharpest, the most beautiful merchant ship in the world, designed to sail at least twenty miles an hour with a whole-sail breeze. See her in the "beauty of her strength," the simplicity and neatness of her rig, flying before the gale and laughing at the rising sea; and then imagine her cumbrous ancester, wallowing from side to side, tearing up the ocean into whitened foam, and drifting perhaps seven miles an hour; yet she was the first ship of her day. Imagine all this, and even a landsman can comprehend the wonderful progress of naval architecture.

Mr. McKay could not have selected a better name for his ship; its historical association is full of instruction, and no ship was ever more worthy of such a name.

Since the opening of the California trade, Mr. McKay has built five large clippers—the *Stag Hound, Flying Cloud, Staffordshire, Flying Fish,* and *Sovereign of the Seas,* but no two of them are alike in model. The *Stag Hound* was 40 inches dead rise at half floor, and convex lines; the *Flying Cloud* 30 inches and concave lines; the *Staffordshire* the same dead rise, and concave lines, but is much fuller in the ends, and has a deck more than any of the others; the *Flying Fish* has 25 inches and concave lines, but shorter ends, though sharper at the extremes, than her predecessors, and more capacity in proportion to her register; but the last and greatest of all, indeed the largest merchant ship in the world, has only 20 inches dead rise, and concave lines, but has the longest and sharpest ends of any ship or ocean steamer, either afloat or building. Owing to the length of her ends, her lines are less concave than those of the *Flying Fish.* A chord from the extreme of her cutwater, to the turn of her side at the load displacement line, (20½ feet draft forward) would only show a concavity of 2 inches. The angle of her bow, at the same line, is 14½ degrees, and of her stern 15½.

Her leading dimensions are as follows:—Length of keel 245 feet, on deck, between perpendiculars 258 feet over all, from the knight-heads to the taffrail, 265 feet; extreme breadth of beam 44 feet, about 20 feet forward of the centre, breadth at the gunwale 42 feet; depth 23½ feet, including 8 feet height of between decks, dead rise 20 inches, swell or rounding of sides 1 foot, sheer nearly 4 feet, and register 2421 tons.

As Mr. McKay built this ship on his own account, he alone is responsible for her success as a sea-boat. He designed that she should be the swiftest sailing vessel in the world, and what is apparent to all, has made her strong enough to carry shot in bulk. Considering the sharpness of her ends, she has large stowage capacity for a clipper, great surface and length of floor, and will be very buoyant, and easy under canvas.

Her lines forward, as they ascend above the water, become convex, to correspond with her outline on the rail, and her bow is plain, without even trail boards, and terminates with the figure of a sea god, half man half fish, with a conch shell raised to his mouth, as if in the act of blowing it. The figure accords with the sheer of the bow, is well executed, and forms a beautiful finish.

Her bow rises boldly, and is beautiful beyond description. The same terms will apply to her model throughout. She is planked flush to the covering-board; her stern is curvilinear, and is formed from the moulding of the planksheer, is very neat and graceful. Her run is long and clean, but still there is not a straight place in her whole model. She is sheathed with yellow metal up to 20½ feet forward, and 21½ feet aft. The rest of her hull is painted black, and her figure head is bronzed sea color.

Her bulwarks are five feet two inches high, surmounted by a monkey rail of 16 inches, and the space between the main and rack-rails is filled in with a heavy clamp, bolted both ways. All her accommodations are on deck. She has a full topgallant forecastle, a large house amidships, and a spacious trunk cabin, in two divisions, built into a half poop deck, with steerage room abaft. Her accommodations forward and aft, are plain, but neat, and are well adapted for all hands.

Her construction, for solidity and strength, is of the highest order. Her frame is entirely of seasoned white oak, and all her planking and ceiling, as well as her deck-frames, and the lower deck, are of the best hard pine, and she is strongly copper fastened and square bolted, and treenailed throughout. In the hold, all her knees are of oak, and all her hooks throughout. The knees in the between decks are of hacmatack, but the hooks and stanchions are of oak. She is 11 feet 8 inches through the back bone, including the moulding of the floor timbers, which is 19 inches, and all her keel and keelson fastening is of 1½ inch copper and iron, driven in the strongest style, and riveted. Her keel is sided 16 inches, and beside the midship keelsons, she has double sister keelsons, one over the other, on each side, which, combined, side 15 inches, and mould 30. Her floor ceiling is 5 inches thick, and commencing below the floor-heads, the ceiling is 14 inches, which diminishes to 10 inches, without a projection; and under the ends of the lower deck hanging knees is a stringer of 14 inches thickness. All this ceiling is scarphed, square fastened, caulked and paved. Her hold stanchions are kneed above and below, and her ends are literally filled with massive hooks and pointers, and are further strengthened with hold beams, which are also strongly kneed. She has three of these beams forward and two aft.

The between decks waterways are 16 inches square, the strake inside of them 10 by 12, and that over them 11 by 16; the ceiling above is 6 inches thick, and the clamp 7 inches. The hold beams are 15 inches square, the upper deck beams 16 by 10 inches, and the hanging knees under them have 20 bolts and 4 spikes in each.

The upper deck waterways are 14 inches square, with thick strakes inside of them, and the planking of both decks is 3½ inches thick.

Her garboards are 8 inches thick, the next strake 6, graduated to 5, the substance of her bottom planking, and she has 25 strakes of wales, each 6 by 7 inches. The covering board and main rail are each 7 inches thick, and the bulwarks 2½ inches, neatly tongued and grooved. Inside she is painted buff-color, and looks well about the decks.

Her windlass, pumps, capstans, ground tackle, &c., are all of the first quality, and are made more for wear than show.

The beauty and strength of her hull are only equalled by her completeness aloft. She has not only the stoutest and most beautifully proportioned set of spars that ever towered above a ship's deck, but the rigging is the very best that could be procured, and the style in which it is fitted reflects high credit on her rigger, Mr. Wm. Dorrian, of New York.

All her lower masts are made from the heads to the steps, each mast in five pieces, bolted and hooped together. Her bowsprit is also a made spar, and all the outside pieces are of hard pine. Her mast rake, commencing with the fore, 6-8ths, 7-8ths, and 1⅛ inch to the foot. The following are the dimensions of her masts and yards.

MASTS.

	Diameter, Inches	Length, Feet	Mast-heads, Feet
Fore	41	89¾	16
Top	19	50	10
Topgallant	14	27½	0
Royal	11½	18	pole 10
Main	42	92¾	17
Top	19½	54	11
Topgallant	14¾	30	0
Royal	12	20	0
Skysail	10	14	pole 8
Mizzen	34	82¾	14
Top	16	43	9
Topgallant	11	24	0
Royal	9½	17	pole 8

YARDS.

Fore	22	80	yard-arms 5
Top	17½	63	5½
Topgallant	14	47	3½
Royal	8	37	2½
Main	24	90	5
Top	19½	70	5½
Topgallant	15	53½	4
Royal	11	42	3
Skysail	9	35	2
Crossjack	20	70	4
Mizzentopsail	15	56	4½
Topgallant	11	43	3
Royal	7	32	2

The bowsprit is made of hard pine, is 20 feet outboard, 34 inches in diameter, and has 4 inches steve to the foot. Jibboom and flying-jibboom in one spar, divided at 15 and 12 feet for the two jibs, with 7 feet end; spanker boom 61 feet long, 2 feet end; gaff 45 feet, with 5 feet end; main spanker gaff 24 feet, with 2 feet end; the other spars in proportion. Her lower masts are only two inches smaller at the truss-bands than what they are at the deck; and instead of holes in the topmast heads, she has double gins for the topsail ties, with gins on the yards and double hilliards. The main topgallantmast has also a gin at the mast head, and a double tie to the yard, the standing part fast aloft.

Her fore and main rigging is of 12 inch wormed, served over the ends and eyes; her topmast backstays of the same size. She has double topgallant backstays on each side, and all the chain and iron work about her bowsprit, masts and yards, now in general use. Her mastheads are crowned with gilded balls; her yards black, booms bright, and lower masts white, and altogether aloft, she is the best fitted ship that ever was built in this port. She will spread between 11 and 12,000 yards of canvas. Her yards are all of single spars, not scarphed and together with the masts, are strong enough to stand till every stitch of canvas blows away.

Her ornamental work was made by Messrs. Gleason & Sons; Mr. T. J. Shelton made her pumps and blocks, and Mr. Mendum was her blacksmith. She was built at East Boston by Mr. Donald McKay, and is the embodiment of his idea of clipper perfection. So perfectly true are her proportions, that, notwithstanding her vast size, there are many freighting ships of half her register, that loom larger to the eye.

At four hundred yards' distance, she does not appear to be larger than 7 or 800 tons. She has been inspected by nautical men from all parts of the country, and we believe, has been the object of unqualified admiration. There are doubtless many ships more tastefully ornamented with carving, gilding and other excrescences; but for beauty of model, strength of construction and completeness of equipment aloft, she has no superior. It is but reasonable to presume that, with a fair chance, she will make the quickest voyage ever performed under canvas. We consider her not only an honor to her enterprising builder, but to the country at large. Americans on distant seas may refer to her with national pride, and challenge a comparison from the commercial navies of the world. She is well named the *Sovereign of the Seas*.

In George Francis Train's "Reminiscences" appears the following account of the building of the *Sovereign of the Seas* in which he claims a personal connection with the conception of the vessel.

"The building of this vessel was a tremendous leap forward in ship-building; but I was not satisfied. I told McKay that I wanted a still larger ship. He said he could build it. And so we began another vessel that was to outstrip in size and capacity the great *Flying Cloud*.

"I was desirous to name this ship the *Enoch Train*, in honor of the head of the Boston house, and had said as much to Duncan MacLane, who was the marine reporter for the 'Boston Atlas.' MacLane had usually written a column for his paper on the launching of our ships. He wanted to have something to write about the new vessel. I told him the story of Colonel Train's life and that we were going to christen the new vessel with his name. I did not consult Colonel Train, thinking that, of course, it was all right.

"The 'Atlas' published a long account of the ship and gave the name as the *Enoch Train*. When I went down to the office that morning Colonel Train had not yet arrived, but he soon came in, walking straight as a gun barrel and seeming to be a little stiff. 'Did you see the Atlas this morning?' I asked. 'Premature,' he replied. That was all he said. He would not discuss the matter. I was nettled that he did not appreciate the honor I thought I was conferring on him. It was not for nothing that a man's name should be borne by the greatest vessel on the seas. I said to myself that the name should be changed at once. The ship was to be of 2,200 tons burden, larger than the *Flying Cloud* and the *Staffordshire*, both of 2,000 tons, and I decided to call her the *Sovereign of the Seas*.

"The news that we were building a still bigger ship was rapidly circulated throughout the world. Many shipping lines wanted to buy her before she was off the ways. Despatches from New York shipping lines making inquiry as to price came almost daily. I invariably replied that we would take $130,000. But this was a little too stiff a price at that time, although the *Flying Cloud* had paid for herself in a single trip.

"I finally sold her to Berren Roosen, Jr. of Hamburg, Germany, through the brokers Funch & Meinke, of New York, for $110,000. She was entered in my name although I was at the time only nineteen years of age. I was quite proud to have the greatest vessel afloat on any water associated with my name. She was sent to Liverpool."

SPARKLING WAVE

MEDIUM clipper ship, built by Mason Barney, at Swansea, Mass., in 1853; 136: 2 x 32: 8 x 22; 655 tons. In May 1854 she was reported sold at New Orleans for $50,000. In 1862 she was owned by Fogg Bros., of New York. In 1863 she was registered as owned in New York, by Brett, Son & Co. In 1864 she was reported sold at London for £3000 sterling, to go under the British flag without change of name.

The *Sparkling Wave* made two passages from eastern ports to San Francisco, on both of which occasions she was obliged to put into ports en route. In the first instance she arrived at destination, Apr. 14, 1855, in 122 days from Philadelphia, via Montevideo, 61 days. Her time from the Uruguayan port is record to this day, while her run of 41 days from 50° South, Pacific, to destination, is also excellent. From San Francisco she went to Honolulu in 16 days and thence in 40 days to Shanghai. Homeward bound she passed Java Head, Aug. 22nd, and was 32½ days to the Cape of Good Hope. She arrived at Boston, Mar. 22, 1856, having had a very rough passage from London, with constant gales. On the passage she took off the crew of the Swedish bark *Petrus* and landed them at Boston. On this voyage she was commanded by Captain Hubbard.

On the second occasion referred to, she arrived at San Francisco, Feb. 6, 1860, under Captain McCarthy, in 324 days from New York, 162 from Rio and 56 from Valparaiso. She was forced into Rio by a bad leak and had to discharge cargo. From Rio she was 24 days to Cape Horn, off which she was 60 days in strong westerly gales. She put into Valparaiso, 97 days from Rio, short of water and provisions. From San Francisco she went to Central America to load hardwood for Europe.

Thereafter, until January 1863, she was engaged in trade between New York and Great Britain and the continent. In April 1862, on a voyage from the Tyne to New York, she grounded on the Goodwin Sands and was badly strained. Her cargo was discharged at the Victoria Dock, London, and she was repaired at the Carter dry-dock at Milwall. She reached New York, July 19, 1862, 37 days from London. After January 1863 she made two voyages from Cardiff to India. In June 1864 she was at St. Helena, bound for London, and Captain Emery furnished Commander McDougal of the U.S.S. *Wyoming*, with information about the *Alabama*, after which vessel the *Wyoming* was in search. Captain Emery had taken command of the *Wave* early in 1861. After her sale abroad her hailing port became Sunderland, Eng., and her owner R. Adamson.

SPIRIT OF THE TIMES

CLIPPER ship, built in 1853, by Cooper & Slicer, at Baltimore, for Aymar & Co., of New York; 191: 7 x 36: 8 x 21: 6; 1206 tons, old measurement; 928 tons, new measurement. Said to have been of sharp model, with 14 inches dead rise.

Under command of Captain Klein she left Baltimore, Jan. 14, 1854, and was 31 days to Liverpool, returning to Baltimore in 26 days. Then went out to Valparaiso in 90 days. On the return passage she lost bowsprit, and fore and main topmasts, off Cape Horn. Arrived at Baltimore, Feb. 1, 1855, under jury rig, 65 days after the disaster. She then loaded at New York for San Francisco, arriving out Dec. 1, 1855, in 160 days' passage. Captain Klein reported being 42 days off the Horn in heavy gales, during which had sails blown away, bulwarks stove, etc. Put into Valparaiso when 117 days out; was in port there two days; had 40 days thence to San Francisco, a fine run, considering that she was becalmed six days north of the line. From San Francisco she went to Mazatlan in 13 days and thence 112 days to Liverpool. From the latter port she went to Rio and New Orleans; thence to Liverpool in a long run of about 60 days. From Liverpool she was 100 days to Calcutta. In June 1858 she was reported at Hong Kong from London.

The *Spirit of the Times* arrived at New York, May 21, 1861, Captain Klein reporting 91 days from Bombay. She was then sold and went under the flag of Hamburg with Kirkland & Von Sach registered owners. Under command of Captain Anderson she sailed from New York, Feb. 16, 1862, and was 104 days to Singapore. Then traded on the Asiatic coast for a time. In 1863 she made a round voyage between Hong Kong and San Francisco. After returning to China she again changed hands and for about a year was known as the *London*. In the spring of 1865 she was sold for £6500, going under the flag of Chile as the *Christine*. In 1868 she appears in registers as the ship *Nina*, of Macao. About three years later she was reported as condemned and broken up.

SPITFIRE

EXTREME clipper ship, launched from the yard of James Arey & Sons, at Frankfort, Me., Sept. 3, 1853; built to the order of Thomas Gray and Manning & Stanwood of Boston; 224 x 40 x 23; 1549 tons, old measurement. Dead rise 15 inches; a gilded eagle was the figurehead. She had long and sharp ends and was one of the most beautiful of the clipper fleet, also proving to be one of the fastest.

Under command of Capt. John W. Arey she sailed from Boston, Oct. 24, 1853, for San Francisco. On Nov. 7th, in latitude 27° North, the fore and main topmasts and the bowsprit were badly sprung and other damage to spars and rigging received. The masts were fished and on Nov. 27th she put into Rio, 34 days out from Boston. Put in new masts and sailed Dec. 16th; made Staten Island, 16 days from Rio and 32 days later she crossed the equator in the Pacific, 48 days out from Rio. During the following 17 days she made 4500 miles, of which the best day was 340 miles. Arrived at San Francisco, Feb. 20, 1854, 65 days and some hours from Rio and a few hours under 100 sailing days from Boston. Captain Arey stated that he was 380 miles from the Golden Gate on the 97th sailing day. Reached port four days ahead of the *Cyclone* whom she had passed after clearing the Horn. At Rio, eight of the crew of the *Spitfire* were discharged for incompetence, the chief mate, Elkanah Crowell saying that his ship wanted only men who "could jump over the fore-yard before breakfast."

The *Spitfire* sailed from San Francisco, Mar. 24, 1854, and was 51 days to Callao; left there guano laden, Aug. 2nd; crossed the line in the Atlantic, 41 days out and arrived at Hampton Roads, Oct. 14th, in 64 days from Callao. Her maiden voyage was exceptionally fast and her run from Rio to San Francisco has only once been beaten by a cargo-laden ship, the *Witchcraft*, in 62 days.

She sailed from Boston, Nov. 30, 1854; was 32 days to the line; on the 57th day out passed through the Straits of Le Maire but was blown back by a severe southerly gale; was 15 days from 40° South, Pacific, to 30° South, in calms and light winds; crossed the equator 97 days out and was thence 21 days to San Francisco, making her passage 118 days from Boston. Was five days making the last 600 miles and had three skysails continually set from latitude 45° South, to port. Arrived 13 days ahead of the *Golden City* whom she had met in the Straits of Le Maire, both ships being then 58 days out. Sailed from San Francisco, Apr. 18, 1855, and was 12 days to Honolulu and 27 days thence to Hong Kong or 39 sailing days from San Francisco. Sailed from Foo Chow, July 13th, about the poorest season of the year and had a long run down the China Sea. Her whole passage to London was 120 days. Then made a round voyage to Hong Kong and on reaching London on the return, was leaking 1000 strokes per hour. Went back to China, arriving at Hong Kong, May 3, 1857, in 110 days from London. Operated on the China coast for a time and later returned to London.

In 1860 the *Spitfire* underwent large repairs after which she returned to the California trade. On Apr. 8, 1861, she arrived at San Francisco in 107 days from Boston, Capt. Samuel R. Leach in command. Was 24 days to the line; passed through the Straits of Le Maire, 52 days out and crossed the equator in the Pacific, 85 days out. Loaded 1640 short tons of wheat and flour and made the passage to Queenstown in 109 days. Discharged at Liverpool and was 26 days thence to New York, arriving Nov. 11, 1861, with a cargo of coal and salt. Again went out to San Francisco, arriving June 3, 1862, in 127 days from New York. Captain Leach reported being 24 days to the line; 52 days to the Straits of Le Maire; 22 days rounding the Horn; 25 days running up the South Pacific and 28 days from the equator to port. Went to Callao in 44 days; left there guano laden, Oct. 25th, and arrived at Queenstown, Jan. 22, 1863, in 89 days' passage. Was ordered to Hull, reaching there Feb. 6th.

In April 1863, the *Spitfire* was at London in a damaged condition and was sold for £9000, going under the British flag without change of name. In 1864 she is registered as owned by W. N. De Matus, hailing port London, and also so appears in registers of 1869. She is not listed in Lloyd's of 1874.

STAFFORDSHIRE

CLIPPER ship, built by Donald McKay, at East Boston, Mass.; launched June 17, 1851, two months after the *Flying Cloud* had left the ways in the same yards, for the same owners, Enoch Train & Co., of Boston. She was built for service in the "Train Line" of Boston-Liverpool packet ships and was named after the celebrated English pottery district where a considerable portion of the Line's homeward cargoes originated. She was one of the few ships of clipper model to be built expressly for trans-Atlantic packet service.

The *Staffordshire* was 1817 tons, old measurement; length of keel, 228 feet; over all, 243; extreme breadth of beam, near amidships, 41 feet; depth of hold, 29 feet; draft forward, 18½ feet, and one foot more, aft; dead rise, 20 inches. Her sheer was three feet, and rounding of sides, 12 inches; she had three complete decks. An image of a witch was her figurehead. Her stern was elliptical, one side of which was ornamented with a carved representation of

"STAFFORDSHIRE," 1817 TONS, BUILT AT EAST BOSTON, IN 1851

From a lithograph showing the ship wrecked on Blonde Rock, near Cape Sable, Dec. 24, 1853

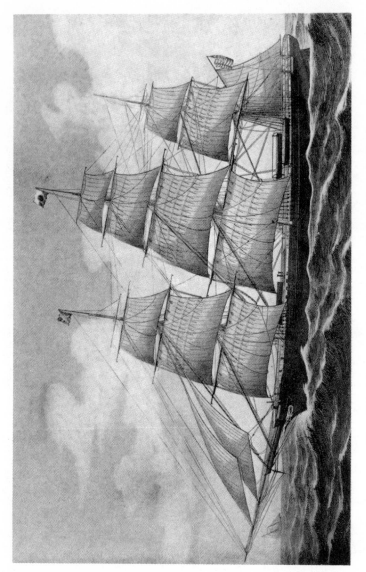

"STAG HOUND," 1534 TONS, BUILT AT EAST BOSTON, MASS., IN 1850

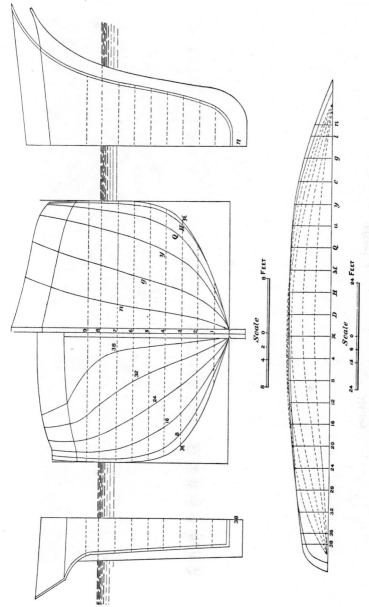

Scale

8 4 2 0   8 Feet

Scale

24 12 6 0   24 Feet

"STAG HOUND," 1534 TONS, BUILT AT EAST BOSTON, MASS., IN 1850
Lines from Hall's *Ship-Building Industry of the United States*, 1884

"STAR OF PEACE," 941 TONS, BUILT AT NEWBURYPORT, MASS., IN 1858
Captured and burned March 6, 1863, by the Confederate cruiser *Florida*

a Staffordshire manufacturing scene, while the other showed the Train counting-house on Lewis' wharf. Below were the name and hailing port flanked, on either side, with a relief of a lion's head. Her masts had the same rake as those of the *Flying Cloud* but she was not so lofty a ship. She was quite sharp, with slightly concave entrance lines but her ends were shorter than those of *Flying Cloud* or *Stag Hound.* Her record for speed during her short career is very good and her last commander, Josiah Richardson, pronounced her a remarkably fast and a fine sea boat, although he acknowledged that his former command, the *Stag Hound,* could outsail her. Under Captain Richardson she logged 15 knots, under topgallants, on one occasion.

On her first voyage the *Staffordshire* sailed from Boston, Aug. 4, 1851, Capt. Albert H. Brown in command, and made the run from her pier to the dock at Liverpool in 14 days and 18 hours. She was up with Tuskar Light when 12 days out, but then had easterly winds; best day, 290 miles; poorest, 180. Her cargo holds were full of freight and all of her elegant and spacious accommodations were occupied by 50 first class, and 150 second class passengers.

Under command of Captain Richardson she sailed from Boston, May 3, 1852, for San Francisco, discharging her pilot at 10 A.M. Arrived at San Francisco Aug. 13th, in 102 days' passage. She crossed the line 25 days out; was thence 27 days to 50° South, and 14 days rounding the Horn; from 50° South, Pacific, she made the very fast run of 17 days to the line and 19 days thence to San Francisco, which time from the Horn to port is very close to record. From San Francisco she went to Singapore in 51 days; thence 21 days to Calcutta. Left the latter port, Jan. 23, 1853, and took her departure from the Sand Heads on the 25th. Arrived at Boston, Apr. 20th, in a passage of 84 days, which was then the record. She was up with the Cape of Good Hope when 39 days out. After arrival home she resumed her place in the Train packet line.

On what was fated to be her last voyage the *Staffordshire* left the Mersey, Dec. 9, 1853, for Boston, her passengers and crew numbering 214 persons. The first part of the passage was prosperous, she having crossed the Grand Bank, 12 days out. On Dec. 24th, the rudderhead was badly sprung in a heavy gale which continued and four days later the bowsprit was carried away close to the knightheads. The foremast and everything above then went overboard breaking the fore-yard at the slings. The temporary rudder was also carried away. While the wreckage was being cleared away to prevent the bow from being stove in, Captain Richardson, who had climbed the fore rigging, fell to the deck and was so badly injured that he was taken to his cabin for treatment by the ship's surgeon. The weather moderated somewhat the next day, the ship standing to the westward under double-reefed maintopsail. At 8 P.M. it was judged that she was 40 miles south of Seal Island and the captain directed the course to remain unchanged until midnight. At 11 P.M. the second mate, who was on watch, discerned lights on the starboard bow and immediately notified chief mate Alden, who had been below to get some needful rest. Orders were instantly given to wear ship to southwest, the wind then blowing strong from N.N.W. All might have still been well but the want of head sail occasioned the ship to pay off very slowly and to cap the climax, some of the gear fouled and prevented the after yards from being swung promptly. At this critical time the ship struck a rock where she remained about five minutes, then slid off and began to sink bow first. In the meantime some of the boats had been cleared and lowered by members of the crew. Captain Richardson, who since his accident had been lying on the cabin table, refused to be moved from his position, saying to Mr. Alden, "If I am to be lost, God's will be done." He and 169 others on board went down with the ship. Mr. Alden jumped overboard from the stern and was picked up by a boat. Altogether 44 lives were saved, including the four mates and one woman who had been in the habit of washing and drying the men's clothes in a spare galley. It was later ascertained that the ship was wrecked on Blonde Rock, about four miles from Seal Island, near Cape Sable. She was valued at $120,000.

STAG HOUND

T HE *Stag Hound* was the first of the very sharp or extreme clippers and when launched, Dec. 7, 1850, was the largest and longest American merchantman. Designed and built by Donald McKay at East Boston, her model was original. The entrance and clearance lines were very long and sharp, slightly convex and her bow favored the appearance of a steamboat more than a ship. The oldest and most conservative authorities were doubtful of her stability and seaworthiness. Mr. Walter R. Jones, the most prominent marine underwriter, than whom there was no one who knew more about a ship, remarked to Captain Richardson, "I should think you would be somewhat nervous in going so long a voyage in so sharp a ship, so heavily sparred." "No, Mr. Jones," was the reply, "I would not go in the ship at all, if I thought for a moment that she would be my coffin." Although the memoranda of the different voyages of the *Stag Hound* show that she generally had but a poor chance, yet in moderate breezes she was conceded to be a very fast ship and in strong winds frequently logged 16 and 17 knots. Her best day's run, so far as can be traced, was 358 miles.

The dimensions of the *Stag Hound* were: keel, 207; between perpendiculars, 215; over all, 226; rake of stem, six feet; rake of stern post, two feet; beam, 39: 8; depth of hold, 21 feet; depth of keel, 46 inches; dead rise, 40 inches; sheer, 30 inches; tonnage 1534, old measurement; about 1100 tons, British measurement. Her stern was small and at eight feet forward of midships of the taffrail, she was only 24½ feet wide. Under full sail she spread nearly 11,000 yards of canvas in a single suit. All the masts raked alike, 1¼ inches to the foot. The foremast was set 50 feet from the center of the stem; thence 67 feet to the mainmast; thence 56 feet to the mizzen, which was 42 feet forward of the sternpost. She was launched in about 100 days from the laying of the keel and was built to the order of George B. Upton and Sampson & Tappan, both of Boston, two of the most prominent owners of the early extreme clippers. Her command was given to Capt. Josiah Richardson, a most skillful navigator who afterwards lost his life in the wreck of the *Staffordshire*.

With a crew, before the mast, of 36 A.B.'s, six ordinaries and four boys, the *Stag Hound* left New York, Feb. 1, 1851, and when six days out, the maintopmast broke off, taking in its fall all three topgallant masts. Soon after the disaster, a west-south-west and westerly gale set in and the *Stag Hound* ran before wind and sea. No maintopsail was carried for nine days and the topgallants were not set until 12 days after the accident, repairs having been made from spare spars. These westerly gales forced the ship to cross the line in 28° 30′ longitude, 20½ days out. Captain Richardson believed that but for this disaster he would have crossed in about 16 days from Sandy Hook. From the line to 50° South, she was 22 days; passed Cape Horn 49 days out and was in 50° South, Pacific, on the 57th day. Nine days later she was at anchor in Valparaiso harbor from which the captain wrote to his owners on Apr. 8, 1851: "Your ship, *Staghound*, is at anchor in this harbor after a passage of 66 days, which, I believe, is the shortest but one ever made and had it not been for the accident of losing some of our spars, I do not doubt it would have been the shortest. . . . We lost at least 800 miles by the accident. The ship has yet to be built to beat the *Staghound*."

The *Stag Hound* was at Valparaiso five days. Thence she had a passage of 42 days to San Francisco in light winds and calms; 21 days to the equator and 21 to destination. Total time from New York, 113 days; sailing days, 108; best day's run, 358 nautical miles. Sailing for Manila, June 26, 1851, the *Stag Hound* is next reported at Whampoa, Sept. 26, 1851, her operations during the interval being missing. She sailed from Whampoa, Oct. 9th; cleared the Straits of Sunda, the 31st and 26 days later was off the Cape. Arrived at New York in 94 days from Whampoa. Her outward cargo to San Francisco had been secured at about one dollar per cubic foot, her freight list exceeding $70,000. Her homeward cargo of tea, for owner's account, was sold at auction and a few days later, when the earnings of the voyage had been computed, it was stated that the ship had paid for herself and divided among her owners a clear profit of over $80,000, earned in ten months and 23 days.

On her second voyage she left New York, Captain Behm in command, Mar. 1, 1852. Had 26 days to the line; passed Cape Horn, 64 days out; was 12 days from 50° to 50°; crossed the equator, 91 days out and was 33 days thence to San Francisco. During nearly the whole passage of 124 days had light or baffling winds. Had three skysails set for 83 days and was within 1000 miles of destination for 20 days. Was in port 17 days, sailing July 21, 1852. Passed Honolulu, ten days out, and arrived at Whampoa, Sept. 6th, a trifle under 45 days' passage. Sailed from Whampoa, Sept. 25, 1852, in company with the *Sword Fish*. Passed Anjer, Oct. 18th, and Java Head, the 19th; thence had 33 days to the Cape and arrived at New York, Dec. 30th, in 95 days from Whampoa. The passage of the *Sword Fish* was 89 days, her gain being mostly in the run down the China Sea. Her run from Anjer was two days less than that of *Stag Hound*.

Sailed from New York, Feb. 25, 1853; had 21 days and 6 hours to the line; passed Cape Horn, 59 days out; was 12 days between the 50's; stopped at Juan Fernandez for water and was detained there by a gale from May 10th to 14th; left the 15th; crossed the equator June 5th, and arrived at San Francisco, July 1st, in 122 sailing days from New York, nearly all in light winds. Had skysails set for 81 days. Sailed from San Francisco, July 16th; passed Honolulu the 29th and arrived at Hong Kong, Sept. 13th. Left Whampoa, Oct. 24th; was at Anjer, Nov. 10th; passed Java Head, the 12th; thence 29 days to the Cape and arrived at New York, Jan. 21, 1854, in 89 days from Whampoa, 70 from Java Head, 41 from the Cape and 19 days from the line.

On her fourth voyage she left New York, Apr. 27, 1854; crossed the line 33 days out; passed Cape Horn, 62 days out; was eight days from 50° to 50°; crossed the equator on the 87th day in 20 days from 50° South, Pacific, and was 22 days thence to San Francisco,— a passage of 110 days. Sailed Aug. 25th and arrived at Hong Kong,

Oct. 14th, in 49 days. Made a round to Manila and went to Shanghai where she loaded for London. Sailing from Shanghai she cleared Java Head, May 29th; was thence 30½ days to the Cape and arrived at London, Aug. 28th, in 91 days from Java Head. Her fifth voyage was from London to Hong Kong and Whampoa, sailing from the latter port, Apr. 21st, and reaching New York, Aug. 21st, in 122 days.

On her sixth voyage she left Boston, Jan. 4, 1857, under Captain Peterson, who had succeeded Captain Behm in the interim. Had 18 days to the line; 43 days to 50° South; crossed the equator, Mar. 28, 1857, and arrived at San Francisco, Apr. 22, 1857, in 108 days' passage. Was off port seven days in light winds. Sailed May 15th and arrived at Hong Kong, July 5th, 50 days out. Sailed from Foo Chow, Aug. 13th, and arrived at New York, Dec. 4th, in 113 days. The seventh voyage of the *Stag Hound* was from Boston, Feb. 6, 1858, to San Francisco, June 7th, in 121 days, Captain Hussey in command, and this was her last westward Cape Horn run. She was 18 days to the line; passed through the Straits of Le Maire on the 46th day out and rounded the Horn five days later. From Mar. 24th to Apr. 20th, experienced very stormy weather,—one continual gale with high seas, hail, snow, rain, thunder and lightning. Crossed the equator 96 days out and then had mainly strong head winds. A newspaper afterwards stated that a fluke of one of her anchors was bent against the stock by the hammering force of the seas off the Horn. She sailed from San Francisco, July 20th, and arrived at Hong Kong, Sept. 17th, in 58 days and was laid up there for a time. In March 1861 she was reported at New York from London, Captain Lowber in command.

The *Stag Hound* sailed from Sunderland, Eng., Aug. 2, 1861, under command of Captain Wilson, with a cargo of coal for San Francisco and was 15 days beating down the Channel, against head winds; then had fair winds and pleasant weather until Oct. 12th, when she was about 45 miles south of Pernambuco. On that day at 1 A.M., in first mate Goodwin's watch, the ship was discovered to be on fire. All hands were called, courses hauled up, head yards hove aback and every endeavor made to keep the fire under until the boats could be got out. At 4 P.M. they had four boats out and saved what few things were possible in the hurry. At 5 P.M. they left the ship and soon after the fire broke out fore and aft and burned so rapidly that in one hour the masts went over the side and the ship was burned nearly to the water's edge. At 6 P.M. the boats started for Pernambuco where they arrived the following morning.

Up to the time of her loss the *Stag Hound* seems to have been unusually free from accidents. True, she lost spars on her first voyage, but so did almost all the early clippers and her after record shows that the underwriters were seldom called on. She had one mutiny on board, at Anjer, in 1860, where the first and second mate were reported stabbed by members of the crew. Captain Hussey was in command at the time.

The following description of the *Stag Hound* is taken from the "Boston Atlas" of Dec. 21, 1850.

This magnificent ship has been the wonder of all who have seen her. Not only is she largest of her class afloat, but her model may be said to be the original of a new idea in naval architecture. She is longer and sharper than any other vessel of the merchant service in the world, while her breadth of beam and depth of hold are designed with special reference to stability. Every element in her has been made subservient to speed; she is therefore her builder's beau ideal of swiftness; for in designing her, he was not interfered with by her owners. He alone, therefore, is responsible for her sailing qualities.

She is 207 feet long on the keel, 215 between perpendiculars on deck, and 226 feet from the knightheads to the taffrail. The whole rake of her stem on deck is 6 feet, and of her sternpost 2 feet. She has 40 feet extreme breadth of beam, 21 feet depth of hold, and will register 1600 tons. Her depth of keel is 46 inches, dead rise at half floor 40 inches, rounding of sides 4 inches, and shear 2 feet 6 inches. She is uncommonly sharp forward, yet her bow bears no resemblance to that of a steamer; it seems to have grown naturally from the fulness of her model to a point, but so beautifully proportioned that the eye lingers on it with delight. It is exceedingly plain, divested of flare or flourish, and is carried up from its leanest to its fullest lines on the rail, without variation in its outline. That is, its angular form is preserved up to the knightheads; consequently, it has neither humps nor corners to mark its bluff. An idea of its sharpness may be formed from the fact that, at the load displacement line (as the cutwater is tapered to an angle), a flat surface applied to the bow from its extreme, would show no angle at the hood ends. Her bow commences at the cutwater, and swells from that point in unbroken curvature. Sharp as she is, her lines are all rounded, and so skillfully, too, that they almost seem parallel to one another.

A carved and gilded stag hound, represented panting in the chase, and carved work around the hawse-holes and on the ends of her catheads, comprise her ornamental work about the bow. She has neither head boards or trail boards, and may be said to be naked forward, yet this very nakedness, like that of a sculptured Venus, true to nature, constitutes the crowning element of her symmetry forward. As she is five feet higher forward than aft, she sits upon the water as if ready for a spring ahead. Broadside on, her great length, the smoothness of her outline, and the buoyancy of her sheer, combined with the regularity of her planking, and the neatness of her mouldings, impress upon the eye a form as perfect as if it had been cast in a mould. She is planked flush to the planksheer, and its moulding is carried from the extreme of the head round her stern. Her stern is elliptical, finely formed, and very light. The eye directed along her rail from the quarter to the bow, would perceive that her outline at the extreme is as perfect as the spring of a steel bow. The planking along the upper part of the run is carried up to the line of the planksheer and there terminates, and this is done too without any irregularity in the width. Below, the planking from the opposite sides meets, and the butts form a series of plain angles down to the stern post. Her run is rounded, not concave like that of most ships, and at the load displacement line, is apparently the counterpart of the bow, for her greatest breadth of beam is about amidships. An idea of the smallness of her stern may be formed from the fact, that at eight feet from the midships of the taffrail, over all, she is only 24½ feet wide. The stern projects about seven feet beyond the sternpost. A stag, her name and other devices, neatly executed, ornament her stern. Mr. Gleason, a young artist of much promise, made her carved work. Her keel is of rock maple and oak, in two depths, which, combined with the shoe moulds 46 inches, and sides 16. The scarphs of the keel are from 8 to 10 feet in length, and are bolted with copper, and the parts of the keel are also bolted together with the same kind of metal. Her top-timbers are of hackmatack, but the rest of her frame and bulwark stanchions are of white oak. The floor timbers on the keel are sided from 10 to 12 inches, and are moulded from 14 to 16, and are alternately bolted with inch and a quarter copper through the keel, and through the lower keelson and the keel. She has three depths of midships keelsons, which combined, mould 42 and side 15 inches. The second keelson is bolted with iron through the navel, every navel timber blunt into the keel, and the upper one is secured in the same style. She has sister keelsons 14 inches square, bolted diagonally through the navel timbers into the keel, and horizontally through the lower midship keelson, and each other. Her hold stanchions are 10 inches square, and are kneed to the beams above and to the keelson below, so that their lower arms form almost a rider along the top of the keelson. Including their depth and the moulding of the floor timbers, she is nine feet through "the back bone."

The ceiling on her floor is 4½ inches thick, square bolted, not tacked on with spikes, and all the ceiling from the bilge to the deck in the hold is seven inches thick, scarphed and square fastened. She has also a stringer of 12 by 15 inches, upon which the ends of the hanging knees rest, and are fayed. The knees connected with the beams of both decks, are of hackmatack. The hanging knees in the hold are sided from 10 to 11 inches, are moulded from 2 feet to 26 inches in the throats, and have 16 bolts and four spikes in each. In the between decks the knees have 18 bolts and 4 spikes in them, are sided about 10 inches, and moulded in the angles from 20 to 22 inches. The hold beams average about 16 by 17 inches, and those in the between decks 10 by 16, and are of hard pine. She has a pair of pointers 30 feet long in each end, three breast-hooks and three after-hooks, all of oak and closely bolted. Her hold is cauled and payed from the limber boards to the deck.

The between decks are seven feet high; their waterways are 15 inches square, the strake inside of them nine by 12 inches, and the two over them combined 10 by 18. These are all cross bolted in the usual style. The ceiling above is five inches thick, square bolted; and all the thick work is carried fore and aft and round the stern. Her between deck stanchions are of oak turned, secured with iron rods through their centres which set up below. The breast hook in this deck extends well aft, and is closely bolted. Her deck hooks, and the hooks above and below the bowsprit, are very stout, and well secured.

The upper deck waterways are 12 inches square, and the two strakes inside of them each 4½ by six inches let over the beams below, and cross bolted. The planking of both decks is 3½ inches thick, of white pine.

Her garboards are seven inches thick, bolted through each other and the keel, and upwards through the timbers and the floor and riveted. The strakes outside of them are graduated to 4½ inches, the substance of the planking on the bottom, and she has 16 wales, each 5½ by six inches. As before stated, she is planked up flush to the covering board. Her bulwark stanchions are eight by 10 inches, and the planksheer and main rail are six by 16 inches. Her bulwarks, including the monkey rail, are 6½ feet high; and between the main and rack rails she has a stout clamp, bolted through the stanchions, and vertically, through both rails. The boarding of her bulwarks is very narrow, and is neatly tongued and grooved, and fastened with composition. More than usual care has been bestowed in driving her bilge and butt bolts, and the treenails, in order to obtain the nicest possible state of finish outside, combined with strength through all.

She is seasoned with salt, and has ventilators in her decks and along the line of planksheer, fore and aft, and also in the bitts, also the foretopsail sheet bitts, are all of choice white oak, and are strongly kneed above and below. Her maintopmast stays lead on deck, and set up to the bitts before the foremast.

She has a topgallant forecastle, the height of the main rail, in the after winds of which she has water closets, for the use of the crew.

Abaft the foremast she has a house 42 feet long by 24 wide, and six high, which contains spacious accommodations for the crew, and other apartments for a galley, store rooms, etc., the upper part of the house is ornamented with panels, which look neatly.

Her cabins are under a half poop deck, the height of the main rail, and have a descent of three feet below the main deck. Along the sides, and round the stern, the poop is protected by an open rail, supported on turned stanchions. On this deck she is steered, and she has a patent steering apparatus, embracing the latest improvements. The deck itself is 44 feet long, and in its front, amidships, is a small square house, or portico, to the entrance of the cabins.

The after cabin is 32 feet long by 13 wide, and six feet eight inches high. Its after division is fitted into a spacious state-room with two berths, and is admirably adapted for the accommodation of a family. Before this there is a water closet on each side, then a state-room; before that a recess of eight feet on each side, and then two state-rooms. The sides of the cabins are splendidly finished with mahogany Gothic panels, enamelled pilasters and cornices, and gilded mouldings. It has a large sky light amidships; and every state-room has its deck and side light also. In furniture and other details it will be as neat as that of a first class packet.

The forward cabin contains the captain's state-room, which overlooks the main deck, on the starboard side; it also contains the pantry, and state-rooms for three mates and the steward. It is 12 by

18 feet, and is neatly painted and grained; and lighted the same as that abaft. Her cabins were designed and finished by Mr. Thos. Manson, whose work on board the ship *Daniel Webster* and other packet ships, has been highly commended.

Inside the ship is painted pearl color, relieved with white, and outside black, from the water's edge to the rail.

She has patent copper pumps, which work with fly wheel and winches,—a patent windlass, with ends which ungear, and two beautiful capstans, made of mahogany and locust, inlaid with brass. She has a cylindrical iron water tank of 4500 gallons capacity, the depth of the ship, secured below the upper deck, abaft the mainmast, and resting upon a massive bed constructed over and alongside of the keelson. The groundtackle, boats, and other furniture are of the first quality, and every way worthy of the ship.

Aloft, she looms like a ship of war. Her masts rake alike, viz., 1¼ inch in the foot. The distance from the stem to the centre of the foremast is 50 feet; thence to the main 67; thence to the mizzen 56; and thence to the sternpost 42 feet. The following are the dimensions of her masts and yards:—

MASTS.

	Diameter, Inches	Length, Feet	Mast-heads, Feet
Fore	32½	82	13
Top	16	46	9
Topgallant	10	25	0
Royal	9	17	0
Skysail	8	13	pole.. 7
Main	33	88	14
Top	17½	51	9½
Topgallant	12	28	0
Royal	11	19	0
Skysail	10	15	pole.. 9
Mizzen	26	78	12
Top	12½	40	8

Topgallant	9	22	0
Royal	8	16	0
Skysail	7	11	pole.. 6

YARDS.

Fore	20	72	yard-arms 4½
Top	15	57	5
Topgallant	10	42	3
Royal	7	32	2
Skysail	6½	24½	1½
Main	22	86	4½
Top	17	68	5
Topgallant	15	53	3½
Royal	10½	42	2½
Skysail	7	32	1½
Crossjack	16	60	4
Mizzentopsail	11½	48	4½
Topgallant	10	36	2½
Royal	7	27	1½
Skysail	6	22	1

The bowsprit is 28½ inches in diameter, 24 feet long, and has 4½ inches steve to the foot; the jibboom is 16½ inches in diameter, and is 38 feet outside of the cap, divided at 18 and 15 feet for the inner and outer jibs, with five feet end; flying jibboom 18 feet outside of the wythe, with four feet end; spanker boom 13 inches in diameter, and 60 feet long, with 2½ feet end; gaff 44 feet, including five feet end; fore and main spencer gaffs each 25 feet long, with two feet ends.

Her fore and mainmasts are fished on each side, in other words, are made masts, and the former is 29½ inches in diameter at the truss-band, and the latter 30. She has pole topgallant, royal and skysail masts, and her topmasts and standing jibboom are of hard pine. The fore and main rigging is 10 inch, four-stranded, patent rope, wormed, and served over the ends up to the leading trucks; the mizzen rigging is eight inch, the fore and main stays 9¾ inch, the topmast rigging 5¼ inch, set up on the ends; the mizzentopmast rigging 4¾ inch, mizzentopmast backstays 7¾ inch, fore and mizzen topgallant backstays and jibboom guys 6½ inch, and the other standing rigging in like proportions. She has chain bobstays, and bowsprit shrouds, martingale stays and guys, and topsail sheets and ties; patent trusses, and the other iron work in general use. Her fore and main chainplates are 1⅞ inch, and all the other iron work connected with her rigging is of the most substantial kind, and remarkably well finished. She has boarded tops, like those of a ship of war, and her caps and crosstrees are both neat and strong.

Her spars look majestically. Her taunt masts and square yards, so truly proportioned, "fill the eye" with admiration. A first class frigate, the most sightly ship of war that floats, is not more imposingly beautiful aloft than the *Stag Hound*; and it is due to Captain Brewster, who rigged her, to say, that he has performed his part of her equipment most faithfully. Her blocks were made by Mr. Thomas J. Shelton, who is well known as one of the best mechanics in New England. Her sails are of cotton duck, 22 inches wide in the cloths, and including the studdingsails and staysails, contain 9500 yards. With a jib-topsail, water-sails, middle royal, and mizzentopmast staysails, gafftopsail and moon sails, not one of which she has, she might spread nearly 11,000 yards. Of course every sailor knows that all these sails can never draw together, still the surface of canvas seems immense, when we call to mind that all these, and even more sails, might be set at the same time upon a ship of 1600 tons. In the light winds of the Tropics and Pacific, such a vast surface of canvas will send her along at the rate of seven or eight knots, when a common freighting ship would have little more than steerage way. The substance of her masts and yards, however, show that she is sparred for stormy weather as well as light breezes. Her spars were made by Mr. Young, and her sails by Mr. Porter, of East Boston. We have examined several of her heavy sails in the loft, and can say that they are well made.

In taking a parting survey of the *Stag Hound*, we cannot speak too highly of her builder, and all who have participated in her construction and equipment.

Although she is sharp beyond all comparison with other ships, still her floor is carried forward and aft almost to the ends, and presents as true a surface to the water, as ever graced the bottom of any vessel of equal length. That she has a long and buoyant floor is evident from the launch displacement. When launched, she drew 10½ feet forward, and 11 feet 6 inches aft, and this, too, including 39 inches depth of keel and shoe, clear of the garboards. Those who have not seen her on the stocks imagine, from her sharp appearance on the water, that she must bury in heavy weather; but this impression is erroneous, for she is, in fact, very buoyant for her tonnage; and what is more, we believe that she will be a remarkably dry vessel on deck in the worst of weather.

She is, as we have already stated, an original, and to our eye, is perfect in her proportions. Her model must be criticised as an original production, and not as a copy from any class of ships or steamers. We have examined her carefully, both on the stocks and afloat, and are free to confess that there is not a single detail in her hull that we would wish to alter. We think, however, that she is rather too heavily sparred; but many New York captains, who have much experience in the China trade, say that she is just right aloft.

Mr. D. McKay, of East Boston, designed, modelled, draughted and built her; he also draughted her spars, and every other scientific detail about her. She is, therefore, his own production—as much so as any ship can be the production of any single mind—and upon him alone, as before remarked, rests the responsibility of her success —always assuming that she will be properly managed at sea. She was designed for speed, and it is the opinion of competent judges, that the vessel has yet to be built that will pass her.

However much Mr. McKay and the workmen employed upon her, are entitled to praise, the owners, after all, have to foot the bills. To their taste for adopting the model, the builder is indebted for this opportunity of showing his skill. Nothing more clearly indicates the taste of a mercantile community than its ships. A merchant selects a model and forms a contract to have it built after, and if the contract is fulfilled, here the builder's responsibility ends. The success or failure of a ship, under such circumstances, ought to be attributed to the merchant alone. This system of building is common in all large seaports, so that a builder rarely has an opportunity to show his skill as a designer. As a general rule, therefore, the merchants, not the mechanics, ought to be responsible for the qualities of their ships. Yet in almost every instance where our mechanics have had an opportunity of displaying their skill, the result, as in the case of the *Stag Hound,* has been most satisfactory.

She is owned by Messrs. George B. Upton and Sampson & Tappan, of this city, and is commanded by Captain Richardson, a gentleman of sterling worth as a man, and a sailor of long-tried experience. In a day or two she will proceed to New York, there to finish loading for San Francisco, and thence will sail for China. We invite the New York mechanics to examine her, for we feel confident that she will bear inspection as well as any vessel that ever graced their waters.

STARLIGHT

MEDIUM clipper ship, launched from the yard of E. & H. O. Briggs, at South Boston, Feb. 11, 1854, to the order of Baker & Morrill of Boston; 190 x 37 x 23; 1153 tons. She was a fine looking ship and maintained a good record for making passages faster than average. She carried a merman for a figurehead.

All of her passages outward from New York or Boston were to San Francisco and were nine in number. The two fastest were in 117 and 118 days. The slowest was in 145 days, when she had very light winds in the North Atlantic and North Pacific for 64 days. Her next longest voyage was in 135 days and the average of the whole nine voyages was 126 days. On her first passage she was 19 days from 50° South, Pacific, to the equator. In 1860 she was only 17 days

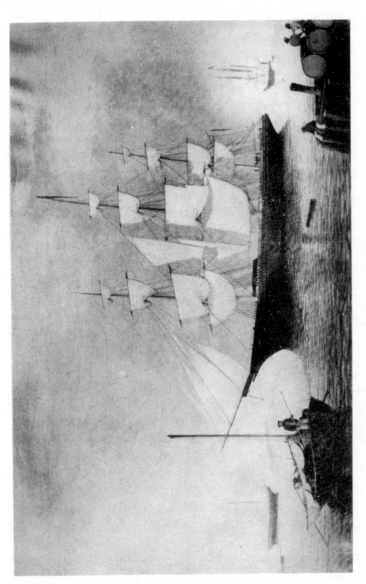

"Starlight," 1153 tons, built at South Boston, Mass., in 1854

From a painting by Lane

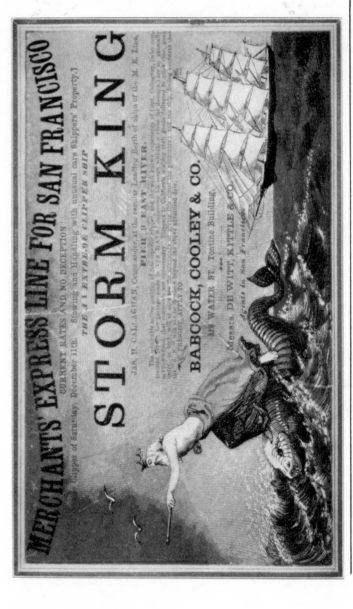

SHIPPING CARD ADVERTISING THE "STORM KING," 1289 TONS, BUILT AT CHELSEA, MASS., IN 1853

From the Peabody Museum, Salem, Collection

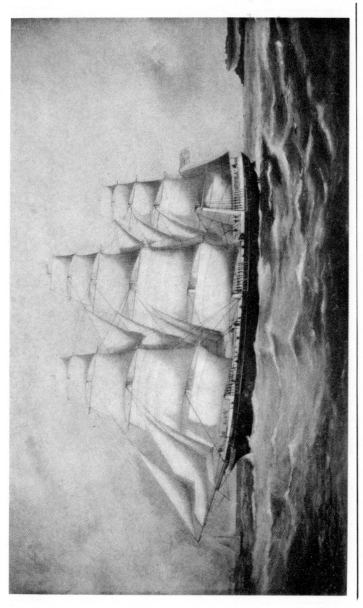

"SURPRISE," 1261 TONS, BUILT AT EAST BOSTON, MASS., IN 1850
From a painting in the Macpherson Collection

"SURPRISE," 1261 TONS, BUILT AT EAST BOSTON, MASS., IN 1850

From a painting by Walters, showing the ship off Dover, England

from the Pacific equator crossing to San Francisco. From San Francisco she had one run to Hong Kong in 46 days and five passages to Manila, of which the shortest was 43 days and the longest 50 days. She made two passages from British Columbia to Australia, in 61 and 60 days; five passages from Manila to New York or Boston, in 107, 113, 130, 114 and 123 days; one run from Manila to Queenstown in 124 days; thence to Bristol, Eng., to discharge, and 35 days thence to New York, with railroad iron. In 1862 she loaded horses at Adelaide, Australia, for Calcutta and was 38 days on the passage; thence 112 days to Boston. In 1864 she was 88 days from Calcutta to Boston, a very fast run seldom equalled and only one week longer than the record.

While at her moorings at Port Adelaide, Australia, from Puget Sound, on Dec. 14, 1861, she was blown on a bank during a heavy gale, but was towed off without injury the following day. The papers stated that her very lofty spars caught the wind so that a tugboat could not hold her during the blow and all her cables were snapped. In May 1862, the *Starlight* left Calcutta 12 hours ahead of the *Belle of the West*, the captains of the two ships being brothers and the chief mate of the *Belle* having a brother aboard the *Starlight*. The two ships sighted each other three times on the voyage to Boston and arrived just 12 hours apart, the *Starlight* first.

In December 1864, the *Starlight*, which had left Boston, July 28th, under command of Capt. N. B. Gibbs, was sold at San Francisco, for $34,000, to be used to transport coolies from China to the guano deposits of Peru. Her name was changed to *R. Protolongo*, after her new owner, a resident of Lima, and her hailing port became Callao. While ready to go to sea from San Francisco, the night of Jan. 26, 1865, she was caught in a severe blow and had to slip both anchors to avoid going ashore; in fact, only a favorable shift of the wind saved her. She was in ballast, but had $180,000 in treasure aboard, and the matter was a case of general average. The ship finally got away Feb. 5th and was 48 days crossing the Pacific to Hong Kong. This was her last appearance at San Francisco.

The first commander of the *Starlight* was Capt. Josiah Chase who, after making two round voyages, was succeeded by Captain Matthews who had the ship for two voyages. Capt. Levi Howes of East Dennis, then had her for four rounds and Captain Gibbs took her to San Francisco on her last passage as an American ship.

STAR OF HOPE

BUILT at Portsmouth, N. H., in 1855; 1097 tons. Owned in Boston. Abandoned near the Cape of Good Hope, June 13, 1861, while on a voyage from Liverpool to Calcutta with a cargo of railroad materials.

STAR OF PEACE

BUILT by N. Currier, Jr., at Newburyport, in 1858; 941 tons; Charles Hill & Co., and M. Davenport of Boston, owners. Captured and burned by the Confederate cruiser *Florida*, Mar. 6, 1863, in latitude 15° North, longitude 54° West, while on a voyage from Calcutta to Boston.

STAR OF THE UNION

EXTREME clipper ship, launched Dec. 9, 1852, from the yard of J. O. Curtis, Medford, Mass. Deck, 185; over all, 200 x 35 x 21: 6; 1057 tons, old measurement; 797 tons, new measurement. Dead rise, 18 inches. She was designed specially for speed and had long and very sharp ends, with concave lines. For a figurehead, there was an excellent image of Daniel Webster, relieved on each side with the American shield and other national emblems. The stern was very light and graceful and was ornamented with gilded carved work. With a bold and lively sheer she could not have been more beautiful, alow or aloft. The main mast was 80 feet long and the mainyard, 72 feet. Her original owners were Reed, Wade & Co., of Boston. In March 1854 she was reported as sold to I. H. Bartlett &

Son of New Bedford, for $70,000. In the '60's, her owners were given as S. G. Reed & Co., of New York. After her arrival at San Francisco, in May 1866, she was offered for sale at a price said to be $35,000, but although her inward freight list had been $26,610.50, there were no takers.

While the *Star of the Union* was conceded to be a fast ship, it remains the fact that she never made any noteworthy rapid passage. On each of her eight passages from New York or Boston to San Francisco, it fell to her lot to have exceptionally unfavorable weather on one or more of the sections of the long voyage. This was particularly the case in the North Pacific where her average from the equator to the Golden Gate is 30 days, 23 being her shortest, with 38 days the longest over this section. On one occasion she was ten days doing the final 500 miles, and on another, 12 days. Her fastest run from an eastern port to the line was 23 days; to 50° South, Atlantic, 53 days; to the equator, 90 days, all these being on different passages. Her fastest direct complete passage was 121 days, although her third run (via Port Stanley), might be considered as 119 sailing days. The others were: 124, 124, 122, 141, 148 and 125 days respectively. On the 121-day run, which was in 1864, she had light winds to the Horn and particularly so in the South Pacific, crossing the equator 98 days out; 11 days thereafter was within 500 miles of the Golden Gate but took 12 days to cover that distance. She arrived in company with the *Hornet,* also from New York, 120 days out, whose captain, Harding, had made a $500 wager with Reed, of the *Star,* at New York, that their respective commands would make the run in 120 days or less. Both technically lost as, although the *Hornet* was off the Heads on the 120th day, she was not anchored within the specified time.

Commencing her third voyage, the *Star* left New York, Nov. 26, 1855; was 31 days to the line; passed Staten Land Jan. 20th; then had a succession of very heavy gales. At midnight, Feb. 1st, while lying to, she was thrown on beam ends and the rudder-head was twisted completely off. After three days Captain Stahl contrived a temporary steering gear and on the 12th of February, reached Port Stanley. Repaired and was in about the position of the accident, 47 days after its occurrence. Was 23 days from 50° South, to the equator and then had 30 days to port. Passed through the Golden Gate, May 10, 1856, after being eight days off port in a dense fog.

Completing her first voyage the *Star* was 58 days from San Francisco to Hong Kong and 105 days from Shanghai to New York; 81 days from Anjer. Her second return was 48 days from San Francisco to Callao and 94 days thence to Philadelphia. The third was direct from San Francisco to New York in 106 days. On the fourth she went from Mazatlan to Liverpool, arriving Feb. 10, 1859; then crossed to New York in 25 days. She was subsequently chartered by the United States Government to return to Africa negroes who had been on various captured slavers. Later, also in 1860, she was reported as making a voyage to Turks Island for salt. She then resumed her place in trade with San Francisco and in 1861-1862 was 81 days from Callao to New York. In 1863 she was 107 days from Callao to Valencia, Spain, later crossing from Cadiz to New York in 35 days, but proceeding to Boston. In 1864 she was 53 days from San Francisco to Callao; sailed thence Oct. 15th, for Cork. Arrived at New York, July 4, 1865, 37 days from Newcastle, Eng., with coal. She took her last departure from San Francisco, June 16, 1866, for McKean's Island, to load guano; arrived at Honolulu on the 30th and left there July 12th. In November she was reported at Rio, in distress, having been in collision off Cape Horn with the British bark *Simon Habley*, which foundered. The *Star* was bound for New York and was badly damaged. An unconfirmed report is that she was condemned and later sold. Her name does not appear in official registers of 1869.

Captain Willis superintended the construction of the *Star of the Union* and was her commander for the first voyage. He had been in the *John Wade*, belonging to the same owners. Capt. F. A. Stahl was in the *Star* 2½ voyages, being succeeded by Captain King at San Francisco, in July 1858. Mr. King was first officer of the *Star* and on Captain Stahl's giving up the ship, on account of sickness, took his place. From 1859 until September 1863, Capt. F. F. Gorham had the ship; thereafter, Captain Reed was in command.

STARR KING

MEDIUM clipper ship, built by George W. Jackman, Jr., at Newburyport, Mass., in 1854. Length over all, 200 feet; extreme beam, 39 and depth of hold, 22½ feet; 1171 tons, old measurement. She was a handsome ship in every way with a good clean run and a beautiful stern. Her Pacific Coast admirers were always confident that she would ultimately make the westward Cape Horn run within 100 days. She was named after the Rev. Thomas Starr King, a popular and brilliant lecturer, writer and preacher, originally of Boston and later of San Francisco. Her principal owners were Baker & Morrill and Bates & Thaxter of Boston.

Under command of Capt. George H. Turner she left Boston at 5 P.M. Apr. 19, 1854, and was 24 days and 22 hours to the line; 52 days to 50° South; passed Staten Island, 55 days out; was 22 days from 50° to 50°, being very close to the Cape for seven days in light winds; then had rough weather in which she lost maintopsail yard and had sails split and bulwarks stove. From 50° South, Pacific, to the equator, had the fine run of 20 days and 16 days thereafter was close to the Golden Gate, a remarkably fast time up the Pacific. For the following eight days, however, she was enveloped in a dense fog bank and did not enter the Golden Gate until Aug. 16th, in a passage of 118 days. Left San Francisco, Aug. 28th, in company with the *Witchcraft*, for a race to Callao and arrived out after a good run of 39 days; but her competitor beat her seven days. Sailed from Callao, Nov. 21st; arrived at St. Thomas, Feb. 1, 1855, and on entering port struck on a reef, losing her false keel. Reached New York, Feb. 17th. On her second voyage she arrived at San Francisco, Aug. 26, 1855, in 124 days from New York. Had 21 days to the line; passed Cape Horn, 61 days out; crossed the equator on the 95th day and thence had light winds and calms to port. Sailed from San Francisco, Oct. 2nd, for Melbourne, thence went to Hong Kong and back to San Francisco, arriving June 26, 1856. Captain Turner reported his time as 58 days to Melbourne; 34 days from there to Hong Kong,—a very fast passage, which was record at that time. From Hong Kong, her time to San Francisco was 44 days. On this latter run she had very light weather in the China Sea, being ten days to the northeast end of Formosa; thence made the passage across the Pacific in the fast time of 30 days, being close to the Golden Gate in 40 days from Hong Kong but unfortunately was then becalmed for four days. In addition to her cargo of rice, sugar and merchandise, she had 375 Chinese passengers. She then returned to Australia, being 64 days to Sydney, thence going to Hong Kong. Again reached San Francisco, Dec. 4, 1857, after a passage of 52 days of very heavy weather. In Captain Turner's sea life of 30 years, which included experiences in one hurricane and two typhoons, he had never seen a more dangerous sea than that of Nov. 13-14. Sails were blown away, bulwarks stove and much damage done on deck, in addition to which the ship sprung a leak.

The *Starr King* sailed from San Francisco, Jan. 18, 1858, and was 52 days to Valparaiso, proceeding later to the Chincha Islands and sailed from Callao, in October, with guano, for Hampton Roads. The next voyage was from New York to Hong Kong, under Captain Ellery. Loaded merchandise and 380 Chinese passengers for San Francisco and sailed Apr. 10, 1860; passed Broughton Rocks, Apr. 27th, and had fine weather thence to San Francisco, arriving May 20th, in 40 days from Hong Kong,—a fine passage. She returned to Hong Kong in 50 days; thence went to Manila and sailed from that port, Oct. 26th, for New York. On her last Cape Horn run she arrived at San Francisco, Sept. 29, 1861, Captain Canfield in command, in 132 days from New York. Was 26 days to the line and passed the Horn 67 days out in moderate weather. Both to the eastward and westward of the Cape, however, she had very severe weather and was forced to throw overboard about 30 tons of cargo from the fore hatch. She was 103 days to the line; thence 29 days in light winds to port. She took her final departure from San Francisco, Oct. 23, 1861, for Puget Sound where she loaded 600,000 feet of lumber for Australia; arrived at Sydney, Feb. 10, 1862, and proceeded to Melbourne to discharge. Went thence to Hong Kong and on her passage thence to Singapore, in ballast, she went ashore on Point Romania, in June, and became a total loss. All hands were saved. The vessel was fully insured.

STING RAY

MEDIUM clipper ship, built at Greenpoint, N. Y., by Eckford Webb, brother of William H. Webb; launched June 3, 1854; 985 tons. Owned by Wakeman & Dimon of New York. Captain Kirby was in command during her career, which was short.

On her maiden voyage she arrived at San Francisco, Dec. 8, 1854, from New York, after a passage of 132 days, light winds having prevailed nearly all the run, particularly in the Atlantic. She was 65 days to 50° South; thence 14 days to the same latitude in the Pacific; thence 26 days to the equator, 105 days out, and thence 27 days to destination. From San Francisco she went to Hong Kong and then returned to the Pacific Coast port in 42 days, arriving May 28, 1855. Captain Kirby reported being nine days in the China Sea, to the south end of Formosa, and light winds throughout the passage. She then went back to Hong Kong in 49 days and loaded for New York.

Sailed from Hong Kong in September 1855; passed Anjer, Oct. 25th, and 26½ days later was off the Cape of Good Hope. On the night of Jan. 9, 1856, being then 76 days from Anjer, she went ashore on Fire Island. A pilot was in charge, Captain Kirby having been sick for 40 days and on arrival at the coast being confined to his stateroom. The ship went to pieces in a gale during the night of January 12th. The *Sting Ray* at the time of her loss, had on board a very valuable cargo consisting of 275,522 pounds of black tea,

18,000 pounds of green tea and a mixed cargo of matting, rattan and silk, the whole valued at over $200,000. Insured in New York for $40,000 on the vessel, $20,000 on the freight money. Most of the cargo was owned in Boston and insured there.

STORM KING

MEDIUM clipper ship, built by John Taylor, at Chelsea, Mass., in 1853, and called the best ship he had produced to that date. Deck, 188; over all, 216 x 39: 6 x 23; 1288 90/95 tons, old measurement; 1148 tons, British measurement. She was built for Snow & Rich of Boston, and was their first venture in clipper ships.

The *Storm King* had long, sharp ends and a beautifully formed clean run; 20 inches dead rise, four inches swell of sides and three feet sheer. Her bow was bold and buoyant, her cutwater forming a dashing curve as it rose. She had as a head the "King of Storms," pointing with his right hand to the sea while his left held the trident of the deep. Her cat-heads were carved and gilded and she had no head or trail boards. Her lower mainmast was 86 feet; main topmast, 48; topgallant, 26; royal, 17; skysail pole, 12 feet; corresponding yards, 78-62-47-36-12. Her masts raked 1, 1¼ and 1½ inches to the foot.

On her maiden voyage she left Boston, Mar. 12, 1853; crossed the line 25 days out; was four days clearing St. Roque; crossed 50° South, 59 days out and was 25 days getting clear of the Cape. Had the topgallant forecastle and the head started; cabin doors stove and two feet of water in the cabin; steering apparatus broken, foretopsail yard and maintopgallant yard carried away. Put into Callao, June 16th, for repairs and was five days in port. Was 13 days thence to the equator and 19 days from there to making the coast near Monterey. Was there five days in the fog. Her passage to landfall, from Boston, was 127 sailing days and from Callao, 32 days, this latter being an extremely good run. Best day on the whole passage,

316 miles. From San Francisco she went to New York via Callao, reaching final destination on Apr. 20, 1854, in 74 days from the Peruvian port, via Hampton Roads. Her second voyage was from Boston to China and return.

On her third voyage she crossed the line in 17 days from New York and passed through the Straits of Le Maire, 48 days out. Off the Horn, while scudding under a reefed topsail and reefed fore-sail, she shipped a sea which filled the cabin and did some damage on deck. Crossed the equator, 86 days out, and was 39 days to port, in light winds and calms being 23 days making 14 degrees of latitude. Reached San Francisco, July 3, 1856, in 125 days from New York. Returned to New York via Shanghai. Her fourth voyage, 1857, was 123 days from New York to San Francisco, she being 66 days to the Horn in light winds. Was seven sailing days making the last 200 miles of the passage. Returned to New York via Hong Kong and Manila. The following voyage was in 1859, in 138 days from New York to San Francisco and was eventful. She crossed the line 22 days out and on the 46th day crossed 50° South; thereafter, for 38 days, she had strong westerly gales. On Mar. 7th she lost a num-ber of sails and had all the spare spars, which were lashed on deck, washed overboard. The main yard was sprung and for eight hours the lee rail was under water with five feet of water in the cabin. The main and after hatch houses were stove in and the ship was not cleared of water until 17 days later. On Mar. 9th, the main sail, foretopsail and foretopsail yard were carried away. She crossed the equator 110 days out and was 11 days making the final 450 miles to port. Sailed from San Francisco, June 14th, and arrived at Hono-lulu in 12 days, landing the mails and proceeding the same day; thence was 39 days to Hong Kong, a long but pleasant passage. On July 25th she passed through a typhoon without damage, although several other ships in the vicinity suffered in spars and rigging.

In 1860, her passage of 149 days, New York to San Francisco, was made in practically all light winds and calms. Had no trades in the Atlantic and was 128 days to the Pacific equator crossing. From

San Francisco she was 16 days to Honolulu; thence 29 days to Hong Kong. In 1861 she was 118 days from Boston to San Francisco, notwithstanding her 35 days to the Atlantic equator. Was close to destination for nine days and hove to in the fog for the last two days. From San Francisco she had the fine run of ten days to Honolulu and was 33 days thence to Hong Kong. Returned to San Francisco, arriving June 8, 1862, a 49 days' passage. Made land June 3rd, 44 days out, and from that time until June 8th she was standing off and on within ten miles of the Heads, part of the time in a heavy gale under close reefed topsails, a large sea running.

The *Storm King* left San Francisco for the last time, July 6, 1862, and went to Hong Kong, arriving Sept. 6th, via Honolulu. She then made two voyages to Bangkok, returning to Hong Kong with rice. In April 1863, she was reported idle at Hong Kong and was sold to go under British colors. She sailed from Hong Kong, May 20, 1863, and arrived at Liverpool, Nov. 8th, with loss of foretopmast. In 1864 she was sold at Liverpool, for £5250. In 1866 she is registered as owned by H. Lefour, hailing port, Liverpool; in 1870 as owned by Mackay & Co., and in 1875, as owned in North Shields, by George D. Dale. The first master of the *Storm King* was Capt. James Collier. In 1856 Captain Callaghan was in command and continued until she was transferred to the British flag, when Captain Harding succeeded.

SUNNY SOUTH

EXTREME clipper ship, launched at Williamsburg, N. Y., Oct. 7, 1854, and was the only sailing ship built by George Steers, the designer of the yacht *America*. Length of keel, 145 feet; at load line, 154; over all, 164: 7; greatest beam (abreast main hatch), at load line, 31: 4; on deck, 28: 6; depth of hold, 16: 6; 776 tons. Dead rise, 28 inches. Her model was somewhat on the plan of the *America*, the entrance lines being slightly concave, long and sharp. She had a good sheer and was light, saucy and very rakish in appearance but her stern was criticized by some as being rather ugly. A scaly monster was the figurehead. Main yard, 66½ feet long; mainskysail yard, 24 feet. Total cost, $70,000. She was built to the order of Napier, Johnson & Co., of New York and her first commander was Capt. Michael B. Gregory.

Although the *Sunny South* had the reputation of being one of the fastest of the clipper fleet, it does not appear that she ever made a passage particularly noteworthy. On her maiden run, which was 141 days from New York to San Francisco, she was forced to put into Rio, but her detention there is not stated. From the Pacific equatorial crossing to within 500 miles of the Golden Gate, she was only 12 days,—very fast time. From San Francisco she crossed to Hong Kong in 51 days, in ballast, and was 102 days thence to New York; 78 days from Anjer. Had left the coast during the unfavorable season.

The voyage quoted was the only long one in which the *Sunny South* was engaged. On arrival at New York, in January 1856, from China, she was put in trade with Brazilian ports and her fastest outward passage to Rio is reported as 37 days. Other runs were 46, 42 and 40 days. Homeward passages from Santos, 47, 41 and 49 days. Under Captain Willis she left New York, Mar. 1, 1856, and her log records;—"Mar. 19; latitude, 13° 17', North; longitude, 30° 24', West; wind at times so strong, could not carry royals; came up with and spoke clipper ship *Whirlwind* which had left New York, Feb. 29, for San Francisco." She crossed the line Mar. 24th, at 7 A.M., 22 days and 15 hours out, and Captain Willis wrote;—"Had I taken Maury's advice and made more south latitude, could have easily made it in 18 days." On Apr. 14, 1858, she arrived at New York from Santos, having on board a portion of the crew of the clipper ship *John Gilpin*, which had foundered off the Falkland Islands, all hands being rescued by the British ship *Hertfordshire* and landed at Bahia.

In 1859, the *Sunny South* was sold at Havana for $18,000, renamed *Emanuela*, and was employed in the slave trade. On Aug.

10, 1860, she was captured in the doldrums of the Mozambique Channel, with over 800 slaves aboard, by the *Brisk*, British screw sloop-of-war. When first sighted in a haze, her occupation was not suspected on account of her size and the unusually large number of staysails and studding-sails set, and when she was hove to, she did so under full sail, without clewing anything up. She was sent in to Mauritius, condemned as a prize and sold to be used as a British cruiser. It was stated that Admiral Keppel was so favorably impressed by her beautiful model that he proposed sending her to England so that naval architects could draw off her lines. She had been regarded as the fastest vessel out of Havana.

SURPRISE

THE *Surprise*, the first clipper ship constructed in East Boston, was launched Oct. 5, 1850, from the yard of Samuel Hall and was built to the order of A. A. Low & Brother of New York, for the China trade. She was modeled by Samuel H. Pook and her construction was supervised by Capt. Philip Dumaresq, who was to command her. Dimensions: 183: 3 x 38: 8 x 22; 1261 tons, old measurement; 1006 tons, new measurement. Dead rise, 30 inches; sheer, 30 inches; swell of sides, nine inches. A finely carved and gilded eagle was the figurehead, while her neatly formed elliptical stern was ornamented with the arms of New York. Her ends were quite sharp although in respect to model and sail area she was surpassed by some other clippers built about the same time, notably the *White Squall, Sea Serpent* and *Game Cock*. Her mainmast was 84 feet long; topmast, 49 feet; topgallant, 28; royal, 17 and skysail-mast, 13 feet. The main yard was 78 feet long; the bowsprit, 30 inches in diameter and 35 feet outboard. Her masts had not the extreme rake of some other clippers, being ⅝, ¾ and one inch to the foot. The foremast was stepped 36 feet abaft the stem; thence 59 feet to the main; thence 53 to the mizzen. She was launched fully rigged and her owners were so much pleased with her that they gave her builder a bonus of $2500.

On account of the activity of California business at the time, the *Surprise* was loaded for San Francisco, in part at Boston, finishing at New York whence she had proceeded in tow. She sailed from New York, Dec. 13, 1850, and arrived at San Francisco, Mar. 19, 1851, in 96 days and 15 hours from Sandy Hook light to anchorage off Clark's Point, San Francisco Bay. She had beaten the time of the *Sea Witch*, her passage being the fastest on record up to that date. From the Pacific equator crossing to port she had the fine run of 16 days and 14 hours and, having been 24 days to the line in the Atlantic, her run between the two equatorial crossings was 56 days. From San Francisco she crossed to Hong Kong in 46 days and was thence 107 days to London. Her outward freight to San Francisco was $78,000 and on the round voyage she earned not only her prime cost and expenses but also a profit of nearly $50,000. From London she went back to Hong Kong, passage 123 days, and returned to London, being 106 days to the Downs. Crossed to New York in 42 days, in continual westerly gales.

The third and fourth outward passages of the *Surprise* were from New York to San Francisco and were each made in 118 days, arrivals out being July 9, 1853, and Aug. 2, 1854, respectively. Her time from Sandy Hook to the line was 19 days, 18 hours, and 18 days, 6 hours; to the crossing of 50° South, Atlantic, 45 and 41 days; rounding the Horn, 24 and 18 days; to the Pacific equator, 87 and 85 days. After these two Cape Horn runs she was engaged continually in trade between New York, China and the Far East.

A résumé of her 14 homeward passages from Asiatic ports, between 1851 and 1866, is as follows. On leaving the coast during the favorable monsoon, 83, 93 and 95 days from Shanghai; 86 and 108 days from Hong Kong and 91 days from Amoy. On leaving in the fair season: 104 and 96 days from Shanghai and 96 days from Foo Chow. On leaving in the bad season: 99 days from Shanghai; 89 days from Batavia; 138 days from Yokohama, all of these being to New York; from Whampoa to London, 107 and 106 days. Her average from Anjer on these passages is 80 days, with 70 days as the shortest and 93 days the longest run. Between the years mentioned, a record is had of one passage to Hong Kong, monsoon favorable, in 91 days; two runs in the fairly favorable season in 106 and 109 days and two in the poor season, 123 and 127 days. There were two passages to Penang, 90 and 89 days; two to Batavia, 88 and 76 days. In 1851 she passed Anjer in 81 days from London and in 1865 in 82 days from New York. In 1858, Woosung to New York 93 days, she was up with the Cape of Good Hope when 46 days out but was 15 days getting around in heavy westerly gales. On her 91-day run from Amoy to New York, in 1863, she was 45 days to the Cape and crossed the line 69 days out.

In 1867 the *Surprise* received extensive repairs at New York, being practically rebuilt. Her single topsails had been replaced by Howes' double topsails and her skysail yards dispensed with. No data is available showing any particularly fast passages made during her later years but her record as a consistently smart ship continued through her whole career and she was always a favorite and popular vessel as well as a money maker.

On what was fated to be her last voyage, the *Surprise* sailed from New York, Sept. 25, 1875, for Yokohama. The first day out she made 240 miles; the 3rd day, 254; on the 26th day, came up with and passed two barks and a barkentine bound in the same direction. Crossed the line, 29 days out, on which day, at 8 A.M. a sail was sighted ahead, which was soon overhauled, a large British ship under full sail, bound for Australia, and at 2 P.M. she was just discernible astern. The *Surprise* passed the latitude of Rio, 36 days out, and on the 68th day, was close to the Island of St. Paul, that day making 315 miles, the best run on the passage. On the 92nd day, was off Timour, making 21 miles that day. Five days later she passed through Manipa Straits and on Jan. 11th, was in the Pacific Ocean, 107 days out. During the night of Feb. 3rd, she received a pilot off the entrance to Yeddo Bay, in a heavy head gale, which, increasing the next day, the ship was put about for shelter in Kaneda Bay. The pilot skirted the Plymouth Rocks too closely and the ship struck, immediately going over nearly on beam ends. The carpenter, third officer, sailmaker and pilot got off at once in the only seaworthy boat at the davits, after which the captain and two men left in the gig, leaving on board, two mates and 13 men, including the only passenger. These, after much difficulty, succeeded in launching the two cutters and got ashore safely. Four days later it was found that the ship had been washed clear of the rocks by the heavy swells and was floating nearly bottom up several miles offshore. A Japanese man-of-war was standing by and rendered valuable aid in salving gear and cargo, a considerable portion of which latter was saved including 10,000 cases of kerosene. An award of $1000 was made to the officers and crew of the Jap. The *Surprise* became a total loss. It was afterwards ascertained that the alleged pilot was merely a beachcomber and that he was intoxicated. He disappeared and later could not be found.

Captain Dumaresq relinquished command of the *Surprise* in 1852 to take the new and larger clipper *Bald Eagle*. Capt. Charles A. Ranlett succeeded him and was in charge many years, after which his son, Charles A., Jr., had the ship until her loss.

SWALLOW

CLIPPER ship, launched Apr. 4, 1854, from the yard of Robert E. Jackson, at East Boston, Mass., for Dugan & Leland of New York and Seccomb & Taylor of Boston. Deck, 210 x 38:6 x 23:6; 1435 tons, old measurement, and 1239 tons, new measurement. Dead rise, 14 inches; swell of sides, six inches; sheer, three feet; a woman draped in white was the figurehead. She was a handsome ship in every way, alow and aloft, with long and sharp ends and slightly concave lines. She was successful during a career of over 30 years and made some passages which were quite close to record. Her first years were spent in trade with the Far East, the majority of her voyages originating in England, where she became one of the best known of the American clipper fleet. In 1862 she was reported as sold to Thatcher Magoun of Boston, for $42,000, and from about that time until 1874, she was engaged in California business. After the latter date she was a general trader. In 1872 she was repaired and overhauled and the following year was purchased by Howes & Crowell, for $44,000. In 1883 she was sold at auction in New York, for $19,000, being then well worn.

The maiden voyage of the *Swallow* was from New York to London; there she was chartered for Melbourne, getting £5500 sterling for the run and returning from Shanghai to London at £6 per ton of 40 cubic feet. Sailed from London, Oct. 10, 1854, from Deal, Oct. 12th, and arrived at Melbourne, Dec. 25th, in 73 days and 18 hours from Deal. Her captain, Benjamin W. Tucker, was much elated over the fact that he had beaten the *Champion of the Seas* by 16 hours and the *Belle of the West* by nine days. From Melbourne, the *Swallow* was 68 days to Bombay, proceeding to Shanghai; left that port, Nov. 8, 1855, and was 138 days to London. Returned direct to Shanghai, with a heavy cargo, in 111 days, arriving out in September 1856. The following year she was 130 days from London to Hong Kong and then took coolies from Macao to Havana in 97 days. On the passage from the latter port to New York, July 1858, she put into Charleston, Captain Tucker reporting most of his crew down with yellow fever, one having died. After arrival at New York, Captain Morton succeeded to the command and sailed Sept. 30, 1858, for Hong Kong.

On Dec. 23, 1860, the *Swallow* sailed from Hong Kong for New York and made the very fast run of 80 days to off Cape Hatteras; there, however, she encountered violent gales and was not able to make New York until Mar. 24, 1861, eleven days thereafter; total passage 91 days.

Between 1862 and 1873 the *Swallow* made nine passages from eastern ports to San Francisco, on two of which she was forced to put into South American ports for repairs. In the first instance she put

"SWEEPSTAKES," 1735 TONS, BUILT AT NEW YORK, IN 1853
From the lithograph by N. Currier

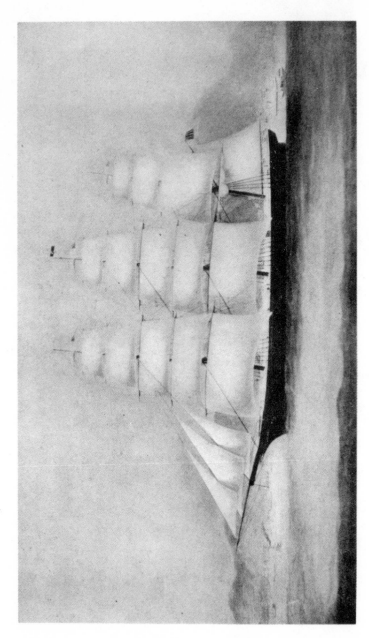

"SWORD FISH," 1036 TONS, BUILT AT NEW YORK, IN 1851
From the painting by Chang Qua, made at Hong Kong

"SYREN," 1064 TONS, BUILT AT MEDFORD, MASS., IN 1851
From a painting made in China

"SYREN," 1064 TONS, BUILT AT MEDFORD, MASS., IN 1851

From a photograph showing her at a New Bedford wharf

into St. Catharine, Brazil, leaky, in August 1862. In the second, she put into Montevideo, May 31, 1867, and Captain McLaughlin reported that on the night of Apr. 27th, in a severe hurricane, the mainmast was sprung and three topsails carried away. The ship was then struck by a heavy sea which twisted the rudderhead and split the rudder port. Repairs cost $5000. The run from Montevideo to San Francisco occupied 80 days. Of the seven direct runs out of the nine passages from eastern ports to San Francisco, five were from New York and averaged 120 days; fastest, 109 days; slowest, 136 days. Two passages were made from Boston, in 131 and 159 days, respectively, the latter being the poorest showing she made over any course during her whole career. On this passage, however, very light winds were experienced in the Atlantic, with 25 days off the Horn. The passage of the *Electric Spark*, which left Boston the day after her, was 155 days, she having encountered the same conditions of wind and weather.

Of return voyages from San Francisco, the *Swallow* made five to Liverpool or Antwerp; average, 111 4/5 days; fastest, 107 days; slowest, 116 days. Two returns were direct to New York in 98 and 101 days respectively. In 1871 she was 38 days from San Francisco to Newcastle, N. S. W., and in 1862 made the run from the Golden Gate to Callao in 37 days, both being excellent passages. Her fastest run from New York to San Francisco was in 1870 in 109 days, when she had favorable weather on all legs of the passage. Was 25 days to the line; thence 25 days to 50°, South; 15 days rounding the Horn; thence 22 to the line, crossing on the 87th day out. From the line she was only 11 days to within 600 miles of the Golden Gate and with continued good weather her total time would have been very close to 100 days. Her last voyage out of San Francisco was in 1876, sailing Oct. 8th, with 1569 short tons of wheat for Antwerp; arrived out Jan. 25, 1877, a passage of 109 days.

In 1885 the *Swallow*, under command of Captain Walsh, left Liverpool for Sydney. Soon after leaving port she began to leak and the pumps becoming choked, the ship was abandoned, all hands being taken off by a passing vessel.

Among the captains who commanded the *Swallow* were, Tucker, Morton, Baker, Small, Dreyer, Daniel McLaughlin, Lester, Bicknell, Bray, Barnabas C. Howes and Walsh.

SWEEPSTAKES

EXTREME clipper ship, launched at New York, June 21, 1853, from the yard of Daniel and Aaron Westervelt, who had previously been associated with their father, Jacob A. Westervelt. Her dimensions were: length of deck, 216: 4; over all, 235 x 41: 6 x 22; 1735 tons, old measurement. She was an ideal clipper, built expressly for speed and very heavily sparred. In comparison with the *Flying Cloud*, of about the same tonnage, her spars were larger and longer; the *Cloud's* lower masts being 82, 88 and 78 feet long, respectively, as against the *Sweepstake's* 86, 90 and 82 feet; lower yards, 70, 82 and 56 feet, as against 78, 83 and 65 feet; topsail yards about the same proportionate difference, while those above were nearly the same in both ships. The *Sweepstake's* spread of canvas was 13,000 yards.

In sliding down the ways on June 18th, the *Sweepstakes* stopped after getting about half her length into the water, on account of too small clearance between her keel and the ground, through which she did not cut her way as expected. She then careened and struck the staging around the clipper ship *Kathay*, then under construction, precipitating a large number of spectators into the water. Steam tugs were unable to complete the launching and it was only after 76 hours' continuous work of two barge-derricks that she was floated. She was then taken to the Brooklyn Navy Yard for inspection and coppering, where it was found that she was badly strained in topsides and joiner work and it is said that the mishap cost the builders all of $20,000 for extra expenses and repairs. She was put on the berth for San Francisco and when about ready for sea, at a banquet aboard, a visitor gave the toast: "Here's hoping that the ship is all right, with a good captain and crew and that she may have a fair wind and no accident." To this, one of the firm of Chambers & Heiser, her owners, responded:—"The ship is all right, the captain is all right, and the crew shall be all right. It's our business to see to this and we've done it. You needn't ask for anything but a fair wind and no accident."

Under command of Capt. George E. Lane, the *Sweepstakes* left New York on her first voyage, Sept. 3, 1853, and was 125 days to San Francisco. In common with other departures at this time she had from the outset light and head winds with no northeast trades and had skysails set for the first 61 days. Was 44 days to the line; passed through the Straits of Le Maire, 75 days out; crossed the equator, 105 days out and then had the fine run of 13 days to within 550 miles of the Golden Gate. But it required seven days to cover that distance, in light winds and calms, and she was within sight of the Heads for four days. On leaving New York she was two feet by the head, due to having heavy boilers on deck. At 10 P.M., Oct. 22nd, in 15° South, Atlantic, she was run into by the Danish brig *Galentine*, being struck in the port fore-chains, but only nominal damage resulted. Her freight list on this passage was $55,000. From San Francisco she was 42 days to Hong Kong. Left Whampoa, Mar. 31st and Macao, Apr. 1, 1854, and was 110 days to New York, 76 from Anjer and 46 from the Cape.

On her second voyage she left New York, Oct. 26, 1854, and was 117 days to San Francisco. Captain Lane reported having moderate weather throughout except for the first 12 days from New York. Reefed topsails twice, only, and furled maintopgallant sail only once. Was 31 days to the line; 57 days to 50° South; ten days thence to 50° in the Pacific and 18 days from there to the equator, crossing when 85 days out, 26 days, only, from passing through the Straits of Le Maire,—exceptionally fast time. Lost the southeast trades in 4° 30′ North, after which had 31 days of light and head winds to destination. Went from San Francisco to Shanghai in 43

days. Sailed from the latter port June 2, 1855, and was 38 days to
Anjer and 85 days thence to London. Crossed to New York, being
23 days from the Lizard to Sandy Hook.

On her third voyage, the *Sweepstakes* left New York, Feb. 20,
1856, discharging pilot off Sandy Hook at 5: 30 P.M. On May
24th, at 4 P.M., she made land three miles distant, about 40 miles
south of San Francisco. The next 24 hours were spent bucking a
strong northwest gale and she took a pilot, ten miles from the
Heads, at 1 P.M. on the 25th and anchored two hours later. Passage: anchor to anchor, 95 days; from pilot to pilot, 94 days and 19
hours and from land to land, 93 days and 23 hours. This run is
the eighth fastest on record and on crossing the equator, May 4th,
when 73 days out, Captain Lane considered his prospects good for a
90-day run, but the trades in the North Pacific forced her too far
to the westward to allow of this. She was 18 days and 8 hours from
Sandy Hook to the line, logging 3896 miles, an average of 8⅞
knots throughout, with the best day only 301, in fresh breezes S.W.
and S. The southeast trades in the Atlantic were light, 23 days being
taken from the line to 50° South, with 286 miles as best day. Passed
Cape St. John, Staten Island, 44 days out and saw the Horn, 30
miles distant, on the 52nd day; was 15 days between the 50's, part
of the time lying to, and for eight days made only 120 miles on her
course. From 50° South, Pacific, to the line, had good to light
trades, being 17 days covering that section, with 306 miles as the
best day. From the line to port was 21 days, winds from the north,
with best days, 241 and 240 miles. Total distance logged—16,062.
She was loaded deep with 2400 tons of general cargo and was drawing slightly more than her depth of hold. Jacob A. Westervelt was
a passenger and naturally was much pleased with her performance.
Continuing this voyage she went to Shanghai in 41 days. Left that
port, Dec. 6, 1856, and arrived at New York, Mar. 17, 1857; passage, 100 days; 77 from Java Head, 46 from the Cape and 25 from
the equator.

On her fourth voyage she left New York, May 9, 1857, and arrived at Bombay, July 22nd, in 74 days' passage, one of the fastest, if not the record over that course. Left Bombay, Dec. 30th, and reached New York, Mar. 20, 1858, in 80 days. Under command of Captain Magill she left New York, Jan. 23, 1859, and arrived at San Francisco, May 8th, in 105 days. Had a succession of heavy gales the first 12 days until she sighted Fayal. Crossed the line, 23 days out; was 57 days to the Horn and crossed the equator on the 86th day. On May 1st, 12 days later and 98 days out, was in 30° North, 137° West, after which had light and baffling winds from the north. Went from San Francisco to Hong Kong in 47 days and thence to Manila. Left that port, Mar. 6, 1860, and arrived at New York, June 12th, in 98 days; 84 from Anjer, 82 from Java Head, 55 from passing Algoa Bay, 47 from the Cape and 28 from the line.

She left New York, Sept. 8, 1860, and arrived at Melbourne, Dec. 11th, in 94 days; thence to Hong Kong in 64 days; thence to Manila in 12 days; thence to Melbourne in 68 days; took a cargo of live sheep to Rockhampton, East Australia, and on return was at Adelaide, Feb. 4, 1862. Arrived at Batavia, Apr. 24, 1862, from Adelaide, in ballast. Had been ashore for ten hours on a reef in the Straits of Sunda. Went on dock at Batavia where a survey showed very extensive injuries; the estimated cost for repairs at the Navy Yard, alone, was 129,440 florins and Captain Magill decided to sell his ship for account of whom concerned. On May 13, 1862, she was put up and sold for 15,000 florins, which ended her career.

SWORD FISH

EXTREME clipper ship, launched from the yard of William H. Webb, at New York, Sept. 20, 1851, to the order of Barclay & Livingston of that city. Sold in 1854, to Crocker & Warren of New York, for about $55,000; 169: 6 x 36: 6 x 20 feet; 1036 tons, American; 730 tons, foreign measurement. She was very sharp, lofty in her spars and carried a great spread of canvas and by some she was considered to be over-sparred. Some of her crews called her a "Diving Bell." She was a handsome ship in every way, and as rakish as a racing yacht. Her first commander was Capt. David S. Babcock, formerly of the ship *Charlestown* and the clipper bark *Race Horse* and later of the clipper ship *Young America*.

The maiden run of the *Sword Fish* was from New York to San Francisco in 90 days and 16 hours, the fourth best passage ever made; arrival out, Feb. 10, 1852. From Sandy Hook to the line she was 23 days; was in 50° South, Pacific, 52 days out and crossed the equator on the 71st day. Carried skysails nearly all the way, light winds prevailing, and for 23 days did not average over three knots per hour. Best day on the run, 325 miles; at periods made 15 knots. Beat the celebrated clipper *Flying Fish*, seven days. From San Francisco she went to Hong Kong in 48 days; made a round voyage to Bombay; sailed from Whampoa, Sept. 25th, against the monsoon, and arrived at New York in 89 days; 70 days from Anjer; best day on the passage, 340 miles.

Her second voyage was made under command of Capt. Charles Collins in 107 days from New York to San Francisco; best day, 340 miles. Was 22 days to the line, sailing 4135 miles; and was becalmed off the Horn four days. Sailed from San Francisco, June 16, 1853, dropping her pilot at 2 P.M. On July 19th, at 11:30 A.M. made Saddle Rock; at 11 P.M. anchored off the entrance to Shanghai to await daylight; passage, 32 days and 9 hours; best on record to this date. Whole log distance sailed, 7200 miles; daily average, 225. On her second day out made 340 miles; was in the passage between the islands of Oahu and Molokai when nine days and two hours out, having averaged 232 miles daily. Sighted the Ladrone Islands, 25 days out, after passing which reduced sail to close-reefed fore and main topsails, there being every indication of an approaching typhoon. Under this canvas made nine knots with the wind abeam. From Shanghai, went to Whampoa and loaded for home. Sailed Oct. 15th and was 97 days to New York. Was in a typhoon shortly after sailing, losing sails, the fore-yard and the mizzen sky-sail-mast.

Capt. H. N. Osgood assumed command and was 110 days from New York to San Francisco, arriving July 23, 1854. Had 18 days and 15 hours to the line; logging 4002 miles, an average of 8.95 knots per hour. Was 48 days to the Horn, coming around in 24 hours in fine weather; crossed the equator in the Pacific 77 days out. Was 42 days from San Francisco to Hong Kong; loaded at Manila and was 102 days to New York. Total time on the voyage around the world, 10 months and 12 days, including 55 days in ports. Logged 39,977 miles, a daily average of 153 miles for her 261 days at sea. Left New York, Mar. 23, 1855; was 24 days to the line; passed Cape Horn 62 days out; then had nine days of heavy weather, during which decks were swept and some damage sustained; was in 50° South, Pacific, 71 days out; then had the fine run of 19 days to the equator, crossing on the 90th day; thence 30 days to San Francisco, being within 100 miles of the Golden Gate for seven days. Completing this voyage she crossed the Pacific and was 91 days from Whampoa to New York.

In April 1856, Captain Crocker took command of the *Sword Fish* and on May 7th she left New York for Panama; crossed the line in 25 days but did not get clear of Cape St. Roque until six days later; was 27 days rounding the Horn, not being north bound in the Pacific until 86 days out. From Panama she crossed the Pacific and finally reached New York, Apr. 29, 1857, in 101 days from Manila. Again under command of Captain Osgood she then went out to Hong Kong in 102 days from New York and returned home in 107 days from Manila. The following voyage, in 1858-1859, was a round between New York and China, the outward passage being 98 days to Hong Kong and the return, 104 days from Shanghai. On Oct. 14, 1859, she was at Shanghai from New York, under Captain Crocker. While running down her easting in a high latitude, she encountered a succession of very heavy westerly gales and being heavily laden and very deep, she took on great quantities of water, tremendous green seas coming on board first on one side and then on the other, while they also often broke over the poop deck. The captain, officers and helmsmen were lashed at their posts and life lines were spread fore and aft the deck. Large holes were made in the bulwarks to let the water run off but marline spikes had to be lashed across them to prevent the men being carried overboard by the suction. The galley was washed out and the cabin, officer's quarters and forecastle were flooded for days together. The only sail which had been carried, a close-reefed foretopsail, was blown out of the bolt ropes, yet the ship scudded under bare poles at the rate of 14 knots. Clothing, bedding, etc., were thoroughly soaked and for over a week all hands had to subsist on ship bread and what few canned goods they could lay hands on. However, the *Sword Fish* was finally worked into fine weather without having sustained any material damage, but with her crew tired, sick, worn out and thoroughly disgusted, swearing that they would desert the "Diving Bell" at the first opportunity and this they did at Shanghai. She sailed from Shanghai, Dec. 12, 1859; passed Anjer, ten days out; was 31 days thence to the Cape and thence 25 days to the line. Arrived at New York, Mar. 3, 1860, in 82 days from Shanghai, 72 from Anjer, 41 from the Cape and 16 days from the line. Her time in covering the last section, is phenomenally fast if, indeed, it is not the record.

Captain Crandall now took over the command and made a round voyage from New York to China, arriving home Mar. 18, 1861, in 102 days from Shanghai. She then loaded for San Francisco, arriving out Sept. 12, 1861, in 136 days' passage. Captain Crandall reported having a very stormy trip during which the first mate, Mr. Macy, was lost from the forecastle head and the boat which was lowered was swamped alongside, its crew being miraculously saved by catching the mizzen chains. The ship then crossed to Hong Kong, having the long passage of 56 days, but on returning to San Francisco she redeemed herself by making the run in 36½ days, which is three days longer than the record. She then crossed back to China, being 47 days to Foo Chow, from whence she went to Shanghai.

The *Sword Fish* left Shanghai, July 9, 1862, with a cargo of cotton for Amoy. She fouled her anchors outside the marks and drifting on the north bank of the Yang-tsze, was forced up by high winds and went to pieces. The wreck sold by auction, July 26th, for 100 taels. The salvage schooner *Frank*, sent to assist, also stranded and was wrecked.

SYREN

MEDIUM clipper ship, launched May 1, 1851, by John Taylor, at Medford, Mass.; 179 x 36 x 22; 1064 tons, old measurement; 876 tons, new measurement. Dead rise, 20 inches. Her entrance lines were fairly sharp and she had a long, clean run. The stern was elliptical and very neat and graceful. Originally she had the image of a mermaid for a figurehead, but this was carried away at an early date and an eagle's head was substituted. She was built to the order of Silsbee, Pickman and associates, of Salem, and in the late 50's was purchased by Joseph Hunnewell of Boston, who, after a few years, sold her to Charles Brewer & Co., of Honolulu. During the final eight or nine years of her career as an American ship she flew the house flag of William H. Besse of New Bedford.

On her maiden voyage the *Syren* sailed from Boston, June 30, 1851, under command of Capt. Edward A. Silsbee, and was 141 days to San Francisco. Between that time and July 1856 she made four additional passages from Boston or New York to San Francisco in 120, 131, 132 and 135 days respectively. Captains Allen and Foster had, in turn, succeeded to the command. Then, after making a round voyage between Boston and Calcutta, she was engaged in trade between Boston, Honolulu and New Bedford, under command of Captain Green. In 1861 she was returned to the California trade and made four successive passages between Boston or New York to San Francisco, in 148, 127, 127 and 152 days respectively. In 1863, Captain Sears took command, being succeeded by Captains Morse and Perkins in turn. In 1866 she was again put on the Boston, Honolulu, New Bedford run and was steadily employed therein for some ten years. In 1870, Captain Johnson was in command and in 1874, Captain Benson. In November 1877, she arrived at San Francisco, under Captain Wood, in 159 days from New Bedford, thereafter going to St. Lawrence Bay, Alaska, to load whalemen's catch for her home port. Arrived off Honolulu, Sept. 16, 1878, from the Arctic and on the 19th resumed her voyage to New Bedford. On Oct. 31, 1879, she arrived at San Francisco, 152 days from New Bedford and returned home with whale oil. Again reached San Francisco, Oct. 5, 1880, in 127 days from New Bedford, returning home as theretofore. Captain Brown in command these two voyages. In May 1882 she arrived at Victoria, B. C., 54 days from Hong Kong; then took a cargo of spars from Seattle to Bath, Me., where she arrived Dec. 5, 1882. On Oct. 26, 1883, she reached San Francisco in eight days from Seattle, with 1208 tons of coal, Captain Crocker in command. She was then laid up in Mission Bay until May 6, 1884, when she sailed for Nanaimo, B. C., to load coal for Port Clarence, Alaska. Arrived at San Francisco, Sept. 7, 1884, 22 days from Port Clarence, and then went to New Bedford, arriving Apr. 30, 1885, in 125 days from the Golden Gate. Returned to San Francisco, arriving Nov. 2, 1885, in 168 days from New Bedford; sailed Dec. 17th and arrived at New Bedford, Apr. 30, 1886, in 134 days from San Francisco.

The *Syren* does not appear to advantage respecting passages from Eastern ports to San Francisco, due to her seeming proclivity for encountering calms, light winds and poor trades and also to generally long and unusual detentions off Cape Horn in heavy weather. In two instances, only, did she have any chance on any section of these voyages these being both in the North Pacific where, in 1852, she was 19 days from the equator crossing to San Francisco, and in 1854, 20 days. A memorandum of her passage of 168 days out from New Bedford, in 1885, shows that she had light winds and very fine weather to the line, followed by heavy head winds and gales to 34° South; then had a month of continuous southwest and westerly gales; passed Cape Horn, 90 days out; was 40 days thence to the equator with practically no trades and then had 38 days from the line to port in light winds, calms and very fine weather.

On routes other than outward to San Francisco, the *Syren* has some good work to her credit. Leaving Boston, June 13, 1857, she was 99 days to Calcutta, returning to Boston in 97 days. Other of her homeward passages from the Far East, completing voyages out to San Francisco, were: two from Calcutta in 104 days each; one from Manila in 105 days and one from Whampoa in 108 days. She made two passages from Baker's Island to Liverpool in 109 and 133 days and one from Batavia to London in 96 days. In 1861 she was 103 days from San Francisco to Boston, beating the *Kingfisher* 17 days; the *Northern Light* and the *Belle of the Seas,* three days each and the *Sierra Nevada* and the *Mary Robinson,* four days each, the four last being bound to New York. From Boston to Honolulu, her passages were very consistent, averaging 118 days; while homeward bound from Honolulu, they figure out about 110 days.

On several occasions the *Syren* met with serious mishaps. In 1853, while on a passage from Honolulu to New Bedford, she was badly damaged off Cape Horn, the head being twisted off, bowsprit and jibboom started, everything on deck, including boats, skylights and hatch, washed overboard and the wheel split. In addition she was struck by lightning and had two men lost overboard. Put into Rio, July 1st, 83 days out; resumed the voyage on the 25th and arrived at New Bedford, Sept. 5th. In 1858, on her passage from Boston to Honolulu, she had the starboard bow stove in a pampero off the Platte, necessitating her putting back to Rio, where she arrived Aug. 15th, 85 days out from Boston. On Apr. 25, 1861, while beating out of the harbor of San Francisco and tacking off Mile Rock, entrance to the Golden Gate, under charge of a pilot, she gathered sternway and struck on the Rock, shivering the bowsprit, opening up the wood ends, etc. She then struck a second time but came off immediately and was squared away back for the harbor with four feet of water in the hold. When beached on the mud flats she was nearly in a sinking condition. Her cargo was discharged and she was taken to the Mare

Island Navy Yard for docking and repairs which cost $15,000. The damage to her cargo was $11,000. In May 1856, off Cape Horn, she had her jibboom carried away, sails split, etc. On her passage from Baker's Island to Liverpool, in 1864, she lost all three top-gallant masts in a squall in the South Atlantic. On Dec. 18, 1870, when near the line in the Atlantic, bound to Honolulu from Boston, she was run into by an unknown vessel and had a close call but fortunately escaped without serious damage.

The *Syren* sailed from Baltimore, Apr. 12, 1888, under command of Captain Merriman, with 1200 tons of coal for San Francisco. On June 25th she was forced to put into Rio, in distress, leaking badly. Her cargo was discharged and after survey she was condemned and sold. Later, she was repaired and as the bark *Margarida* of Buenos Ayres, owned by J. Hurley, she is listed in Lloyd's of 1920, thus having the distinction of being the longest lived of the old clipper fleet.

TALISMAN

MEDIUM clipper ship, built in 1854, by Metcalf & Norris, at Damariscotta, Me.; 194 x 37 x 23: 6; 1237 tons, old measurement; owned by Crocker & Warren of New York. She was a beautiful ship, with fine lines and has a good record for speed. Capt. Francis Bursley, formerly in the *Alert* and later in the *Skylark*, is said to have been in command for a short time, but during most of her career, including the five passages she made to San Francisco, Captain Thomas was in charge. Captain Howard took her over in March 1863, and was in command when she was burned by the *Alabama*.

The *Talisman* arrived at San Francisco, Oct. 24, 1857, in 140 days from New York; was thence 53 days to Callao and from there, 90 days to Hampton Roads; proceeded to New York, arriving June 20, 1858. On her second passage to San Francisco she reached port Jan. 17, 1859, in 135 days from New York. Sailed Feb. 10th and arrived at New York, May 18th, in 96 days' passage, beating by four days the *Great Republic* which had passed through the Golden Gate the same day that she did. Her third run out to San Francisco, arriving Jan. 6, 1860, was in 142 days. Other ships going over the route about this time were equally long. The *Talisman* was 44 days to the line, 20 days making the Cape Horn passage and was not up with the Cape until 80 days out. Crossed the equator on the 115th day. Completed this voyage by returning east via Callao. On Apr. 13, 1861, she reached San Francisco, 112 days from New York. Crossed the equator in the Pacific, 83 days out and, but for having ten days of calms in latitude 24° North, should have made the whole run in 103 days. From San Francisco she was 108 days to Queenstown, her cargo being 1579 short tons of wheat and flour. After discharging at Liverpool, she crossed to New York in ballast, arriving Nov. 6, 1861, in 34 days' passage. Her last arrival at San Francisco was on Apr. 15, 1862, in 115 days from New York. She was 60 days to 50° South, Pacific, and crossed the equator 84 days out. Then went to Callao in 55 days and loaded guano at the Chincha Islands for England. Arrived at New York, Mar. 6, 1863, in 36 days from London in ballast.

The *Talisman* sailed from New York, May 2, 1863, bound for Shanghai. On June 5th, in latitude 14° 35' South, longitude 36° 26' West (34 days out, showing good time to have been made) at about 4 o'clock A.M., she found herself close aboard and standing towards a strange vessel lying to, which proved to be the *Alabama*. The latter then filled away, set topgallant sails and bore down on the *Talisman*, firing a blank cartridge to bring her to. A boat's crew from the privateer then boarded and took possession of the ship which they set afire at nightfall. In the interim the *Alabama* supplied herself with provisions and other articles of value from the captured ship, among the spoils being four brass 12-pound guns mounted on ships' carriages, as well as a quantity of powder and shot originally intended for fitting out a steam gunboat. The *Alabama* took aboard the crew of the *Talisman*, as well as her four passengers, one of which was a woman. The next day, passenger Murphy and wife were transferred to a British ship bound to Calcutta. On June 20th the *Alabama* captured the bark *Conrad* of Philadelphia and the following day Semmes commissioned her as the Confederate cruiser *Tuscaloosa*, to be tender to *Alabama*, using two of the 12-pound guns taken from the *Talisman* as part of her armament.

The claim filed with the Alabama Prize Commission, for loss of the *Talisman*, was:—for vessel, $101,950; for freight, $38,579; for cargo, $90,371; wages of 44 men for eight months, $8560; personal effects, $8305. Total, $247,765. In addition, the claim for war risk insurance premiums previously paid, amounted to $115,500.

TAM O'SHANTER

BUILT by Enos Soule, at Freeport, Me., in 1849; 777 tons. Owned by the builder. Abandoned and foundered off Cape Cod in December 1853, while on a voyage from Calcutta to Boston.

TELEGRAPH

EXTREME clipper ship, launched in May 1851, by J. O. Curtis, at Medford, Mass., for P. & S. Sprague & Co., of Boston; designed by S. H. Pook; keel, 173 feet; deck, 178, her fore-rake being but five feet; beam, 36; depth of hold, 21: 6; 1078 tons, old measurement, but could barely carry that amount in dead weight; dead rise, 27 inches, sheer; two feet. A female image was her figurehead. She was very sharp and in her design combined the best points of the *Surprise* and *Game Cock*. Cost, $70,000. Although she proved to be a fast sailer her whole career was one continual run of disaster.

On her maiden voyage she left New York, July 13, 1851, under Capt. Kimball Harlow, and arrived at San Francisco in 125 days. Had five days of dead calms, otherwise mostly head winds and there were only two days on the run when she had any kind of chance. Her best day was 325 miles and best speed, 16 knots. On her second voyage, Capt. C. W. Pousland in command, she was 114 days from

Boston to San Francisco with generally unfavorable weather throughout; best day, 300 miles. Was on the equator in the Pacific, in longitude 110° when 93 days out and twelve days later was within 600 miles of the Golden Gate. Returning home from Valparaiso and a few days out, she struck an unknown floating object at 2 A.M., which stopped her headway and caused so serious a leak that she was forced to put back for repairs, which were made by divers in marine armor. On finally reaching Boston, Aug. 20, 1853, it was stated that her passage was 58 days, the fastest on record. In the South Atlantic, a whirlwind crossing her bows took the head sails out of the ropes. On her third voyage, leaving Boston, Dec. 2, 1853, Captain Harlow again in command, she was eight days beating through the Straits of Le Maire and had bad weather off the Horn during which she lost her bowsprit and head sails and had the yards on the main mast sprung. Was forced to put into Valparaiso for repairs which took 15 days. Made Point Reyes, near the Golden Gate, in 34 days from Valparaiso, the fastest time on record, and arrived in port four days later in 119 sailing days from Boston. Completing this voyage she went home via Manila, reaching Boston, Oct. 13, 1854, in 76 days from Anjer. Again left Boston, Dec. 21st, and on the third day out was in collision with the ship *Spark of the Ocean*, New Orleans for Europe. Lost her maintopgallant mast and all attached forward except the foremast and bowsprit. Was 88 days to the Pacific equator crossing and anchored in San Francisco bay, 109 days from Boston. Went from San Francisco to New York in 106 days and is said to have been the first ship to take a cargo of merchandise over that run.

In November 1855, the *Telegraph* arrived in the Humber, from Archangel for London. It was stated that when the blockade of the White Sea was raised, she, in company with some 80 other vessels, many being Americans, slipped into the Dwina and discharged their inward cargoes; by great dispatch about half of them were able to get away. The *Telegraph* was reported in the Cattegat, prior to Jan. 11, 1856. On returning to Boston she was sold for $34,000 and loaded for Australia but was forced to put into Savannah, leaky, and when repaired and ready to sail took fire, Jan. 26, 1857, and was scuttled. The fire was thought to have been set by the crew. She was sold as she lay for $6200 and was raised and repaired, being re-named *Henry Brigham*. The repairs on the *Telegraph-Henry Brigham* were completed in the early part of February 1857 and some time prior to Mar. 18th, she was reported to have dragged her anchors and gone ashore at Tybee. She was got off and Apr. 10, 1857, one-fourth of the ship was sold at auction, in New York, to satisfy a mortgage of $5000. The fraction sold brought $5150, the buyer to pay his share of the ship's bills.

She arrived at San Francisco, Dec. 6, 1858, under Captain Dow, in 131 days from New York and was again at the Pacific Coast port, Feb. 25, 1860, in 125 days from New York, Captain Potter in command. These two voyages were completed by her taking guano from Jarvis' and Baker's Islands, respectively. On Sept. 5, 1861, she arrived at San Francisco with a cargo of coal, in 141 days from Liverpool in very severe weather; started the cutwater, stove bulwarks, lost sails and was for a time on her beam ends, necessitating some jettison. On arrival she was seized by the United States authorities on account of her ownership being with rebels. It was developed that she was owned by Lothrop Brothers of Savannah, although Lloyd's Register quoted her as then belonging to Atwater & Mulford. While anchored in the stream in San Francisco bay, November 1861, she was fouled by the ship *Inspector* and damaged to the extent of about $1000. On Aug. 5, 1862, she was sold by the U. S. Marshal for $15,250 to C. Meyer & Co., of San Francisco. After making two round voyages to China, Captain Potter still in command, she went to South America and reached New York, Oct. 8, 1864, in 88 days from Arica.

The following passage was her last as an American ship, in 168 days from New York to San Francisco, arriving out Aug. 3, 1865. Captain Potter reported having adverse winds all the way; 38 days to Cape St. Roque; thence 39 days to 50° South; 21 days rounding the Horn; thence 40 days to the equator and 30 days from there to

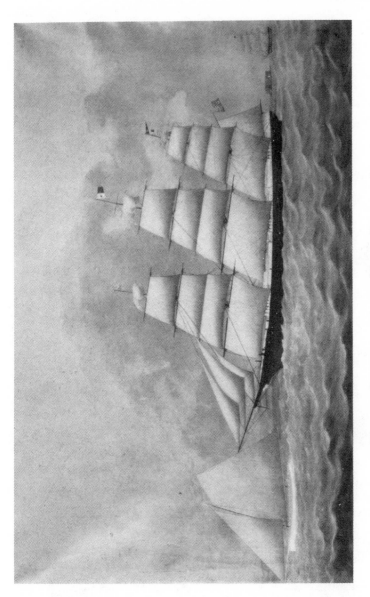

"TWILIGHT," 1482 TONS, BUILT AT MYSTIC, CONN., IN 1857

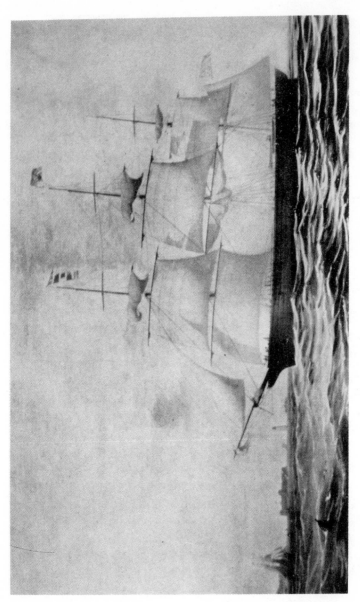

"TYPHOON," 1611 TONS, BUILT AT PORTSMOUTH, N. H., IN 1851
From the painting by Walters, at the Portsmouth Athenaeum

"WAR HAWK," 1067 TONS, BUILT AT NEWBURYPORT, MASS., IN 1855
From the painting by J. G. Denny, 1880

"WESTWARD HO," 1650 TONS, BUILT AT EAST BOSTON, MASS., IN 1852

port. Shortly after reaching port she was sold by her then owners, said to be Rich & Brother of San Francisco, to the Maritima Company of Peru, for the coolie trade, as a companion to the *Twilight* which had been purchased by the same parties a short time previously. She was renamed *Compania Maritima del Peru, No. 2,* the *Twilight* being No. 1. In 1866, the name of No. 2 was changed, at San Francisco, to *Galileo* and as an Italian ship she operated several years in the Pacific, registers giving her owner as Nicholas Larco, who was the San Francisco agent of the coolie-ship owners. On her first passage as *Galileo,* from San Francisco to Hong Kong, she reached destination partially dismasted and the following year (1867) she had a similar experience, repairs costing $8000. In 1868 she was reported as having been burned at sea.

THATCHER MAGOUN

MEDIUM clipper ship, built in 1856, by Hayden & Cudworth, at Medford, Mass., for T. Magoun & Sons, prominent shipowners of Boston. She was named after the senior member of the firm, whose lifelike image she carried as a figurehead. Thatcher Magoun had originally been a builder of ships and was called the father of shipbuilding on the Mystic River. He died the year the ship was launched, aged 81 years.

The *Magoun* was a fine looking ship, conceded to be a fast sailer and credited with a record of 16 knots. Her entrance lines were concave below, merging into convex; the oval stern was very neat and handsome and was ornamented with gilded scroll work. Her length of keel was 173 feet; deck, 190, and over all, 200 feet; extreme beam, 40 feet; depth of hold, 24 feet. Dead rise, 18 inches; swell of sides, nine inches; sheer, 20 inches. Tonnage, 1248, old measurement; 1155, new measurement. She had Howes' double topsails. The mainmast lengths were: lower, 86 feet; topmast, 46; topgallant, 23; royal, 16½; skysail mast, 12. The main yard was 80 feet; lower topsail yard, 68½; upper topsail yard, 59; topgallant, 48;

royal, 38½; and skysail yard, 22 feet. It is said that she set no studdingsails.

From her maiden voyage, in 1856, until the end of 1873, all except one of her outward passages from Eastern ports were to San
Francisco, and were as follows: five from Boston, of which the fastest was 113 days and the slowest, 152 days; seven from New York;
fastest, 117 and slowest, 149; two from Liverpool in 150 and 115
days. The average of the 14 is 128.7 days. On her maiden trip she
was nine days making the final 600 miles yet her run was the second
fastest made about that time, she beating such ships as the *Sea Serpent, Flying Dutchman, Robin Hood* and *John Gilpin* from 4 to
18 days. Her run was 121 days. In 1857, her time being 125 days,
she had the jibboom carried away. In 1861 her time was 121 days.
She passed Cape Horn on the 54th day out but was driven back. In
1862 her time was 127 days, but she was nine days within 100 miles
of the Golden Gate. In 1863 it was 130 days; she was 350 miles
from destination when 116 days out. On her next passage, which
was her fastest (113 days) she was 6½ days between the two 50's
and 87 days to the equator. In 1866 she was 45 days from the
equator to San Francisco, her whole passage being 150 days from
Liverpool.

From San Francisco to Liverpool, the average of the *Magoun's*
eight passages is 121 days; fastest, 114 and slowest, 136 days. In
1861 she was 104 days to New York; made Fire Island Light on
the 97th day and was then fog bound for seven days. On Mar. 15,
1869, she arrived off Sandy Hook in 96 days from San Francisco;
grounded on the East Bank, outside of Gedney's Channel; lightered
a portion of her cargo and was got off by tugs without having sustained any material damage. On three of her homeward runs she
carried guano from the Chincha Islands. In 1858 she went to Callao
from San Francisco but there being no guano charters offering, she
proceeded to Singapore. In 1872 she made two round voyages between San Francisco and Newcastle, N. S. W., in the good time of

4 months and 15 days and 5 months and 25 days, respectively, including detentions at the antipodes.

The first master of the *Magoun* was Capt. Alexander Baxter who was followed by Capt. Asa Lothrop. In 1861, Capt. Otis Baker assumed command and made three voyages. Capt. Albert H. Dunbar, who lost the fine ship *Grecian* in 1889, made one voyage in the *Magoun*. Captain Peterson was in command from 1866 until 1873 and Captain Nugent had her one voyage in 1873-1874. Shortly thereafter she was sold to go under the Norwegian flag as the *Hercules* and engaged in trans-Atlantic trade. She is reported to have been lost off the coast of Africa in the early 80's.

TINQUA

EXTREME clipper ship, launched Oct. 2, 1852, from the yards of George Raynes, Portsmouth, N. H., for Olyphant & Co., of New York, who had been greatly pleased with the performances of their clipper *Wild Pigeon*, a production of the same builder. The models were very similar save that clear forward the lines of the *Tinqua* were hardly as fine as those of the *Pigeon*. She was 145 x 31: 9 x 19 feet; 668 tons; and for figurehead she had a ferocious dragon whose tail was extended on both trail boards. She was named after one of the most prominent Hong merchants of Canton, a close business connection of her owners. Capt. Jacob D. Whitmore superintended her construction from keel to truck and became her commander. During her short career she gave evidence of being very fast.

She left New York, Nov. 24, 1852, and made 2666 miles the first 14 days. Crossed the line in 19 days and 19 hours, in spite of having encountered considerable light winds, squalls and heavy seas which necessitated her being hove to on several occasions to set up slack rigging. On the 24th day out she was clear of Cape St. Augustine; was south of Rio on the 30th day; then had light winds to Cape San Diego, 52 days out, which was seven days longer than

Captain Whitmore had anticipated; was clear of Cape Horn, 62 days out, after which had heavy gales and was 25 days to the equator, 87 days out; then had 11 days of calms; arrived at San Francisco, Mar. 19, 1853, in 115 days' passage. After being discharged and on account of having an insufficient amount of ballast aboard, a strong puff of wind caused her to careen to such an extent that her spars went flat down on the wharf. She was however righted without material damage. From San Francisco she proceeded to Whampoa via Honolulu, and was 33 days from the Island port to destination. Left Whampoa Aug. 15th, the poorest season, and was 42 days to Anjer. Experienced severe gales for 12 days north of Bermuda and reached New York, Dec. 9th, 116 days from Whampoa and 74 days from Anjer,—a good run considering the season.

From New York she went to Philadelphia and loaded for San Francisco. From the Delaware Capes to the line she was 20 days, and to 53° South was 49 days; between the entrance to the Straits of Magellan and Le Maire was detained ten days by strong head gales, so was 22 days from 50° to 50°; crossed the equator, 96 days out and was four days off the Golden Gate in fogs and calms; total time on passage, 122 days; 118 days from land to land. From San Francisco she was 14 days to Honolulu and 31 days thence to Shanghai.

She sailed from Shanghai, Sept. 14, 1854, bound for New York, with a cargo valued at $300,000. Cleared the Straits of Sunda, 38 days out; passed the Cape 31 days later and crossed the line, Dec. 13th, 90 days out. During the night of Jan. 12, 1855, she struck on the outer shoal off Cape Hatteras and 24 hours later her stern was knocked out and her bottom gone and she became a total loss. Was valued at $40,000.

TITAN

MEDIUM clipper ship, built by Roosevelt & Joyce, at New York, in 1855. Owned by Capt. Daniel C. Bacon of Boston, and later by his two sons. She was 1985 tons register, old measurement, and in 1857, was called by the "London Times"—"the largest and finest clipper in the world." Her first master was Capt. Oliver Eldridge of Yarmouth. In 1855, while she was engaged as a French transport, Capt. J. Henry Sears, formerly in the *Wild Ranger*, took command and continued in her until her loss.

After crossing to Europe on her maiden voyage, the *Titan* was chartered by the French Government to carry troops and munitions of war between Marseilles and the Crimea, during that war. On Nov. 26, 1855, she arrived at Malta from Kameisch and Constantinople, with 1174 officers and privates. In letting go her anchor in Valetta Harbor she narrowly escaped running on the Point. She then came in collision with the iron screw transport *Marley Hill*, receiving considerable damage. In January 1856 she was at Marseilles loading stores in company with the American clippers *Great Republic, Ocean Herald, White Falcon, Monarch of the Seas* and *Queen of Clippers*. After the close of the war, in 1857, the *Titan* went to New Orleans and there loaded for Liverpool, the largest cargo of cotton ever carried in any ship previously,—6900 bales. On entering the port of Liverpool in a heavy gale, while in charge of a pilot, she was unmanageable, due to a leak allowing so much water to enter as to prevent her answering the helm. She was nearly on beam ends when it was deemed necessary to cut away the main and mizzen masts to set her upright, after which she was towed into port, a wreck aloft.

After repairs were made, the *Titan*, under charter to the "White Star Line," took on board 1030 passengers and with a large cargo in her holds made a successful voyage to Melbourne. She thence went to Peru and loaded guano at the Chincha Islands. Sailed from Callao, Dec. 24, 1857, for Queenstown; had heavy weather off the Horn and in the South Atlantic and on Feb. 14, 1858, was found to be leaking badly. Four days later she was abandoned, Captain Sears and his crew of 49 men taking to the boats. They were 1100 miles from the coast of Brazil and a course was steered for Rio. After being afloat one week they were all picked up by the Spanish ship *Golconda* and landed at Pernambuco.

TORNADO

CLIPPER ship, launched in January 1852, from the yard of Jabez Williams, at Williamsburg, N. Y., for account of W. T. Frost & Co., and Benjamin Mumford, formerly of Murray & Mumford, all of New York City. Deck, 229: 6; over all, 248: 6 x 42: 4 x 28: 2. She had three decks. Her timbers and general construction were said to have been as strong as those of a vessel of war. She was heavily sparred and in port her lofty yards overtopped all others. While not of the extreme clipper type, she had sharp ends; the floor was flat, the dead rise being very small. Tonnage, per register, 1802; carpenter's measurement, 2376; foreign measurement, 1721. On her maiden voyage she loaded 3300 tons of general merchandise at New York for San Francisco. Under command of Capt. Oliver R. Mumford, formerly in the ships *Palestine, Wisconsin* and others, she left New York, Feb. 21, 1852. The passage was made in 131 days, light winds prevailing throughout. Of her 86 days to the Pacific equator crossing, 17 were at an average of 70 miles; on 29 of the 45 days required from the line to destination, her average was only 52 miles. Total distance logged on the run, 17,575 miles. Her homeward run from San Francisco to New York, in ballast, was remarkable. At 2 A.M. on Sept. 11th, then 35 days out and in latitude 46° South, Pacific, and about 1000 miles from Cape Horn, sea smooth, little wind, ship going three knots under short canvas on account of a steadily falling barometer, a whirlwind crossed her bow. Instantly the bowsprit, which was 36 inches in diameter, was broken off close to the knight heads, the whole mass of wreckage being carried inboard on the port side. The foremast followed, close to the deck, being lifted from between the mainstays and carried over the side tearing away the rails. The immense weight lying across the main-stays, together with the surge of the ship due to increasing seas, jeopardized the mainmast, and had to be cut adrift; the mainmast was then found to have been sprung. Ship was hove to, refitting until the 18th, but her yards could not be crossed for another week, due to the high sea. When rerigged and again put on her course, Sept. 25th, it was found that she was about 12 miles from where the disaster occurred. From there to New York she was 51 days, reaching port Nov. 15th, 86 sailing days from San Francisco, 100 days including the detention. In appreciation of Captain Mumford's successful completion of the voyage without putting into a port in distress, the underwriters presented him with a set of seven pieces of plate suitably inscribed, each piece being engraved with a view of the *Tornado*, dismasted.

On her second voyage, the *Tornado* left New York, Jan. 11, 1853, and arrived at San Francisco, May 2nd, in 111 days' passage. Was 22 days from the equator in the Pacific to the Golden Gate and was within 300 miles the final seven days. She had crossed the line in the Atlantic, 22 days out, after logging 3989 miles; logged during February, 3897 miles; on noon on the 52nd day out, Cape Horn bore north, 38 miles distant and could be clearly seen. Shortly after clearing the Horn, spoke the *Phantom*. The latter led into San Francisco by 11 days, having had the exceptionally fine run of 15 days from the line to destination. The *Tornado* completed this voyage via the Chincha Islands, making the passage from Callao to New York in 71 days. She then made a round voyage to Havre and then one to Liverpool, crossing over in 16 days and returning in 28 days. She was again at San Francisco, Apr. 10, 1855, in 135 days from New York, having had light winds and calms all the way except for 16 days off the Horn. Total distance sailed, 18,156 miles. For 48 days averaged but 60 miles; 12 days before reaching destination she was 500 miles due south of the Farallon Islands. From San Francisco she went to the Chincha Islands via Acapulco, and was 72 days from Callao to New York, arriving Sept. 26, 1855.

The *Tornado's* last visit to San Francisco was made in March 1856, when she arrived after a passage of 112 days from New York. Was 21 days to the line; 90 days to the crossing in the Pacific; was within 500 miles of the Golden Gate for 12 days and sailed 16,869 miles on the passage. When 13 days out from New York she was spoken by the clipper ship *Antelope* which had sailed two days after her. The *Antelope* had 19 days to the line, 81 days to the Pacific crossing and 97 days into San Francisco, thus beating *Tornado* on each section of the passage. The *Tornado* returned home via Callao. She subsequently made a number of voyages between Liverpool and Melbourne and is reported to have made an outward run in less than 75 days. There was, however, a New Brunswick-built *Tornado* engaged on the same run so that it is difficult to separate their voyages. The American *Tornado* arrived at Melbourne, in March 1858, with mutiny aboard, the mate having shot three men, of whom one had died. The ship proceeded to Callao, having a very long passage.

In 1856, the *Tornado*, then 56 days out from Callao for Hampton Roads, was spoken just north of the equator in the Atlantic, by the McKay clipper *Lightning*, 47 days from Melbourne for Liverpool. The weather was variable and squally. The *Tornado* had the wind and was going by the *Lightning* in a heavy squall which split her sails and caused her masts to buckle like fishing rods. On board the *Lightning* all possible sail was set and trimmed most carefully, but still the *Tornado* gained and some on board the *Flyer* thought she was going to be beaten. When, however, she did get the full strength of the wind she gradually dropped the *Tornado* astern and as her log states, "Bid him good bye." The *Lightning* while crediting her opponent with being a first rate sailer, added, that in a steady breeze, "She could not manage us."

On Sept. 9, 1861, the *Tornado* left Cardiff and arrived at Manila, Jan. 27, 1862. Sailed from Manila, May 1st, and arrived at New York, Aug. 29th, Captain Mumford reporting strong westerly gales from 70° West to the Cape of Good Hope. In 1863 the *Tornado* was sold in England for £12,750, name not changed. Captain Mumford was in command during her whole career under the American flag, retiring from the sea after the ship was sold. He had been a master 28 years and was accepted as an authority on matters of navigation.

While under the British flag the *Tornado* changed owners several times. In 1864 she was reported as owned in America, by Page, Richardson & Co. Lloyd's Register of 1866 gives her owners as Wilson & Chambers of Liverpool and Captain Underwood as commander. In 1875 she was owned by Bilbrough & Co., of Liverpool, with Captain Marshall as master. In 1875 she was burned at New Orleans; vessel and cargo valued at $100,000. She was sold as she lay for $3825 to Brady & McLellen.

TRADE WIND

EXTREME clipper ship, launched at New York, Aug. 12, 1851, from the yard of Jacob Bell, successor to Brown & Bell, and was the longest and largest sailing ship built in the United States to that date. Keel, 235; over all, 265 x 43 x 25 feet; 2030 tons. After her first voyage a flush deck was added, improving her general appearance and increasing her capacity about 500 tons. On her second voyage she loaded at New York, 3300 tons of general cargo against 2800 theretofore. A portion of the space on the upper 'tween deck was utilized for passengers, officers and crew accommodations, galleys, etc., the ground tackle being also worked there. A carved billet took the place of a figurehead, the stern was round and handsome and altogether the ship was regarded as a model of perfect symmetry. During her short career she proved to be a fast sailer, being credited with having made at times 17 knots when deeply laden. The best day's work, however, reported on her three outward passages, was only 293, 289 and 270 miles respectively. Her owners were Booth & Edgar of New York, and William Platt & Son of Philadelphia. Her hailing port was the latter city.

The *Trade Wind* completed three round voyages, the outward

passages being to San Francisco, the first two from New York, in
121 and 102 days and the third from Philadelphia, in 125 days.
The homeward runs were, in order: San Francisco to Panama, 32
days and thence 86 days to New York; San Francisco to New York
in 86 days, she being off Cape Hatteras when 78 days out; and the
same route, in 1854, in 89 days. On all of these homeward runs she
was in ballast.

Capt. W. H. Osgood, who was in command on her first outward
passage, reported being 16 days off Cape Horn and 18 days from the
Pacific equator crossing to destination, being off the Heads the last
four days with a pilot on board for two days. In common with other
arrivals about that time had much light and head winds on the run.
At San Francisco she was fitted up for passengers of which she embarked 214 and sailed for Panama, Mar. 3, 1852, arriving out Apr.
4th, but Captain Osgood reported his run as 28 days, he being four
days beating up the Bay of Panama. On Mar. 17th, a fire had broken
out but it was immediately gotten under control. Captain Sweeney
assumed command and arrived at New York, Sept. 10th, in 86 days'
passage. Capt. Nathaniel Webber now took the ship and left New
York, Nov. 13, 1852, crossing the line, Dec. 6th, 22 days out. Two
days previously fire had been discovered in the 'tween decks which
was extinguished by forcing water through holes chopped in the upper deck, but for eight hours the ship had to be run before the wind,
resulting in her falling to leeward of Cape St. Roque and Captain
Webber figured that he lost two days beating around; had crossed
the line in longitude 34. Crossed 50° South, Atlantic, 48 days out;
was 12 days thence to 50°, Pacific; 25 days from there to the equator, crossing Feb. 7th, 86 days out; and was thence 16 days and odd
hours to port. Discharged and loaded 600 tons of ballast and 14
days after arrival was on the Pacific, homeward bound. On her third
outward run, she was in competition with five other first class clippers, all arriving at San Francisco on Dec. 10-11, 1853, as follows:
Witch of the Wave, 117 days; *Raven,* 119 days; *Mandarin* and
Hurricane, 123 each; *Trade Wind,* 125; and *Comet,* 128 days.

After arrival at New York, Captain Smith took command and sailed from Mobile, June 5, 1854, with 4657 bales of cotton, a crew of 34, and 25 to 30 passengers. At 11 P.M., June 26th, the weather being dark and thick and blowing fresh, she came in collision with the ship *Olympia* of Boston, from Liverpool, May 24th, for Boston, laden with hardware and iron, 13 in the crew and with 40 passengers. The position was latitude, 41° 50′; longitude, 57° 20′. The *Olympia* was crossing the bows of the *Trade Wind* when discovered, too near to be cleared. She was cut down between fore- and mainmasts, all of her masts going by the board. *Trade Wind's* bows were entirely stove in and she was a mass of wreckage from stem to stern. The *Olympia* swung fore and aft, alongside, hung on a few moments and then drifted away. While in contact, the captain and some of the crew of *Olympia* got aboard the *Trade Wind*, believing her chances for floating better. At daylight the *Olympia* was seen some miles distant and her captain and his men started in a boat to inspect her, believing the *Trade Wind* in no immediate danger. Almost immediately, however, the latter was found to be settling fast, when Captain Smith sent his long boat, filled with passengers, towards the *Olympia*. The quarter boat, in being launched, was capsized and lost by the now demoralized crew, leaving Captain Smith and 25 men to climb into the mizzen top. In the meantime the *Olympia* had foundered and before the long boat had returned to the *Trade Wind* she, also, had gone down with Captain Smith and some 15 men. The Belgian bark *Stadt Antwerpen*, Captain Wyteerhoven, now fortunately appeared and rescued the survivors, some of whom had saved themselves on floating spars. The total loss of life on both ships is said to have been 24. The *Trade Wind* was valued at $100,000; her cargo, at $250,000 and freight money, $50,000; all covered by insurance. The *Olympia*, owned by George Callender & Co., of Boston, was valued at $50,000; cargo, $200,000, and freight money, $15,000; partially insured.

TWILIGHT

MEDIUM clipper ship, launched from the yard of Charles Mallory, at Mystic, Conn., Oct. 6, 1857, for Gates & Co., of Mystic; 215 feet over all x 40: 4 x 22: 7; 1482 tons register; capacity, 2500 tons, California cargo. She was built under the supervision of Capt. Gurden Gates, who was her commander until she was sold in 1863. She had a half poop deck to the mainmast; convex lines, with a fine run, and 29 inches dead rise; a lively sheer and a handsome round stern. Her record as a fast sailer will compare favorably with many clippers of extreme model.

On her maiden passage she discharged Sandy Hook pilot at noon, Jan. 5, 1858, and passed Fort Point, Golden Gate, San Francisco, at 8 A.M. on April 16th, in 100 days and 20 hours' passage. In latitude 45° South, Atlantic, spoke the *Dashing Wave* and led her into San Francisco two days. The *Andrew Jackson* reached the same port 12 days after the *Twilight*, reporting 99 days from New York, but her time was actually 100 days and 16½ hours. The *Twilight* had 20½ days to the line; 45 days to the Horn, very fast time; and was in 50° South, Pacific, when 50 days out; crossed the equator on the 74th day and was 900 miles from destination when 89 days out. The *Jackson* was 81 days to the equator and thereafter had favorable winds. From San Francisco the *Twilight* was 50 days to Hong Kong, via Honolulu, and homeward bound was 85 days from Anjer to New York.

On her second voyage she arrived at San Francisco, July 26, 1859, in 114 days from New York. Had a good run of 20 days to the line and was only 12 days from 50° to 50°; crossed the equator in the Pacific 87 days out. Went to Callao in 50 days; thence to Hampton Roads, with guano, continuing on to Rotterdam and thence to New York in 29 days. Her third voyage was in 1861, in 109 days from New York to San Francisco, returning direct to New York in 100 days. On the homeward run she was up with Cape Horn in 45 days; passed the Bermudas, 84 days out, but thereafter had 16 days of heavy northwest gales. Her fourth voyage, in 1862, was in 137 days from New York to San Francisco in light and head winds; returning to New York direct in 99 days.

The *Twilight* was then sent to Mystic where thorough repairs and overhauling occupied five months after which she was reported as being sold and Capt. Joseph Warren Holmes of Mystic, took command. His first voyage in the ship (1863-1864), was 121 days from New York to San Francisco, returning to New York in 95 days. The outward run was made with light winds throughout, excepting that portion from 50° to 50° which occupied but ten days. On the following outward passage Captain Holmes reported being 115 days from New York and shortly after his arrival at San Francisco he sold the *Twilight*, for account of Merchant & Cadman of New York, to N. Larco of San Francisco, who was the agent of Peruvian parties engaged in the coolie trade between China and the guano deposits. She was renamed *Compania Maritima del Peru, No. 1,* and sailed for Hong Kong via Honolulu. She was apparently soon resold at Macao as, on her return to San Francisco, in April 1866, in 39 days from Callao (a good passage), she appeared as the Portuguese ship *Dom Pedro 1st* and as such she returned to China. Her next appearance at San Francisco was in March 1877, in 42 days from Callao, in ballast. Was bound for Puget Sound to load back with lumber. She was then under the Costa Rican flag and named *Hermann.* Her captain reported leaving Callao, Feb. 1st, crossing the equator on the 18th and then taking very strong northeast trades with a heavy head sea which caused the ship to strain considerably. Some of her lower beams were broken and she sprung a leak which continued until arrival in port. It was found inexpedient to make repairs and in May she was sold at auction for $4575, to be stripped and broken up. As though objecting to this ignominious end, she floated off the beach one night at high tide, drifted through Raccoon Straits into the upper bay and stranded near California City. From there she was towed back to Sausalito, securely beached and then broken up and burned.

TYPHOON

EXTREME clipper ship, launched Feb. 18, 1851, from the yard of Fernald & Pettigrew, at Badger's Island, Portsmouth, N. H., to the order of D. & A. Kingsland & Co., of New York. She was fully rigged on the stocks and with skysail yards crossed and colors flying she took the water in the presence of a large crowd of admirers. Length for measurement, 207 feet; over all, 225 x 41 x 23; 1611 tons, old measurement; 1215 tons, new measurement; dead rise, 30 inches. She had sharp ends and a leaping horse, life size, surrounded by clouds and lightning, was her figurehead. The handsome round stern was ornamented with a gilded eagle and intricate scroll work. The poop deck was 63 feet long; the rake of masts, 1¼, 1½ and 1¾ inches to the foot; and the spars on fore and mainmasts were the same size, the lower yards being 80 feet long and the topsail yards, 64. She was built for the China and California trade.

Under command of Capt. Charles H. Salter of Portsmouth, she left Portsmouth at 9 A.M., Mar. 12, 1851, and anchored in the Mersey at noon on the 26th, in a passage called 13 days and 22 hours, allowing for difference in time. On two consecutive days she made 313 and 346 miles and frequently took 15½ knots off the reel. Had some light winds and calms and was twice struck by lightning on the 16th, one of the crew being burned and the cabin damaged. Captain Salter's prediction of making the run across in 15 days was more than fulfilled and his ship attracted much attention at Liverpool, not only on account of the fast passage but also because she was the first American clipper and the largest merchant ship that had ever called there. With some freight and 393 passengers she left Liverpool, Apr. 20th, and arrived at New York, May 17th. The packet ship, *Parliament*, sailing two days after the *Typhoon*, reached Boston, May 19th, both making the passage in 27 days.

Loading for San Francisco the *Typhoon* sailed Aug. 2nd and arrived out Nov. 18th, in 108 days. She was in competition with the small clipper *Raven*, from Boston, and the celebrated *Sea Witch*, from New York, which were 106 and 111 days, respectively, on the run. The *Typhoon* was 79 sailing days from San Francisco to the Sand Heads, Calcutta, and was thence 107 days to London. From the Sand Heads to the Cape of Good Hope she was only 37 days, a run never beaten and equalled only by that of the *Witch of the Wave*, according to Lieut. Maury's list of Calcutta passages. She loaded at Liverpool, sailing Nov. 14th, and was 25 days to New York.

On arriving at San Francisco, June 8, 1853, Captain Salter reported his passage as 133 days which did not include four days detention in the fog outside the Golden Gate. Had adverse winds in the Atlantic, not being up with 50° South, until Apr. 1st, when 69 days out. Was eight days rounding the Cape of which four days were calms. Crossed the equator 106 days out. On proceeding to sea from San Francisco in ballast for China, on June 27th, while beating out in the fog she struck Mile Rock, off the South Head, and stove a hole in her bottom and returned and on reaching Rincon Point had 10½ feet of water in her. After repairing she sailed again, Aug. 16th, and arrived at Shanghai in 44 days. Had touched at Honolulu, 16 days out. Sailed from Shanghai, Nov. 4th, passed Anjer, the 24th, and arrived at Deal, Feb. 18, 1854, in 106 days' passage. She then made a round to Calcutta, under Captain S. Goodhue, being 87 days going out and 80 days only from the Lizard to the Sand Heads. The return was in 94 days to Deal.

Captain Salter again took command and continued in the ship until some time after she was sold. During 1856-1857 she was engaged in trans-Atlantic trade, thereafter returning to the Indian and later to the China business with England. On Apr. 2, 1858, near the line in the North Atlantic, she lost all three topmasts in a heavy squall. In the summer of 1862 she left Whampoa and later Manila, for Cork. Nov. 16th she stopped at St. Helena and proceeded the same day and on Dec. 24th put into Fayal, in distress, damaged and leaky, with the loss of the first officer and five men through over exertion. Shortly after arrival several other members of the crew died. Finally arrived at Liverpool on Feb. 19, 1863.

Sailed Apr. 15th and from Newport, Eng., on May 5, 1863, for Hong Kong. Towards the end of that year she was reported at Singapore, sold for $39,000. In May 1865, the *Typhoon*, Captain Salter, was reported at Hong Kong from Saigon. In 1869 she was registered as the British ship *Indomitable* of Dublin, John Martin and Sons, owners.

UNCOWAH

BUILT by William H. Webb, at New York, in 1856; 169 x 36 x 22; 988 tons. Owned in New York. Sold to go under the Peruvian flag in 1865, to carry coolies. Burned in the Pacific Ocean in 1870.

UNDAUNTED

MEDIUM clipper ship, built in 1853, by Hall, Snow & Co., at Bath, Me.; 198 x 38 x 23; 1371 tons, American measurement, 1075 tons, British. Owned by W. H. Foster & Co., of Boston. She was built for general trading, was a good carrier and made some passages which rank as better than average.

The *Undaunted* was first put on the run to New Orleans, returning to her port of departure direct or via Liverpool. On Feb. 3, 1854, she arrived at Boston, in 18 days from the Southern port. In May 1854, there left New Orleans, within a few days of each other, the *Nabob, Panther, Bostonian* and *Undaunted,* all for Liverpool, and their passages were remarkably close, being 37¾, 37, 38 and 38 days respectively. On returning to New York, the *Undaunted* sailed on Nov. 13, 1854, for the west coast of South America. Left Callao, Sept. 7, 1855, and arrived at Valencia, Spain, Nov. 26th, a good passage of 80 days. She then loaded at New York for San Francisco and her only arrival at the latter port was on Jan. 20, 1857, her passage being 132 days. Capt. William Freeman, who was in command, reported being 70 days to 50° South, Atlantic; 15 days rounding the Horn; 24 days in the South Pacific and 23 days from the equator crossing to destination. From San Francisco she went to Callao in 46 days and thence to England with guano from the Chincha Islands. Sailed from Liverpool, July 2, 1858, and arrived at Calcutta, Oct. 1st, a fine run of 91 days. After returning to England she loaded at London for Sydney and is reported to have made the passage in 81 days, an excellent run. Sailed from Akyab, Apr. 6, 1861, and was 139 days to Liverpool.

In 1862-1863, the *Undaunted* was under charter to the U. S. Government for transport purposes, on one occasion taking horses to Ship Island. On Mar. 27, 1863, she is reported as reaching New York, in 17 days from New Orleans, consigned to the U. S. Quartermaster, Capt. Benjamin Tay being in command. She then loaded at New York for San Francisco and in Sept. 1863, put into Rio in distress and was condemned and sold. Her cargo was forwarded by the *Fleetwing*. The *Undaunted* was bought by J. Lane of Liverpool, and under the name of *Caprice*, operated until 1867, when she appears as the Norwegian ship *Halden*, of Frederickshald, owned by A. & T. Weil.

On one occasion a portion of the crew of the *Undaunted* mutinied shortly after the ship left Boston and severely wounded Captain Freeman. Assisted by his officers he proceeded and finished the voyage to St. John. Captain Freeman had previously been in the ship *Maine* which was lost on the bar at the mouth of the Kennebec River, in November 1853. In 1862, Captain Freeman had the *Kingfisher*. In August 1874, his command, the *Mogul*, was burned in the South Pacific while on a voyage from Liverpool to San Francisco. All hands reached the Marquesas Islands in three boats, sailing 1500 miles in 12 days. Later, he was in the ships *Ocean King* and *Jabez Howes* and subsequently went into steam being in the *Zenobia, Palmyra* and *Edward Everett*. He was a native of Beverly, Mass., and after retiring from the sea made his home at Brewster.

UNION

CLIPPER ship, built at Baltimore, in 1851, and owned by S. Lurman & Co., of that port; 184 x 35: 7 x 21: 8; 1012 tons, old measurement; 853 tons, new measurement. She had no figurehead, a billet substituting. Was of sharp model and a fast sailer. Captain Buxton was in command during her early career and Captain Wiley had her during the last six or seven years that she was under the American flag.

The *Union* left New York, June 1, 1852, for San Francisco and arrived out Sept. 28th, in a passage of 119 days. Her best day's work was 340 miles; poorest, 20 miles. She was 25½ days to the line; 30 days thence to 50° South; 15 days making the Cape Horn passage; 21 days running up the South Pacific to the equator, which was crossed 91 days out; and thence 28 days. From San Francisco she was 44 days to Hong Kong, thence proceeding to Shanghai and loading for New York, sailing Mar. 6, 1853. On June 10, 1854, she again arrived at San Francisco, from New York, in 126 days. Captain Buxton reported that on Apr. 1st, off the Cape, she shipped a heavy sea which carried away the head rail and part of the cutwater and caused a leak of 12 to 15 inches per hour. For the remaining 70 days of the passage both pumps were kept going every hour. She was 23 days from the Pacific equator crossing to destination. From San Francisco she went to Shanghai in 40 days and thence to New York in 94 days, arriving Feb. 15, 1855.

The *Union* made no further passages to California but was kept in the China trade principally. On Aug. 7, 1861, she left Shanghai and had a long and tedious passage down the China and Java seas, entering the Indian Ocean through the Straits of Allass, Oct. 24th, in 78 days from Shanghai. Light and variable winds continued throughout the remainder of the run she not reaching New York until Jan. 28, 1862, 58 days after passing the Cape of Good Hope and 38 days from the equator. Captain Wiley reported that on Christmas day he had been boarded by an officer from the sailing cruiser *Morning Light* and warned to be on the lookout for the Confederate privateer *Sumter*.

Shortly after her arrival at New York, Apr. 23, 1863, after a light-weather passage of 47 days from Rio, the *Union* was sold to go under the French flag. She was renamed *Eugene & Adele*, her hailing port being Marseilles. In June 1872 she sailed from Marseilles for San Francisco, under command of Captain Jobet. On Aug. 22nd she put into Rio, leaking and badly strained. Her cargo was discharged and the damaged portion sold. That which was sound was forwarded to San Francisco by the French ship *Reine du Monde*. In December, the *Eugene & Adele* was condemned.

VICTORY

B UILT at Newburyport, in 1851; 670 tons; Benjamin A. Gould and others of Boston, owners. Sold later to D. Knight & Co., of New York. Lost near Cape Henry, Feb. 9, 1861, while on a voyage from Callao and the Chincha Islands to Hampton Roads.

VIKING

C LIPPER ship, launched from the yard of Trufant & Drummond, at Bath, Me., Nov. 30, 1853, 230 (over all) x 41: 9 x 22: 9; 1349 54/95 tons. A Scandinavian warrior in armor was her figurehead. She was a handsome ship, finely proportioned and had a beautiful sheer. She was built to the order of George Hussey of New Bedford. In the early 60's, after being thoroughly overhauled and repaired at an expense of $24,000, she was purchased by W. J. Rotch of New Bedford, for $82,000. Capt. Zenas Winsor, Jr., formerly in the *Monsoon*, was in command until June 1860, Captain Young then succeeding at San Francisco and taking the ship thence to New York in 109 days. In 1861-1862, on a round voyage from New York to San Francisco and return, via Mazatlan and England, Captain Smith had charge, and was succeeded by Captain

Townsend. The *Viking* made six passages from Boston or New York to San Francisco, in 116, 122, 108, 134, 125 and 128 days respectively. On her maiden run she arrived out a few hours ahead of the clipper *Fleetwing* which had left Boston six days before her. The *Viking* was 83 days to the Pacific equator crossing and 33 days thence to port. On her second passage out she was off the Platte 46 days out and 18 days thereafter was in 50° South, Pacific; was 33 days from the equator to the Golden Gate and was within 200 miles of destination for ten days.

In 1858, her passage being in 108 days, she was 19 days to the line; was off Rio, 28 days out; was 48 days to the Horn and 89 days to the equator crossing and thence 19 days. Had she not encountered light winds in the South Pacific her passage would have been very fast. On her next voyage she left New York, May 1, 1859, crossed the line, June 3rd; rounded Cape Horn, July 6th, and was off it for 14 days in constant gales during which, for three days, the ship was completely hedged in by ice and became unmanageable. She was driven back and rounded the Cape, July 20th, for the second time; crossed the equator, Aug. 15th, and was 28 days thence to destination; passage, 134 days. On her passage in 1861 she encountered very heavy weather during which she sprung a bad leak and her cargo was delivered badly damaged. Her last arrival at San Francisco was on Jan. 23, 1863, in 128 days from New York. Had 43 days from Sandy Hook to the line but her time of 47 days from Cape Horn to destination, 17 days from the equator, was excellent. On this passage she is said to have made 330 miles in 24 hours as against her previous best day's record of 321 in 1855.

Some of her intermediate passages were:—46 days from San Francisco to Callao and thence 92 days to Boston, including a stop at Hampton Roads;—63 days from San Francisco to Calcutta and thence 131 to Deal;—94 days from Deal to Callao and thence 91 days to Antwerp, thence 32 days from Flushing to New York, with 378 passengers; on this latter run she lost spars and sails in heavy weather;—84 days from Callao to New York via Hampton Roads;

—51 days from San Francisco to Hong Kong, returning in 45 days and thence 109 days to New York;—44 days from San Francisco to Hong Kong, in 1863,—her last completed passage.

She left Hong Kong May 17, 1863, for San Francisco, in ballast, but with 400 Chinese passengers. At 1 o'clock in the morning of June 4th, she went ashore on Princess Island, off Simoda, having been driven there by adverse winds and strong currents. All hands were saved and taken to Simoda by the U. S. steamer *Wyoming*, and her passengers reached San Francisco, Sept. 15th, on the *Don Quixote*, which also had the Chinese passengers of the clipper *Ringleader*, wrecked while on a similar voyage. The *Viking* was abandoned and sold as she lay. She was insured for $38,000.

VITULA

BUILT by E. & H. O. Briggs, at East Boston, in 1855; 180 x 38 x 23; 1187 tons; Williams & Daland of Boston, owners. Sold in November 1859 to Samuel G. Reed of Boston. Condemned at Rio in June 1867 while on a voyage from New York to San Francisco. Repaired and went under the British flag as the *Bessie & Annie* of Liverpool. Later renamed *James Rowan*.

WAR HAWK

THE medium clipper ship *War Hawk* was launched Jan. 3, 1855, from the yard of George W. Jackman, Newburyport, Mass. Her original owners were Bush & Comstock and others, of Boston and New York, who employed her in the Cape Horn and China trade until she was sold in 1871, at San Francisco, to S. L. Mastick & Co. Her new owners used her to transport lumber from their mills at Fort Discovery, Puget Sound, to San Francisco, until she was burned in 1883.

She was 1067 tons, old measurement; 1015 tons, new; was 182 x 35: 6 x 23 feet depth of hold and was sister ship to the *Daring*. In the Cape Horn trade she made ten passages from eastern ports to San Francisco; three from Boston and seven from New York. Fastest run from Boston, 128 days, her maiden effort; slowest, 144 days. Fastest from New York, 121 days; slowest, 156 days. Average of the ten passages, 134.2 days. She had two passages from San Francisco to Hong Kong, each in the good time of 45 days, on one of which she was but 31 days from Honolulu to her port of destination. In 1858 she was 114 days from Honolulu to New Bedford. In 1859 she was 104 days from Callao to Baltimore, via Hampton Roads. In 1856 she took 900 coolies from Swatow to Havana in about 110 days, being 84 days from her sailing port to the line in the Atlantic. In 1861 she was 29 days from Liverpool to New York with cargo of coal. In 1863 she had a long passage from Manila to Queenstown, 132 days. In 1867 she went direct from San Francisco to New York in 121 days. These various runs show a very fair average for a good carrier.

On her last voyage as a general trader, she left Liverpool, June 20, 1870; put into Rio, in distress, Oct. 27th, and was there repairing some six months. She finally reached San Francisco, Sept. 2, 1871, 440 days from the time she left Liverpool. She was then sold under bottomry bonds for $11,000. Insurance reports show partial loss $38,000 and total loss, $20,000.

Her career as a lumber drogher was very successful and it was said that up to the time she was destroyed by fire she had paid for herself ten times over while so engaged. On her first coasting trip she left San Francisco, Dec. 22, 1871, arriving at Fort Discovery, Jan. 7, 1872. Her second round up the coast, for lumber, was but 25 days, being the record to that time, considering the large cargo she brought down,—750,000 feet. She had left San Francisco, Feb. 19, 1872, and arrived at Fort Discovery on the 23rd, a four days' passage. She loaded in 16 days, sailed Mar. 10th, and was at San Francisco again on Mar. 15th. The best previous record had been 23 days by a vessel handling only 250,000 feet. These figures for the round have since been beaten though it is doubtful if the actual sailing time has been. There was great rivalry among various former Cape Horn and China medium clippers which ultimately had been sold to go into this trade and the *Dashing Wave* was a particularly formidable competitor of the *War Hawk*, being generally considered the faster vessel although the latter consistently made good passages to the end.

On her last voyage she sailed from San Francisco, Apr. 1, 1883, and arrived at Fort Discovery on the 11th. The following day she was found to be on fire and became a total loss. The hatches were battened down and she was scuttled, going on her beam ends under water. Insurance $9000.

Capt. Lemuel B. Simmons commanded her on her first voyage and had her until 1863, except for the second voyage, 1857-1858, when Captain Freeman had charge. In 1863 Captain Scudder was in command for one voyage; then Captain Dunbar, followed by Captain J. S. Williams who retained command until she was sold. Captain Commo had been master for some time prior to her destruction.

WATER WITCH

CLIPPER ship, launched from the yard of Fernald & Pettigrew, at Portsmouth, N. H., May 6, 1853. Keel, 178; deck, 182: 6; over all, 192 x 38: 3 x 21; 1204 tons, old measurement. Built under the superintendence of Capt. Benjamin Tay for Stephen Tilton and others of Boston. She was a handsome ship with sharp ends, neither head nor trail boards, but a beautiful female figure in flowing garments ornamented her bow, while her neat, oval stern had a carved sea scene with three mermaids sporting in the center. Her dead rise was 24 inches; swell of sides, nine inches and sheer, three feet. Her lower masts were 76, 80 and 73 feet long, respectively, and lower yards, 70, 76 and 58 feet.

On her maiden voyage she left Boston, July 31, 1853, under

Capt. Washington Plummer and on Sept. 16th, put into Rio with four feet of water in the hold and dismasted. Was forced to discharge her entire cargo for repairs. Sailed from Rio, Dec. 31st, and was off the Horn ten days in strong gales. Crossed the line in the Pacific, 51 days out from Rio and was within three days' sail of the Golden Gate for ten days. Arrived at San Francisco, Mar. 16, 1854, Captain Plummer reporting her passage as 116 sailing days from Boston and 76 from Rio. She then went to Callao in 52 days; thence 64 days to Hampton Roads and arrived at New York, Oct. 20th, in 75 days from Callao, including detention at the Roads.

On her second and last voyage she arrived at San Francisco, Apr. 11, 1855, 120 days from New York. Captain Plummer reported 59 days to the Horn; off which she was ten days in heavy gales; was 26 days from the equator to destination in light winds. Sailed from San Francisco, Apr. 30th, and was reported arriving at San Blas after a fine run of eight days. Thence proceeded to the roadstead of Ypala to load dye-woods. On the night of June 1st, at the time being half loaded, during a violent gale she dragged both anchors and though the masts were cut away and everything done to save her, she went on the rocks and bilged. The steward and one seaman were drowned. The officers and the rest of the crew got a line ashore and were saved. The vessel was sold as she lay for $500. Said to have been fully insured on a valuation of $68,000.

WAVERLEY

BUILT by Joshua Magoun, at Charlestown, Mass., in 1853; 161 x 34 x 22; 749 tons; Thomas Curtis, Thaddeus Nichols and others, of Boston, owners. Sailed from Coringa, Sept. 21, 1862, for Calcutta and never after heard from.

WEBFOOT

MEDIUM clipper ship, built in 1856, by Shiverick Brothers, at East Dennis, Mass., for Prince S. Crowell, who was her manager and principal owner; relatives had a small interest; 180 x 37: 6 x 22; 1091 tons, old measurement; 1061 tons, British measurement. She proved to be a good sailer and was a large carrier. In 1859 she had 2160 weight and measurement tons of general merchandise from New York to San Francisco and drew on arrival out, 20½ feet. In 1861 she had 1443 short tons of wheat from California to Liverpool, while the *Lookout*, of 200 tons greater register, had only 1471 tons.

The *Webfoot* was commanded during the whole of her career as an American ship by Capt. Milton P. Hedge. She made five passages from New York to San Francisco, between 1857 and 1862, inclusive, in 119, 120, 152, 124 and 146 days respectively. On her longest run she sailed at the poorest season and was 33 days off the Horn in very heavy weather during which she had bulwarks carried away and main hatch stove. She also encountered very unfavorable weather on the 1862 passage of 146 days. The other three runs were good. In 1857 she was 110 days from San Francisco to New York; in 1859 she was 85 days from Calcutta to New York, an exceptionally fast passage, and in 1861 her time of 115 days from San Francisco to Liverpool was only beaten, at about the same dates, by the clipper *Jacob Bell's* 110 days to London. The *Webfoot* had beaten the *Chariot of Fame* 25 days on the run to Liverpool.

In 1863 she went to Melbourne from New York and thence to Callao and the Downs. On entering Dunkirk, Apr. 8, 1864, she stranded on a bank and was badly strained, with bottom severely damaged. Was taken to London where she was sold in July for £2882 to Jenkins & Co., of London, continuing as a British ship under original name. Was later sold to W. J. Woodside and re-rigged as a bark, hailing from Belfast. In November 1886, under Captain Yeaton, she left Puget Sound, lumber laden, for Callao.

Outside of Cape Flattery she sprang a leak in a gale and jettisoned deck-load. Was returning in distress when she was found to be afire in the after hatch and was finally taken in tow and beached, all hands having been obliged to abandon her. When the tide receded the hulk broke up.

WESTWARD HO

E XTREME clipper ship, launched from the yard of Donald McKay, at East Boston, Mass., Sept. 24, 1852, and built to the order of Sampson & Tappan of Boston; 210 x 40: 6 x 23: 6; 1650 tons, old measurement. Her ends were very long and sharp, the greatest beam being 12 feet forward of amidships, while at 20 feet from the apron she was only 12 feet wide. Her lines were slightly concave up to the wales and convex above. A full-length representation of an Indian warrior was the figurehead. Her masts raked somewhat less than those of other clippers of the period, the slant being ¾, ⅞ and 1⅛ inches to the foot, respectively. She was a trifle less lofty than the *Flying Cloud* and *Flying Fish* but her yards were more square, notably all those on the foremast and all royal and skysail yards. She was sparred as follows:

MASTS.

	Lower	Topmasts	Topgallants	Royals	Skysails
Fore.	82	46	24	16	12
Main.	88	49	27	18	14
Mizzen.	78	38: 6	21	14	10

YARDS.

	Lower	Topmasts	Topgallants	Royals	Skysails
Fore.	75	60	45	36	29
Main.	80	64	48	39	31
Mizzen.	57	46	34	26	20: 6

Under command of Captain Johnson the *Westward Ho* sailed from Boston on her maiden voyage, Oct. 16, 1862, and arrived at San Francisco, Jan. 31, 1853. Her passage was reported as being 103 days but sailing and arrival dates, confirmed by her log, show that a full 107 days were taken. She was 29 days to the line; thence 23 days to 50° South; was 13 days making the Cape Horn passage; 23 days in the South Pacific, crossing the equator 88 days out and thence 19 days to port. A few hours after her arrival the *Flying Fish* dropped her anchor after a passage of 92 days and 4 hours from New York harbor and two days later the *John Gilpin* showed up in 93 days and 20 hours from New York, pilot to pilot. From San Francisco the *Westward Ho* went to Manila in 39 days, beating the *Flying Fish* one day on the run, both passages being exceptionally fast. Remained in port three weeks, thence going to Batavia in 29 days and from that port was 82 days to New York. Lost her jibboom in a heavy squall after rounding the Cape and was 35 days from St. Helena to destination. The voyage around the world occupied eight months and ten days including all detentions.

Captain Johnson was now superseded by Captain Hussey who took his departure from New York in the *Westward Ho*, Nov. 14, 1853, and arrived at San Francisco, Feb. 27, 1854, in a passage of 105 days. Was 24 days to the line; 18 days off the Cape in heavy gales and had the fine run of 18 days from the Pacific equator crossing to port. From San Francisco she went to Calcutta in 87 days and thence to Boston in 103 days. Loaded for San Francisco and on Apr. 24, 1855, dropped her anchor in that harbor, 100 days and 18 hours from Boston Light, having sailed by log 17,123 miles. The distance made to the equator crossing in the Pacific was 14,034 miles, a daily average of 175.42 miles. Best day's run, 315 miles, as against 376 miles on the prior passage; frequently logged 16 knots. Was 23 days to the line; 12 days off the Cape in strong gales and crossed the equator 80 days out. The clipper ship *Neptune's Car* reached port the day after the *Westward Ho* in 100 days and 23½ hours from New York and it was claimed that her passage should be considered faster than that of the *Westward Ho* from Boston. Both ships left San Francisco, May 13th, for Hong Kong, the *Car* arriving out 11 days ahead of her rival and it was fortunate for Captain Hussey that the *Car* had no backers to cover the large wagers he was offering to make on the passage of his ship before leaving San Francisco.

Instructions to the effect that their ships should not engage in the coolie carrying trade had been forwarded by Sampson & Tappan but before these were received in China, both their ships, *Westward Ho* and *Winged Racer*, had been chartered and had sailed from Swatow for Callao with laborers for the guano deposits. Captain Hussey does not appear to have had any trouble with his cargo of 800 human chattels although he had a long run down the China Sea to Anjer. Arrived at Callao, Feb. 4, 1856, and sailed June 12th, for New York.

The following voyage was the last made by the *Westward Ho* under the American flag. Leaving New York, Dec. 16, 1856, she anchored in San Francisco bay, Mar. 26, 1857, another fine run of 100 days. Captain Hussey reported being 20 days to the line; came around Cape Horn on the 51st day out and made the Pacific equator crossing on the 81st day. At San Francisco the command was transferred to Captain Jones who took his charge to Callao where she was purchased by Don Juan de Ugarte of Lima, to be used in the coolie trade. She went under the Peruvian flag without change of name, her hailing port becoming Callao. Leaving Callao, Oct. 13, 1857, she went to Hong Kong in 61 days. Then took coolies to Havana, but after this voyage is said to have been operated entirely on the run between Peru and China. Her end came on Feb. 27, 1864, when, at anchor in the harbor of Callao ready to leave for China, she caught fire and burned until she sank at her moorings, proving a total loss.

WEST WIND

MEDIUM clipper ship, built by Joshua Foster, at Medford, Mass.; launched in March 1853; 180 x 36: 6 x 24; 1071 tons, old measurement. With fairly sharp lines she was a good carrier, having on her maiden voyage 2000 tons of weight and measurement cargo. Her dead rise was 15 inches and sheer 24 inches. She had no figurehead but on the stern was a carved representation of a ship under full sail by the wind. Her lower masts were 76, 81 and 73 feet long, respectively. Fore and main yards, 68½ feet each. she carried but one skysail, the main. She was nearly identical in model and dimensions with the *National Eagle,* a product of the same yard in 1852. Her owners were J. & A. Tirrell of Boston.

The maiden voyage of the *West Wind* was from Boston to San Francisco, under Capt. G. W. Elliott, arriving out, Sept. 26, 1853, in 135 days. In heavy weather off the Cape the cutwater was started and head rails and knees carried away. In 1855 she went over the same route in 129 days encountering light winds, particularly in the Pacific. When 119 days out was within 400 miles of destination. In 1856-1857 she was 122 days over the same course, Captain Hatch in command. In 1858, Capt. Allen Baxter had 137 days from Boston to the Golden Gate and in 1859-1860 he reported his run from New York as 170 days, being 46 days to the line and 37 days rounding the Cape. Her last westward Cape Horn run was in 1861-1862, in 133 days from Boston, Captain Elliott in command.

The continuation and completion of the above voyages were as follows: on the first she was 51 days from San Francisco to California and thence 97 days to Hampton Roads. On the second she was 54 days to Singapore, thence 21 days to Calcutta and 116 days from that port to Boston. In 1857 she also returned to Boston by way of Calcutta. In 1858-1859 she was 13 days from the Golden Gate to Honolulu, and thence to New Bedford, arriving Apr. 16th. In 1860 she went to Callao and Hampton Roads. Later she was at New Orleans, sailing thence Mar. 28, 1861, and reaching Naples,

June 7th. On her last voyage as an American ship she left San Francisco, Feb. 28, 1862, passed Honolulu, Mar. 15th, and arrived at Hong Kong 26 days later. Went to Melbourne, Batavia and Calcutta, sailing from latter port Dec. 26th and the Sand Heads the 29th, arriving at New York, Apr. 11, 1863, in 102 days' passage. Shortly after her arrival at New York she was sold for $40,000 to go under the British flag. She was renamed *Lord Clyde*, her hailing port becoming Calcutta and her owner, M. McLean.

WHIRLWIND

EXTREME clipper ship, built by James O. Curtis, at Medford, Mass., and launched Sept. 13, 1852, for W. & F. H. Whittemore of Boston; 185 x 38 x 21; 960 44/95 tons. Dead rise, 18 inches; swell of sides, nine inches; sheer, three feet. Her ends were like those of a steamboat, very sharp; bow, wedge-shaped with slightly hollow entrance lines; the stern was round. The "Goddess of the Winds" holding a lighted torch in the left hand, was her figurehead.

Under Capt. William H. Burgess, the *Whirlwind* left Boston, Nov. 12, 1852, and was 28 days to the line with 18 days off the Horn and 22 days from the equator to San Francisco, arriving Mar. 11, 1853, 119 days out. Went to Callao in 55 days and was 76 days thence to New York, arriving Nov. 26, 1853. Sailed again Feb. 4, 1854, and was 27 days to the line; 54 days to the Falkland Islands; off the Horn 22 days, in heavy gales; crossed the equator 102 days out and reached San Francisco, June 13th, in a passage of 129 days. Was 54 days thence to Callao and 84 days from there to New York. Capt. John R. Giet then took command and left New York, Mar. 28, 1855, arriving at Port Philip, June 11th, in 75 days' passage. She was 26 days to the line and only 16 days thence to crossing the prime meridian, a very fast run. From off St. Roque to Port Philip her time was 48 days which has seldom been equalled or beaten. From Melbourne she went to Calcutta in 40 days and was 94 days thence to New York, arriving Jan. 12, 1856. Again left that port Feb. 29th and arrived at Melbourne, May 19th, in 80 days' passage. Went to Manila and was 116 days thence to New York. Sailed from New York, Jan. 21, 1857; arrived at Melbourne, Apr. 10th, in 79 days; went to Manila in 43 days and was thence 113 days to New York, arriving Nov. 10, 1857. Again sailed Jan. 18, 1858, and was reported as arriving at Melbourne, Mar. 31st, which would be 72 days, the second best passage on record; one day, only, longer than the celebrated run of the *Mandarin*. From Melbourne she went to Calcutta in 40 days and thence to New York in 102 days. Then loaded for San Francisco, arriving out June 5, 1859, a 120 days' passage and crossed to Hong Kong in 49 days.

In the spring of 1860, she, with other American clippers then at Hong Kong, was tendered to the British Government to load stores, troops and horses for the campaign in the north of China. The *Game Cock* was taken up at 22 shillings per month, per ton register, for six months, but the *Whirlwind* did not get a charter in that service. Later in 1860 she was at Bangkok; in September, at Penang and under date of Nov. 27, 1860, was reported in port at Calcutta to proceed to Bombay. Efforts to trace her future movements or history have been without avail. In 1862, then appearing in registers as owned by Francis Burrett & Co., of New York, it was reported that she was sold to go under British colors for operation in the "Black Ball Line" of Liverpool-Australia passenger ships, but registers show that the *Whirlwind* of that line was a ship built in Scotland.

WHISTLER

CLIPPER ship, launched from the yard of George W. Jackman, Jr., at Newburyport, Mass., June 15, 1853, for account of Bush & Wildes of Boston. Keel, 159; deck, 171; over all, 185; x 36 x 22 feet; 820 tons, old measurement. Dead rise, 17 inches; swell of sides, 12 inches; sheer, 30 inches. She was quite sharp, with convex entrance lines and was without ornaments, having no figurehead and her round stern was free from any carved work.

On her maiden passage she left Boston, July 16, 1853, under command of Capt. Charles H. Brown, and made the run out to San Francisco in 131 days. Was 32½ days to the line; 60 days to 50° South and was ten days thence to the same latitude in the Pacific. Crossed the equator, 37 days later, 107 days out, and was thence 24 days to port. On the passage had the bowsprit badly sprung in a heavy gale. From San Francisco crossed to Hong Kong in 44 days. Loaded at Whampoa for New York. Left Macao, Mar. 3, 1854, and made the passage in 106 days, 81 days from Java Head.

On her second and last voyage she sailed from Boston, Aug. 1, 1854, and was 130 days to San Francisco. Passed Cape Horn 66 days out and then had a succession of heavy gales for 14 days; crossed the equator 102 days out and was 28 days to destination in light winds; was within 50 miles of the Golden Gate for two days. Then crossed to Hong Kong in 48 days and went thence to Melbourne. Sailed from Port Philip, May 19, 1855, in ballast for Singapore and went ashore and became a total loss, when four days out, on King's Island, Bass Straits. Captain Brown was still in command. The steward and one seaman were drowned.

WHITE FALCON

CLIPPER ship, built at Pittston, Me., in 1853; 190 x 38 x 23; 1372 tons. Of quite sharp model her carrying capacity for dead weight cargo was but little over her register. She was owned by M. O. Roberts of New York, and was engaged in trade principally with China and the west coast of Central America and was never on the San Francisco run. During the winter of 1856-1857, in company with the *Great Republic, Queen of Clippers* and other fine American ships, she was under charter to the French Government carrying stores from Marseilles to the Crimea. On Mar. 16,

1859, she left Callao for Hampton Roads, for orders, with a cargo of guano.

Early in 1862 she was reported as ashore at Foo Chow, being floated with the loss of a portion of her keel. Was docked and repaired at Hong Kong, later proceeding to Manila. Sailed thence Mar. 2nd and arrived at New York, June 20th. Captain Winsor, then in command, reported that on Apr. 26th, in a heavy westerly gale off the Cape of Good Hope, the foretopgallantmast, maintopmast and jibboom with the spritsail yard were carried away and the foremast badly sprung. A leak of 14 inches per hour developed forward. After strenuous work for seven days a chain was successfully passed through the hawse pipes around the stem to the windlass, and a purchase forced the stem into place, it having been opened 2½ inches. The leak was gradually got down to four inches per hour where it continued until they reached port. On May 5th, in latitude 28° South, she met the British ship *Shalimar*, 58 days out of Calcutta for Liverpool, who ran across her bows. The *Falcon* was making seven knots at the time and the ships cleared by only some ten feet,—a very close call for both.

Shortly after her arrival at New York, on this passage, the *Falcon* was seized by the Government on account of her ownership then being with Southerners. On Aug. 12, 1862, she was sold by order of the Prize Commissioners for $21,000 to Boston parties. Under command of Capt. William L. Merry, in later years one of San Francisco's most prominent merchants, she left New York, Oct. 10, 1862, with 1400 tons of coal to be distributed at San Juan del Sur to the steamers of Commodore Vanderbilt's Nicaragua Line. On Nov. 16th she put into Rio, leaky; repaired and sailed Dec. 10th. Arrived at San Juan, Feb. 23, 1863, in 75 days from Rio, with head winds and gales alternating with calms and baffling airs throughout the passage. She was 123 sailing days from New York. On her arrival out it was found that the Line was having some trouble with the local government, the steamer *Moses Taylor* being detained in port with her passengers aboard. The *Falcon* therefore proceeded to San Francisco, with her cargo intact, arriving Apr. 4th, after a passage of 37 days in light winds and calms. She was in port at San Francisco two weeks after which she returned south to Acapulco, with her inward cargo for its original consignees. While lying at the latter port, Dec. 11, 1863, she had her jibboom carried away and was otherwise damaged forward through being fouled by the ship *Kate Prince* which was outward bound for Callao.

After her cargo was distributed, the *Falcon* returned in ballast to San Francisco, arriving Jan. 3, 1864, in 21 days from Acapulco. She was soon after sold for $28,000 gold to Canavero & Co., of Lima, N. Larco of San Francisco becoming her agent. She became the Peruvian ship *Napoleon Canavero* and was used to transport coolies from China to the Chincha Island guano deposits. On a passage from China to Callao, early in 1866, her coolie passengers became rebellious and were driven below by force of arms, after which the hatches were put on and secured. The coolies rather than be suffocated, set fire to the ship and the crew finding they could not extinguish the flames, left in the boats without opening the hatches, thus leaving the 650 unfortunates below to perish most horribly. The crew were later picked up by a passing ship.

WHITE SQUALL

EXTREME clipper ship, built in 1850, by Jacob Bell, successor to Brown & Bell, New York. A very handsome ship, somewhat similar in design and general appearance to the *Oriental* and *Samuel Russell*, preceding products of the same yard, the *White Squall*, however, being sharper and having greater dead rise; 190 x 35: 6 x 21; 1119 tons, old measurement. Cost, including stores and provisions for one year, $90,000. Her freight list to California on her maiden voyage was $74,000; that from Canton to London was $58,000 and in addition she had a number of passengers at $600 each for the trip from San Francisco to New York via China and

London. Her performances on her first round voyage were so satisfactory to her owners, William Platt & Sons of Philadelphia, that they at once procured two other Bell-built clippers, purchasing the *Messenger* from New York owners and having the *Trade Wind* built for their account.

On her maiden voyage the *White Squall*, Captain Lockwood in command, left New York, Sept. 5, 1850, and when 50 hours out lost all three topgallant masts. She crossed the line 32 days out and put into Rio to refit. On arrival at San Francisco, Jan. 8, 1851, her captain reported being 118 sailing days from New York; 73 days from Rio; 39 days from latitude 50° South, Pacific (which time has seldom been beaten), and 14 days from the equator crossing, which is within a few hours of record. Crossed to China and left Whampoa, Sept. 5, 1851, and was in a typhoon when a week out. Had light winds between Natunas and Gaspar; was two days at anchor off Anjer and lost maintopmast off Madagascar, being under easy sail the following three days. Arrived off the Isle of Wight in 102 days and in the Downs in 104 days from Whampoa, the fastest passage made that season. Captain Lockwood wrote from London: "Our teas were discharged in fine order which fact and our general appearance has caused great excitement here. It is conceded that the *White Squall* bears off the palm and is the finest ship that ever entered this port." She had beaten the *Surprise* and other Boston clippers whose backers were loath to acknowledge the fact.

The second voyage of the *White Squall* was 111 days from New York to San Francisco, Capt. Samuel Kennedy in command. She was in 50° South, in the Pacific, when 60 days out and was on the line on the 85th day. Crossing to China she then went to New York from Whampoa in 103 days, being 79 days from Anjer. Had lost spars in a squall near Gaspar Straits. Proceeding to Philadelphia she was thence 117 days to San Francisco and returned direct to New York in 97 days, arriving out Dec. 20, 1853. Crossed the line in the Atlantic 68 days out, 26 days from the Horn.

On the night of Dec. 26th, while lying at pier 27, New York, she caught fire from sparks from a conflagration on shore and soon became a mass of flames. The mate, Mr. Poole, cut the moorings and she was towed clear of the shipping and drifted down the stream and finally grounded at the foot of Hudson Street and burned to the water's edge. She was sold as she lay, for $5500, and was raised and rebuilt as a bark with but one deck. New register, 896 tons; draft, 15 feet.

She sailed from New York, Dec. 22, 1854, for San Francisco and two days later shipped a heavy sea which stove in the cabin and bulwarks, besides doing other damage. The captain and three men were injured so she bore off for New York reaching there Jan. 15, 1855. After repairing she sailed again, Feb. 17th, under Capt. E. J. Harding and lost all three topmasts in a gale four days out and put into Rio in distress, Mar. 25th. As repairs would cost about $13,000 and no funds could be obtained under bottomry at less than 75 per cent premium, she was made ready for sea through the proceeds of sale of a portion of the cargo. The master left the ship and first mate Burke was appointed to command. A financial mixup ensued resulting in a law suit. The ship returned to New York in February 1856 and again sailed and was reported in September as at Montevideo in distress. She was sold there for $15,000 and went under the French flag as the *Splendide* of Marseilles, C. Verminck being owner. She appears in the Register of 1875 as above. In 1877 a French vessel named *Splendide*, Captain Levet, from Rouen for Barcelona, was reported as beached at Gibraltar in sinking condition.

WHITE SWALLOW

EXTREME clipper ship, launched by Hayden & Cudworth, at Medford, Mass., Mar. 26, 1853, for account of William Lincoln & Co., of Boston; subsequently and at the time of her loss, owned by Joseph Nickerson of the same place. Keel, 176; deck, 186; over all, 192 x 37 x 22: 10; 1192 tons, old measurement;

985, new. She was very sharp, modeled expressly for speed, with long, concave entrance lines and a long, clean run. The cutwater was boldly inclined forward, terminating with a female figure in white with wings outstretched. The stern was neatly arched and embellished with carved work. Dead rise, 18 inches; rounding of sides, six inches; sheer, three feet. She was painted black outside and buff, relieved with white, inside. The waterways were black. The bulwarks, including the monkey-rail, were five feet, five inches high and the stanchions and hatch coamings were of polished teak. She had a house for the crew and two beautiful cabins, the after one being under a half poop deck and elegantly fitted up. Mainmast, 80 feet long; main-yard, 73 feet, and she was otherwise heavily sparred. In San Francisco she was always regarded as one of the most beautiful, neat, trim and best proportioned vessels ever seen at that port.

The principal features incident to the work done by the *White Swallow* on her passages to San Francisco from eastern ports are as follows:—between the years 1853 and 1868 she made three runs from Boston and six from New York; the fastest was 110 days and the slowest, 150; average of the nine, 130 days; average of the fastest four, 122 days. On three of these runs she took her departure during the summer months, the poorest season for prospective fast passages. Her maiden passage, sailing from Boston, May 27, 1853, was 150 days and is the poorest showing she ever made over any course during her whole career. On this run she was 51 days to the line; 86 days to 50° South; 102 days to 50°, Pacific, and although she then had the excellent time of 19 days to the equator, head winds were thereafter encountered and she was 29 days from the line to port; was near the Golden Gate for six days. Best day's run on the passage, 280 miles only, head winds prevailing practically throughout. Her fastest westward Cape Horn run was from Boston, sailing Apr. 18, 1860, and making land 40 miles south of the Golden Gate on Aug. 1st, 104 days out. The following six days were spent in a dense fog with practically a dead calm and the pilot was on board for 30 hours before she was able to anchor in

San Francisco bay, Aug. 7th, 110 days from New York. She had been 22 days from Sandy Hook to the line; passed through the Straits of Le Maire, 55 days out and was on the Pacific equator on the 84th day. On her second outward passage to the Pacific Coast she left New York Feb. 21, 1856, the Highlands of Neversink bearing west, 15 miles distant at 5 P.M. On Mar. 9th, at 6 A.M., she crossed the line, 17 days and 13½ hours from Sandy Hook. When 60 days out she was up with the Horn, off which had bowsprit sprung, crossjack yard and spanker gaff carried away. Crossed the equator 98 days out and was thence 36 days to San Francisco in light winds and calms. In 1864, her outward passage being again 134 days, she crossed the Pacific equator 107 days out and 13 days later was 500 miles from the Golden Gate. On her passage of 130 days in 1867 she was in a hurricane on the third day out from New York and for three days was under close-reefed maintopsail only, being hove-to for 24 hours. Both in the South Atlantic and the South Pacific very heavy gales were encountered during which the figurehead was lost, sails split and mizzen topsailyard carried away. Crossed the equator in Pacific 101 days out.

Her passage out in 1865 was a momentous one. She was 31 days to the line and 63 days to the Cape; was 18 days between the 50's; four days off the San Francisco Heads in a fog and experienced light winds and calms most of the entire run of 136 days. She had left New York, Sept. 14th, under command of Capt. Elijah E. Knowles, with her rigging in rather poor condition and according to the story of the crew, they were put to unnecessarily hard and particularly dangerous work, forced by brutal beatings with brass knuckles, belaying pins and the like. One particular grievance was that they were put over the side on stagings while the ship was going ten knots and rolling and pitching heavily in a bad sea. Two men were lost overboard. The crew finally took matters into their own hands, securing the captain and mates without harming their persons, and confiscated their weapons. For three days the captain and his two mates were kept in irons although Captain Knowles was allowed on deck to direct affairs, take observations, etc., all his orders being fully obeyed. A written agreement was then drawn up and signed wherein the crew were absolved of blame or intention to do harm or damage, and they were further promised good treatment and no unnecessary or extra hazardous labor, with watch and watch whenever possible. Under these conditions the voyage was concluded but on arrival at San Francisco six of the crew, claimed to be the ringleaders, were arrested and prosecuted with vigor. The case attracted much attention and occupied over a week and aided by the admissions of the officers and the testimony of the passengers was decided in favor of the crew, the verdict being in accordance with the charge of the Judge. For many years the "White Swallow Case," unique of its kind, was a principal topic of conversation in seafaring circles throughout the ports of the world.

On her second and fourth outward passages from eastern ports, the *White Swallow* was diverted from the San Francisco run. Leaving Boston, Nov. 21, 1854, she was 35 days to Cape St. Roque and thence 55 days to Melbourne; total, 90 days. Returned home by way of China. In 1857 she made the run from New York to Hong Kong in 89 days. Had sailed June 28th and arrived out Sept. 23rd, the poor season at both ends. Crossed to San Francisco and went home via Jarvis Island.

Between San Francisco and ports in China her record is as follows; from San Francisco:—to Shanghai, in 1856, 49 days;—to Hong Kong, 1861, 59 days; 1862, 48; 1866, 56 and in 1868-1869, 49 days. From Hong Kong to San Francisco:—in 1858, 59 days; 1861, 43 days, with all light westerly winds; beat clipper ship *Nor'wester* ten days; in 1862 she had 71 days of which 16, only, were of fair winds the remainder being steady head winds from northeast to east. On five passages, while en route from San Francisco to China or the Pacific guano islands, she stopped at Honolulu and has the following excellent record:—in 1858, 11½ days to Honolulu and thence in seven days to Jarvis Island; in 1859, 12 days, thence going to McKean's Island; in 1861, 13 days, and 46 days thence to Hong

Kong; in 1867, 15 days, 50 days thence to Hong Kong; in 1862, 16 days and 31 days thence to Hong Kong. In 1853 she was 51 days from San Francisco to Callao and in 1860, 72 days from the Golden Gate to Melbourne.

The record of the *White Swallow*, homeward bound with guano cargoes, is as follows: in 1854, Callao to Hampton Roads, 66 days;— in 1858, Jarvis Island to New York, 84 days;—in 1858-1860, Mc-Kean's Island to Hampton Roads, 90 days. In September 1864 she was at both Baker's and Howland's Islands, waiting her turn to load, but severe gales occurring about a week apart caused several ships to be driven on the reefs. The phosphatic guano becoming the consistency of pea soup, due to the heavy and unusual rainfall, Captain Prince deemed it unsafe to remain longer and proceeded to Manila. The *White Swallow* arrived there Nov. 12th and obtained a charter for Boston.

From China and the East Indies the *White Swallow* made passages as follows. Leaving Foo Chow, Aug. 25, 1855, season unfavorable, she had 38 days to Anjer; thence made the very fine run of 26½ days to the Cape; thence 50 days to New York, arriving Dec. 19th, in 115 days from Foo Chow and 77 from Anjer. On Jan. 19, 1857, she left Shanghai and cleared Java Head, Feb. 9th; thence was 31 days to the Cape and 49 days from there to New York arriving Apr. 30th, in 101 days from Shanghai and 80 days from Anjer. Left Manila, June 7, 1862, and was 48 days to Anjer, against a strong monsoon. Arrived at Boston, Oct. 7th, in 122 days from Manila and 74 from Anjer. Left Manila, Dec. 8, 1864, and was 103 days to New York.

The *White Swallow* was at Hong Kong, Apr. 28, 1870, from Melbourne. In September she proceeded to Manila and finally was chartered for Boston. Sailed Dec. 22nd and although the date of her arrival home is not ascertainable, yet it must have been a short passage. In five months and seven days after leaving Manila she took her departure from Boston for Hong Kong, having in the interim made the homeward run, discharged her inward cargo, loaded 1015 tons of

ice for account of the Tudor Company, cleared and sailed. Captain
Winslow, who had succeeded Captain Knowles, took his departure
from Boston, May 29, 1871, and on June 17th was forced to abandon
his ship, being then about 180 miles southwest of Fayal, at which
port the crew arrived safely in their boats. A cutter was sent out to
locate the derelict but could find no trace of her. She was insured for
$40,000.

The first captain of the *White Swallow* was F. W. Lovett who died
of cholera shortly after completing his first voyage in the ship. Captain Gore was then in command, being succeeded by Capt. Nat.
Brown, in 1856, he making one voyage. Captain Ingersoll then made
one voyage and was followed by Capt. Freeman Crosby, Jr., who
made two. Captains Ellery, John Bunker and Prince made one voyage each. Capt. Elijah E. Knowles was in command about five years
and was succeeded by Captain Winslow. Captain Crosby was lost with
his ship *Liverpool Packet* which, in 1863, bound to Shanghai from
Hong Kong, was posted as missing. Captain Knowles after leaving
the *White Swallow,* was in the ships *Nonantum* and *Landseer* and
retired from the sea in 1882 to reside at his home town, Brewster,
Mass.

WIDE AWAKE

CLIPPER ship, built by Perrine, Patterson & Stack, at Williamsburg, N. Y., in 1853; 168: 6 x 31 x 17: 10; 758 tons, old
measurement. She was of sharp model and in every way a handsome
ship, although small. She was owned in New York which was her
hailing port.

On her maiden voyage she arrived at San Francisco, Dec. 13,
1853, in 112 days from New York. This passage and that of the
Fearless, also 112 days, were the fastest made about that time, such
ships as the *Raven, Witch of the Wave, Hurricane* and *Northern
Light* being from 4 to 11 days longer. From San Francisco the *Wide
Awake* went to Hong Kong, in 45 days, later proceeding to Singapore. She left that port, Apr. 10, 1854; passed Anjer, the 28th and

arrived at New York, July 15th, in 96 days from Singapore. There-after she was engaged in trade between New York and Singapore making consistently good passages of about 80 days.

She last sailed from New York in July 1857 and after arrival out was sold at Bangkok, going under the Siamese flag without change of name. Her future operations were on the coast of Asia.

WILD DUCK

CLIPPER ship, launched Apr. 13, 1853, from the yard of George Raynes, at Portsmouth, N. H., and was his fiftieth vessel. She was built to the order of Olyphant & Co., of New York, who were much pleased with the performances of their clipper *Wild Pigeon,* a prior product of the same builder. The newcomer is said to have much resembled the *Pigeon,* being quite sharp though a some-what heavier carrier. The *Wild Duck* was 175 x 33: 6 x 20; 860 tons. An eagle on the wing was her figurehead while on her hand-some round stern there was a sporting dog, surrounded by gilt scroll work.

Under command of Capt. A. G. Hamilton, formerly of the ship *Luconia,* the *Wild Duck* sailed from New York, July 2, 1853, and was 134 days to San Francisco. Except for 12 days of violent gales off the Horn, nothing but light winds were experienced and for the final 40 days skysails were set. She was within 300 miles of port for six days. From San Francisco she had a long run of 72 days to Shanghai; left there Mar. 5, 1854, and was 105 days to New York. On her second voyage she left New York, Aug. 8, 1854, and Cap-tain Harrison reported another passage in light winds, excepting off Cape Horn. Crossed the equator in the Pacific 98 days out and was within 600 miles of destination for 15 days. Did not start a royal for 40 days after getting into the Pacific. From San Francisco she was 68 days to Shanghai and 143 days thence to New York. From Anjer she was 105 days, from the Cape of Good Hope, 70 days and from St. Helena to the line, 17 days; thence 37 days. On her third and last outward passage she arrived at San Francisco, Mar. 9, 1856. Captain Ellery, then in command, reported having the same experience of light winds as did his predecessor; 33 days to the line; 65 days to Cape Horn; 100 days to equator in the Pacific; was north of the latitude of San Francisco, ten days; passage 131 days.

She left San Francisco, Mar. 22, 1856, for Hong Kong; went to Foo Chow and when sailing thence about Oct. 1st, for New York, she went ashore on the bank of the river Min and was sold as she lay, it being seemingly impossible to get her afloat. A later report was that she had been floated and towed to Foo Chow but there is no record of her having resumed operations as a sailing ship. Insurance on vessel and cargo, $250,000.

WILD HUNTER

CLIPPER ship, built by Shiverick Brothers, at East Dennis, Mass., for Capt. Christopher Hall and associates of that place; launched Nov. 22, 1855. Soon afterwards she was purchased by Bush & Wildes of Boston and in March 1866, following her return to Boston after a round voyage to San Francisco, she was sold to G. C. Lord & Co., for $33,000. Dimensions: 178: 7 x 36: 2 x 22: 6; 1081 tons, old measurement and 999 72/100 tons, new measurement. She was of a sharp model, carried a large spread of canvas including three skysails and was conceded to be a fast ship. Capt. Joshua Sears of East Dennis, a great "driver," was in command during the first five years of her career; yet, in the face of these favorable points the stern fact remains that no noteworthy passage appears in such list of her voyages as is at present available.

On her maiden voyage the *Wild Hunter* left Boston, Jan. 8, 1856, and made the run to San Francisco in 112 days; was 25 days to the line, 56 days to the Horn, 93 days to the equator and 19 days thence to port. From San Francisco she was 85 days to Calcutta; sailed thence Oct. 27th and arrived at Boston, Jan. 27, 1857, in 98 days from the Sand Heads. Had a heavy gale in the Gulf Stream,

11 days before arrival, losing bowsprit, foretopmast and maintopgallant-mast. She again loaded for San Francisco and arrived out July 15, 1857, in 131 days from Boston. Was 24½ days to the line; 60 days to 50° South; 18 days rounding the Cape and 102 days to the equator crossing. From San Francisco she was 77 days to Singapore; thence 22 days to Akyab and thence 106 days to Falmouth, arriving June 7, 1858. Proceeded to Bremerhaven; then to Cardiff where she loaded for Ceylon. Sailed from Cardiff, Sept. 5th, and arrived at Point de Galle, Dec. 20th, 106 days out. Later she went to Rangoon in 30 days' passage; thence 12 days to Singapore and 30 days from there to Hong Kong. Then crossed to San Francisco in 56 days, arriving Feb. 25, 1860. Captain Sears reported that in a severe squall off Formosa, three men were washed overboard and lost, the jibboom was carried away and the bowsprit sprung. From San Francisco she went to Callao in 60 days and from there was about 83 days to New York. Made the trip in ballast as there were no guano charters offering.

Captain Baldry then succeeded to the command and made a round voyage to Liverpool, reaching New York on return, Dec. 31, 1860, after a boisterous passage of 34 days; lost and split sails, etc. She then returned to Liverpool and in attempting to enter the dock, Mar. 7, 1861, took the ground and drove the anchor through her bow; made considerable water and was beached when it was found that three-quarters of her cargo was more or less damaged. After repairing she made a round voyage between Liverpool and Coquimbo and on return to Liverpool loaded for San Francisco, Arrived out Feb. 16, 1863, in 149 days' passage; was 43 days to the line; 80 days to 50° South; 18 days rounding the Cape and 125 days to the equator. She then went to Phoenix Island, Pacific Ocean, and loaded guano for England. Arrived at New York, June 21, 1864, 39 days from London, with a cargo of iron.

Capt. Thomas Prince Howes assumed command and on May 22, 1865, reached San Francisco after a rough passage of 156 days from New York. Had heavy gales in the Gulf Stream during which jettisoned 70 carboys of vitriol, deck cargo. Was 66 days to 50° South and 24 days rounding the Horn in heavy westerly gales; from the equator to port was 31 days in very light winds. From San Francisco she went to Boston in 108 days.

The *Wild Hunter* was then withdrawn from the California trade and her subsequent operations are said to have been mainly in the Atlantic. In 1873 she was re-rigged as a bark and in 1875 her owners are still given as G. C. Lord & Co., of Boston, her master being Captain Kelley since 1868. Her name does not appear in Registers of 1884.

WILD PIGEON

EXTREME clipper ship, launched July 31, 1851, from the yard of George Raynes, Portsmouth, N. H., and in many respects resembled his prior famous productions, the *Sea Serpent* and *Witch of the Wave*. She was 189 feet long, over all x 39: 9 x 20; 996 tons, American; 768 tons, British measurement. Dead rise, 26 inches; swell of sides, six inches; sheer, three feet. Her bow was wedge-shaped, with but little flare, and she had neither head nor trail boards. A pigeon was the figurehead and two gilded pigeons ornamented her handsome oval stern. Her entrance and clearance lines were very long and sharp. She was well sparred, crossed three skysail yards and her masts raked 1¼, 1⅜ and 1½ inches to the foot. The lower mainmast was 85 feet long; topmast, 47 feet; topgallant, 26; royal, 16½; and skysail mast, 12½ feet. The corresponding yards were in length; 76 feet; 61, 41, 27¾ and 23 feet. She was an out and out clipper in model, rig and general appearance, being one of the most beautiful and jaunty ships afloat in her time. Her owners were Olyphant & Co., of New York, who were engaged largely in trade with China.

She arrived at New York, Aug. 27, 1851, under her own sail, in 40 hours from Portsmouth, in ballast and under command of Captain Buckingham. Capt. George W. Putnam, formerly master of the packet ship *Sunbeam* then succeeded and on Oct. 13th, the *Wild*

Pigeon left New York for San Francisco. On arrival out, Jan. 28, 1852, Captain Putnam reported his passage as 107 days in light winds. Was under three skysails for 75 days and for 24 successive days in the Pacific had skysails and royal studding-sails set and never shifted a rope. Her best day's run was 300 miles, on the wind. From San Francisco she returned to New York via Whampoa. Left New York, Oct. 12, 1852, and was 118 days to San Francisco; thence 38 days to Hong Kong and 110 days from Whampoa to New York, having a long beat down the China Sea against the monsoon.

On her third voyage Captain Hanson was in command and his passage from New York to San Francisco was 126 days; thence to Hong Kong in 50 days; and Whampoa to New York in 107 days, the season being again that of the adverse monsoon. She and the clipper ship *Sweepstakes* passed Anjer, in company, the *Flying Fish* having passed four days previously. All four ships arrived at New York the same day, the *Pigeon* first, her time and that of the *Sweepstakes* being 76 days from Anjer. All had fallen in with each other on more than one occasion during the run. The *Pigeon* again loaded at New York for San Francisco and made the passage out in 139 days, Captain Hanson reporting a succession of calms and light winds throughout. Was 43 days to the line and in the South Pacific was 16 days making seven degrees of latitude. From San Francisco she went to Hong Kong in 40 days and thence to Foo Chow where she loaded tea for London.

After making a round voyage to China, the return being from Shanghai to New York in 98 days, arriving Mar. 23, 1857, the *Pigeon* was put in trade between New York and ports in Chile and under command of Captain Mayhew became a very popular ship, both for cargo and passengers. Her passages outward and homeward averaged well, some being very close to record. In the fall of 1861, when homeward bound from Valparaiso, she put into Rio and was thence 34 days to New York. On the 13th day from Rio, she was in latitude 11° 33' North, and passed Cape Hatteras on the 22nd day, but this remarkable passage was spoiled by a subsequent 12-day spell of fogs and calms. She then went out to San Francisco in 130 days; thence to Valparaiso; arrived at New York, Feb. 21, 1863, in 78 days from Caldera. She was then put under the British flag and without change of name and still commanded by Captain Mayhew, she went from New York to Shanghai, later crossing from Hong Kong to San Francisco in 47 days. Thence to New York via Valparaiso and back to the latter port, arriving Apr. 7, 1865, in 80 days from New York. There she was reported sold for $35,000. In registers of 1868 she appears as the Spanish ship *Bella Juana* of Barcelona. Later her name was changed to *Voladora*. On Feb. 17, 1892, being then rigged as a bark, she was abandoned in a sinking condition in latitude 27° North, longitude 68° West.

The clipper ship *Wild Pigeon*, 997 tons, old measurement, loading at New York in October 1851, was asked by the representative of Bingham & Reynolds, San Francisco, for a rate on 1000 barrels, Haxall and Gallego flour, which was then on board of a schooner just arrived from Richmond, Va. Freights at the time were firm and advancing and as this quantity would fill the ship, an option was given for two hours of $6.50 per barrel and primage, equivalent to $1.00 per foot, at that time the highest rate. Before the time allowed had expired the rate was accepted, the schooner came alongside and the freight was taken in. The *Wild Pigeon* arrived out at San Francisco, Jan. 28, 1852, in 107 days' passage.

WILD RANGER

CLIPPER ship, built by J. O. Curtis, at Medford, Mass.; launched Apr. 7, 1853; 177 x 35: 4 x 22: 8; tonnage, 1044, old measurement; 930, new measurement. A carved hound was her figurehead. A rakish ship, crossing three skysail yards, she was beautiful in every way. She was owned by the Searses and Thatchers of Cape Cod and on her first voyage was commanded by Capt. J. Henry Sears, subsequently one of Boston's most prominent shipowners. Capt. Elisha Freeman Sears succeeded and had command for some six years, after which Captain Chase was master.

The first three outward passages of the *Wild Ranger* were from Boston or New York to San Francisco and were made in 125, 125 and 134 days respectively, but she had no chance to show her sailing ability on either run. On the first she had the mainmast sprung and was otherwise damaged off Cape Horn and was 12 days covering the last 300 miles of the passage. On the second, light winds prevailed throughout; the line was not crossed until she was 47 days out; the topsails were reefed only once on the passage and the skysails were continually set from Cape Horn to destination; from 50° to 50°, she was 11 days, in light winds and fine weather. On the third run, she was becalmed off Cape Horn for three days; had light winds in the Pacific and was ten days making the final 600 miles. Her first two homeward passages were in 48 and 44 days from San Francisco to Callao; thence 78 days, to Hampton Roads in both instances. The third return was via Calcutta, from which port she was 102 days to Boston.

Sailing from Boston, Dec. 12, 1856, she went to India and on the return arrived at Deal, Sept. 10, 1857, in 109 days from Calcutta and 46 days from St. Helena. After crossing to Boston, she went out to Melbourne in 87 days; thence to Valparaiso in 50 days; thence in 89 days to London, via Cork where she had put in for orders. From London she was 96 days to Sydney; thence to Calcutta and from there was 103 days to Boston. Sailed from Boston, Feb. 25, 1860, and arrived at San Francisco, July 19th, in 144 days, with light winds throughout. Was 30 days to the line and not up with Cape Horn until 74 days out and was 47 days thence to the equator crossing. From San Francisco she went to Melbourne in 79 days and thence to Calcutta, Colombo, Rangoon and London.

The *Ranger* sailed from London, Dec. 28, 1861, and Gravesend, the 31st, for Boston. On Jan. 3, 1862, she was in collision with the British ship *Coleroon*, from Madras for London. The starboard bow of the *Ranger* was badly stove, the cutwater damaged, bowsprit

"White Swallow," 1192 tons, built at Medford, Mass, in 1853
From the painting by W. B. Eaton. 1884

"WIDE AWAKE," 758 TONS, BUILT AT WILLIAMSBURG, N. Y., IN 1853

"WILD HUNTER," 1081 TONS, BUILT AT EAST DENNIS, MASS., IN 1855
From a Chinese painting showing the ship off Hong Kong

"Wild Ranger," 1044 tons, built at Medford, Mass., in 1853

sprung and foretopgallant-mast carried away. She put into Falmouth, Jan. 5th, and discharged her cargo which was forwarded per
Nonantum. The collision occurred during the daytime and the
Ranger was adjudged to be in fault. She was libeled for £12,500 and
was sold at auction under writ, realizing £4550. She was renamed
Ocean Chief, registers giving her owners as Angel & Co., of Liverpool. On a voyage to Rio, in 1872, she is reported as having foundered after being in collision with a steamer.

WILD ROVER

MEDIUM clipper ship, built in 1853, by Austin & Hall, at
Damariscotta, Me.; owned by Alpheus Hardy & Co., of Boston, until about 1869, when she was purchased by J. C. Nickels of
the same port; 187 x 36 x 22; 1100 tons, old measurement; 1036
tons, new measurement. She was of quite sharp model and was called
a smart ship. Prior to 1869 her captains were Thomas Crowell, Bena-
jah Crowell, Jr., Thomas Sparrow and Horace S. Taylor. Capt.
Charles R. Null was her last commander.

The *Wild Rover* was first employed in trans-Atlantic trade, being later diverted to the California and East Indian business. On
Jan. 26, 1855, while bound to Liverpool, the foremast was struck
by lightning and soon after the mainmast was also struck. Fire in her
cotton cargo developed and some 35 bales were thrown overboard.
The fire was gotten under control after several hours of pumping
water aboard. On her return from England she loaded at Boston
for San Francisco and arrived out Dec. 31, 1855, after a passage of
136 days in light weather. Returned to Boston from Calcutta. Again
loaded for San Francisco and made the run out in 126 days. The
voyage started auspiciously, the line being crossed on the 19th day
from port but thereafter nothing but light winds were encountered
excepting 23 days of very heavy weather off Cape Horn. From San
Francisco she went to England via Callao and thence back to Callao,
arriving May 28, 1858, in 94 days from London. On Nov. 20, 1859,

she reached San Francisco, 178 days from New York, of which 60 days were spent making the Cape Horn passage. On four occasions she was up with and had passed the Cape but was driven back. The first time was on Aug. 11th, then 78 days out. She again passed the Cape on Aug. 13th. The third time was on the 17th and the final passage was made on Sept. 4th. From San Francisco she went to Hampton Roads via Callao. She then went out to the East Indies and thence to Amsterdam, England and Boston.

On Feb. 8, 1863, she arrived at San Francisco, in 121 days from Boston. When 111 days out she was 200 miles from the Golden Gate, being in that position when only 15 days from the equator crossing. On Jan. 25th the fore and main topmasts and maintopgallant mast were sprung. Sailed from San Francisco, Mar. 11, 1863, for Puget Sound where she loaded a cargo of lumber for Shanghai. She had a long passage of some eight months from Shanghai to Boston, having as a passenger the first Japanese to come to the United States in search of learning. He had been smuggled out of Japan, locked in the storeroom of a ship. After the arrival of the young foreigner at Boston, Mr. Alpheus Hardy had him educated and sent through college and lived to see his protege serve Japan and there found Doshisha University.

The last visit of the *Wild Rover* to San Francisco was in May 1868 when she reached port in 132 days from New York, having experienced one continual series of light winds. Crossed the line 25 days out and was thence 72 days to a similar crossing in the Pacific; was 21 days rounding the Horn. She returned home via Manila. In 1871 she went ashore at Jones Inlet, Long Island, and became a total loss.

WILD WAVE

MEDIUM clipper ship, built in 1854, at Richmond, Me., by G. H. Ferrin, for Benjamin Bangs of Boston. Capt. Josiah N. Knowles was in command during her brief career. Of 1547 tons, old measurement, she was a particularly handsome ship, of a fine model for speed and carrying capacity, but her principal prominence came later, in the romantic incidents attending the experiences of Captain Knowles and his crew after their ship had been wrecked.

On Aug. 4, 1855, the *Wild Wave* left Gravesend, England, for Callao; went thence to the Chincha Islands and loaded 1600 tons of guano; then back to Callao for clearance; thence to Genoa, where she arrived in February 1856. Time on the round voyage, including all detentions, was 198 days; covered about 25,000 miles. On Jan. 23, 1858, she arrived at San Francisco, in 140 days from New York. Captain Knowles reported being 46 days to the line; 19 days thence to 50° South; 20 days rounding the Horn, having the maintopgallant mast carried away, two topsails split, and the cutwater and forward house started; was 30 days in the South Pacific, in light winds, and 25 days from the equator to destination, taking six days to make the final 150 miles in strong southeast gales. Sailed from San Francisco, Feb. 9, 1858, in ballast, for Valparaiso, having a crew of 30 all told with ten passengers and two boxes containing $18,000 in gold coin. On Mar. 5th, at 1 o'clock A. M., she went ashore on the coral reef of the atoll of Oeno, in latitude 24° South, longitude 131° West, the chart position of which was later found by observations to be some 20 miles out of the way. The following details of the wreck are condensed from the diary kept by Captain Knowles.

At one o'clock in the morning of Mar. 5, 1858, the *Wild Wave* was 24 days out from San Francisco and making 13 knots when the lookout reported breakers under the lee bow. In attempting to go about, she mis-stayed, and wearing, struck the coral reef. In five minutes she had bilged and was full of water, the sea breaking all over her, even stripping off the copper and casting the sheets on deck. Daybreak showed that she had struck on the smoothest part of the reef; otherwise, all hands would have been lost. A landing was made on the low, brush-covered strip of sand about a half mile in circumference which constituted the island, and some provisions and sails, as well as the live stock on board, were gotten ashore. Tents were erected; sea birds and eggs were found in abundance; fish were plentiful and water was obtained by digging. It was determined to rig one of the boats and make the 80 mile trip to Pitcairn Island, which was supposed to be inhabited. A heavy surf prevailed until the 13th, when Captain Knowles, mate Bartlett, and five men, with the treasure, were able to get out to sea. The second mate was instructed to also proceed to Pitcairn in case assistance had not reached his party within four weeks. After an exhausting trip of three days and a very narrow escape from being swamped and all hands drowned, the party was able to effect a landing on Pitcairn, although they could not reach Bounty Bay. No inhabitants were seen and a search of the houses resulted in the finding of various notices stating that all the residents had moved to Norfolk Island, distant about 3300 miles, west by south. Plenty of fruit, such as oranges, bananas, cocoanuts and breadfruit were found, as also sheep, goats, bullocks and chickens. The treasure was landed and buried. A day or two after reaching the island, the boat was stove and finally demolished by the heavy surf. With some axes and a few other tools found in the houses, the construction of a small schooner was begun. Trees were felled but as no saw could be found, all planks and timbers had to be hewn. Some of the small houses were burned to obtain metal and nails, but they were forced to make and use many wooden pegs. After an immense amount of labor, the material was assembled and on Apr. 29th the keel of their vessel was laid. They picked oakum from old pieces of rope and with an improvised walk, made some 45 fathoms of cordage. On June 4th, the hull was finished. It was 30 feet long, eight feet beam and four feet deep. A small pump was rigged; an old anvil served for an anchor and a copper kettle was made to do duty as a stove. An ensign was made from the red hangings of the church pulpit, an old white shirt and a blue overalls. On July 23rd the launching took place, the boat being christened *John Adams,* after one of the original settlers of the island. She was laden with a supply of fruit, chickens and goat meat; and soon after noon, June 4th, she set sail for Tahiti under jib, foresail and mainsail, with the treasure also on board. Three men, preferring to remain on the island, were left behind. The wind was ahead for Tahiti and soon developed into a gale, so a course was made for the Marquesas Islands, via Oeno. Contrary winds prevented their being able to pass close to the latter island.

After being at sea for 11 days, during all of which time everybody suffered greatly from seasickness, they made the island of Ohitahoo, one of the Marquesas, but learning that there were no Europeans at Resolution Bay, and the natives appearing very savage and warlike, they refused pressing invitations to anchor and pressed on for Nuka-hiva. This island was reached Aug. 4th and to their great surprise but intense delight, they found there the United States sloop of war *Vandalia,* Captain Sinclair. Captain Knowles sold his boat to a missionary for $250 and later on the same day, the *Vandalia* got under way for Tahiti, arriving there six days later with the castaways on board. The following day she left for Oeno, with mate Bartlett, and in due time the castaways there were rescued. It was found that they had built a boat out of material obtained from the wreck but it proved to be so large that all their efforts to effect its launch were unsuccessful. One of the party had died on the island. From Oeno, the *Vandalia* proceeded to Pitcairn and picked up the three men who had chosen to remain there.

At Tahiti, Captain Knowles accepted the invitation of the commander of the French sloop of war *Eurydice* which was about leaving for Honolulu and after a pleasant voyage of 16 days he was duly landed at that port. He reached San Francisco in the bark *Yankee* on Sept. 27, 1858, 11 days from Honolulu, and was greeted by his friends as one risen from the dead. By the first Panama steamer, which was the *Golden Gate*, he proceeded to his home in Brewster, Mass.

Captain Knowles was born in Eastham, Mass., May 26, 1830. In addition to the *Wild Wave*, his commands were the ships *Kentuckian*, *Charger* and *Glory of the Seas*. After giving up the sea he became one of the most enterprising and prominent shipping merchants of San Francisco and died at his home in Oakland, California, on June 10, 1896. His mate in the *Wild Wave*, J. H. Bartlett, afterwards commanded the ship *Ellen Sears*, which was named after the wife of Captain Knowles. In this ship he sailed from San Francisco, Oct. 10, 1867, for Liverpool, but never arrived and no trace of vessel or crew was ever found.

WINDWARD

BUILT by Trufant & Drummond at Bath, Me., in 1854; 159 x 35 x 21; 818 tons; owned in New York. Wrecked on Whidbey Island, Puget Sound, December 1875, while on a voyage from Seattle to San Francisco.

WINGED ARROW

MEDIUM clipper ship, built at South Boston, Mass., in 1852, by E. & H. O. Briggs; deck, 176; over all, 183 x 36 x 22; 1052 tons, old measurement; 933 tons, new measurement. Dead rise, 20 inches; figurehead, a flying dragon with darting tongue. Her owners, Baker & Morrill of Boston, were so well pleased with her that they had the Briggs Brothers build a duplicate, the *John Land*, which was launched in March 1853. The first master of the *Winged Arrow* was Capt. Frank Bearse of Hyannis, who was succeeded by Captain Berry. In 1866, Capt. E. P. Chase took command and remained master until she was sold in 1868.

The *Winged Arrow* proved to be a fast sailer and a successful ship. While the shortest of her nine runs from Atlantic ports to San Francisco is 113 days, yet on different voyages her fastest time over the five several sections aggregates but 96 days. As will appear, her runs up the Pacific from 50° South to the Golden Gate were particularly fast and remarkably uniform, an average of six of them being but 43 days and over this section her work is fully equal to that of any other vessel engaged in the trade, not excepting the extreme clippers. Her time of 36 days from San Francisco to Manila has been equaled in a few instances but never surpassed.

On her maiden voyage the *Winged Arrow* sailed from Boston, Aug. 5, 1852, and reached San Francisco, Nov. 27th, in 113 days' passage. Had much light weather, her best day being only 260 miles. The prominent feature of the run was her 38 days up the Pacific, being 20 days from 50° South to the line and 18 days thence to pilot off the Farallons. From San Francisco she was 52 days to Singapore; thence to Calcutta. Left the Sand Heads, Apr. 23, 1853, and was 102 days to Boston. Sailed from Boston, Sept. 11, 1853, and was 126 days to San Francisco. The only chance she had on this run was in the North Pacific when she was 18 days from the equator crossing to port. During one stretch of 12 days in the North Atlantic she covered only 100 miles and on the whole passage had 25 days of calms. From San Francisco she went to Manila in 36 days. Left there Apr. 1, 1854, and was 112 days to Boston, being 84 days from Anjer, 52 from the Cape and 28 from the line.

On her third voyage she left Boston, Oct. 15, 1854, and was 115 days to San Francisco. Had light winds until reaching 50° South, Pacific, 76 days out, but thereafter did some fine work. From 50° South to the line she was only 19 days and thence to 300 miles from the Golden Gate, only 15 days, which time is very close to record. She then went to Manila in 47 days; sailed thence May 5, 1855, and arrived at Boston in 101 days; 76 from Anjer, 46 from the Cape and 23 from the line. On Jan. 4, 1856, she was again at San Francisco in 125 days from Boston. Had three heavy gales off Cape Horn; lay to for 32 hours; had chain plates broken and sails split; was in 50° South, Pacific, 80 days out; thence 26 days to the line and thence 14 days to 100 miles off the Golden Gate but five days were required to cover that small distance. Again returned to Boston from Manila, arriving home Aug. 6th, in 116 days; 90 from Anjer, 56 from the Cape and 26 from the line. Her fifth voyage was 117 days from Boston to San Francisco, arriving out Jan. 12, 1857. Was 15 days rounding the Horn and crossed 50° South, Pacific, 67 days out; made the run from the line to port in 18 days. Went to Hong Kong in 52 days and returned to San Francisco in 52 days also. Then went to Guaymas and was 111 days thence to Queenstown.

On Nov. 16, 1860, the *Winged Arrow* arrived at San Francisco after a momentous passage of 150 days from Boston. On Aug. 4th, when near the Platte, she was struck by a sudden squall lasting 30 minutes, which took away the mizzenmast and all attached, the maintopgallantmast with all its yards and sails and also the main yard; spare spars were set up for a jury mizzenmast and she proceeded bark rigged. Was 26 days rounding the Cape and had light winds thence to destination. From San Francisco she took wheat to Cork in 122 days. She then went out to Otago, N. Z., from Glasgow, with emigrants and sheep, arriving Nov. 1, 1861; thence to Rangoon and Liverpool, which port was reached Mar. 3, 1862. After crossing to Boston she loaded for Singapore, sailing in October. On Dec. 6th she put into Rio for repairs and was detained three weeks; arrived at Singapore, Mar. 16, 1863. Left there Apr. 1st, for Bassein and sailed thence May 15th, for Liverpool. Had a tedious run down the Bay of Bengal and was not up with the line until three weeks out. She arrived at Boston, Dec. 28th, from Liverpool.

The *Winged Arrow* arrived at San Francisco, July 16, 1864, limping into port 141 days from Boston. While lying to under close-reefed topsails, at 2 A. M. on June 24th, in latitude 10' North, Pacific, the head of the mainmast broke off close to the eyes of the rigging, taking with it the fore and mizzen topgallant masts, the whole mass of sails and yards going overboard. Nothing could be saved on account of the heavy rolling of the ship. Captain Berry had great difficulty in working his ship to port of destination in 22 days after the disaster and repairs at San Francisco cost $8900. Completing this voyage, the ship went to Honolulu, Singapore, Calcutta and New York. Sailed from New York, Nov. 3, 1866, and was 122 days to San Francisco. Had two very severe gales in the North Atlantic, the ship laboring hard in a high, irregular sea, taking on board large quantities of water; the close reefed main-topsail was split. Crossed the line 34 days out; passed Cape Horn on the 62nd day and was thence 40 days to the equator and 20 days from there to port. Sailed Mar. 26, 1857, and was 102 days to Liverpool, her passage being the fastest made over the course about that time. The whole voyage from New York to San Francisco, Liverpool and Boston occupied ten months and four days, including all detentions. Sailed from Boston, Oct. 23, 1867, on her last voyage as an American ship and arrived at San Francisco, Feb. 20, 1868, in 119½ days' passage. When seven days out from Boston she had the courses and close reefed topsails split in a severe gale, after which, for 24 days, she had very light winds and averaged but 82 miles daily. Crossed the line 35 days out; off the Platte had part of the figurehead washed off and the head rails and knees were badly strained and was forced to go to the eastward of the Falklands. Passed Cape Horn, 74 days out; crossed the equator on the 106th day and 13 days later was up with the San Francisco bar, which latter time is the fastest recorded to the present date.

Shortly after her arrival at San Francisco, the *Winged Arrow* was sold to Wasserman & Co., representing the Russo-American Fur Company who were discontinuing operations in Russian America (or Alaska) following the purchase of that territory by the United States. Her name was not changed and under command of Captain Sands she sailed from San Francisco, Mar. 20th, for New Archangel (Sitka). She made the passage up in nine days and after visiting the various stations of the Company returned to San Francisco, arriving July 28th in eight days from Sitka. Her time on the upward as well as on the return run is regarded as being very fast. She then went back North and on leaving Sitka in December, for Cronstadt, with some 300 passengers, it was stated that she had thus nearly depopulated the town. On Jan. 2, 1869, she put into Honolulu for supplies, being then 25 days out. Sailed Feb. 2nd and was reported as arriving at London, July 24th, en route to St. Petersburg. In 1871 she was still listed as being owned by the Fur Company, Captain Bergeman being in command.

WINGED RACER

THE clipper ship *Winged Racer* was built by Robert E. Jackson, at East Boston, and launched in November 1852, for the account of Seccomb & Taylor who shortly after disposed of her to Sampson & Tappan of Boston, whose fleet included such beautiful models as the *Nightingale, Flying Fish* and *Westward Ho*. At the end of her career, however, the *Racer* hailed from New York and was reported as belonging to R. L. Taylor.

She was of 1767 44/95 tonnage; her length of keel was 198 feet; of deck between perpendiculars, 210 feet; over all, 226 feet; breadth of beam, 42½ feet; depth of hold, 23 feet; dead rise, 24 inches and sheer, three feet. She carried a flying horse, with wings extended, for a figurehead. She was designed by Samuel H. Pook, had a long sharp bow with slightly convex lines and was in every way the beau ideal clipper. Her lower masts, counting from the foremast, were 81, 87 and 76 feet and the corresponding yards, 71, 81 and 61 feet. Her command was given to Capt. William Homan of Marblehead, a master mariner from 1830 and well known all over the world in connection with the once prominent ships *Sweden, Jamestown* and others.

The *Winged Racer* reached San Francisco on her maiden voyage, Mar. 30, 1853, 108 days from New York. On his arrival Captain Homan wrote to his owners:—"I arrived off the bar at San Francisco, Mar. 27th, in 105 days but owing to the fog was obliged to lay off until Wednesday. I was 53 days to Cape Horn, 85 to the equator in the Pacific and 20 here. The New York clipper *Jacob Bell*, left New York three days before us and is not in yet; heavy bets were laid on the result." On this passage Captain Homan had followed the sailing directions as laid down by Lieutenant Maury and in his report to that officer, he states, that while he would follow his directions again, he believed, with the wind as it was, he would have saved five days on the passage by going east of the Falklands. From San Francisco the *Racer* went to Manila in 52 days; thence to Batavia and had a good run of 75½ days from that port to Boston.

On her second voyage the *Racer* left Boston, Jan. 25, 1854, under Capt. Francis Gorham of Barnstable, and arrived at San Francisco, May 23rd; passage, 118 days. She reported 15 days off the Horn in heavy westerly gales. From San Francisco she went to Manila in 51 days and thence to Boston in 133 days, 79 from Anjer. The commencement of the third voyage was auspicious, the Horn being reached in the good time of 45 days, but her slow run of 75 days thence to the Golden Gate offset this; total passage, 120 days. Twenty-three days out, in 10° South, she spoke the clipper *Herald of the Morning*, which had left New York the day after the *Racer* had left Boston. The *Herald* led the *Racer* by one day to the Horn and thereafter had exceptionally favorable wind and weather, making the Cape Horn passage in eight days, the equator in 79 days and the whole passage in 99 days and 12 hours, arriving at San Francisco May 16th. The *Racer* did not get in until June 2nd, due to being off the Horn 17 days and then having light winds to port.

Resuming her voyage the *Racer* went to Hong Kong in 50 days and from there to Swatow where she took on a load of coolies for the Chincha Islands. She was ready to sail Dec. 14, 1855, but it was reported that Captain Gorham was alarmed at the mutinous state of his cargo of 700 coolies and had flogged 60 in one morning. This report, whether true or false, caused comment in Boston and Sampson & Tappan issued a statement that in 1854 they had sent out an agent to investigate the coolie trade and on his report that the trade was perfectly legitimate, if properly conducted, they had written to the captains of their ships *Winged Racer* and *Westward Ho* to fill up with coolies, stipulating, however, that the coolies should not be employed in the Peruvian guano islands. Later they had written countermanding the order to fill up with coolies, but the vessels were already under contract and loaded. The *Racer* made her voyage safely, arriving at Callao, Mar. 19, 1856, in 82 days from Anjer. From Callao she went to Baltimore in 94 days. After the *Racer* and *Westward Ho* had completed their voyages, Sampson & Tappan made no more ventures in the coolie trade.

In 1857, the *Racer*, Captain Gannett, was caught in ice eight inches thick, near Annapolis, and began to leak. Two tugs were sent down to her and she was beached at Greenbury's Point in 18 feet of water. Her cargo of 30,000 bushels of wheat was damaged and lightered. She was soon after sold to W. L. Taylor, for $35,000. She then made a couple of round voyages between New York and China and on Dec. 31, 1860, arrived at New York, under Captain Trundy, from Foo Chow, Sept. 2nd, and Anjer, Oct. 15th. On Dec. 16th, during a gale, she lost all her topmasts and was towed into New York. At New York, Capt. George Cumming was placed in command and the ship loaded for San Francisco.

On arriving at San Francisco, Aug. 10, 1861, Captain Cumming reported having had a good run of 19 days to the line but unfavorable winds and weather for the balance of the passage which was made in 127 days. Continuing her voyage on Oct. 23rd, she cleared for Liverpool with 30,244 bags of wheat, 85 bags and ten boxes of silver ore and three cases of books, to the total value of $64,045. On the morning of Oct. 3rd, while proceeding down the bay under sail in charge of a pilot, the tide set her on a sunken rock between Alcatraz Island and Arch Rock, knocking a hole in her bottom. She soon swung off, however, and was taken to North Point wharf with eight feet of water in her hold and leaking badly. The cargo was discharged and the ship taken to Mare Island where she was drydocked, having a portion of her keel replaced, with some new planking, besides being caulked and recoppered. She reloaded and sailed Dec. 10th, arriving at Liverpool, Mar. 30, 1862, after a passage of 110 days. The damage due to her stranding amounted to $42,000. She returned to China in 1862 and was on that coast about a year, part of the time at

Bangkok. She finally went to Manila and loaded for New York, sailing Oct. 8, 1863, with 5000 piculs of sugar, 11,880 piculs of hemp, 100,000 cigars and 178 quintals of indigo. The *Winged Racer* reached the Straits of Sunda and was there captured and burned by the Confederate privateer *Alabama*.

The log of the *Alabama* says:—"Tuesday, November 10, 1863,— ran through the Straits of Sunda about 2 P.M. and soon discovered a clipper-looking ship under topsails standing toward North Island. Gave chase in the midst of a rain squall and in 15 minutes made him show colors; found him to be the *Winged Racer*, a vessel for which we had been hunting outside the Strait. Sent him to anchor about three miles from North Island, we anchoring near. Got every thing out we wanted by 2 A.M. and sent off his crew in his own boats; fired ship and were out of sight of land by daylight. Our appraisement: value of ship, $87,000; of cargo, $63,000; total, $150,000."

Semmes' memoirs contain more details as follows:—"On the morning of November 6, we boarded an English ship from Foo Chow, which informed us that an American ship called the *Winged Racer* had come out of the Gaspar Strait in company with her. That afternoon we captured the bark *Amanda* of Boston, from Manila for Queenstown, with hemp and sugar; a fine rakish looking ship. Burned her at 10 P.M. Next day ran through the Straits in full view of the town of Anjer. Just where the Strait debouches into the China Sea, we descried in the midst of a rain squall, to which we were both obliged to clew up our topgallant sails, a tall clipper ship, evidently American. She loomed up through the passing shower like a frigate. We at once gave chase and in a few moments hove the stranger to with a gun. It was the *Winged Racer* which our English friend had told us had passed out of the Strait some days before in his company. She was a perfect beauty; one of those ships of superb model, with taunt, graceful masts and square yards, known as clippers. We anchored her near North Island and came to ourselves for the purpose of 'robbing' her. She had sundry provisions aboard, particularly sugar and coffee, of which we stood in need. She had besides a large supply of Manila tobacco and my sailers' pipes were beginning to want replenishing. It took the greater part of the night to transport to the *Alabama* such things as were needed. The captain was presented with all the *Winged Racer's* boats with liberty to pack as much plunder as he chose. He left about 1 P.M. proposing to make his way to Batavia and report to his consul for further assistance. The prisoners of the *Amanda* took passage with him."

Captain Cumming was later known as commander of the famous ships *Young America* and *Three Brothers*. A friend of the captain recounts the following:—Captain Cumming could spin many a yarn of his voyages and if worked up to a concert pitch would tell of the capture of his ship *Winged Racer;* how the baby carriage of his child was destroyed and himself treated very shabbily by a craft that approached him carrying British colors for the occasion. In remembrance of this he would never acknowledge the salute of a vessel carrying the British flag while he was in command of an American vessel.

According to the records of the Geneva Conference, the claims filed on account of the destruction of the *Winged Racer* aggregated $385,867.91, of which value of vessel was $56,833; cargo, $256,-983; wages of 62 men for ten months, $13,700.

WINGS OF THE MORNING

CLIPPER ship, launched Oct. 28, 1852, by Edwin Achorn, at Waldoboro, Me., for account of John Bulfinch and Captain H. A. Lovell, the latter taking her command; 915 tons, old measurement; 770 tons, new measurement. She had sharp ends and was a fast sailer.

Her maiden voyage was full of mishaps. Leaving New York, Jan. 21, 1853, she experienced a very heavy gale when five days out which carried away the jibboom and flying-jibboom, all three topgallant masts and the slings and truss of the main-yard; had skylight stove and received damage on deck. For several days thereafter the only sails that could be carried were two topsails, the foresail and the spanker. Following that, to latitude 16° North, which was crossed 32 days out, she had head winds, except for two days, and for two days was under single reefs in very squally weather. Crossed the line 41 days out and put into Rio for repairs. Off the Platte had the jibboom carried away a second time and suffered considerably in sails and rigging. Was 21 days off the Horn in heavy weather, having head rails and part of the stern mouldings carried away. Was 34 days from the equator to San Francisco in light winds. On arrival, July 23rd, Captain Lovell reported his passage as 183 days from New York; 109 days from Rio. From San Francisco she crossed to Shanghai in 47 days and sailed from that port, Nov. 30th; passing Anjer, Dec. 22nd.

Her second voyage was from New York to Melbourne, sailing July 15, 1854, and making the run out in 102 days. George Francis Train, formerly of Boston, who was engaged in the shipping business at Melbourne at the time, wrote to "Hunt's Merchants Magazine";—"The *Wings of the Morning* came in day before yesterday from New York but the Utter-Most-Parts-of-the-Sea has not yet been heard from. Snail, Tortoise or Drone I would suggest for the next clipper, just for a change. I am tired of these always-a-little-faster names."

From Melbourne the *Wings* went to Callao; sailed thence Mar. 31, 1855, and was 85 days to Hampton Roads; reached Philadelphia, June 30th. Sailed from Philadelphia, Sept. 27th, and was 144 days to San Francisco. From the Delaware Capes she was 39 days to the line; 29 days thence to 50° South; 12 days to 50°, Pacific; thence, 32 days to the equator and ran from there to within 500 miles of the Golden Gate in 16 days; then had light winds and calms for ten days to port. Sailed from San Francisco, Mar. 4, 1856; crossed the equator 15 days out; thence 52 days to Callao. Sailed from Callao, July 3rd, and arrived at Havre, Oct. 17th, in 106 days' passage; beat the *Red Rover* by 19 days.

Shortly after her arrival at Havre she was sold to go under the French flag, being renamed *Surat*. In 1868 her hailing port is given as Toulon; Brunet & Co., owners.

WITCHCRAFT

EXTREME clipper ship, launched from the yard of Paul Curtis, at Chelsea, Mass., Dec. 21, 1850, for account of S. Rogers and William D. Pickman of Salem, which was her original hailing port. She was designed for speed rather than for cargo capacity. Length, over all, 193 feet; beam, 39:6; depth of hold, 22 feet; 1310 tons, old measurement. Dead rise, 35 inches; swell of sides, six inches; sheer, two feet. Her figurehead was a tiger crouching for a spring and her handsome curvilinear stern was ornamented by a huge serpent in the act of uncoiling. The lower masts, counting from the foremast, were 79, 84 and 72 feet; topmasts, 48, 49 and 39; topgallants, 25, 28 and 21; royals, 16, 17 and 15; skysail masts, 12, 15 and 10. The corresponding yards were, 68, 78 and 56 feet; 52, 60 and 42; 39, 47 and 32; 31, 38 and 21; 25, 30 and 19.

The *Witchcraft* was placed under command of Capt. William C. Rogers, son of one of her owners, and sailed from New York, Apr. 4, 1851. The *Ino* had sailed shortly before, while the *N. B. Palmer*, *Flying Cloud* and *Witch of the Wave* were getting ready, the latter at Boston, all bound for San Francisco. All five were new ships and experts classified their sailing ability in the following order, as to prospective passages: the *Palmer* and *Flying Cloud*, each 95 days; *Witch of the Wave*, 105 days; *Ino* and *Witchcraft*, 100 and 115 days respectively. The sequel was that the *Flying Cloud* beat expectations by five days and the *Witchcraft* by eight days (in actual days at sea), while the others failed to make good as prophesied. Like most of the early extreme clippers, the *Witchcraft* suffered loss of spars and put into Rio for repairs. There she found the *Game Cock* which had left New York a month before her and been obliged to put in with a sprung mainmast. The *Witchcraft* was at Rio 21 days and arrived at San Francisco, Aug. 11, 1851, in 107 sailing days from New

"Winged Racer," 1767 tons, built at East Boston, Mass., in 1852

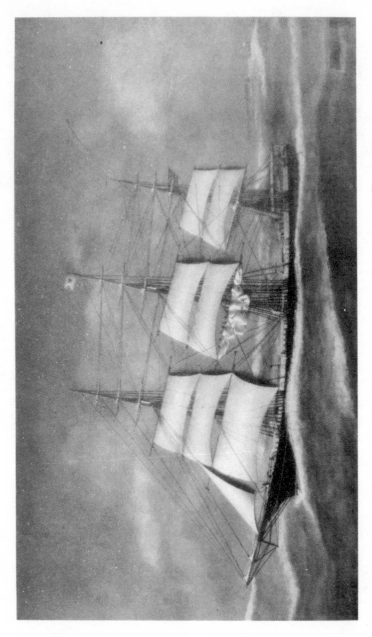

"Witch of the Wave," 1498 tons, built at Portsmouth, N. H., in 1851

"WITCHCRAFT," 1310 TONS, BUILT AT CHELSEA, MASS., IN 1850

"Young America," 1961 tons, built at New York, in 1853

York, being 62 days from Rio, which is the fastest on record to the present date. She sailed from San Francisco, Oct. 2nd, and was 61 days to Hong Kong. When 42 days out she lost her three topmasts with everything attached, in a squall. It was found impossible to obtain suitable spars at Hong Kong and she was detained three months while they were fashioned out of teak wood, her whole bill for repairs amounting to $28,832. She left Hong Kong, Mar. 30, 1852, and was 44 days to San Francisco; thence went to Shanghai and was 111 days from there to New York.

Under command of Capt. Josiah Dudley she left New York, Mar. 19, 1853, and was 110 days to San Francisco. Passed Cape Horn, 58 days out, and was on the Pacific equator crossing when 79 days out, with excellent prospects of completing the passage in two figures. However, north of the line she experienced light winds and for 13 days lay practically motionless. From San Francisco she was 48 days to Callao and thence 63 days to Hampton Roads. After her arrival at New York she was purchased by T. Magoun & Sons of Boston, for $66,000, and Capt. Benjamin Freeman, formerly in the clipper *Climax*, was placed in command. She sailed from New York, May 9, 1854, and arrived at San Francisco, Aug. 15th, a passage of 98 days. Was 22 days to the line and 21 days from the Pacific equator crossing to port; came around the Horn in fine weather and had generally moderate weather conditions throughout, with 340 miles as her best day's work and 50 miles as the poorest. When 91 days out she was 700 miles from the Golden Gate, having made the equator crossing on her 77th day. Sailed from San Francisco, Aug. 28th, and was 32 days to Callao, the record to the present time. From Callao she was 67 days to New York.

From San Francisco, Captain Freeman wrote his owners as follows:—"I have met with no accident on the passage, not so much as parted a rope yarn; did not close reef topsails once. I am at a loss to explain how I like the *Witchcraft*; we never know when the weather is bad."

On July 13, 1855, the *Witchcraft* arrived at San Francisco, Captain Freeman reporting his passage as 122 days of which 98 were days of head winds. She then went to Callao in 40 days and was thence 64 days to Port Louis, Mauritius. Left there, Jan. 10, 1856, with a cargo of sugar at £300.6 a ton and made the passage to Falmouth, England, in 85 days. Crossed from London to Boston in 32 days, arriving June 16, 1856. Captain Boolt then assumed command and sailed from Boston, Feb. 7, 1857, for Melbourne; made the run out in 97 days. Thence was 55 days to Hong Kong, later proceeding to Manila. Left that port Sept. 30th and cleared Java Head, Nov. 7th; was 15 days off the Cape in heavy weather, losing an entire suit of sails and arrived at Boston, Feb. 4, 1858. Sailed from Boston, Mar. 13, 1858, and had head winds nearly all the way to the Horn, with much heavy weather from the Platte until after the Cape had been passed. On June 9th, off the Cape, lost foretopmast and bowsprit and 12 days later put into Valparaiso for repairs, which occupied 20 days. Arrived at San Francisco, Aug. 30th, in 150 sailing days from New York, 49 days from Valparaiso. Left San Francisco, Sept. 26th and was 48 days to Sydney, N. S. W. Sailed from Melbourne, Dec. 14th and was 62 days to Shanghai. Loaded at Foo Chow and had part of her false keel twisted through grounding in the river. Sailed Oct. 14, 1859; passed Anjer, Nov. 15th; the Cape, Dec. 28th, and arrived at New York, Feb. 8, 1860; rarely made ten knots on the whole passage.

On her last voyage the *Witchcraft* left New York, Mar. 20, 1860, for San Francisco. Was 25 days to the line; passed Cape Horn, 67 days out and crossed the equator, 100 days out. On the 115th day was 840 miles from the Golden Gate but took 16 days to cover that distance. Off the Horn was in company with the *Jacob Bell* which led into San Francisco by 15 days, having had good trades and winds up the Pacific. The *Witchcraft* went to Callao from San Francisco and left the Peruvian port, Jan. 16, 1861, for Hampton Roads. On Apr. 8th, at 4 A.M. she went ashore on Chickamaconic, with the lights of Cape Hatteras and Bodie Island both in sight. The watch had just been called to tack ship. The sea made a clean breach over her and in a little over an hour she had gone to pieces. Chief mate Pitts and second mate Cass, with 12 of the crew, were drowned or killed by falling spars. Capt. John Hayes, his wife and child, passengers from Callao, were also drowned.

WITCH OF THE WAVE

EXTREME clipper ship, launched from the yard of George Raynes, at Portsmouth, N. H., Apr. 6, 1851, for account of Glidden & Williams and Hunt & Peabody of Boston; and Capt. John Bertram of Salem, from which latter port she hailed; 220 x 40 x 21; 1498 tons, old measurement; 997 tons, foreign measurement. Dead rise, 40 inches; swell of sides, six inches; sheer, 42 inches. Her bow was ornamented with the representation of a female figure in flowing white garments and on the stern there appeared a witch floating in a sea shell, which was accompanied, on the port side, by an imp riding on a dolphin, this elaborate work having been done by John A. Mason of Boston. Each cat head was gilded and two eyes looked forward from the bow. Her first cabin contained staterooms for her captain and officers; the second had seven staterooms, magnificently furnished, for passengers; the third, or great cabin, was finished in gothic panels of birdseye maple with frames of satin wood, relieved with zebra, mahogany and rosewood and surmounted with curiously carved capitals. The upholstery was rich velvet and speaking tubes connected the several cabins. There was a fine library of 100 volumes. Her cost was $80,000.

She was sparred by Martin Fernald and it speaks well for the work done that on her first voyage around the world, she did not lose as much as a studding-sail boom. The foremast was stepped 45 feet aft of the stem; thence to the mainmast, 67 feet; thence to the mizzen, 53 feet; thence 37 feet to the taffrail. The masts raked 1¼, 1½ and 1¾ inches to the foot. The masts, counting from the foremast, were in length as follows: lower masts, 84, 90 and 79 feet; topmasts, 47, 50 and 41; topgallants, 26, 28 and 22; royals, 16, 18 and 14; skysail masts, 11, 12 and 9½ feet. The corresponding yards were: 71, 81 and 61 feet; 57, 63 and 44; 43, 48 and 37; 34, 38 and 30; 29, 30 and 24 feet. The bowsprit was 28 feet outboard and the jibboom, 35 feet outside the cap. The spanker boom was 50 feet long and gaff, 38 feet. The main rigging was of 10½ inch hemp.

Having aboard a large company of friends of the builder and owners, the *Witch of the Wave* was towed from Portsmouth to Salem, May 2, 1851. Before she started, an inspection of the ship was made and Ephraim F. Miller, Collector of the Port of Salem, proposed the following toast:—"Success to the newest and youngest of the Salem witches. She, perhaps, includes in her composition an equal amount of craft with her unfortunate predecessors. Had they possessed a proportional share of her beauty, we are confident that the sternest tribunal before which any of them were arraigned would never have had the heart to subject a single one to the trial to which their successor is designed, the 'Trial by Water.'"

In May 1851, when the *Witch* started loading at Boston for San Francisco, there were at New York, similarly employed, the clippers *N. B. Palmer* and *Flying Cloud*. All three ships were new and shipping experts classified their ability in the following order, as to prospective passages on their maiden voyages: the *Palmer* and *Flying Cloud*, each 95 days; *Witch of the Wave*, 105 days. The new clippers *Ino* and *Witchcraft* had sailed several weeks before, being slated to make the run in 100 and 115 days respectively. The *Flying Cloud* beat expectations by five days, the *Witchcraft* by eight days (in actual days at sea), while the others failed to make good as prophesied. The *Witch*, under command of Capt. J. H. Millet, left Boston, May 20, 1851, with 1900 tons of general cargo; was 25 days to the line; passed Rio, 35 days out; rounded Cape Horn on the 63rd day out; crossed the equator on the 90th day and reached San Francisco in 123 days from Boston. Best day's run, 300 miles; best speed, 16 knots, with the wind one point forward of the beam; logged 13 knots on a taut bowline. From San Francisco she made the fine run of 40 days to Hong Kong. Sailed from Whampoa, Jan. 5, 1852, in the full strength of the northeast monsoon and was up with Anjer in 7 days and 12 hours. Passed the Cape of Good Hope in 37 days from Whampoa, a run within some hours of record, and then had adverse winds to the Western Islands. Received her pilot off Dungeness, Apr. 4th, in 90 days from Whampoa and arrived at London the following day, the record fast passage to that time. The "London Shipping Gazette" said of her:—"She worked up the English Channel to windward of 400 sail of vessels and not a ship could keep up with her. Her best day's run on the trip was 338 miles." The "Illustrated London News" had her picture showing her under three royals and port and starboard studding sails on the mainmast as high up as royals. The "London Times" published quite an article including the following statements:—"The *Witch of the Wave* has been received into East India dock from Canton, having made one of the most rapid voyages on record and brought one of the most valuable cargoes of tea that has ever entered London—19,000 chests of the first quality. She was built at Salem, near the port of New York, last year." (An amusing ignorance of American geography) "From China she made the passage to the Downs in 90 days and had she not encountered a strong easterly wind in the Channel, she would have done it several days sooner. As it was she was four days beating up the Channel from the Chops to river, while some of our large English vessels were two weeks. She is the object of much interest as she lies at the dock. Her bows are similar to those of a large cutter yacht."

The *Witch* left London, Apr. 22nd, and was 23 days to Boston where she loaded for San Francisco and sailed June 22, 1852, arriving out in 119 days, although Capt. Benjamin Tay, who was then in command, reported his passage as 116 days. She had light weather throughout, being 27 days to the line and 64 days thence to a similar crossing in the Pacific. She then crossed to Hong Kong in 41 days. On Jan. 23, 1853, when nine days out from Hong Kong bound for Calcutta, she put into Singapore to repair the rudder, damaged by collision with the bark *Spartan*. At Calcutta she loaded for Boston and took her departure from the Sand Heads, Apr. 13th; passed the Cape of Good Hope, 37 days out, a run never beaten and equalled only by that of the *Typhoon,* according to Lt. Maury's list of Calcutta passages. She crossed the equator in the Atlantic, 58 days out and reached Boston, July 3rd, in 81 days from the Sand Heads, the record from Calcutta to any American Atlantic port to the present time.

On her third voyage, the *Witch of the Wave* sailed from Boston, Aug. 16, 1853, Capt. Lewis F. Miller in command, and arrived at San Francisco, Dec. 11th, 117 days out, beating five first-class clippers, all reaching port within the space of 30 hours:—the *Trade Wind, Comet, Mandarin, Raven* and *Hurricane.* The *Witch* was 28 days to the line; 23 days thence to 50° South; 19 days rounding the Horn; 21 days running up the South Pacific and 26 days from the equator to port. Sailed from San Francisco, Dec. 25th, and arrived at Singapore, Feb. 10, 1854, a fine passage of 46 days; 18 days later she was at Calcutta. Homeward bound she left the Sand Heads, Apr. 1st; was 57 days to the Cape and arrived at Boston, July 12th, in 102 days' passage. Captain Shreve then took command and sailing from Boston, Sept. 6, 1854, went out to Batavia in 76 days; loaded there for Amsterdam and sailed Feb. 12, 1855. On arrival she made a favorable impression in every way and was chartered for a round voyage to Batavia which was accomplished successfully and in good time. On her return to Amsterdam, she was purchased by merchants of that city, who renamed her *Electra* and under the flag of Holland she was operated a number of years. She is listed as late as 1871; owners, Van Eighen & Co., of Amsterdam.

WIZARD

EXTREME clipper ship, built in 1853, by Samuel Hall at East Boston, Mass., on his own account and was his 84th production and his masterpiece. On arrival at New York, May 9th, she was purchased by Slade & Co., for $95,000. She was 210 feet between perpendiculars and 225 feet over all x 40: 6 x 25: 9; 1601 tons, old measurement. She had beams for a lower 'tween deck on which were laid four strakes along both sides her whole length between the fore and mizzen masts, this deck being completely laid at both her ends. Her entrance and clearance lines were very long and sharp and a finely graduated sheer of three feet gave her ends just sufficient rising to impart a saucy look. An Oriental magician, with his book of spells under one arm, was the figurehead and her handsome rounded stern was richly ornamented with gilded work. The fore and mainmasts were "made sticks," 86 and 90 feet long and 36 inches in diameter. The mizzen mast was a single stick, 82 feet long. The lower yards, on fore and main, were each 80 feet and the crossjack, 62 feet.

On her maiden voyage the *Wizard* left New York, July 24, 1853, Captain Slade in command and passed Cape St. Roque 27 days out. When south of the Platte she had the bowsprit carried away and was so badly damaged in spars and rigging as to warrant her being put about for Rio where she arrived Sept. 18th. Repaired and sailed Oct. 11th. Was 14 days to 50° South; 12 days rounding the Horn and 21 days thence to the equator, 47 days from Rio. Was 22 days from the line to San Francisco, being ten days making the final 500 miles in the face of a heavy northerly gale. Her passage from New York was equivalent to 104 sailing days while her time of 69 days from Rio is the fourth fastest on record for a cargo-laden ship. From San Francisco she went to Hong Kong in 44 days. Sailed from Whampoa, Mar. 22, 1854, and arrived at New York, June 18th, 88 days' passage, 73 days from Anjer, 45 from the Cape. Left New York, Aug. 10th, and was 78 days to Singapore; thence to Hong Kong and Manila; left the latter port, July 24, 1855, and was 98 days to New York; 74 from Anjer. Arrived at San Francisco, June 27, 1856, in 117 days from New York. Captain Slade reported being 15 days off the Horn in heavy weather; crossed the equator 86 days out and in latitude 10° North was in a dead calm for 13 days which spoiled a prospective fine passage. From San Francisco she crossed to Hong Kong in 48 days; thence 39 days to Akyab; returned to Hong Kong in 45 days; thence to San Francisco in 45 days, arriving June 28, 1857. Returned to Hong Kong where Captain Slade died and Captain Woodside took the ship. Left Hong Kong, Dec. 18th, for Melbourne; thence to Manila from whence took her departure June 26, 1858, and reached New York, Oct. 23rd, in 119 days' passage, the only run over 100 days she ever made over that course. On Aug. 8th, ten days after passing Anjer, she lost a whole suit of sails and carried away the mizzen topgallantmast in a strong gale.

On arrival at San Francisco, June 24, 1859, Captain Woodside reported a very stormy passage of 144 days from New York. Left Sandy Hook, Jan. 31st, and on Feb. 3rd, in a heavy gale, split the double-reefed foretopsail, had the cutwater and figurehead started, lee ports knocked out, cabin skylights started and the cabin and decks filled with water. Next day, the wind suddenly died out, leaving the ship in the trough of the sea, rolling rails under and carrying away the masts, etc., refitting being done under great difficulties. Was in 50° South, when 66 days out; passed Cape Horn, Apr. 14th, 73 days out, in light, pleasant weather and five days later took a succession of west-northwest and west-southwest gales which continued for 18 days, the ship being constantly flooded with water and straining badly. Fourteen members of the crew were laid up from exposure. Crossed the equator 118 days out and had light easterly and head winds to port. Continuing her voyage she was 52 days from San Francisco to Hong Kong; thence went to Bangkok, returning with a cargo of rice; then loaded in part at Whampoa, finishing at Manila. Left that port, Jan. 11, 1861, and arrived at New York, Apr. 5th, a passage of 84 days, the fastest on record to the present date. She was 72 days from Anjer, 44 from the Cape, 34 from St. Helena and 19 days from the equator.

Under command of Capt. H. G. Dearborn, the *Wizard* left New York, Jan. 31, 1862, for Acapulco, with a cargo of coal for the "Pacific Mail Steamship Co." On Mar. 22nd, 50 days out, in 45° South, 62° West, had a heavy gale from south-southwest which lasted 48 hours. The decks were swept by heavy seas, bulwarks stove, head rails started and a bad leak developed. After the pumps had been continually going for 24 hours without reducing the water which was four feet deep in the hold, a course was steered for Port Stanley, Falkland Islands, and on Mar. 25th the ship was anchored in the harbor. A portion of the cargo was discharged and everything possible done to stop the leak. The voyage was resumed Apr. 11th with the crew still at the pumps, but the following day the leak was found to have increased and a return to Stanley was made. Here, all the cargo was discharged except sufficient for ballast and on June 11th the *Wizard* set out for New York, with the pumps still going. The equator was crossed 18 days out and on the 29th day the ship was in latitude 25° North. From 22° 49′ South, to 25° 20′ North, she was but 18 days; then experienced light and baffling winds, with a dense fog on the coast and did not arrive in New York until July 28th, in 41 days from Port Stanley.

After undergoing necessary repairs, Tappan & Starbuck of New York, who were then her owners, sent the *Wizard* across to London, where, in November 1862 she was sold for £7000 to Mackay, Baines & Co. She was renamed *Queen of the Colonies* and made some passages in the "Black Ball Line" between Liverpool and Australia. In August 1869 she arrived at San Francisco, in 60 days from Sydney, with 1669 tons of coal, against her British register of 1346 tons. Her master, Captain Jones, reported having very heavy weather throughout the trip; lost an entire suit of sails; had a boat carried overboard from the davits and started a leak; several members of the crew and some passengers were injured.

The *Queen of the Colonies* appears listed in Lloyd's of 1874, owned by W. Williams of London, but she is reported to have been wrecked the same year while on a voyage from Java to Falmouth.

WIZARD KING

BUILT by T. J. Southard at Richmond, Me., in 1854; 199 x 38 x 23; 1398 tons; and owned by the builder. Sold to go under the British flag in 1863. Renamed *Munsoory*, hailing port Moulmain.

YANKEE RANGER

BUILT at Rockland, Me., in 1854; 707 tons; Abbott, Kimball & Co., of New York, owners. Sold and went under the flag of Bremen. Renamed *Franklin*.

YOUNG AMERICA

EXTREME clipper ship, launched Apr. 30, 1853, from the yard of William H. Webb, at New York, and was the last clipper he built, as well as his masterpiece. Keel, 239: 6; deck, 243; beam, 43: 2; depth of hold, 26: 9; draft, 22 feet; 1961 tons, old measurement; 1439 tons, in 1865, and 1380 tons, in 1883, according to changes in rules for computing tonnage. Dead rise, 20 inches. Had no figurehead, a billet substituting; the trail boards were ornamented with carvings of national emblems. The stern was elliptical and very graceful. A poop deck, 42 feet long, contained cabins handsomely fitted up and for many years she carried a number of passengers. She had three complete decks; was diagonally braced with iron plates five feet by 3¾ inches, four feet apart, bolted at intersections, forming a network of the utmost strength. That she was built of the best materials is evidenced by the fact that she saw 30 years of the hardest service. She was very lofty and heavily sparred, in her prime swinging a 104 foot mainyard, while her spanker boom was 86 feet long. Under her original rig of single topsails, her whole complement was 75 men, there being four mates and 60 seamen. For beautiful lines and general handsome appearance she was not excelled by anything afloat. She cost $140,000.

The *Young America* was always a prime favorite with shippers, commanded the highest freight rates, and proved to be a veritable mint to her owners. The freight list on her maiden passage, New York to San Francisco, was $86,400. In 1866 it was $50,442, while that of the new ship *Seminole,* loaded at the same time and a larger carrier, was $45,600. She also proved to be a money maker for friends and admirers as her passages were the subject of betting for larger aggregate amounts than was the case with any dozen other ships, and she never failed to realize expectations. A single run from San Francisco to Liverpool netted her Pacific coast and European backers as much as $40,000. On her maiden passage, her builder offered to wager $20,000 that she would beat the *Sovereign of the Seas,* in a race to San Francisco, but the latter went to England and Australia, a matter of regret to all interested.

During nearly all of her career, the *Young America* was engaged in trade between San Francisco and New York or Liverpool. Between 1853 and 1882, excepting the years 1857-1858 and 1860-1862, all her passages from eastern ports were out to San Francisco, there being 20 from New York, three from Liverpool and one from Antwerp. Her last western run was from New York to Portland, Oregon, in 1883. The passage from Antwerp was in 1881-1882, 142 days, with generally adverse winds throughout. The runs from Liverpool were: 99 days, in 1872-1873; 117 days, in 1874, and 111 days, in 1880-1881. The total time consumed on her 20 passages from New York is 2362 days, an average of 118; fastest, 102½ days, in 1880; two were of 107 days each; one of 109; two of 110; one of 112; one of 116; five of 117 each, that of 1859 being actual days at sea, she having put back to Rio from near the Platte and being 70 days from Rio to San Francisco. The remaining seven of her runs to San Francisco were one each, in 120, 122, 125, 130, 131, 136 and 139 days. On her longest run she was 38 days to the line and was within 400 miles of destination for ten days. On the 136-day passage, violent easterly gales, the first 13 days out, prevented any progress to speak of being made and thereafter nothing but adverse conditions prevailed. On the 131-day run she was 34 days to the line and was within 750 miles of the Golden Gate for seven days. On her 130-day passage she was 19 days off the Horn and was becalmed ten days in 20° North, Pacific, being 33 days from the equator to destination. On the 125-day run, she crossed the Pacific equator, 95 days out and in 33° North, was seven days making 20 miles on her course. In 1863, her passage being 117 days, she was 600 miles from destination when 105 days out. From New York to the line, her fastest time was 19 days; to 50° South, Atlantic, 41 days; to 50°, Pacific, 57 days; and to the equator, 79 days, all on the occasion of her fastest passage, 102½ days.

On her famous passage of 99 days from Liverpool, she left the Mersey, Oct. 12, 1872, and discharged the Channel pilot off Coning-beg light ship, near Tuskar, on the 16th; crossed the line, the 31st in 15 days and 6 hours from pilot, the record; passed Pernambuco, Nov. 3rd, 17 days and 19 hours out and Cape Horn, Nov. 29th, 43 days and 12 hours from pilot. Was in 50° South, Pacific, 51 days out; from 30° South, to 20° South, Pacific, she had light winds and calms requiring seven days to cover the 727 miles, which spoiled the prospects of an unprecedentedly fast passage. Crossed the equator, Jan. 3, 1873, and on the 18th was 100 miles southwest of the Golden Gate, 94 days from pilot, but the wind then came out north-northeast and she had to tack and stand off shore. Anchored in San Francisco Bay, Jan. 20th, 99 days from Liverpool and 96 days from pilot, both being record runs, good to this date.

From San Francisco to eastern Atlantic ports, direct, the *Young America* made 20 passages, of which 13 were to New York, six to Liverpool and one to Antwerp, her time on the last mentioned being 118 days. Those to Liverpool were:—125, 108, 105, 106, 103 and 106 days, an average of 108. The average of the 13 to New York is 98 2/13 days, there being seven of 99 days or under, to wit: 99, 83, 86, 92, 97, 99 and 92. The longest was 114 days. On her fastest run, 83 days, which is the record for a cargo-laden ship, she left San Francisco, Mar. 15, 1870; was 16 days to the equator; passed

Cape Horn, 42 days out and was on the line in the Atlantic on the 64th day. At 8 A.M. on June 4th, she was ten miles from Sandy Hook light ship, 81 days out, but a thick fog setting in and no pilot appearing, she had to haul off shore. Took pilot the next day, 20 miles east of the light ship, 82 days from the San Francisco pilot. Best day's run, 325 miles. Going over the same course the following year, she left San Francisco, Apr. 7th and arrived at New York, July 2nd, 86 days out, which is the second fastest passage for a loaded ship. In 1875 she was 91 days and 12 hours from San Francisco to Sandy Hook lightship, having sailed Feb. 9th and made the light at 7 A.M. May 12th. During the first three days out, made but 236 miles yet she crossed the equator 15 days and 22 hours out and was up to Cape Horn in 41 days and 1 hour. Crossing 50° South, Atlantic, 44 days out, had a strong northwest gale with a very heavy sea, the water flying over everything under lower yards. The ship was under courses and single reefed topsails going over 11 knots. At 10 A.M. made a sail on the lee bow; at 11 was up with her, the *City Camp*, 77 days out from Portland, Oregon, going five to six knots under lower topsails and at noon she was out of sight astern.

On her passage of 103 days from San Francisco to Liverpool, she sailed Mar. 12, 1874; was 17 days to the equator; passed Cape Horn, 41 days and 10 hours out; was in 38° 28′ South, 39° 16′ West, on the 49th day and thereafter had light or contrary winds. Passed Cape Clear, 98 days out and arrived at Liverpool, June 23rd, 102 days and 12 hours, from bar to bar. One day, in the Channel, she passed 20 ships bound the same way. The following day, 19 were in sight, all close hauled on the starboard tack, but only one, a large skysail ship, proved anything like a match for the *Young America*, the two sailing nearly side by side for 36 hours. The race started with skysails set and ended when topgallants had to be furled and the stranger tacked. On this voyage the *Young America* covered 16,-317 miles, an average of 158½ per day, and beat the *Glory of the Seas* 15 days.

Completing voyages from San Francisco, otherwise than by going direct thence to eastern ports, the *Young America* on her first, was 12 days to Honolulu and 96 days from there to New York, arriving home Apr. 7, 1854. Continuing her second voyage, she left San Francisco, Nov. 8, 1854, and was 42 days to Hong Kong; eventually loaded at Manila for New York, sailing Sept. 21, 1855, and making the run home in 101 days. In continuation of the third voyage she left San Francisco, Aug. 5, 1856, and was 44 days to Hong Kong. Then took 800 Chinese coolies to Melbourne; thence went to Singapore and Rangoon; left the latter port July 31, 1857, and was in port at Mauritius, Sept. 3rd and arrived at Falmouth, Oct. 30th; proceeded to Bremen to discharge. Then went to Liverpool and loaded for Melbourne. Sailed Apr. 18, 1858, and arrived out June 20th, in a passage of 63 days, which is the record to the present time. From Melbourne she went to Singapore; sailed thence Sept. 24th; passed Anjer, Oct. 5th and the Cape of Good Hope on the 30th; arrived at New York in December.

In the spring of 1860 she again went out to Melbourne and was 49 days thence to Callao, arriving Sept. 20th. Sailed Nov. 8th and arrived at Liverpool, Feb. 2, 1861; reached New York, Apr. 26th, 39 days from London, in ballast. Left New York, July 27th, for Liverpool and was the first vessel chartered from Europe to Oamaru, N. Z. Loaded at Glasgow, her cargo consisting of merchandise and live sheep. Sailed Nov. 1st and arrived out Feb. 2, 1862. Was forced to put to sea again immediately, with loss of anchor and chain, taking the beach master, Captain Sewell, along. Later she caught the ground at Lower Point and the steamer *Samson* went from Otago to render assistance, if required. On May 21st she was at Callao from New Zealand. Sailed Aug. 4, 1862, for Antwerp and put into Plymouth, England, Oct. 30th, in distress. In a tornado in latitude 9°, longitude 32°, had lost foretopmast, fore and main-topgallant masts, spars and sails and had the main topsail yard sprung. Arrived at New York, Mar. 21, 1863, in 32 days from Flushing, in ballast. The only subsequent occasion on which she was diverted from the Cape Horn run was in 1865, when, leaving San Francisco, Jan. 14th, she was 45

days to Hong Kong and later proceeded to Manila. Left that port
Apr. 16th; cleared Java Head, May 18th; passed the Cape, June
10th; crossed the line July 2nd, and took pilot off Barnegat, July
23rd, in 65 days and 12 hours from Java Head, one of the fastest
passages recorded and only three days longer than the phenomenal
run of the *Sea Witch*.

Aside from complete passages which have been mentioned as
record runs, the *Young America* covered different sections of various voyages in remarkably fast time and many of the following instances are also unequalled. During voyages from New York towards
San Francisco, she was 19 days to the line on two occasions. To 33°
South, she was 33 days, being 12 days from the line. To 35° South,
on a different trip, she was 35 days, being 14 days from the line. Another time she was 41 days to 50° South, and 22 days from the line.
On one occasion she passed Cape Horn 54 days out, and on another,
58 days out. On an entirely different trip she was 57 days to 50°
South, Pacific, the time of passing the Cape not being stated. She has
been on the equator in the Pacific, in 79 days and in 80 days. On her
99-day run from Liverpool to San Francisco, she was in 50° South,
Atlantic, in 39 days and 6 hours from pilot. Other details of this
passage have already been mentioned. From 50° South, Atlantic, to
50°, Pacific, she was six days in June 17-23, 1876; in November
1869, she was seven days and in August 1853, 8½ days. From 50°
South, Pacific, she made the equator in 18 days and port in 40 days,
in 1853; in 1879 it was 18 days and 42 days; and in 1875 it was 19
days and 43 days. From the equator to San Francisco the run was
made in 16 days in January 1881, of which the final 60 hours were
spent in a storm within 84 miles of the Golden Gate. In 1866 she was
17 days, with pumps continually going to control a bad leak. In 1873
she was 17 days and in 1854, 18 days. From the equator, Atlantic, to
the equator, Pacific, she was 52½ days in 1853; 54 days in 1869;
56 days in 1856 and again in 1873. From the equator, Atlantic, to
San Francisco she was 74 days in 1853; 77 days in 1881; 80 days in
1873; 81 days in 1869 and in 1872; and 83 days in 1876 and in

1880. It will be seen that although the fastest time made from New York to San Francisco by the *Young America* was 102½ days, yet a total of her best performances over the various sections, on several voyages, aggregates but 79 days.

Bound eastward from San Francisco she made the following noteworthy runs:—to the equator; 15 days and 22 hours in 1875; 16 days in 1870 and 17 days in 1874. She passed Pitcairn's Island 24 days out in 1874 and again in 1875. Passed Cape Horn in 41 days and 1 hour in 1875 and in 41 days and 10 hours in 1874. Was in 38° 28′ South and 39° 16′ West, 49 days out, in 1874 and the following year when the same time at sea, was in 39° 23′ South and 34° 24′ West,—very even sailing. She crossed the equator, Atlantic, 64 days out, in 1870. Was 39 days from the pitch of the Cape to Sandy Hook light ship and 17 days from the line, in 1870. In 1875 she was 16 days and 20 hours from the line to the same light ship. In 1870, her run from the equator, Pacific, to equator, Atlantic, was 48 days. As to the time made on round voyages, there are the following:—from San Francisco to New York and return (August 1867 to April 1868), 8 months and 15 days gross or 208 sailing days; from San Francisco to Liverpool and return (May 1880 to January 1881), eight months and ten days gross or 217 sailing days; from Liverpool to San Francisco and return to Liverpool and thence to New York (October 1872 to August 1873), 9 months and 27 days gross; days in ports, 68; actual sailing days, 228; from New York to San Francisco and return (January 1868 to September 1868), eight months even, gross or 218 sailing days; from New York to San Francisco and thence to Liverpool (October 1873 to June 1874), 7 months and 24 days gross or 209 sailing days.

While the Cape Horn route does not offer the same opportunities for great daily runs for protracted periods such as occur in the South Atlantic and Indian Oceans in Australian passages, yet the *Young America* has some notable performances to her credit. In 1872, on the fourth, fifth, sixth and seventh days out from Liverpool, she made 340, 268, 230 and 300 miles and the following seven days she covered 1609 miles, a total of 2747 for the 11 days. On her passage of 99 days from San Francisco to New York, in 1876, her runs for four consecutive days were 365, 358, 360 and 340 miles. On a similar voyage in 1870, her best week was 1780 miles. In 1875, on the same course, she crossed the equator in the Pacific, Feb. 25th and during the month of March she sailed 6435 miles, an average of 207½ daily. In one week made 1802 miles, an average of 257½, with 270 miles as the best day. On Apr. 25th she was seven miles north of the equator in the Atlantic and on May 2nd her position was 19° 26′ North; 59° 48′ West, giving for the seven days, 1667 miles, an average of 238, with 260 miles for the best day.

Considering her long life the *Young America* was singularly free from mishaps, particularly those incident to the passage around Cape Horn where on only two occasions did she receive damage, the most serious being the breaking into three pieces of her jibboom while lying to during the night of May 18, 1856. On her passage from New York in 1870, she struck a reef off Cape St. Roque about 5 A.M. on Oct. 2nd and jettisoned some cargo and came off after four hours, not leaking nor having sustained any serious damage; insurance loss, $14,000. On Dec. 3, 1868, while off the Platte, 41 days from New York, bound to San Francisco with a full cargo of railroad iron, she was, without warning, struck by a whirlwind, swinging off some 12 points, then being taken aback and becoming unmanageable. With his ship lying on her beam ends Captain Cumming ordered shrouds and stays cut away but before the order could be executed the gale shifted, carrying away the fore royalmast, maintopgallant and cutting the mizzen down to the lower mast head. The ship was laboring heavily and it was feared that her dangerous cargo had shifted but it was found to have been skilfully stowed and intact. After four hours the gale subsided but the ugly cross sea continued. Passengers assisted the crew at the pumps and finally the hold was freed from the water which had been taken aboard. The standing rigging had kept the wreckage of spars alongside and by the fifth day a jury mizzenmast had been completed. Ten days later the maintop- and topgallant sails were sent up and the ship was on her way again. On arrival at San Francisco, Captain Cumming received great praise for bringing his ship into port under jury rig, looking like a yacht, with standing rigging well set up and everything taut and shipshape and only 117 days out from New York. Underwriters presented him with a purse of $1000 in gold for had he put into Rio, the ship would have had to discharge to step a new mast, which would have meant her practical confiscation. She was repaired at San Francisco at a cost of $18,000. When commanded by Captain Brown she had had an experience at Rio, putting in there in March 1859, with loss of only her maintopmast and mizzen topgallantmast, —yet repairs had taken two months. As heretofore stated she had also been dismasted in October 1862, but Captain Carlisle took her into Plymouth under jury rig. In February 1866 she sprung a bad leak south of the equator in the Pacific, the pumps being kept going until arrival at San Francisco. She then went on dry dock at Mare Island and was repaired and thoroughly overhauled at a cost of about $40,000.

On her last voyage as an American ship she left New York, Sept. 7, 1882, and arrived at Portland, Oregon, Feb. 5, 1883, in 151 days' passage. Was thence seven days to San Francisco with a part cargo of wheat. Left San Francisco for the last time June 2nd and put into Rio, leaking, when about 62 days out. Repairs took some 20 days and she arrived at New York, Oct. 6th, about 100 sailing days from San Francisco. She was then sold for $13,500 and went under the Austrian flag under the name of *Miroslav*, hailing port Buccari. Continued in trans-Atlantic trade some two years. Sailed from the Delaware Breakwater, Feb. 17, 1886, and was never thereafter heard from.

The *Young America* was built to the order of George B. Daniels of New York. About 1860 her registered owners were given as Abram Bell's Sons, they being succeeded a few years later by Robert L. Taylor. From about 1870 until 1880 her owners were George Howes & Co., of New York and San Francisco. Thereafter, until sold foreign, she was the property of John Rosenfeld of San Francisco, who had taken over the business of the Messrs. Howes. Her first master was Capt. David S. Babcock, formerly of the *Sword Fish*, who had superintended her construction and he was in command until 1869. Capt. Nat. Brown, Jr., then had her for one voyage, he being succeeded by Captain Carlisle who continued in her until early in 1863. Captain Jones then made one voyage, Capt. George Cumming whose fine ship *Winged Racer* had been burned by the *Alabama*, succeeding in the summer of 1864. Captain Cumming left the *Young America* in June 1874 at Liverpool, to supervise the alteration of the steamer *Vanderbilt* into the ship *Three Brothers* and was succeeded by Capt. John L. Manson. In April 1876, Capt. E. C. Baker, formerly in the *Black Hawk*, took the command and in 1882-1883 it was held by his brother, H. T. Baker. Capt. Charles Matthews took her at San Francisco, in May 1883 and was her last American master.

YOUNG BRANDER

BUILT by Jotham Stetson at Chelsea, Mass., in 1853; 194 x 36 x 24; 1467 tons; Brander, Williams & Co., of Boston, owners. Later owned by Edward Matthews of New Orleans. Sold in April 1855 to go under the British flag; renamed *Timour*. Resold and renamed *Golden Dream*, hailing port Liverpool. Abandoned September 1873 while on a voyage from Pensacola to Liverpool.

YOUNG MECHANIC

MEDIUM clipper ship, built at Rockland, Me., by T. W. Rhoades, and launched Feb. 2, 1855; 199: 6 x 38: 6 x 22: 6; 1375 tons, old measurement. The builder, attracted by the fine, graceful lines of a model whittled out of a block by his young son, laid down a ship from it, hence the name given the finished product. She proved to be a fast ship and was also a good carrier. Her owner was William McLoon of Rockland, and her first master Captain Freeman. Later, Captain McLoon was in command. He died at Calcutta in 1865 and his body was taken to Boston in the ship on her return, with Captain Richardson in command. Captain Grant then succeeded on what was to be the last voyage of the *Young Mechanic*.

The *Mechanic* was engaged in general trade and has some fast passages to her credit. On her maiden voyage she went to Savannah and made the passage from that port to Liverpool in 17 days. In six successive days she covered 1730 miles. On June 3, 1862, she arrived at San Francisco in 127 days from New York, this being her only call at that port. She was 22 days to the line and crossed the parallel of 50° South, Atlantic, 47 days out; was 25 days rounding the Horn in heavy gales, losing the main-yard; had head winds in the South Pacific and was 28 days from 50° South to the equator and thence 27 days to destination, in light or head winds with five days of dead calms. The extreme clipper ship *Spitfire* reached San Francisco the same day having the same length of passage. The two ships left within a few days of each other for Callao, the *Spitfire* making the run in 44 days from the Golden Gate against the *Mechanic's* 46 days. The latter loaded for Europe and arrived at Antwerp, Jan. 29, 1863. Sailed from Sunderland, Apr. 9th, and arrived at Rio prior to June 2nd.

She left New York, Nov. 2, 1864, with a cargo of coal for San Francisco. In heavy gales she sprang a leak and was forced to put into St. Thomas. The cargo was discharged and sold, the ship later sailing for New York for repairs. On Feb. 17, 1865, she put into Newport, in distress, with sails and yards carried away and rigging badly damaged. One man had been lost overboard in continued heavy gales. After repairs had been made she was chartered by the Tudor Company to take a cargo of ice to Madras and Calcutta and sailed from Boston, May 4, 1865. Shortly after her arrival at Calcutta the cholera broke out on board and on Sept. 9th, Captain McLoon, his second mate and three of the crew died. Others were stricken but eventually recovered. Under command of Captain Richardson she left Calcutta,

Oct. 22nd; cleared the Sand Heads, Nov. 1st, and arrived at Boston, Jan. 29, 1866, her passage being reported as 88 days. The *Antelope*, of and for New York, left in company and the two met in the South Indian Ocean when 36 days out. Both reached their ports of destination the same day. Six days later the ship *Longwood* reached New York in 86 days from the Sand Heads, so that that period appears to have been favorable for fast passages.

The Tudor Company were so well pleased with the passages out and home that they engaged the *Young Mechanic* for another voyage and under command of Captain Grant she left Boston, Mar. 5, 1866, with a cargo of ice, pitch, kerosene, etc., for Hong Kong. In latitude 11° South, longitude 33° West, fire was discovered in the pitch, stowed forward, and in less than two hours the vessel was entirely destroyed. The crew took to the boats, losing all their belongings. On Apr. 10th they were picked up by the French bark *Eugene* which landed them at Pernambuco the following day. The fire was supposed to have been due to spontaneous combustion.

INDEX

Architect, 20, 21.
Arco Iris (bark), 236.
Arctic (packet ship), 488.
Arcole (ship), 458.
Arey, Capt., 168, 182.
   Capt. John W., 610.
Arey & Co., James, 182, 610.
Arey, 22.
Argonaut, 22-24, 137, 432, 440, 469, 541, 548.
Argonaut (ship), 40.
Ariel, 23, 242.
Arquit, Capt., 99.
Asa Eldridge, 24, 25.
Aspasia, 25.
Asterion, 25-27.
Atalanta, 28, 29, 105.
Atmosphere, 29, 30.
Atwater & Mulford, 660.
Atwood, D., 347.
Auchincloss, Capt., 166.
Aulick, Commodore, 57.
Aurora, 30-32, 189.
Austin & Co., 43.
Austin & Hall, 709.
Australia, 32.
Avalanche (ship), 107.
Avery, Capt. Latham B., 226.
Avon (ship), 112, 113.
Aymar & Co., 609.

B. F. Hoxie, 32.
Babcock, Capt. David S., 650, 743.
   James D., 106.
Bacon, D. G. & W. B., 409, 476.
   Daniel C., 214, 522, 665.
   William, 522.
Bacon & Sons, D. C., 267.
Badger & Co., 253.

Bailey, Capt., 241, 389, 392.
Baines & Co., James, 44, 73, 75, 135, 189, 292, 295, 352, 364, 404, 451, 459, 518.
Baker, Capt., 24, 42, 401, 646.
   Capt. E. C., 743.
   Ezra H., 589.
   Capt. H. T., 743.
   Capt. Judah, 572.
   Capt. Judah P., 195.
   L. E., 40.
   Capt. Otis, 663.
Baker & Morrill, 3, 313, 496, 498, 585, 594, 628, 633, 714.
Balch, Capt. John W., 476.
Bald Eagle, 33-35, 179, 181, 348, 468, 643.
Baldry, Capt., 705.
Ballard, Capt., 174, 494.
Baltimore-built vessels, v, 12.
Bangs, Capt., 321.
   Benjamin, 91, 304, 711.
Bangs & Co., W. H., 382.
Barber, Capt. Harry, 213.
Barclay & Co., 421.
Barclay & Livingston, 649.
Barnaby, Capt., 5.
Barney, Mason, 608.
Barrett, Capt., 158.
Barstow, Capt., 236, 237, 242.
Bartlett, ——, 431.
   Capt., 169.
   J. H., 712, 714.
   Capt. W. H., 418.
Bartlett & Son, I. H., 630.
Bates, Capt., 108, 204.
   John, 419.
Bates & Co., E., 222.
Bates & Thaxter, 633.